THE
CHURCH

A TRILOGY

The New Testament Church
Robert C. Shannon

The Church
Through the Centuries
John W. Wade

The Restoration Movement
Enos E. Dowling

Reprinted 2000 and 2019.

This edition of *The New Testament Church* is made possible through an arrangement with the original publishers, Standard Publishing (© 1964) and College Press (© 1984).

The Church Throughout the Centuries and *The Restoration Movement* in this edition are published with permission of the Standard Publishing Company, Cincinnati, OH © 1964.

FORWARD

THE CHARACTER OF A MOVEMENT BY ROLLAND STEEVER

The CHRISTIAN RESTORATION ASSOCIATION is to be commended for reprinting the study books bound into this convenient single volume. Opportunity is offered to readers of this generation to become acquainted with important material which did not reach a wide enough readership at the time of original publication.

CURRENT THOUGHT

The present membership of our Churches of Christ/Christian Churches is often shockingly unaware of the biblical principles for which we stand, that have been faithfully conveyed throughout many centuries of time by wonderfully dedicated people. An increasing number of people and congregations, along with too many preachers, reflect an attitude of callous indifference concerning the place our own Restoration Movement occupies in such a glorious thread of history. Any consistent preaching of the message which will save fallen humanity from sin and death is now considered passé. The more popular message of the day is presented on an entertainment level and aimed at people in an effort to make them feel good about themselves. Any talk about sin and its consequences is studiously avoided. The glowing reports from many such assemblies exude over their enthusiasm, their multi-million-dollar building achievements and the exceedingly large body count. These are the kinds of reports that giant corporations send to their shareholders.

WE MUST BE HONEST IN AN ASSESSMENT
OF
PAST HISTORY

Within our own Restoration Movement, a number of historians have sought to describe us to be part of a historical on-going reform within the church "catholic," rather than one of many other strong religious movements which in each case have claimed to be "Restorationists". A new terminology has emerged, suggesting that we are the Stone-Campbell Reform, or conversely, the Campbell-Stone Reform. The rationale behind such thinking is that in reality the requirement for reform has been an ever-present necessity *within* the church since its inception in the first century. Much of the corrective teaching in the New Testament epistles address this very point. As pagan philosophies and human innovation of every kind seeped into the life of the church in the earliest years, their leaders would use the New Testament scriptures as the standard by which all error would be measured, and corrections made. Honesty compels us to recognize that often such errors were major in character and the drift from Biblical teaching was profound, but corrective voices never failed to speak out. It was not uncommon for such to often be ruthlessly and cruelly silenced; but at no time was the church completely obliterated. Jesus spoke of such times when he said, "the gates of Hades *will not prevail* against it" (Matthew 16:18). Copies of the Scriptures were not always available to everyone in the early years of the church because of the tremendous amount of labor and cost involved to produce multiple copies; *but they were preserved!* Another declaration of Jesus is verified, for He had said, "My words *shall not pass away* (Matthew 24:35). The church was mightily blessed with the advent of the Gutenberg printing press in Germany during the fifteenth century. Reformers for the next two hundred years had a better means to print and distribute their writings to the general public and to make Bibles available in their own languages.

The gigantic strides of progress made in reform during the next two centuries would form something of a crucible from which would flow the substance of thought to open the way for the work developed amidst the people who were moving in an ever-westward direction in that new nation called the United States. Thomas Campbell and his son, Alexander, together with a new immigrant named Walter Scott and American born Barton Stone, would become primary figures in that work. Religious movements, like any other, are the product of a series of changing events that take place over a considerable period of time. They almost never emerge spontaneously as an impulsive action. This fact points to the importance of our careful study of the long view of previous history.

A LAGGING SPIRITUALITY IN EARLY AMERICA

After our Revolutionary War and into the early nineteenth century, the population had grown quite indifferent to the church. A well-entrenched clergy in the several denominations tenaciously defended the tenets of their creeds and confessions of faith. They seemed more anxious to defend their institutions than meeting the spiritual needs of people. It was this situation that reformers of that period opposed.

A diligent effort was made to persuade people both in and out of the church to accept the Bible alone as the basis for faith and practice. Jesus Christ was proclaimed as the only Savior as revealed in the gospels, and that every Christian should live in obedience to His word and will. Such faithful disciples can then be united by His love and present to a lost world the unity for which Jesus prayed as recorded in John 17.

Put into plain language, freed from the crushing oversight of a denominational hierarchy, people were attracted to such teaching and preaching. It resulted in a great movement for reform springing into life throughout the population west of the Allegheny Mountains. It is a joy to read of victories achieved within the work of the Campbell-Stone Reform from 1800 till 1850. A wise man once observed that "the story of history was the story of man's struggle to be free." Jesus had taught much earlier that "if the Son therefore shall make you free, you shall be free indeed" (John 8:36).

IT IS IMPORTANT TO UNDERSTAND WHAT OUR EARLIEST LEADERS BELIEVED AND TAUGHT

Alexander Campbell wrote numerous essays in his MILLENNIAL HARBINGER (1830-1834) on "Restoring The Ancient Order." In these he urged a departure from those things which formed the church into a variety of sects and denominations. The Bible was a sufficient guide to instruct concerning salvation and the need to be molded into a life which reflected the image of God. He studiously avoided the use of the word restore or restoration, believing that it resulted in conflicting views about the nature of the first century church and produced a polarizing effect that would give rise to separate parties opposing one another. Barton W. Stone nourished a burning passion for the unity of the church and voiced as his goal the words, "Let Christian unity be our polar star." In a short, simple sentence he defined the thrust of the pioneer preachers.

Walter Scott and his co-workers in the Western Reserve, (northeastern Ohio), during the years 1827-1830 learned to sum up the redemptive plan in a few carefully chosen words. They were FAITH— REPENTANCE— BAPTISM—REMISSION (of sins)—(gift of the) HOLY SPIRIT. Alexander Campbell liked to add one more, HOPE (of eternal life). As they brought people within the embrace of this singular concept, the rapidly increasing numbers during the pre-Civil War years defined church growth with the purest characteristics.

THE POST CIVIL WAR YEARS

The tragic consequences the nation suffered because of this catastrophe did have some adverse effects within the churches in spite of valiant efforts exerted to avoid any disastrous feelings that would divide Christian brethren.

It also marked something of a watershed period as the first generation of the reform was passing from the scene of action and a new generation grasped "the baton" to continue this great spiritual race. It is not uncharacteristic for the second generation of any movement to defect somewhat from the course pursued by its earlier founders. The Campbell-Stone Reform did not escape this problem. Opinions once kept as private judgments now began to emerge as matters of concern and soon formed into matters of faith. Some issues became *doctrinal* matters of faith. The basis for discussion of such slanted judgments was based upon the principle of "where the Scriptures speak we speak, and where they are silent we are silent."

In addition, it was the period of time when humanistic liberalism began to seep into the college classrooms and the pulpits, to insidiously undercut the credibility and authority of the scriptures. These issues, along with other matters, slowly created cracks in the structure of the reform and eventually brought about open division. It was a heart-rending experience to see this mighty unity movement drift toward partyism and separation that it had taught against for years.

INTO THE TWENTIETH CENTURY

By the year 1927 there were three distinct fellowships quite at odds with each other. Those, who in the terminology of J. D. Murch in his book CHRISTIANS ONLY, were the Centrist group, made a new effort to fulfill the goals of the original reformers. Direct support for missionaries, new bible colleges, different resources for books and printed materials, and all the other necessities for pursuing this important task were implemented as quickly as possible. Most of us who will read this book are aligned with this Centrist group. It is not my purpose to develop the claims of the other two groups, but each feels that they too are the rightful heirs of the Campbell-Stone pioneer work. By this time any reference made of the movement describes it as the RESTORATION MOVEMENT. Any serious student of historical backgrounds is strongly urged to read histories from all three "wings" of the movement, and to read as many histories as possible in order to get an adequate picture. In addition to the above new resources mentioned this Centrist group has developed one of the most significant family-oriented, national religious gatherings each year under the name of the NORTH AMERICAN CHRISTIAN CONVENTION. When one is in attendance at this annual gathering, it is to witness the worldwide growth of the Movement since the years of World War II.

2000 AND BEYOND

As the future is viewed, it is with some anxiety. The past forty years have witnessed a great change in our national life, and in the life of the church. The incoming leadership of both is a curious mixture. Moral values are blurred for most and it is not clear to many which direction to pursue. The paralyzing influence of a grossly secular and materialistic society adds to this deadly malaise.

The politically correct structure of our present society had rendered so many things off limits that it has blunted the true evangelistic thrust of the gospel message. This new language forbids the "upsetting talk" about sin, death and hell. We are now told that it is more important to build personal self-esteem than to deal with the issue of sin, and in that way reduce the anxiety level present in people's lives. Too few realize that they are stewards of the most important message to be proclaimed to a perishing generation of humanity. It is shocking to Christian sensitivity to hear preachers speak of MY deacons, MY elders, MY church. Such declarations betray a misunderstanding of the words of the Lord Jesus who said, "Upon this rock I will build MY church" (Matthew 16:18). Another unsettled issue on the current scene is the question of authority in the organizational structure of the local congregation. The consequent power struggle has continued with devastating effects, all of which could be avoided if all parties involved would again carefully read the last recorded words of Jesus to the Eleven, "*All authority* in heaven and on earth is *given unto me* …. therefore, etc.*" No human on earth has one speck of authority, only enormous responsibilities.

A survey done a few years ago in a well-known Indiana city sought to get an evaluation of any current evidence present from a highly organized and publicized "gimmicky" campaign that had been conducted there twenty-three years previously. The response was a total zero. Only a handful of people recalled the campaign. Reports of the campaign spoke very positively of its great success, and of hundreds that had been won to Christ.

However we report our successes, and whether we call our movement a Reform, a Restoration or a Renewal, the end product is not to be measured by a well-publicized success story, but by how the grace of God is permitted to work within each individual so that they have been so *transformed as to reflect the image of God in their lives*. Any other standard for measurement contradicts God's measurement of success.

(Scripture quotations are KJV)

TABLE OF CONTENTS

FOREWORD

The old Greek adage, "Know thyself," is good advice both for individuals and for institutions. The church knows no greater need than to understand itself! Since the church is faced with grave problems and graver responsibilities, what study could be more valuable to it than a study of its own nature, mission, and destiny? As R. Newton Flew has so aptly said, "The conviction is growing that the need of Christian people is a fresh vision of the church of Christ as God meant it to be, His own creation, the instrument of His age-long purpose, the reconciling body in which all mankind might meet in a worship and service which would extend to the farthest boundaries of human life."[1]

As vital as it is to study the life of Christ, that study is not completed until one learns of the church that He built to be an extension of His life into modern times. Indeed, how could one grasp the significance of the life of Christ if he remained ignorant of the body of Christ? That is precisely what the church is! When Christ was on earth, He performed all His mighty deeds of power through one human body. Christ acts in our world today, and He acts through a body. It is a spiritual body, a mystical body, at once a visible and an invisible body. Still, it is a body nonetheless, and that body is the church. Through it Christ seeks to influence our world and bring His salvation to our generation.

This course seeks to present briefly the nature and ministry of the church as it is found in the New Testament. The author is deeply indebted to many who have written about this grand theme. The first of these is C. J. Sharp, whose book entitled *The Church of the New Testament* precedes this volume. Of great value have been such books *as*

The Nature and Mission of the Church, by Donald G. Miller; *Jesus and His Church,* by R. Newton Flew; and *The Church and the Sacraments,* by P. T. Forsyth. Though I have sometimes found myself in disagreement with these great men, their works are extremely valuable and highly stimulating. Karl Barth's *The Teaching of the Church Regarding Baptism* has proved to be very interesting reading.

Certainly the primary source book has been the New Testament itself. A list of pertinent Scriptures is provided at the beginning of each chapter. It is recommended that these be studied before beginning a study of the chapter itself. Then, as the student thoughtfully reads the chapter, he should look up every reference, perhaps comparing two or more translations. The questions at the end of each chapter will help the student to satisfy himself, that he has mastered the material. The ambitious student will perhaps want to secure some of the books mentioned above. Additional resource material may be found in such books as *Church Polity,* by W. L. Hayden (Old Paths Book Club); *The Church of Christ,* by T. W. Phillips (Standard Publishing); *Scheme of Redemption,* by Robert Milligan (Christian Board of Publication); *That They May Be Won,* published privately by its compiler, F. J. Winder; *Churches of Today,* by L. G. Tomlinson (Gospel Advocate Company); and *The Church in the Bible,* by Don DeWelt (Ozark Bible College Press).

It is intended that this little book be used as a study course in the churches. Perhaps the teacher can make use of the books indicated by assigning students to read and report on one or more of these volumes. It would also prove valuable if the major chapters in the New Testament on this subject were assigned to various members of the class. One could make Acts 2 his specialty, another Ephesians 4, etc. Thus each member of the class would be a resource person, able to enrich the learning experience from his own individual research and study. Whatever the use to which this study booklet may be put, it must never come to be regarded in any sense as authoritative in its field. Only one book can claim that distinction, and that book is the New Testament itself. The best that any of us can offer is an effort to collect in one place the Biblical teachings on the subject, offer some definitions of the terms used, and share the thoughts of many others who have studied long and hard. If it serves no other purpose, at least may this booklet be used to underscore the awesome significance of the church, which Christ viewed so highly that He "gave himself for it."

---

[1] From *Jesus and His Church*, by R. Newton Flew. Copyright by The Epworth Press, London, England. Used by permission.

WHAT IS THE CHURCH?

Matthew 16:13-19; Ephesians 1:19-23; 5:23-32;
Colossians 1:12-20

WORDS AND THEIR MEANINGS

Definitions of the Word "Church"

A little girl became lost in the maze of the city's streets and a policeman was trying to help her. "If I can just find the church," she said, "I can find my way home." This is the cry of all humanity. Hopelessly lost in sin, we still can make our way home if we can find the church. To find it we must know what we are looking for and where to look. We must define carefully what we mean by "church" and even more carefully what is meant by "The New Testament Church." The word "church" is commonly used today to convey a variety of meanings. Sometimes it refers to a building set aside for worship, sometimes to the worship service itself, sometimes to a particular congregation, sometimes to a specific denomination, and sometimes to the whole body of obedient Christian believers.

Its Use in the Bible

In the Bible the word "church" is used to translate the Greek word *ekklesia*, which literally means "called out." To the Greeks the term referred to an assembly of citizens in a free and democratic society called out by the herald that they might discuss and act upon public business. The Hebrews also used a word that is translated "church" in the New Testament (Acts 7:38). The word appears often in the Old Testament where it is usually translated "congregation." To the Jews a church was the congregation or the community of Israel—not a self-governing body, but a theocratic assembly, i.e., one controlled by God. If we put the two ideas together, the Greek and the Hebrew, we have a fair idea of what the church really is: a community of men and women, free under Christ, following His orders when given and otherwise governing their own affairs. As Lindsay describes it, "a theocratic democracy." We may say, then, that the word "church" as it is used in this course and as it is used in the New Testament refers to the people whom God has called out of the world into a society dedicated to serving Him.

Jesus' Use of the Word

Interestingly, Jesus used the word "church" on only two occasions. This does not mean that Jesus did not have a lot to say about the church. He used a different term to describe it. Jesus' favorite term for the church was the broader expression, "kingdom." We are generally safe in saying that Jesus often used the terms synonymously. The best illustration of this is in Matthew 16:18, 19, where both terms come in the same breath and are obviously intended to describe the same thing. That Jesus should use the term "kingdom" rather than "church" is quite natural. His ministry was altogether among the Jews. All their Messianic hopes were built around the idea of a kingdom. When Jesus spoke of the kingdom, they knew at once that He referred to the society promised by God and described by the prophets.

It is equally appropriate that the apostles should use instead the word "church." By the time the Acts and the epistles were written, the church already had broadened out to include the non-Jewish world. To these Gentiles there would be little of the rich background the Jews saw in the word "kingdom." For them the word "church" would express the idea far more perfectly. Thus we find that the word "kingdom" appears but rarely in the Acts and in the epistles.

The Ideal Church

We shall study what Paul had to say about the perfect church. We shall keep in mind that the epistles were written to correct the faults of the church of the first century. They can also serve to correct the faults of the church in any century. The only perfect church is in the mind of

God. The New Testament letters were written to bring the church as it existed in Bible times more closely in line with God's ideal for it. It should be the objective of every sincere Christian to endeavor to make the church of this century like the church of God's intent. There never has been a perfect church and perhaps none now is exactly as God intended. But just as the first-century Christians used the epistles to become more like God's ideal church, so may we.

A Common Objection

This may help to explain a common objection raised when one says, "We want to be a New Testament church." It is often asked, "Which New Testament church do you want to be like? The one at Corinth, where men became drunk at the Lord's Table? The church at Galatia that wanted to hold on to the Old Testament law? The church at Ephesus with its false teachers?" The answer, of course, is that no one wants a church exactly like any of these. The point is that God had, and yet has, a plan for what His church ought to be. That perfect plan for the church is revealed in the New Testament. Then, as now, there was no perfect church. This church, God's ideal church, is the object of our study and, hopefully, our imitation.

Three Meanings

When the word "church" is used in the New Testament, it is used in at least three different senses. Sometimes it refers to the local congregation in a given city or a given community. Examples of this can be seen in 1 Corinthians 16:19; Colossians 4:15; and Philemon 2. In other instances the term refers to the church in its universal rather than its local sense. This wider meaning is seen in such passages as 1 Corinthians 10:32 and 12:28. There is a third use of the word, which we may call an ideal sense. This is the church as it exists in the mind of God: the church as God intended it to be and as eventually it shall be when the kingdoms of this world become the kingdom of our God and of His Christ. Which of these "churches" will be studied in this course? All three. We shall study the local congregations to see what they did and how they were constituted. We shall study what Jesus and Paul had to say about the church universal. We shall study the ideal church that it may become our example.

Use of the Old Testament

To some the phrase, "New Testament church," implies ignoring the Old Testament. Such an inference is wholly unwarranted. No man can hope to understand the Biblical doctrine of the church apart from the Old Testament. It provides the background and the explanation of the New. Still, it is the New Testament that records the founding of Christ's church, relates its early history, points out its errors and its virtues. It is only by a study of the New Testament, with constant reference to the Old, that man can ever understand the nature and mission of the church.

Use of the Term "New Testament Church"

The term "New Testament church" became prominent in our vocabulary when men began to notice striking dissimilarities between the various denominations and the church as God intended it. The term was and is used to distinguish those who yet strive to return to the divine pattern from those who seem content with the established traditions. Those human traditions slip so easily into our lives that we may often be unaware of their presence. Men have sometimes searched the Scriptures, not to find the truth, but to locate some proof for what they already practice and already have decided to believe. Such an approach to the study of the Bible often leads to gross misinterpretations and misapplications of Scripture. To say, "We are a New Testament church," implies that we have a perfect understanding of God's will and that we are following it exactly. Since no congregation wishes to appear that arrogant, many have said, "We are striving to be a New Testament church."

THE CHURCH JESUS BUILT

A Gift From God

When Jesus promised, "I will build my church" (Matthew 16:18), He referred to a society or kingdom He intended to found. He did not have in mind something that men make by their own efforts or devise by their own ingenuity. The church was God's kingdom, and citizenship in it a gift from Him. While in some instances in the New Testament the word "kingdom" refers to the eternal kingdom (heaven), in a great many passages the church may be meant. (See Matthew 3:2; 13: 24ff.; 19:24; Colossians 1:13; 2 Timothy 4:18; 2 Peter 1: 10, 11.)

Names for the Church

This church is called by many names in the New Testament. In Acts 20:28; 1 Corinthians 1:2; 11:22; 15:9; 2 Corinthians 1:1; 1 Thessalonians 2:14; and 1 Timothy 3:5 it is called the "church of God." In 1 Timothy 3:15 it is called the "church of the living God." In Romans 16:16 we are told, "the churches of Christ salute you." In 1 Corinthians 14:33 it is called "the church of the saints." Paul refers to the churches of Galatia and the churches of the Gentiles, but most often the term used is simply "the church" or "the churches." There are ninety-three such instances.

THE CHURCH—CHRIST'S BODY

A Living Body

We have seen that when Christ promised to build His church He had reference to an organization of men and women. But the word "organization" does not do justice to the church. It is much more than this. It is an organism, a living body. Nor is it just any sort of body. It is Christ's body, and He is its head. "And hath put all things under his feet, and gave him to be the head over all things to the church, which is his body, the fulness of him that filleth all in all" (Ephesians 1:22, 23). "For the husband is the head of the wife, even as Christ is the head of the church: and he is the saviour of the body" (Ephesians 5:23). "But speaking the truth in love, may grow up into him in all things, which is the head, even Christ" (Ephesians 4:15). "And he is the head of the body, the church: who is the beginning, the firstborn from the dead; that in all things he might have the pre-eminence.... Who now rejoice in my sufferings for you, and fill up that which is behind of the afflictions of Christ in my flesh for his body's sake, which is the church" (Colossians 1:18, 24).

A Living Christ

If Christ had not risen from the dead, if He were not alive today, it might have been necessary for the church to have some earthly head. Since Christ lives, no man has the right to take the Lord's place at the head of His body, the church. As long as Christ lives, the church needs no earthly head, and since the headquarters are where the head is, there is no place on this earth that may be pointed out as the headquarters from which Christ continues to govern and direct His body. What a tragedy it is when a man's physical body does not obey the head. In such a situation, there can be no meaningful activity. Greater still is the tragedy so often repeated in church history, when the body of Christ has refused to obey its head. The authority of Christ must never be usurped by a man nor by any group of men. Christ is as capable of directing the affairs of His kingdom today as ever. He has never delegated His authority as head of the church to any man.

A Loving Christ

When we press a little further this figure of the church as a body, we get a beautiful picture of the care and concern that Christ has for us. We know that when one portion of a human body suffers pain a message is immediately transmitted to the head, and it shares that suffering. It is the head that instructs the other parts of the body to go to the aid of the stricken area. If it is an infection, the heart pumps faster to keep the blood supply moving, the tiny armies that fight disease are dispatched to the scene, and the whole body goes into action to stamp out the infection. If it is a wound to be healed, a similar process occurs. How comforting it is to know that whenever the church suffers from disease or injury Christ suffers too. Not only so, but He mobilizes for us spiritual forces that can cure our diseases and heal our wounds. In a lonely and often friendless world, it is a great satisfaction to belong to an institution whose all-wise head can anticipate every situation and move at once to correct it. When the human body is severed from the head, death is certain. To preserve its own life, the body must not cut itself off from its head. That is why prayer and the daily study of God's Word are so essential. By these means we keep in contact with the headquarters of the church, receive our instructions from the living Christ, and, more than this, receive His power as well.

A United Body

In this connection it is good to recall that Paul said in Ephesians 4:4, "There is one body." How are we to reconcile this statement with the fact that there are hundreds of church bodies in the world, each claiming our allegiance and support? There are some who declare that this is an acceptable condition. They contend that God is not displeased with the divided condition of Christendom, that such a situation is good and wholesome. Certainly such a view is not in harmony with Scripture. Read Paul's condemnation of the divisions at Corinth (1 Corinthians 1:11-13) and you will see how seriously he regarded such a situation to be. What is the answer to such a problem? Is Christian unity possible? Can all believers in Christ be brought together in one body today? Upon what basis can unity be accomplished?

Answers to these questions are to be found in the New Testament. Let us refer to that time in history when the church was united, when there was one body. Let us be determined to have a church in our time that is striving in every way possible to be like God's ideal church. Then we may call upon men to discard the doctrines and practices that have grown up in the years since the New Testament was written, and on the basis of the Bible and the Bible alone Christians can be united. The person perplexed and confused by denominationalism can be given the opportunity of being "just a Christian." So many are asking, "Which church shall I choose?" The answer always ought to be, "Find the religious group that is most like the church described in the Bible and affiliate with it."

THE CHURCH—CHRIST'S BRIDE

Obedient to Him

Paul wrote in Ephesians 5:22-24, "Wives, submit yourselves unto your own husbands, as unto the Lord. For the husband is the head of the wife, even as Christ is the head of the church: and he is the saviour of the body. Therefore as the church is subject unto Christ, so let the wives be to their own husbands in every thing." In Paul's day the husband was the undisputed head of the household. His wife never questioned his judgment. This is the illustration Paul uses to show the relationship of the church to Christ. He is the head of the spiritual household. The church is His bride. The church has no right to question the wisdom of the Lord. If He has dictated that His church shall follow a certain pattern in organization, worship, or service, then the church is bound to do His will. To refuse to do so would be to disown His authority and supplant it with our own. No human being is wise enough to chart the course of the kingdom of God. Neither man nor group of men has either the ability or the right to do this.

Awaiting His Coming

Revelation 19:6-9 says, "And I heard as it were the voice of a great multitude, and as the voice of many waters, and as the voice of mighty thunderings, saying, Alleluia: for the Lord God omnipotent reigneth. Let us be glad and rejoice, and give honour to him: for the marriage of the Lamb is come, and his wife hath made herself ready. And to her was granted that she should be arrayed in fine linen, clean and white: for the fine linen is the righteousness of saints. And he saith unto me, Write, Blessed are they which are called unto the marriage supper of the Lamb. And he saith unto me, These are the true sayings of God." Revelation 21:9 adds, "Come hither, I will shew thee the bride, the Lamb's wife." These verses indicate that the actual marriage is yet to take place; that the church is betrothed to Christ; and that she awaits the marriage supper; which will initiate her eternal life with him. What a beautiful illustration this is! In our country an engagement is not legally binding, and may be easily broken. This was not the case in Bible times. It will be recalled that Joseph was betrothed to Mary when the Holy Spirit visited her, and that at first he was tempted to divorce her (Matthew 1:18-21). It was only by a divorce that a betrothal could be broken. The church is betrothed to Christ. Though the wedding awaits the return of the Lord, the church belongs to Him and must remain faithful to Him.

QUESTIONS

1. What are some of the meanings of the word "church" as it is commonly used today?

2. What is the meaning of the Greek word that is translated "church" in the New Testament?

3. Compare the Greek and the Hebrew ideas of an assembly.

4. What synonym for the word "church" did Jesus generally use?

5. In the New Testament the word "church" has three meanings. What are they?

6. What are some of the names by which the church is called in the New Testament?

7. What lessons may be learned from the picture of the church as the body of Christ?

8. What lessons may be learned from the picture of the church as the bride of Christ?

9. Was the church in New Testament times a perfect church?

10. How may we discover God's ideal for the church?

WORD PICTURES OF THE CHURCH

1 Peter 2; Romans 11; Ephesians

In attempting to express the complex nature of the church, the New Testament makes use of many word pictures. These suggest various aspects of the church's life and nature. Man can better understand the church when he is told that it is like a family, or a kingdom, or a bride. In considering these passages, however, it must be kept in mind that the church is not exactly like a family nor exactly like a kingdom. Only in certain aspects does the resemblance hold true. The church is not like any family you have known, nor like any kingdom history has recorded, nor like any bride. Perhaps by putting many of these word pictures together and viewing them all at once, we may gain an accurate view of what the church really is.

PICTURES DRAWN FROM FAMILY LIFE

The Household of God

Few relationships of man are dearer than the family relationship. What grand ideas of peace, security, love, and contentment we associate with the home. Ephesians 2:19 shows in very eloquent fashion how God has gathered the homeless, the separated, those with almost nothing in common, and made of them a family. "Now therefore ye are no more strangers and foreigners, but fellow-citizens with the saints, and of the household of God." What a beautiful expression is this, that partakes of all our precious memories and builds upon them a picture of a home that will never know sin or sadness, an eternal home filled

19

with unfailing love and unending happiness. It is ours, now, in the church!

The Bride of Christ

We have already seen what a powerful figure of speech this is. Here we need only add that there is a wide range of parallels between the church and a bride. The bride's manner of dress suggests purity. Her marriage ceremony demands lifelong loyalty. A bride is the object of honor and praise, as the church must be. Since she is the bride of Christ, the church is worthy of respect and reverence and must never be degraded or debased. Paul says that this is a great mystery! No man can understand how two people become one flesh in the marriage ceremony, and no one can comprehend fully the intricate and intimate relationship that exists between Christ and His bride, the church.

A Brotherhood

In its original sense. the word "brotherhood" had reference to those who were actually brothers. Now it has come to carry a fraternal rather than a filial significance. Our society knows many brotherhoods. Some are social, some are economic. They range from college fraternities to lodges and labor unions. Each brotherhood draws men together upon the basis of common interests. The Christian brotherhood possesses a stronger tie. In that fraternity, men are drawn together upon the basis of a common Father. So our brotherhood resembles current brotherhoods in that it draws men from many and various backgrounds and unites them in a common purpose. It partakes of the original idea of brotherhood because the basis of the relationship is the fact that each has been adopted into the family of God. Christ then takes His place in this family relationship as the elder Brother (Matthew 12:50).

PICTURES DRAWN FROM POLITICAL LIFE

The Church as a Kingdom

The first essential of a kingdom is a king. The term may suggest the absolute rule of a dictator. It has been said that a dictatorship is the most efficient form of government ever devised. Unfortunately, however, a dictatorship may be good or bad depending upon the character and intelligence of the dictator. In the church One of unchallenged character and of undisputed wisdom reigns supreme.

Another essential of a kingdom is territory. There must be a realm to rule. As a great hymn of the church declares, the world now lies in the grip of a usurper who has tried to supplant the world's rightful sovereign. The usurper is Satan whom the Bible characterizes as "the prince of this world." It is necessary that an all-out offensive be pressed forward so that the kingdoms of this world may become the kingdom of our God and of His Christ, and He may reign forever and ever (Revelation 11:15). Kingdoms are further characterized by laws. How else shall the subjects know what is expected of them? How else can one measure his allegiance to the king? It must be pointed out that while there are many laws of conduct in the church, and that while they must be obeyed, still one's salvation rests not in law but in grace. The distinction is a difficult one, and often has been misunderstood.

A Holy Nation

In a dramatic passage (1 Peter 2:9), the apostle indicates that Christians are citizens as well as subjects. From every nation they come to be united in this new and spiritual nation. Unlike the nation of Israel, this is a holy nation. Its codes and laws are the highest imaginable. Its blessings are likewise beyond compare. Great spiritual freedom exists, but, spiritually as politically, it is liberty within law. Indeed, where there is no law there can be no lasting liberty. Law is liberty's safeguard. Politically, law keeps men free by keeping them safe from themselves. God's laws are given solely for the protection and welfare of His children. They reflect His incalculable wisdom and love.

The Church as Community

We are apt to think of the word "community" in a geographical sense. Actually, the word can have a much wider significance. The dictionary defines the term as basically meaning "a body of people having common organization or interests," or "common character; likeness." Thus there are economic communities, political communities, and religious communities. In its earliest beginning, the church possessed a deep sense of community, as evidenced by the communal living described in Acts 2. Whether or not communal living is practiced, the church must always have this sense of community, this sense of belonging. Indeed, the sense of community knows no geographical bounds, and one may feel this kinship with those whose faces he has never seen and about whom he knows little. Such is the fellowship of the church, and only of the church. As Dwight E. Stevenson has said, "Where is the belonging that will assuage that lonely heart? In the answer we find the church's reason for being. The cry for community is deeper and more urgent than the cry for human friendship; it is a cry that rises to heaven and calls, 'Father!' "[1]

PICTURES DRAWN FROM THE OLD TESTAMENT

A Royal Priesthood

For long centuries the Hebrews had looked upon their priests with respect and honored them as the spiritual intercessors between their nation and God. This did not mean that a Jew could not go directly to God in prayer; but it did mean that when the awful matters of sin, judgment, and forgiveness were involved, the priest was the mediator between sinning man and forgiving God. With this heritage so much a part of his background, it is easy to see why Peter was so impressed with the priesthood of all believers. He considered it no small matter to be able to say in 1 Peter 2:9 that Christians constitute "a royal priesthood." He mentions it also in 1 Peter 2:5. John declares in the Revelation that God has made us priests (1:6; 5:10; 20:6). It may be interesting to speculate whether we are each individually priests of God, whether corporately, as the church, we constitute a royal priesthood, or both. Whatever the case, there is a sense in which the church occupies that favored position of ministering to God in worship and sacrifice, a position once held dear by a sacred few.

The People of God

In that same passage in which the apostle Peter likens the church to the priesthood, he echoes the prophet Hosea, and calls the church "a peculiar people." A better translation would be "a people peculiarly God's," or "a people of God's own possession." Hosea's daughter was named, at God's direction, Loruhamah, which means "I will no more have mercy." The next child, a son, was named Loammi, which means "ye are not my people." Later God instructed Hosea to change the children's names to Ruhamah, "I will have mercy," and Ammi, "Ye are my people." It is with this dramatic story from the prophets in mind, that Peter writes of those "which in time past were not a people, but are now the people of God: which had not obtained mercy, but now have obtained mercy."

Assembly of God

The phrase, "people of God," is particularly interesting when we compare it with our English word "church." Why was this word chosen to translate *ekklesia*? Would not the word "assembly" have been better? What about the word "congregation" or "community"? The handicap that all of these words share is that they are not distinctive. There are many kinds of assemblies, congregations, and communities. Is the church just another assembly, another gathering for a worthy cause? Many believe that our English word "church" stems from a word that means "that which belongs to the Lord." When we consider that the church is the people of God, the bride of Christ, the body of Christ, the assembly of God, the household of God, and the kingdom of God, then suddenly the word appears to be most expressive of what the *ekklesia* really is. The distinctive thing about it is that it belongs to God, that it is made up of people whom God has called out. Despite its ambiguity, the word "church" is distinctively religious, tied inseparably to God, and it is a most appropriate equivalent to *ekklesia*.

Israel of God

In Galatians 6:16 Paul refers to the church as "the Israel of God." Surely he has a similar idea in mind when in 1 Corinthians 10:18 he distinguishes the Hebrew nation as "Israel after the flesh." Paul sees in the church the spiritual continuity of the chosen people. From the call of Abraham and the deliverance by Moses, through the war-torn days of the judges, the golden age of David and Solomon, and on through the long years of oppression and servitude, Paul sees God at work to bring the church to fulfillment. This is not merely Hebrew heritage; it is Christian heritage. Spiritual Israel is made up of all those who will accept God's call by faith, as Abraham did. Just as He called the patriarch out of Ur and out of Haran, and just as He called Moses out of Midian and Israel out of Egypt, so today the church consists of "the called out ones."

Abraham's Seed

This is why Paul sees Christians as descendants of Abraham. They are not necessarily his physical descendants, but because they live by faith they are his spiritual descendants. In Romans, chapter nine, Paul argues long upon this point. In Galatians 3:7 he again asserts, "They which are of faith, the same are the children of Abraham." John the Baptist intimated this when he declared, "Begin not to say within yourselves, We have Abraham to our father: for I say unto you, That God is able of these stones to raise up children unto Abraham." While the Old Testament's dramatic events may be thought of as preparatory to the coming of Christ and the church, there is a sense in which the church becomes the spiritual and eternal continuation of that which began with the patriarchs of long ago.

OTHER WORD PICTURES

Christ's Body

We have already seen that one of Paul's most popular figures of speech for the church was that of a body. We may ask, "Is this a good illustration of the church?" Perhaps if we are thinking of our bodies as they are besieged by disease, subject to injury, destined to death and decay, we might say that there are few parallels. But it is not our bodies that illustrate the church. It is Christ's body, and His body was indestructible! It came forth from the grave! Just as He triumphed over death, so shall the church triumph over sin and Satan. The church is destined to endure. She may suffer for a time, as Christ in His physical body suffered, but she will never be destroyed. Men may imagine that they have buried the church beneath the debris of history, but as surely as Christ came forth from the grave, so will He ever resurrect His church. It is a body that even death cannot destroy.

A Full-grown Man

In Ephesians, chapter four, the apostle Paul declares the object of all Christian service to be this: that the church and its members may be brought to spiritual maturity. While Jesus taught us to be childlike, we are not to be childish. Paul declares that Christian living is a matter of growing up; that through the various ministries of those who serve we may come to know Christ better, and through that knowledge be more like Him. We shall someday, He says, be a full-grown man. The church will know "the measure of the stature of the fulness of Christ." How beautiful is the picture of a church, struggling through many centuries to be like Christ, and at the very best failing repeatedly, but assured that someday she shall indeed succeed.

A Building of God

No student of the Hebrew religion can miss the significance attached by Jews to their places of worship. Elaborate precautions surrounded the tabernacle, that movable house of worship in the wilderness. Only those divinely designated could so much as touch its sacred furnishings. Great wealth was invested in Solomon's temple, and strict and unyielding rules governed its use. To a people whose religion was so unmistakably tied to a particular place and to a certain building, Christianity must have seemed barren and colorless. The Christian religion was tied to no special city, no temple, no geographical location, no building. Instead, says Peter, we have a spiritual house. Each Christian is a living stone in this building of God! As such, says Paul, we are "built upon the foundation of the apostles and prophets, Jesus Christ himself being the chief corner stone; in whom all the building fitly framed together groweth unto an holy temple in the Lord: in whom ye also are builded together for an habitation of God through the Spirit." The hopes of Christians are never tied to a collection of stones and brick and mortar. They are themselves the stones and love is the mortar. Thus bound together, they constitute the loveliest and holiest temple ever built.

An Olive Tree

In a very beautiful passage reminiscent of Jesus' words, "I am the vine, ye are the branches," Paul characterizes the people of God as an olive tree. He devotes the greater part of the eleventh chapter of Romans to this theme. He sees the Jews as the natural branches, the Gentiles as branches from a wild olive tree. Because of unbelief, the natural branches were cut off, and in their place God grafted in branches from the wild olive. Paul warns the Gentiles that they must not be filled with pride, for God will cut them off just as He did the natural branches, if they do not believe. Moreover, the original branches will be grafted in again if they believe. God was no respecter of persons in selecting either the Jews or the Gentiles. In every case, God demands faith in Him.

It goes without saying that once a branch is separated from the tree, it withers and dies. It can live and bear fruit only as it remains connected to the vine. Notice also that the individual is a branch. Sometimes these parables have been used as justification for a divided Christendom. As Jesus and Paul viewed it, the branches were not denominations but persons. Each person must keep himself united with the parent tree, from which comes his strength and his very life.

WORD PICTURES OF THE CHRISTIAN

Each of these word pictures of the church suggests corresponding terms to characterize the individual Christian. When the Bible describes Christians as sons and brothers, we think at once of the family relationship. When Christians are described as citizens, subjects, servants, soldiers, or ambassadors, our minds turn to the parallels between the church and political government.

When Christians are described as stones or branches, we find these terms beautifully suggestive of our duties and nature. When the Bible refers to God's children as strangers and pilgrims, we think at once of the world's antagonism for Christ and of its rebellion against His will. Indeed, so wide is the scope of Christianity that all these terms are necessary to even a partial understanding of God's plan for men. No single word or combination of words can ever fully express all that is involved in the Christian system. In its broader ramifications, it is as complex as God himself. In its immediate application, however, its requirements are so plain that the most unsophisticated and unlearned may thoroughly know what God requires.

QUESTIONS

1. In what sense is the church like a family?

2. What ideas associated with a bride are also true of the church?

3. What three things are necessary to a kingdom? Does the church possess these?

4. Discuss the word "community" as it is commonly used, and in its wider significance. How is the church a community?

5. What parallels are there between the priesthood of the Old Testament and the church?

6. Why does Paul call the church "The Israel of God"?

7. Who are Abraham's seed? Who are his seed by faith?

8. What is the Christian temple and of what material is it constructed?

9. In the parable of the olive tree, as given by Paul, identify the wild branches and the natural branches.

10. How many word pictures of the Christian, found in the New Testament, can you name?

---

[1] *From The Church—What and Why*, by Dwight E. Stevenson, page 7. Copyright by the Christian Board of Publication of St. Louis, Missouri. Used by permission.

PREPARING THE WAY

Hebrews 7:1-28; 8:1-13; 9:1-28; 10:1-22;
Romans 2:11-24; 3:1-31; Galatians 4:1-31; 5:1-26

When God set His infant church in the midst of a hostile world, He did not do so thoughtlessly nor carelessly. Its beginning marked the climax of centuries of preparation. Though the world of the new church was almost immediately antagonistic toward it, it was nonetheless a world prepared for that great event. That preparation is recorded in the Old Testament, in secular history, and in the New Testament.

PREPARATION IN THE OLD TESTAMENT

Preparing a People

God began by preparing a people to be the cradle of the king; a people that could produce a Mary, humble enough and faithful enough to bear the Christ child; a nation that could produce an Anna and a Simeon to bear witness to that child; a nation that would serve as a nucleus for an international kingdom.

He prepared these people by revealing himself to them. As the centuries rolled by, more and more knowledge and truth about God was unveiled. We may well believe that, had God in the very beginning fully revealed himself to sinful man, man would have been totally incapable of receiving it. Before the fulness of that revelation could come in the purpose of Christ, humanity had to be conditioned by a gradual revelation of the glory of God. The vehicle of this progressive revelation was the Hebrew people. God spoke to them through the patriarchs and the prophets, developed in them a deep religious consciousness, and through them made himself known to all men.

He further prepared them by victory and defeat, thus showing the power of God and showing that God was absolutely indispensable to man. By blessing and punishment He showed them that "the way of transgressors is hard," but "blessed is the man that walketh not in the counsel of the ungodly."

Preparing a Vocabulary

How is it possible to describe to a man something that he has never seen? It can be done only in terms of that which he has seen. How could God convey the revolutionary concepts of the church to men? How could He ever hope to make man understand? The answer lay in the preparing of a vocabulary that would be adequate. The law of Moses served this purpose, for it gives us the nomenclature of the New. When John the Baptist pointed Jesus out as the "Lamb of God," no one wondered what He meant. They had seen hundreds of lambs offered on the sacrificial altars of the temple. Their prophets had told them of a suffering servant, to whom these offerings pointed. How could one understand terms like atonement and propitiation without the rich background of the old law and its manifold sacrifices and burnt offerings? Indeed, the very word "sacrifice" is rich with meaning because of our knowledge of the offerings of bygone days. The very idea of grace and mercy is made plainer to us when we see the mercy seat in the temple and understand its true significance. In the book of Hebrews the writer draws heavily upon the Old Testament vocabulary, declaring that Christ is our high priest, though we all are priests of God, that heaven is the holy of holies into which Christ has at last entered, having offered himself for our sins. The person who has read Leviticus will be thrilled when in Hebrews he learns that Christ is at once the perfect sacrifice and the perfect priest to offer that sacrifice. As a little exercise, try to eliminate from your vocabulary all terms borrowed from the Old Testament and see how few songs are left in the hymnal, how meaningless are the sermons, how empty the lessons!

The Law—a Schoolmaster

No child begins his formal education in high school; so humanity could not begin with Christ and His kingdom. Paul says in Galatians 3:24 that the law was our schoolmaster to bring us to Christ. The spiritual maturing of the human race began with its great teacher, the law of Moses. Many indeed are the lessons learned from that schoolmaster. Paul devotes the greater portion of the book of Romans to outlining them. Perhaps chief among them was the lesson that no man could ever be justified by the works of the law. The law proved once and for all the utter sinfulness of men; proved that man by his own good works could never deserve God's forgiveness or a heavenly home. Man's crying need for the grace of God was made plain. The law further taught mankind the faithfulness of God. It showed that God remains righteous, no matter how sinful His creatures may become. His divine faithfulness underscores human unfaithfulness, and points out the void that only God's grace can fill.

PREPARATION IN HUMAN HISTORY

God Sets the Scene

Secular history also contains a record of God's preparation for His church. It may not be possible for us to decide to what extent God interfered in history to prepare for His Son and the church. Did God manipulate history, or merely make use of it? While we may never be able to agree as to the extent of His interference, there can be no doubt that divine providence provided an ideal time for the church to be born. Galatians 4:4 says that Christ came in "the fulness of time." That fullness was characterized by many factors, political, social, economic, and spiritual. At no point in history was the time riper for the coming of the promised Messiah than in the first century A.D.

Political Preparation

To the person reared in the atmosphere of a free republic, it might appear that the church was born at a most unlikely time. All the civilized world lay under the power of one of the most totalitarian dictatorships ever known. Rome ruled with an iron hand (though not always with a cool head) all the lands of the Mediterranean to the farthest reaches of

31

the known world. Christianity, however, was not concerned with politics. It is a good lesson for every age that Christianity had its beginnings under a cruel and pagan dictatorship and can survive under any political system.

Roman rule offered many advantages to the infant church. The first of these was peace. It was an uneasy and an enforced peace, to be sure. But when nations are engaged in great wars they become so preoccupied with military conquest that there is little time for religious speculation and contemplation. When the nation is at peace, people find time to turn their thoughts inward and consider the state of their souls. Peace also means that there are few restrictions on travel. In this case, the advantage was increased by the fact that there were few national boundaries to cross. With Rome in control of so vast a portion of the world, there was no need to secure visas or passports. The long waiting periods and the interminable red tape so much a part of modern missions were unknown then. With persecution attending the church almost from its inception, and with opposition to it growing rapidly in intensity, time was a precious commodity to the early church. The absence of restrictions on travel helped conserve that precious time.

Economic Preparation

The first century was a prosperous era for Rome, though it was not so for the far-flung provinces. Lands like Israel were bled white by the oppressive taxation of Rome, but part of those taxes were used to build the fine highways of ancient times. The Roman roads that sped the tax collectors and the armies on their way also provided a speedy route for the evangelists of the church of Christ. So splendid were those roads that some of them remain to this day. Over them hurried the feet "shod with the preparation of the gospel of peace" to fulfill Isaiah's prophecy, "How beautiful upon the mountains are the feet of him that bringeth good tidings, that publisheth peace; that bringeth good tidings of good, that publisheth salvation" (52:7). The first century also was an era of great commercial activity. From Rome marched armies and procurators, and to Rome came caravan after caravan bringing the precious commodities of the East. Thus the gospel was spread not only by those who sought places of opportunity, but also by those to whom travel was incidental to their professions. Merchants and soldiers and public officials were converted to Christ, and wherever their professions took them they witnessed for Him. Every Christian became an evangelist, and the unprecedented commercial activity of the time became the current that bore the witnesses of Christ to the farthest reaches of Roman rule.

Social Preparation

Though the Romans held political sway over the world, the Greeks continued to control the minds of men. Militarily they had been defeated by Rome, but intellectually they continued to rule the world throughout the Roman era; and their influence even in our time is considerable. Thus it came to be that every educated person in the time of Christ spoke Greek. It was so widely used that the New Testament books were written in Greek. Here again we can see an inestimable advantage for the church. How many years a missionary must spend learning the language of his people! How valuable it would be if this were not necessary. To be sure, there were those who did not speak Greek, and God on occasion miraculously provided the gift of tongues to overcome that difficulty. But almost any man who could read knew Greek, and the New Testament was, from the first, a book for all the people. It is worth noting, too, that the Greek language was one of the most precise languages ever to be used. There is a word for every shade of meaning. Often one English word will be used to translate three or four different Greek words, simply because our language has no word to express the exact meaning. Such precision made it possible for God to convey His will to man with exactness and accuracy. No more expressive language could possibly have been chosen.

Spiritual Preparation

We have already learned of the spiritual preparation that God undertook in making ready for the church. There was, in addition, incidental spiritual preparation that is significant. The old religions were all breaking down. The paganism of Rome was kept intact only because of the political power of the emperor-god, Caesar. The Greeks loved to debate their heathen religion, but few really had any faith in the old gods. Even Judaism, the worship of the true and living God, had turned into a hollow mockery. The hypocrisy of the priests was common knowledge. Men were bound to Israel more by political, sentimental, and family ties than by a real spiritual concern. Certainly many still worshiped the God of Israel sincerely, but many others had lost their confidence in the old ways. Messianic expectation was high. While it is true that men expected a political Messiah, and that they longed for freedom from Rome more than for freedom from sin, still there existed a great spiritual void, crying to be filled.

NEW TESTAMENT PREPARATION

The final steps in preparing the way for the church were taken by Jesus himself, and are recorded in the four Gospels. During His ministry Jesus revealed, more fully than ever before, the nature and character of God. He laid down the perfect example for every man's life. He preached the good news, healed the sick, and raised the dead. Despite the hectic days filled with activity and despite the continuous pressure of the crowds, He found time to train the twelve for their duties. Finally He brought His ministry to a climax by dying on the cross for the world's sins and by His resurrection from the dead. Certainly it would be a mistake to say that Jesus did all this simply by way of preparation for the church. The incarnation of God in Christ was itself the climax of all the hopes and dreams of the human race. The church is the extension of that incarnation, so that just as God was in Christ, so in some lesser sense He may be in all men. The church and its members were to bear witness in every generation to these facts about Christ: His life, His death, His resurrection. "Ye shall be witnesses unto me," Jesus said. That the witness of the twelve might be effective they were promised remarkable gifts of the Holy Spirit: inspiration, revelation, miraculous abilities to heal, speak in foreign tongues, and to raise the dead. Thus empowered they were ready for the awesome task of preaching the gospel to every creature.

The last step in preparation for the church was prayer. Just before His ascension Jesus instructed the apostles to wait for the promised power that God would give them. The Bible records that the ten days between the ascension and Pentecost were spent in meditation and prayer. It may be truly said that the church was born out of a prayer meeting. It was the final step and an essential step in preparing the way for the kingdom of God.

COMPARING OLD AND NEW

The entire book of Hebrews is devoted to a comparison of the old covenant and the new. Such a comparison reveals striking dissimilarities and even more striking parallels. The Old Testament church was national, while the New Testament church is international. The old was temporary, the new, eternal. The old had its beginning in Abraham, the new in Christ. The members of the old lived by the law of Moses, those of the new by the grace and truth of Jesus Christ. The old law was written on stone, the new in the heart (2 Corinthians 3:1-8). The old was entered by physical birth, the new by a spiritual birth. The old had a sign, circumcision; the sign of the new is faith (Galatians 5:6). The Jewish church had endless animal sacrifices, the new is sanctified by the blood of Christ. Worship in the old centered in the temple at Jerusalem. The emphasis of worship in the new is on "spirit and truth." Loaves of unleavened bread lay on the table in the old and they are on the table of the new. The old had a high priest chosen from among men, the new has an eternal high priest without beginning of days or end of life. The Old Testament church fulfilled its purpose by ushering in the new. The new will have its fulfillment in the bringing of mankind to eternal life with God.

THE CHURCH IN PROPHECY

Beginning at Jerusalem

In Isaiah 2:1-3 the following prophecy is recorded: "The word that Isaiah the son of Amoz saw concerning Judah and Jerusalem. And it shall come to pass in the last days, that the mountain of the Lord's house shall be established in the top of the mountains, and shall be exalted above the hills; and all nations shall flow unto it. And many people shall go and say, Come ye, and let us go up to the mountain of the Lord, to the house of the God of Jacob; and he will teach us of his ways, and we will walk in his paths: for out of Zion shall go forth the law, and the word of the Lord from Jerusalem." The prophecy occurs again in Micah 4:1-4. Jesus reiterated it in Luke 24:46-48: "Thus it is written, and thus it behoved Christ to suffer, and to rise from the dead the third day: And that repentance and remission of sins should be preached in his name among all nations, beginning at Jerusalem. And ye are witnesses of these things."

Ye Shall Receive Power

Both Joel and Jesus predicted that the inaugural day of the church would be attended by manifestations of divine power. In Acts 2, Peter quotes Joel 2:28-32 and shows that Pentecost is the fulfillment of the promise, "I will pour out my spirit upon all flesh." Just before His ascension Jesus had said "Tarry ye in Jerusalem, until ye be endued with power from on high" (Luke 24:49; Acts 1:4). Acts 2:3, 4 records the fulfillment of the promise. Cloven tongues of fire appeared on the heads of the twelve, and they spake in foreign tongues the wonderful works of God.

QUESTIONS

1. How did God go about preparing a people?

2. How many terms can you name which are used in the church, but which were borrowed from the Old Testament?

3. What did the law prove to man?

4. What advantages were offered the early church by being under Roman rule?

5. What advantages did the church enjoy because of the wide use of the Greek language?

6. What were the social and economic factors that made the time appropriate for the church to be born?

7. What did Jesus do to prepare for the coming of the church?

8. Make two lists. In one write down as many similarities between the Old Testament and the New Testament as you can. In the other, write down as many dissimilarities as you can.

9. According to Old Testament prophecy and the promises of Jesus, in what city was the church to be launched?

10. How did God show that He had given divine power to the twelve?

WHEN THE CHURCH WAS BORN

Acts 2; Joel 2:28-32; Acts 3

THE DAY OF PENTECOST

The Evidence

The New Testament does not state precisely on what day the church began. All evidence, however, points to Pentecost. For the first time the church is spoken of as being in existence (Acts 2:47). In previous references to the church in Matthew 16 Jesus used the future tense. The passage in Matthew 18 either refers to Israel, or else to what should be done when the church was itself finally established. The apostle Peter regarded Pentecost as the beginning (Acts 11:15).

There is a sense in which the church is the spiritual continuation of the people of God, Israel. Yet Jesus' oft-spoken words, "The kingdom of God is at hand," indicate a decisive beginning rather than a gradual blending of one into the other. Some would date the beginning of the church with the calling of the twelve. Certainly the twelve were, in a sense, the prototype of the church. Jesus calls them "Little flock" (Luke 12:32), and it may well be that this was the beginning of that larger flock that was to embrace all who would accept Christ. Some have held that the church began with the last supper. If the church did begin at some time prior to Pentecost, then certainly it is true that the church did not begin its work before "that great and notable day." It must also follow that if the church was begun sooner it was a powerless church, for Jesus' promise (Luke 24:49 and Acts 1:4) was not fulfilled until then. The better view is that the calling of the twelve and the last supper are but part of the prelude, the

37

foreshadowing, of things to come. Pentecost stands out as the most momentous day in human history, apart from the crucifixion and the resurrection.

The Jewish Feast

For nearly fifteen hundred years the Jews had celebrated this joyous feast. It was their harvest festival, when the grain was ripe and ready for harvesting. From this harvest the Hebrew brought an offering to God to thank Him for the bounty. How appropriate that at the feast of first fruits the gospel should bear its fruit for the first time. How fitting that God's reapers should move out into fields white unto harvest just at the time that every Hebrew farmer began to reap. Just as the grain was ripe in the farmers' fields, so the time was ripe in the history of man. Just as the Jews engaged in solemn worship before the harvest, so did the apostles spend ten days refreshing their spirits through prayer and fasting before the harvest began.

The Crowds

Multitudes thronged Jerusalem's narrow streets at Pentecost, and a symphony of sound echoed from its walls. Lambs bleated and donkeys brayed, children cried, and old friends hailed one another. The merchants called out their wares and the temple priests chanted out their rituals. Worshipers had come from every corner of the civilized world. They were people steeped in the traditions of their fathers and schooled in the law and the prophets. The stage was set, the crowd was assembled, the participants were ready. The curtain was about to be rung up on that unforgettable drama: the birth of the church.

A DAY OF POWER

Divine Manifestations

At the very climax of the festival Christ fulfilled His promise to the twelve. "Ye shall receive power," He had said, and receive it they did. They were all in one place, perhaps somewhere in the temple area, when cloven tongues like as of fire appeared.

These were the visible tokens of an unseen power that was to grip the minds and the mouths of the apostles. Not only were they guided in the content of their message, they were miraculously enabled to preach it to those who spoke neither the Hebrew of their birth nor the Greek of their school. According to Acts 2, Jews from more than a dozen lands were present, yet each heard the message in his own tongue. Bible scholars are not agreed as to the nature of this miraculous event. Some take the view that the twelve spoke in only one language, but that every man heard in his own. Others object saying that this is not consistent with the language of the text, and that it makes the miracle in the hearing rather than the speaking. They contend that either one apostle spoke one language and another a different one, or that in turn they spoke the various tongues of the crowd. There is no way to resolve this point, and it really does not matter. The vital point is that in a miraculous way each man heard in his own tongue the gospel message.

A Universal Church

From the very beginning God made it evident that this was to be a universal kingdom, not limited by national or racial boundaries. The fact that "each in his own tongue" heard the good news demonstrated that Christianity was not an exclusive religion. One did not need to learn Hebrew or Greek in order to share in the kingdom. The implication is strong that one must not confuse customs with Christianity. Missionaries have sometimes been accused of giving more attention to Americanizing than to Christianizing. The Christian need not adopt any man's way of life, only Christ's.

A DAY OF PROCLAMATION

The cloven tongues of fire did more than signal the miraculous gift of speaking in foreign tongues. They were further symbolic of the burning eloquence with which the message was delivered. Perhaps each of the twelve preached that day, but only one sermon is recorded, that of Peter. He "lifted up his voice," and that voice continues to be heard in every age. He proclaimed that the events of this Pentecost were prophesied in the Old Testament, that God had said beforehand that this was what He would do. Taking his text from the prophet Joel, Peter declared that what they were witnessing was the fulfillment of Israel's hopes and dreams.

Peter further showed that the events of Pentecost, A.D. 30, were rooted in the mighty acts of God. Jehovah himself had intervened in human history, had in fact *entered* human history in the person of Jesus Christ. Peter counted the crucifixion and the resurrection chief among His mighty acts. They, too, said Peter, had been prophesied beforehand. From the psalms of David he showed that the Messiah must experience both death and resurrection, and that far from disqualifying Him, these were the very things that fitted Him to be made "both Lord and Christ."

Peter's message was quite personal and pointed. He next accused his audience of being personally responsible for the death of Christ. Those words were themselves tongues of fire. They burned their way to the very hearts of all who heard. Had some there actually been a part of the crowd that cried to Pilate, "Crucify him"? Perhaps. But all Israel was guilty, for "he came unto his own and his own received him not." Indeed, all humanity must share the guilt, for it was not the nails that held Christ on the cross, but our sins. Who could fail to react to such a message in just the same fashion as the audience at Pentecost? "Men and brethren, what shall we do?" What minister would not like to preach today with such power that convicted sinners would interrupt the message and cry out, "What shall we do?"

Peter's Reply

The apostle does not respond to the cry with a call to believe. It is evident that his hearers had come to faith. They now must act upon that faith by repentance and baptism. The phrase, "in the name of," means by the authority of Jesus Christ. Peter claims to be offering the divine remedy for men convicted by sin. Both repentance and baptism are understood to be for the remission or forgiveness of sins. What is the gift of the Holy Spirit Peter promises? Will it enable them to also speak in tongues? That is not implied here or anywhere else in the New Testament. A close reading of Corinthians and Romans makes plain the fact that not all Christians are expected to do miraculous signs and wonders. It is also made plain in those epistles that every Christian is to view his body as the temple of the Holy Spirit who dwells within him.

A DAY OF VICTORY

The Response

How magnificent was the response of Peter's hearers! About three thousand turned to the Lord. They were baptized that very day. It has sometimes been argued that the twelve could not immerse three thousand persons in one day. However, there is no reason to assume that there were not others of the 120 who helped perform the rite. As a matter of fact, could not the newly baptized in turn baptize other converts? The teaching that only a certain few can administer baptism is foreign to the Bible.

So completely overwhelmed were these new Christians that they immediately liquidated their assets and began a communal life. It is sometimes said that this was an experiment in communism. Let it always be understood that there is a vast difference between communal living and communism in the Marxian form we see today.

Their hearts filled with praise, the Christians met in various houses in the city, and worshiped God both there and in the temple. Though the old law which that temple preserved was now superseded by the new, the Christians saw nothing wrong with returning to its sacred rooms to worship Christ, the "new and living way."

Added to the Church

If you have read carefully the second chapter of Acts, you have noted that the word "church" does not appear until the very last verse of that long chapter. That final verse is nonetheless quite significant. It indicates that those saved from their sins that day were not left to their own devices, were not left to battle alone against temptation. Christ had called these men out from the world in order to gather them together in a fellowship. Donald Miller calls it "the fraternity of the forgiven." The church consists of the called. They are called out from the world. They are called to the Lord, and they are called together in a world-wide assembly of saints. Certainly it falls far short of the mark to say that the church is simply a fellowship, an assembly of people. It is this, but it is much more than this. Its members have fellowship one with another because they have fellowship individually and severally with the living, risen Christ. They have become a part of Him, of His flesh and of His bones (Ephesians 5:30), and it is through them the world will be redeemed.

A Day of Tongues

The great events of Pentecost may well be summarized by pointing out the many voices heard. The cloven tongues of fire bespeak the Holy Spirit who made possible the foreign tongues of miracle. The proclaiming tongues of Peter and the apostles quickened the inquiring tongues of convicted sinners, and before the day was over both were blended in the praising tongues of worship and witness. Are not we who study together this great event constrained to say with David, "And my tongue shall speak of thy righteousness and of thy praise all the day long"?

Unparalleled Results

Mohammedanism did not make one hundred converts in the first year, but Christianity made three thousand the first day. Within a few days five thousand more were added (Acts 4:4). Each convert became himself an evangelist, a witness. From this magnificent beginning in Jerusalem would come the seed that would bring forth churches everywhere. The Christians were scattered by the winds of persecution (Acts 8:4), and every Christian became the seed for a new congregation, leading men in his own community to accept Christ too. Within Paul's lifetime it could be said that the news had reached every corner of the civilized world (Colossians 1:6). What an auspicious beginning for God's new covenant with men!

The Cost of Pentecost

Such stupendous results were not easily attained. We must remember that Pentecost was the climax of long centuries of preparation. We must recall that it cost Christ the glory of heaven, the fellowship of the angels, and the immediate presence of the Father. We must remember the cost to Him in terms of toil and tears and sweat and hunger. Above all, we dare not forget the cost in pain and agony and death. It was a victory not easily won. Still, it was a decisive victory, and it was Christ's victory. We cannot explain the results of Pentecost upon any basis other than the power of God. It has often been asked how so much was accomplished by ignorant and unlettered fishermen.

The answer is that it was not accomplished by them at all. "Thanks be to God, which giveth us the victory through our Lord Jesus Christ"!

RECAPTURING PENTECOST

It has been asked, "Can we in our time have another Pentecost?" In a sense Pentecost can never be recaptured. It was the church's inaugural day and that cannot be repeated. But is the church today without power? Certainly we do not expect and perhaps do not need today the cloven tongues of fire or the foreign tongues of miracle. But is not God's Word yet mighty and is not preaching "the power of God unto salvation"? If we can become the kind of vessels of that power that the early church was, then surely we can know in our time a new resurgence of victory in the church. What characteristics made those first Christians such effective channels of God's power? They were unseparated in their fellowship. None of the petty and trivial differences that separate the people of God in our time were allowed to disrupt the "one accord" of Pentecost.

They were unsparing in their generosity. The infant church was born without funds, but was hardly more than a day old before the treasury was filled, filled by the sacrifice of men and women to whom the church meant everything! They were outspoken in their witness. Commanded by the authorities not to teach, they continued unabated. Placed in prison, they converted the jailer. Brought to trial, they pleaded for their judges to accept the living Christ. They found it impossible to keep to themselves the wonderful news that the resurrected Lord is a redeeming Saviour.

First Things First

Pentecost was also known as the "feast of first fruits." The first of the harvest's bounty was brought as an offering to God. Thus did the Jews dramatically demonstrate that God must come first in men's lives. The new converts who on that day of first fruits became the first Christians were ready at once to put God first too. Houses, lands, and businesses were sold so that the infant church might not want for funds. The day on which all these events occurred was the first day of the week. It was not by accident that the church should be born on this day. Nor is it by accident that the church still meets on the first day of the week. By deliberate and divine design we bring together our offerings on the first day of the week, and in the weekly Communion seek for strength to truly put God first ourselves.

The first day of the week does not, however, commemorate Pentecost. It commemorates the resurrection of Jesus from the dead. When it is noted that Paul called Jesus "the firstfruits of them that slept" (1 Corinthians 15:20, 23), we see how singularly appropriate it is that He should rise from the dead on the same day of the week that the feast of first fruits had been observed for fourteen centuries. What a rich heritage is ours when we meet together on the first day of the week!

QUESTIONS

1. What evidence is there that Pentecost was the birthday of the church?

2. Describe this Jewish festival.

3. Not only did the gift of tongues show that the apostles spoke by divine direction, but it also provided an object lesson regarding the nature of the church. What lesson can we learn today from that phenomenon?

4. What two Old Testament writers did Peter quote in his sermon at Pentecost?

5. Memorize verbatim Peter's response to the cry of the multitude, "What shall we do?"

6. How many converts were made that day?

7. To what were they added? By whom?

8. What qualities of the early disciples will we have to imitate in order to repeat, in any measure, the results of Pentecost?

THE CHURCH AND ITS MEMBERS

Acts 2:36-47; 8:5-40; 9:1-22; 10:1-47; 16:13-40; 22:1-16

CHURCH MEMBERSHIP AND SALVATION

Identical Terms

It is not generally understood that in the New Testament becoming a Christian and becoming a church member were the same thing. Today, in the thinking of many, the two are almost entirely separate. Acts 2:47, however, declares "The Lord added to them daily those that were saved" (A.S.V.). In Biblical language, to be saved, to become a Christian, and to belong to Christ's church all meant the same thing. It is still true today that when men become Christians, Christ adds them to His church. The fallacy lies in the contention of some that after being saved one must then join some denomination. If the Lord adds the saved to His church, what additional church membership is necessary or desirable? It will be well to note here that the term "joining the church" does not appear in the New Testament. The Scriptures rather speak of joining Christ and His adding such persons to the church. This may seem like a rather fine technical point, and perhaps it is. Still, it is worth pointing out that as head of the church it is Christ who determines its membership. He has indicated in the Bible that those who meet the terms of salvation will be added.

The Terms of Membership

What are the terms of membership in the New Testament church? How does one become a Christian and thus be in a position to be added to the church? To answer this question one need only to turn to the book of Acts. This is the only book in the Bible that offers a record of conversions. Eight case histories of conversion are described there. An analysis of these accounts reveals that in every case the persons converted did three things: (1) Believed on Christ as the Son of God; (2) repented of sin; (3) were baptized into Christ. Believing on Christ is not mentioned in all cases, but it is strongly implied. Repentance is not mentioned in all cases, but it, too, is implied. Baptism is mentioned in every case. These items will be studied in detail in the chapters that follow. In today's lesson we want to take a close look at the first conversion recorded in Acts. It gave us the text, "And the Lord added to the church daily such as should be saved."

The Conversion of Three Thousand

The opening verses of Acts 2 set the scene. Peter's sermon is interrupted at verse 37 by a cry from the multitude asking, "What shall we do?" They are told, "Repent, and be baptized." There is no mention of believing, for it is evident from their question and the sermon that prompted it that they do believe. Also, there is a strong implication in the words, "Now when they heard this, they were pricked in their heart." So, we have here the elements faith, repentance, and baptism. In the thirty-eighth verse we have the extent ("every one of you"), the authority ("in the name of Jesus Christ"), the reason ("for the remission of sins"), the result ("the gift of the Holy Ghost"). The added blessing of church membership is indicated in the final verse of the chapter.

The Corinthians

The briefest case history of conversion occurs in Acts 18:8 and is told in a single verse. It shows that Paul and Silas taught the same requirements for conversion that Jesus taught. "He that believeth and is baptized shall be saved." No one should be disturbed by the absence of the word "repentance," since the very act of turning to God, or the decision, is itself repentance.

Simon the Sorcerer

The second case history of conversion appears in Acts chapter 8 (unless we include Acts 4:4). The meager information given regarding the five thousand render it of little value in the present connection. The case of Simon, however, presents some interesting information. When in 8:13 we are told he believed and was baptized, one thinks at once of Jesus' words in Mark 16:16: "He that believeth and is baptized shall be saved." The sorcerer, however, finds the world still very much with him and commits a serious sin almost immediately after his baptism. Still, no doubt is cast upon the validity of his conversion, nor is he told to be baptized again.

This is important information for every Christian. The fact that you have sinned since accepting Christ does not necessarily reflect upon your initial conversion, nor does it demand a second baptism. It is for the alien sinner that faith, repentance, and baptism are indicated as steps to forgiveness. To the sinning Christian, repentance and prayer are the remedy.

Philip and the Eunuch

A third case history of conversion also appears in the eighth chapter of Acts. Here the treasurer of the Ethiopian queen is returning from Jerusalem where he has gone to worship God. The Spirit directs Philip, an evangelist, to him. From the Scriptures that the eunuch has been studying, Philip shows that Jesus Christ is the fulfillment of Isaiah's prophecy. At verse 36 the eunuch requests baptism. While the thirty-seventh verse is not included in some translations, due to its absence from many manuscripts, it is not logical that Philip would have made no response to the eunuch's question. The question of whether or not verse 37 should be included is, of course, a very technical one. However, we are safe in assuming that what was said is not out of harmony with the teachings and practice of the early church. There is a hint regarding the manner of administering baptism in the fact that both men went down into the water. It should be noted that it was not until after he had been baptized that it is said the eunuch rejoiced. He must have seen baptism as the final step in his acceptance of the Christ.

The Conversion of Saul

There are three accounts of Saul's conversion, and each one must be read in order to understand the story thoroughly. Compare the ninth chapter of Acts with the twenty-second and the twenty-sixth. Notice that Christ's purpose in miraculously appearing to Saul was not to convert him (Acts 26:16). Notice also that even after the vision, the fasting, and the prayers Saul was still a sinner (Acts 22:16). Saul's conversion, then, was not really unlike the others, despite its dramatic and miraculous aspects. He believed on Christ (Acts 9:6; 22:8, 10). He surely repented, for he fasted for three days and nights. The fact that he was baptized, and the reasons are clearly set forth (Acts 22:16).

The Conversion of Cornelius

Notice in Acts 10 and 11 that Cornelius is unsaved (Acts 11:14) though he is a good man, a generous man, a man of prayer, and a man who has witnessed a heavenly vision! That these Gentiles truly believed in Christ, and were therefore worthy candidates for church membership despite their national origin, is shown by God himself. He gives to the ones gathered in the house of Cornelius the same miraculous outpouring of the Holy Spirit that the apostles received at Pentecost. (Compare Acts 2:1-4; 10:44-46; 11:15-17.) This dramatic demonstration was necessary to convince both Peter and the rest of the apostles that Gentiles were to be included in the Christian faith. The miraculous gift of the Spirit was wholly incidental to their conversion. This is seen, first, in the fact that it does not appear in any other case history of conversion. Second, the very language of the story indicates this. In Acts 11:14 we learn that Peter is to tell them words whereby they shall be saved. Peter's only command is recorded in 10:48: "And he commanded them to be baptized in the name of the Lord."

The Conversion of Lydia

While baptism is the only act specifically mentioned here (Acts 16:15), we may be certain that Lydia also believed on Christ and repented of her sins. It is interesting to note that of the three items mentioned, faith, repentance, and baptism, only one is ever challenged. No one denies that faith has a part in salvation, yet faith is not mentioned in every case. No one denies that repentance has a part in salvation, yet repentance is not mentioned in every case. Many deny that baptism has a part, yet baptism is mentioned in every case!

The Philippian Jailer

In this dramatic story (Acts 16) the jailer asks, "What must I do to be saved?" The first part of the answer is given in the thirty-first verse:

"Believe on the Lord Jesus Christ, and thou shalt be saved, and thy house." That this is not the complete answer can be seen in the very next verse, "And they spake unto him the word of the Lord, and to all that were in his house." That he repented is clearly evident, for he washed from their backs the very stripes that he himself had helped to place there. He was baptized the same hour of the night. Then, like the eunuch, after his baptism he rejoiced.

Summary

From a study of these cases it can be clearly seen that three human responses are involved in conversion. While God's grace is always the ground of salvation (Ephesians 2:8, 9), man is expected to respond by faith, repentance, and baptism. This is seen not only in the case histories of conversion, but also in the commands of Christ himself (Mark 16:15, 16; Matthew 28:19, 20; John 3:3-5; Luke 24:27, 46). Faith changes men's hearts (Romans 10:10). Repentance changes men's lives (Acts 3:19). Baptism changes a man's state, i. e., his relationship to Christ (Galatians 3:27).

RELATIONSHIPS AND RESPONSIBILITIES

Relationship to Christ

It must continually be emphasized that what we have in the church is not simply a group of people joined together for some noble humanitarian or social purpose. What we do have is a group of people joined to Christ, and dispatched by Him to perform His will. The Bible speaks of Christ as the head and the church as the body, but even this does not give a complete picture. Thus we find the words "Christ" and "church" used almost synonymously in some of the epistles. Paul seemed to see the two flow together and become one as he wrote, "But speaking the truth in love, may grow up into him in all things, which is the head, even Christ: from whom the whole body fitly joined together and compacted by that which every joint supplieth, according to the effectual working in the measure of every part, maketh increase of the body unto the edifying of itself in love" (Ephesians 4:15, 16). Notice the phrases "grow up into him" and "from whom the whole body." We must not use the term "church of God" or "church of Christ" in a way that will suggest that this is just one community among many. The church is unique, and it stands alone. Perhaps it is precisely because they saw this that early Bible translators did not use a word like "assembly" or "community" to translate *ekklesia*. Such usage might suggest that the church is just another good organization among many similar organizations. That is not the case at all. It is the-church-of-God, incomparable and without parallel.

Relationship to One Another

The new relationship with Christ brought about a new relationship with one's fellow men. It swept away all human distinctions. Class, race, national origin, economic situation, land, and language—all were obscured by the larger fact of newness in Christ: "There is neither Jew nor Greek, there is neither bond nor free, there is neither male nor female: for ye are all one in Christ Jesus" (Galatians 3:28); "Where there is neither Greek nor Jew, circumcision nor uncircumcision, Barbarian, Scythian, bond nor free: but Christ is all, and in all" (Colossians 3:11); "For there is no difference between the Jew and the Greek: for the same Lord over all is rich unto all that call upon him" (Romans 10:12). The American Standard Version uses the word "distinction" here rather than "difference." Certainly there were differences between Jew and Greek, just as there were between slaves and free men, but there were to be no distinctions between any. World-wide brotherhood is the avowed aim and purpose of the church. The Bible conceives all humanity as rightly belonging in one great family. The problem lies with sin, which separates men from their heavenly Father and alienates men from one another. Christ came to restore the proper relationship, that men may be adopted back into the family of God (Romans 8:15). It is worth pointing out that just as in the human family we do not choose our own brothers, so in God's family we do not determine who shall be our brethren. The word "fellowship" is never a verb. Fellowship is not something we do; it is something we have. Brotherhood, then, and fellowship are not based upon our poor human judgments of truth and error. As Carl Ketcherside has so aptly said, "We are brothers because we have the same Father, not because we have the same opinions."[1]

The Responsibilities of Church Membership

Church membership is a sacred trust. Since the Lord adds us to His church, it is no small thing to be a member of that body. Great responsibilities fall upon every member. First, he bears the responsibility of regular attendance at worship. Notice that those first Christians continued steadfastly in the apostles' doctrine, fellowship, breaking of bread, and in prayers (Acts 2:42), and were daily in the temple praising God (Acts 2:46, 47). Worship was and is the very lifeblood of the Christian. Without it the church cannot survive, and its members cannot survive.

The worship of the early church was accompanied by an insistent witness. Everyone felt it his responsibility to spread the good news. Some did it publicly and some privately, but every Christian was a bearer of good tidings, an evangelist, a soul-winner.

Along with the responsibilities of worship and witness, there are numerous other areas of responsibility. Benevolence, church administration, and Christian education are all personal obligations of every church member. The selection of leaders is a responsibility its members must never take lightly. They bear also financial responsibility for the program of the church. Just as the Jews supported with their tithes the Old Testament priesthood, so must Christians undergird financially the work of the church and its ministry.

Membership Revoked

Once a person attained membership in that church of the New Testament was it ever revoked? The story of Simon the sorcerer in Acts 8 answers the question clearly. Read this story and see that Simon was truly converted, for it is said that he believed and was baptized. Jesus promised that "he that believeth and is baptized shall be saved." Since it is an inspired man who tells us Simon believed, we can be certain that he truly did have faith in Christ. He was saved from his past sins and made a Christian. Still, the pull of the world was strong. Seeing the miraculous gifts of the apostles and the leaders in the church, he tried to purchase it with money. Peter regarded this as a very grave sin, and urged him to repent and pray lest he be lost. Here it is obvious that one can indeed lose his membership in Christ's church. Here also is the divine formula for the forgiveness of those who do fall away. They need not be baptized again, but are required only to repent and pray in order to be reinstated by Christ.

Church Discipline

Does a congregation have the right to withdraw fellowship from one who persists in behaving in a shameful and disorderly fashion? The New Testament indicates that a congregation does possess this right, but that it should be exercised sparingly. As a matter of fact, there is only one case of such church discipline recorded. In the fifth chapter of 1 Corinthians Paul instructs the Corinthian church to "put away" a member. Why is this one singled out, when others who are drunken (11:21) or divisive (1:11) or even guilty of fornication (5:1; 6:18) are not cast out? A close study of chapter five, especially verses 9-12, indicates that it is the persistent refusal to repent that is the key point. Only after one has tenderly and prayerfully worked with an individual over a very long period of time should such action be considered. Even then, the purpose of discipline is not merely to preserve the purity of the congregation, but to save the person ejected (1 Corinthians 5:5). The act is to be done in love and pity. That this procedure succeeded in this instance is implied in 2 Corinthians 2:1-11. Another passage of Scripture dealing with this subject is 2 Thessalonians 3:6. Two facts must be kept in mind in considering this subject. Wholesale excommunication of groups of persons is out of harmony with New Testament teaching. In the only example we have it was an individual matter. Second, such discipline is to be exercised only in the most extreme case, and even then it is to be done in love. The motivation must ever be the salvation of the person involved. The need for such action might not arise more often than once in a lifetime. When the need does arise, the church's duty is clearly seen.

NAMES OF THE MEMBERS

Various Names Used

What terms were used in New Testament times to designate the members of the church? In their relationship to their Lord they were known as believers or disciples. In their relationship to one another they were called brethren. In their relationship to the world they were saints. The word "disciple" means learner, pupil, or follower. All the great philosophers had their disciples. The Jews had long used the term "brethren," and it was not a new name. Too, the term "saint," coming from the familiar Old Testament word "sanctify," had been long in use. One name applied to these church members was a new name. One name fulfilled the prophecies of Isaiah 62:2 and 65:15. That was the name "Christian." It was and is the distinctive name of those who belong to Christ.

A Divinely-given Name

God had prophetically declared that such a name should be given to His people. In Isaiah 62:2 we read the promise: "And thou shalt be called by a new name, which the mouth of the Lord shall name." In the American Standard Version, Isaiah 65:15 reads, "And the Lord Jehovah will slay thee; and he will call his servants by another name." In Acts 11:26 we find that the disciples were called Christians first at Antioch. As C. J. Sharp said: "Here the promised new name first appears. The Greek word used here for 'call' is not the word *kaleo*, which means an ordinary calling, but is *chrematizo*, which means divinely called or called by the will of God." Thus Isaiah's prophecy is fulfilled as God calls His people Christians. Jesus himself prayed "Holy Father, keep them in thy name which thou hast given me, that they may be one, even as we are" (John 17:11, A.S.V.). James 2:7 asks, "Do not they blaspheme that worthy name by the which ye are called?" If that worthy name did not include either the name of God or of Christ, how could its misuse be termed blasphemy? Revelation 2:13 finds Jesus commending the church at Pergamos because "thou holdest fast my name."

A Unifying Name

What possible value could come from substituting some other name for God's people or for His church? In every age in the church's history such action has only further divided Christian believers. (Consider in this connection 1 Corinthians 1:11-13.) It is enough to say simply, "I am a Christian." To add qualifying adjectives and distinguishing names to the Scriptural names for God's people is only to perpetuate the sad division of Christendom. If all who believe in

Christ would wear no names but those divinely given, that alone would carry us a long way down the difficult road to Christian unity.

The Best Name

The special significance of the name "Christian" is indicated by many passages of Scripture. "If a man suffers as a Christian, let him not be ashamed; but let him glorify God in this name" (1 Peter 4:16, A.S.V.). "And whatsoever ye do, in word or deed, do all in the name of the Lord Jesus, giving thanks to God and the Father by him." Consider also the following passages:

1. His name is to be above every name (Philippians 2:9).

2. Salvation is in His name and His alone (Acts 4:12).

3. We are baptized in His name (Acts 2:38).

4. We are to pray in His name (John 14:13).

5. We are blessed when we meet in His name (Matthew 18:20).

6. Unity is in His name (1 Corinthians 1:10-13).

7. The disciples were called Christians (Acts 11:26).

8. His name is to be in our foreheads (Revelation 22:4, 5).

QUESTIONS

1. What relationship exists between the terms of salvation and the terms of church membership as laid down in the New Testament?

2. What is the first case of conversion recorded in the book of Acts? What is the briefest?

3. How many case histories of conversion are recorded in Acts?

4. Are there case histories of conversion in any other New Testament book?

5. What does the story of Simon the sorcerer teach us concerning sins after baptism?

6. Discuss briefly the conversion of Saul.

7. What are some of the responsibilities of church membership?

8. Explain the relationship of church members to one another. To Christ.

9. Under what circumstances is church membership revoked? How may one then be reinstated?

10. What is the distinctive and divinely given name for Christ's followers?

---

[1] From *Mission Messenger*. Used by permission.

FAITH IN THE LIFE OF THE CHURCH

Hebrews 11; Romans 10:4-17; John 20:26-31

THE SIGNIFICANCE OF FAITH

Christians Are Believers

The significance of faith in the life of the church is seen in the fact that the first and most popular name for the followers of Christ was "believers." This continued to be a very popular term throughout New Testament times, and it appears often in Acts and in the epistles. The term is not quite so definitive today, when a great many people claim to be believers but make no claim to be Christians. Such a condition did not exist in Bible times. Perhaps the threat of persecution was instrumental in separating those who really believed from those who only claimed to believe. At any rate, and in any age, a Christian must be a believer. Whatever else he may be, he *must* be a believer; whatever else may be required of him, faith stands out as a basic requirement. We may well ask, then, "What is faith?" The question is not easily answered, and much confusion exists regarding it. Some have made a distinction between belief and faith. Others have distinguished between simple faith and saving faith. Neither of these distinctions is made in the Bible. In New Testament language a man believed or disbelieved, and which position he took made all the difference in his life. In defining faith, we must be careful to avoid two extremes. Faith must be defined as something more than simple mental assent to a proposition. We must equally avoid the opposite extreme, which makes faith a miraculous manifestation of God.

The nearest thing to a definition of faith in the Bible is found in Hebrews 11:1. The King James Version reads: "Now faith is the substance of things hoped for, the evidence of things not seen." The American Standard Version translates the passage: "Now faith is assurance of things hoped for, a conviction of things not seen." The rendering of this verse in Phillips' translation of the New Testament is: "Now faith means putting our full confidence in the things we hope for; it means being certain of things we cannot see."[1]

Faith has sometimes been defined as reliance or trust. Perhaps the following quotations should be called descriptions of faith, rather than definitions. St. Augustine wrote, "What is faith, save to believe what you do not see?" Thomas Aquinas said, "Faith has to do with things that are not seen, and hope with things that are not in hand." Calvin described faith as "a knowledge of the benevolence of God toward us, and a certain persuasion of His veracity." Pascal said: "Faith affirms what the senses do not affirm, but not the contrary of what they perceive. It is above and not contrary to." Wordsworth described a believer as:

One in whom persuasion and belief
Had ripened into faith, and faith become
A passionate institution.

Perhaps the easiest way to define faith is to say what it is not. Faith is something less than knowledge. When we are trying to express a very firm faith we may sometimes say, "I know," but that is only a way of being emphatic about our faith. Faith is something less than knowledge. Faith is something more than superstition. It is not simply a guess. Faith in God is not to be compared with carrying a rabbit's foot or nailing a horseshoe over the door or finding a four-leaf clover. Faith, then, lies somewhere between knowledge and guess, somewhere between actual experience and superstition. We may say, then, that faith is a conviction, based on facts but projected beyond the facts. Indeed, faith must often be projected into areas where facts and experimental knowledge cannot exist. Here is a simple illustration: I have faith in a friend. He tells me something that I cannot corroborate in any possible way. I believe it. I believe it because he has always told me the truth before, and I have never known him to lie. This is exactly the position of Christian faith. No man can corroborate a story like the creation. Facts cannot be gathered to give us absolute knowledge of what occurred. Since, however, we have found the Bible true in those areas where it could be compared with history, science, and other branches of knowledge, our faith tells us that it is also to be trusted in those areas where corroboration is impossible.

THE SOURCE OF FAITH

Comes by Hearing

Romans 10:17 says, "So then faith cometh by hearing, and hearing by the word of God." It is a strange fact that men have so often missed this important passage. The source of faith has been variously defined. Some have held that faith comes by accident; that if one grows up in a religious family, or is thrown into surroundings favorable to Christian faith, he will believe. Others have felt that faith comes by predestination; that God has already and eternally predetermined who shall be saved and who shall be lost; that faith is a miracle that God has wrought in some men and not in others. There are some who deny the predestinarian view, but who continue to look upon faith as a miraculous gift of God. Some have thought that faith comes by prayer. Dwight L. Moody once said that for years, he had prayed for a stronger faith. Then one day he read Romans 10:17, and discovered that "faith comes by hearing, and hearing by the word of God." It is true that the father of an afflicted boy said to Jesus, "Help thou mine unbelief." While there may be nothing amiss in this request, its circumstances do not justify our concluding that faith comes by prayer. Indeed, the man had already declared, "I believe" (Mark 9:24). Faith comes by hearing the Word of God, whether that Word is communicated through preaching, through reading, or through simple conversation. John 20:31 puts its quite plainly: "These are written, that ye might believe."

To say that "faith comes by hearing" is another way of saying that faith is a matter of deliberate choice. Men choose to believe, or they choose to disbelieve. If this were not so, how could Jesus condemn them for unbelief? Yet He does just that. In Mark 16:14, He "upbraided them with their unbelief." Man, then, is held personally responsible in the matter of believing. In this connection, study 2 Thessalonians 2:12; Jude 5; 1 John 3:23; 2 Timothy 3:8; Romans 1:28 and 10:14.

If we compare Romans 10:17 with Matthew 13:15, we will see that hearing is more than listening. It is more than simply being exposed to the Bible. Not all students of the Bible are believers. Many have ears but do not hear, have eyes but do not see. (Compare Revelation 2:7, 11, 17, 29; 3:6, 13, 22.) When men are willing to hear the Word of God, when they listen with open minds, they will be led to faith.

A Growing Faith

We are not to think of faith as stagnant. Faith grows as one's knowledge of the Bible increases and as his experience with God broadens. That is why we may need to speak of the point where faith begins. We must agree that one begins with faith in God as the almighty Creator and loving Father. The next step is faith in Jesus as the Christ, God's only begotten Son. Then will come growing confidence in the efficacy of prayer, the power of the gospel, the omnipotence of God, the wisdom in His will for our lives.

We keep our faith growing by continually studying the Bible, by communing with God in prayer and meditation, and by exercising ourselves in serving Him. Faith, like all living things, must grow or die. Every living plant is either growing or decaying. In every living animal there are continual processes of growth, or of death. Faith is never static. The amount of it one possesses either increases or diminishes day by day.

THE SCOPE OF FAITH

A Definite Faith

Perhaps the simplest answer to the question, "What must one believe to be a Christian?" is this: he must believe that the historical Jesus was and is the prophesied Christ, the Son of God; that the man from Nazareth is the Messiah, God's anointed. Of course, such a statement presupposes faith in God himself. Hebrews 11:6 is basic: "He that cometh to God must believe that he is, and that he is a rewarder of them that diligently seek him." Such a faith in God is presupposed in Philip's answer in Acts 8. The eunuch had asked, "What doth hinder me to be baptized?" Philip's answer was, "If thou believest with all thine heart, thou mayest." What was he to believe? The very next verse gives the eunuch's response. "I believe that Jesus Christ is the Son of God." The nature of faith then is centered upon the nature of Jesus. That is why Jesus asked, "Whom do men say that I the Son of man am?" That is why He was so pleased with Peter's answer, "Thou art the Christ, the Son of the living God."

It is important here to define our terms. The word "Christ" is the Greek equivalent of the Hebrew word "Messiah," and means "God's Anointed." Thus the proper view of Jesus is inseparably tied to the Old Testament and its many prophecies concerning Him. One must believe that Jesus was the fulfillment of Israel's hopes and dreams, that He was the one of whom the prophets spoke. All that they have written of Him may be summarized in the single word "Christ." There is then considerable significance in saying "Jesus is the Christ." Jesus is likewise concerned about what men think concerning His origin. In Matthew 22:42, He is even more specific than in Matthew 16:18, 19. "What think ye of Christ, whose son is he?" Faith begins with a belief in Jesus as the only begotten Son of God. Christian faith demands rejection of the old rumors raised at His birth and raised again in our time, that Jesus was the illegitimate child of Joseph or some other man. The virgin birth occupies a strategic place in Christian faith.

It may not be wise to say what is the bare minimum of faith. Perhaps we ought not to ask what is the least one may believe and still be said to have faith. Still, we must consider that the Bible points out at least one specific detail about Jesus that must be believed. Romans 10:9 says: "That if thou shalt confess with thy mouth the Lord Jesus, and shalt believe in thine heart that God hath raised him from the dead, thou shalt be saved." There are many who are willing to confess Jesus as Lord, but have some reservations about His being raised from the dead. Until they change their views they cannot be saved. The resurrection of Christ occupies a key position in the Christian religion, and one must believe that God raised Him from the dead.

How essential is faith? Compare Mark 16:15, 16; Acts 16:31; and Ephesians 2:8, 9. These passages state what ought to be perfectly obvious: that without faith it is impossible to please God (Hebrews 11:6).

A Motivating Faith

The relationship of faith to life is clear. We often speak of one who lives uprightly as "faithful." Literally, "faithful" means "full of faith." Faith, then, is the mainspring of Christian action. It is the headwaters from which flow all the streams of Christian virtue and obedience. It was faith that prompted people at Pentecost to cry, "Men and brethren, what shall we do?" It was faith that led the jailer at Philippi to wash the stripes from the backs of Paul and Silas and to be baptized. It was faith that led the first Christians to sell homes and businesses that the infant church might have funds. It was faith that led men to forsake the pagan way of sin in which they once lived for the austere but happy life of the Christian.

The illustrations of faith as a motivating factor are many. The eleventh chapter of Hebrews offers a long chronicle of them, beginning with Noah and Abraham and on through the long history of Israel. Whether we are thinking of the performance of Christian duty, or the avoidance of temptation and sin, faith is the key. Modem religious psychologists have caught the gleam of this truth and used it to help many. Sometimes, though, in the process they have denuded faith of its true meaning and its genuine power. One must have more than just faith in himself, faith in the future, or faith in democracy. All of these are well and good, but only faith in Christ and His Word will motivate us to be Christians. Motivating faith rises above mere optimism or self-confidence. It places its trust not in man but in God, not in one's self but in one's Saviour.

A Confessed Faith

This is not the sort of faith one can keep quiet about. Indeed, the early Christians were continually testifying of their faith. Their witness could not be stopped by stones, prison bars, or even by death itself. All too often we think of confession as a formal, one-time affair. The Biblical picture is that of continual witnessing. Certainly the man who comes seeking baptism may properly be called upon to declare his faith as the eunuch did (Acts 8:37). Still, this formal and initial confession is only the beginning of a life that is a continuous testimony to what one believes about Christ.

It will be noted that in coming to forgiveness, one confesses his Saviour, not his sins. There may be certain value in confessing one's sins. The New Testament mentions it at least twice. In James 5:16, we learn that we should confess our faults to one another. This does not imply a public recital of our misdeeds, nor does it suggest that we must confess to some practitioner of religion. There is no precedent in the New Testament for this. Certainly such a procedure is not implied in 1 John 1:9, where we are instructed to acknowledge our sins. The implication is strong that we confess our sins to Christ, who alone can forgive us.

There is ample precedent in the New Testament for confessing the Saviour. The New Testament records statements of faith by Martha, Peter, and the eunuch from Ethiopia. It declares that Timothy and that Christ himself made such a profession (1 Timothy 6:12, 13). The importance of confessing Christ is clearly seen in Matthew 10:32, 33; Romans 10:9, 10; and 1 John 4:15. While the Bible does not give us a specific wording for the confession of faith we should use, certainly we are safe in saying that it is not out of order to ask him who comes to Christ to make some formal profession of faith.

The term "confession of faith" is used in another sense in Christendom. It is often used to describe long and involved statements of doctrine. Many denominations are governed by such confessions. To bind upon men any human creed or any man-made statement of faith or practice is, of course, to depart greatly from the will of God. He has given us the Bible for this purpose. With it we are "thoroughly furnished unto all good works" (2 Timothy 3:16, 17). Man needs no other authoritative or binding statement of doctrine. Certainly any man, or any group of men, has a right to compose and offer to the world a summary of the Christian religion as he views it. It is equally certain that no man, and no group of men, has the right to make such a confession of faith binding upon the consciences of others.

QUESTIONS

1. What was the first and most popular name for the followers of Christ?

2. Discuss how one might define faith.

3. What is the source of faith?

4. What is the confession of faith made by the eunuch in Acts 8?

5. What does the word "Christ" mean?

6. What event connected with the ministry of Christ is an essential part of true faith?

7. Discuss the relationship of faith to the problems of daily living.

8. Why do we confess our Saviour rather than our sins?

9. What importance does the New Testament give to a confession of faith?

10. Explain the difference between the way the Bible uses the idea of confession of faith and its use in modem denominationalism.

---

[1] From *The New Testament in Modern English*, © J. B. Phillips 1958. Used by permission of The Macmillan Company.

REPENTANCE IN THE LIFE OF THE CHURCH

Luke 13:1-5; Luke 3:7-18; Revelation 2:5, 16, 22; Acts 17:29-31

BIBLICAL BACKGROUNDS OF REPENTANCE

"Thus saith the Lord God; Repent, and turn yourselves from your idols; and turn away your faces from all your abominations.... Repent, and turn yourselves from all your transgressions; so iniquity shall not be your ruin." With words like these, the prophet Ezekiel addressed himself to Israel (14:6; 18:30). "Turn ye again now every one from his evil way, and from the evil of your doings, and dwell in the land that the Lord hath given unto you and to your fathers for ever and ever." This, said Jeremiah (25:5), was the message of all the prophets. "Bring forth therefore fruits meet for repentance"—thus did John the Baptist begin to prepare the way for the Son of Man. "Except ye repent, ye shall all likewise perish," declared Jesus himself. "God," said Paul, "now commandeth all men every where to repent."

It is easy to see how large a place repentance occupies in the Word of God. The word appears 110 times in the King James Version of the Bible, though not always with the same significance. If one word had to be chosen to summarize the message of God's spokesmen in both Old Testament and New, that word would be "repent." Apostles and prophets from the time of the exodus to the close of apostolic times were all preoccupied with the need of men to turn from sin and turn to God.

Repentance in the Old Testament

Repentance figures large in the Old Testament. Hosea, Ezekiel, and Job all had something to say about it. Under different terms the subject was pressed upon the people by Isaiah and Jeremiah, by Joel and Amos and Jonah and Zechariah. This was, in fact, the burden of the prophets' messages to their contemporaries, that men should turn from their wicked ways to serve the living God. The first instances in the English Old Testament in which the word "repentance" appears are verses concerned with God and His dealings with men. While we cannot in this course concern ourselves with the problems associated with these passages, it must be pointed out that when God is said to repent, the word is understood in a different sense than when man is said to repent. Attributing human emotions to God is no more out of place than attributing physical characteristics to God. We do not need to be disturbed when the Bible speaks of the arm of God. Neither do we need to be disturbed when the Bible speaks of God's repenting. In both cases human attributes are used to convey an idea that is not easily communicated. God does not repent in the same sense that man does any more than God has an arm in the same sense that man has.

Two Hebrew Terms Involved

Two Old Testament terms express ideas associated with repentance. The one most commonly translated "repent" means "to pant," "to sigh," or "to groan." Since grief is naturally associated with repentance, the term is related to, but not identical with, Biblical and current ideas of repentance. First Samuel 15:29 declares that God "is not a man, that he should repent." God then may be said to have grief, but does not repent in the sense that man changes his mind and conduct.

This idea of a change of mind and conduct is expressed in another Old Testament term that is generally translated "turn" or "return." This word expresses the ideas generally associated with the word "repentance" as it is used today. This God does not do. This men must do, and this the prophets continually urged upon the people. It was because they did not repent that affliction came upon Israel, that other nations subjugated them, that their land lay desolate and their citizens were exiled. Of all these calamites Israel was warned as the prophets urged them to turn to God.

Repentance in the Preaching of John the Baptist

The forerunner of Christ made repentance the keynote of his message. When he stood before vast multitudes in the wilderness of the Jordan Valley, he urged them to repent. When he was given audience before Herod, the governor, he indicted him for taking his brother's wife and urged his repentance. The preaching of this noble and fearless man was blunt and direct. "Generation of vipers" he called his hearers. Swiftly he cut down their pride in being Abraham's children and called them back to personal faith and obedience. He declared, in effect, that national attachment to God was no substitute for personal allegiance to Him. His sermons were permeated with a note of urgency. "The kingdom of heaven is at hand"; "the ax is laid unto the root of the trees"; "[His] fan is in his hand." Something was about to happen. The people must repent in preparation for it. John's preaching of repentance prepared the way of the Lord. Surely the preaching of repentance will prepare the way that He may come again.

Repentance and the Preaching of Jesus

The program upon which Jesus embarked was much longer in range than that of John the Baptist. John's preparatory ministry was geared to the short-term proposition of preparing for the coming Christ. Jesus, on the other hand, had to keep constantly in mind the long years that lay ahead for His kingdom.

So repentance did not occupy as large a place in Jesus' preaching as in John's. In His public addresses and private talks alike, Christ had to cover numerous aspects of Christian attitude and conduct. Still, He did have much to say on the subject of repentance. He began His preaching ministry by reiterating John's refrain: "Repent: for the kingdom of heaven is at hand." In outlining His purposes, He declared that He came to call sinners to repentance. When the twelve were sent forth two by two, they preached that men should repent. In Luke 13:3, 5, Jesus issued a stern call to repentance.

The parables of the rich man and Lazarus, the lost sheep, the lost coin, and the prodigal son are all concerned, directly or indirectly, with repentance. In His post-resurrection appearance on the way to Emmaus, Jesus indicated that repentance would continue to be preached by the witnesses whom He was about to send to all nations.

THE MEANING OF REPENTANCE

Repentance Involves the Intellect

Two different but closely related words are translated "repent" in the New Testament. One of these words means "to think differently, to reconsider," and it implies a reversal of thinking. What once was disbelieved is now believed; what once was denied is now affirmed. Biblical repentance, then, involves a change in what one thinks about God, Christ, sin, and self. It may be likened to the "renewing of the mind" in Romans 12:2. John the Baptist used the word in this way in Matthew 3:2. Jesus made a similar use of it in Mark 1:15, likewise Peter in Acts 2:38. This word for repentance is often joined to baptism, with baptism being the outward manifestation as repentance was the inward manifestation of conversion. Consider Mark 1:4; Luke 3:3; Acts 13:24; 19:4.

Repentance Involves the Emotions

It must be emphatically declared that repentance is much more than sorrow for sins. Still, repentance is inseparably tied to the emotions. "Godly sorrow worketh repentance," said Paul in 2 Corinthians 7:9, 10. Sorrow then is seen as the seed of repentance, and not repentance itself. The second Greek word that is translated "repent" in the New Testament is a word that means "to care afterward, to regret." It may be translated "to be concerned." Repentance may then correctly be said to involve a change of heart as well as a change of mind. That which one once loved he now hates, and that which he once hated he now loves. This change in heart wrought by repentance has considerable impact upon the convert—so much so that he often mistakes repentance for the whole process of conversion. His mind and heart were once unsettled on the subject of sin and the Saviour. Now that condition no longer exists. Because he has settled the matter in his mind and heart, the convert may assume that therefore the matter has been settled before God. Scripture does not warrant such an assumption. As tremendous as the impact of repentance is, and as necessary as it is, it must not be mistaken for the entire process of conversion. As an examination of the Scriptures will surely show, baptism is inseparably related to pardon (Acts 22:16; 1 Peter 3:21). In a sermon published many years ago, J. S. Sweeney pointed out that there is considerable difference between the term "conversion" as it is popularly used, and the term "pardon." Conversion takes place in the sinner. Pardon takes place in the mind and heart of God. While the two are intricately related, they are not identical. Repentance with its strong emotional impact is an important step on the road to pardon. Its importance cannot be overemphasized, but its nature can be, and has been, misunderstood.

Repentance Involves the Will

A third term in the New Testament may be thought of as a corollary to the word "repent." This word is translated "turn" in Acts 9:35; 14:15; 11:21; 26:20; 1 Thessalonians 1:9, and elsewhere. Twice it is translated "be converted" (Matthew 18:3 and John 12:40). True repentance involves a determination to do the will of God. It is inseparably related to decision, to a reversal of direction in life. It is a mistake to see repentance as a period of probation, wherein one tries to live the Christlike life to see if he can do it. Repentance can take place in a moment, but its effect may endure a lifetime. It involves a firm decision of the will, based upon the thoughts and feelings of the changed mind and the changed heart. Its certain result is a changed life.

ASPECTS OF REPENTANCE

A Comprehensive Term

Our English word "repentance" is, then, a very broad and comprehensive term. Its meaning is well summarized by Byron DeMent, as "A consciousness of spiritual poverty dethroning pride, a sense of personal unworthiness producing grief, a willingness to surrender to God in genuine humility..."[1]

Repentance From Sin

Repentance has two aspects. In the first place, it involves a turning from sin. One turns his back upon the past and upon the world. He is sorry that he ever walked in the ways of sin. He knows now that there is a better way. He is determined that he will never go back to the old life. So complete is this turning from sin that the Bible calls it "putting to death the old man."

Repentance Toward God

When a man turns to God, in the same act of repentance he turns away from sin. He looks toward heaven, to the new way of life that Christ ordained. So in Acts 20:21, we find Paul speaking of "repentance toward God." Man faces away from something in order to look toward something. He leaves behind his sins and embraces a Saviour. Thus many have defined repentance by the military term, "about face."

REPENTANCE AND CONVERSION

Prerequisite to Baptism

Acts 2:38 points out that repentance is necessary before baptism can be properly performed. "Repent, and be baptized every one of you in the name of Jesus Christ for the remission of sins, and ye shall receive the gift of the Holy Ghost." In the story of the conversion of the Philippian jailer, we see repentance in action as he washes and treats the wounds of Paul and Silas. In Saul's conversion, his repentance is amply demonstrated in the three days and nights of fasting. Perhaps each convert will demonstrate his repentance in a little different way, but each one must repent before he can be Scripturally baptized. As Julius R. Mantey says, "the fact that baptism was then regarded as a sort of public confession of faith makes it very unlikely that the unrepentant would submit to baptism."

Repentance and Faith

The order of faith and repentance sometimes has been debated. Some have declared that one must repent of his unbelief first, and then he may come to faith. Others have argued that if one did not first believe, why should he repent? Upon what basis would his change of mind and heart rest, if not upon his faith? It will be noted that in Acts 11:21 it is said that a great number that believed "turned to the Lord." Here the order is faith first, then the turning. Still, when all is said and done, the point is hardly worth arguing. It may be a mistake to even attempt to isolate faith and repentance by making them totally separate steps. The two are interwoven, and interact one upon the other. The more one believes, the deeper his repentance. The more fervent his repentance, the firmer his faith.

A Continuing Action

It would be a grave mistake to think of repentance as occurring only upon one's initial response to the gospel. In the Bible, repentance is seen as a continuing need, an action that will take place often in the Christian's life. We learn in Acts 8 that when a person sins after baptism, the remedy is repentance and prayer. The Christian who is alert to internal affairs of his own soul will see almost daily the need to repent. It is just such an attitude that makes prayer meaningful and effective. Perhaps at some times repentance will seem to be a more profound experience than at others, but at every crossroad man must remember the wreckage sin has wrought in his life, be filled with regret for his wrongs, and be firm in his determination to walk in God's ways.

QUESTIONS

1. What place does repentance hold in the Old Testament?

2. Discuss the two Hebrew terms that mean about the same as our word repentance.

3. Relate the place of repentance in the preaching of Jesus and of John the Baptist.

4. Discuss the three words in the New Testament that are related to repentance. Show how the intellect, the emotions, and the will are involved.

5. What does one repent from? Toward whom does one repent?

6. What relationship exists between repentance and baptism?

7. How important is repentance in conversion? Explain.

8. Why is repentance sometimes misunderstood and regarded as the entire process of conversion?

9. Is repentance to come only upon one's conversion? Explain.

---

[1] From the *International Standard Bible Encyclopedia*, Volume 4. Used by permission of the Wm. B. Eerdmans Publishing Co.

BAPTISM IN THE LIFE OF THE CHURCH

Acts 8:26-39; Romans 6:1-7; Matthew 18:19, 20; Mark 16:15, 16

CEREMONY OF INITIATION

Baptized Into Christ

To be a Christian, to be saved from one's sins, is to be in Christ. Certainly no one can be saved outside of Christ. The Bible teaches that a sinner is "baptized into Christ." This is not to say that baptism alone will save. Without faith baptism is meaningless (Acts 8:36, 37). Without repentance baptism is not valid (Acts 2:38). When these first two steps have been taken, when the candidate is prepared in heart by faith and in life by repentance, then baptism marks his initiation into Christ. That is exactly what Paul says in Galatians 3:27. "For as many of you as have been baptized into Christ have put on Christ." The sacred rite of baptism is not to be waved aside as a mere formality or just a ceremony. Ceremonies often mark the turning points in men's lives.

It is the wedding ceremony that changes one from a single state to a married state. It is the ceremony of naturalization that changes one from the status of an alien to that of a citizen. It is the ceremony of baptism that marks the change from the state of a sinner to that of a Christian. Certainly the person who comes to the wedding ceremony must be prepared by love, and the person who comes to the naturalization ceremony must be prepared by knowledge. In the same way, he who comes to the ceremony of baptism must be prepared by faith and repentance. The one who thus comes is thereby formally inducted into the kingdom of God, the church of Jesus Christ.

Baptized Into His Death

Study carefully Romans 6:1-7. Then consider these facts. We are saved by the blood of Christ. This the Bible teaches everywhere, and on this point all who claim to be Christians are agreed. When was Christ's blood shed? There is no record of Jesus ever shedding His blood except in death. To be baptized into the death of Christ is to come in contact with His blood. That is why Ananias said, "Arise, and be baptized, and wash away thy sins, calling on the name of the Lord" (Acts 22:16).

If we study carefully these verses in Romans 6, we see that baptism has a dual thrust. It is not only Christ's death that is involved, but our own as well. The old man is crucified, and in baptism there is signified his death and burial. In his place a new creature is resurrected. Thus our death to sin, as well as Christ's death for sin, are both wrapped up in baptism. Karl Barth points out that just as circumcision was coming under the threat of death, and that just as Israel's baptism in the Red Sea (1 Corinthians 10:1, 2) placed their lives in jeopardy, so in baptism a man comes close to death—and that signifies the real death of the old man of sin.

Baptized Into His Body

One of the tragedies of modern times is that in their thinking men have separated Christ and His body, the church. In the New Testament, to be in Christ was to be in His body. It was inconceivable that one could be in Christ and be outside His body. That is why the Bible not only says we are baptized into Christ, but also declares that we are baptized into His church. First Corinthians 12:13 declares, "For by one Spirit are we all baptized into one body." Thus the final step in becoming a member of the church is baptism. To be Scripturally baptized, then, is to come into Christ, into His death, and into His body, the church.

WHICH BAPTISM?

Several Uses of the Word

The word "baptism" is used in more than one way in the New Testament. There is the baptism of the Holy Spirit, the baptism of fire, the baptism of suffering, and the baptism in water. If baptism is so very important to us, if it does stand as the final step in coming into Christ, into His body, the church, it is imperative that we know which of these baptisms is meant.

Man Commanded to Administer

If we study closely these baptisms, we see that there is only one that man can administer. Only the Lord could baptize with the Holy Spirit (John 1:33; Matthew 3:11). He alone could baptize with fire. In Matthew 20:22, 23 and in Luke 12:50 we see the baptism of suffering. This is administered by the enemies of the gospel and the persecutors of the church. The only baptism that Christians are commanded to administer is baptism in water. When Jesus therefore commands us to baptize (Matthew 18:19, 20), He obviously has reference to baptism in water.

Man Commanded to Receive

Not only is man commanded to administer baptism; he is also commanded to be baptized. Since the Lord gives the baptism of the Holy Spirit and the baptism of fire to whom He chooses, man could not logically be commanded to do something that only God could do for him. Yet, baptism *is* commanded (Acts 10:48). The baptism of suffering is administered by God's enemies. No man can sensibly be commanded to receive such a baptism. So when Jesus commanded baptism (Mark 16:15, 16), there can be no doubt as to which baptism He had in mind. The only baptism that man could be commanded both to administer and receive is baptism in water.

Example and Precept

That this is the baptism that brings one into Christ is amply demonstrated by example and by precept in the New Testament. "See, here is water; what doth hinder me to be baptized?" (Acts 8:36); "Christ also loved the church, and gave himself for it; that he might sanctify and cleanse it with the washing of water by the word" (Ephesians 5:25, 26); (Acts 10:47), "Can any man forbid water, that these should not be baptized?" Hebrews 10:22 speaks of "bodies washed with pure water." First Peter 3:20, 21 reads: "Eight souls were saved by water. The like figure whereunto even baptism doth also now save us." Jesus said that to be born again a man must be "born of water and of the Spirit" (John 3:5). A synonym for the term "born again" is used in Titus 3:5, where we are told that God saved us "by the washing of regeneration."

ONE BAPTISM

Do the Scriptures Contradict?

We have learned that there are at least four baptisms in the New Testament. What then does Paul mean in Ephesians 4:5 when he says there is one baptism? Is this a contradiction? Not at all. Paul is saying just what we have been saying: there is one baptism men are commanded to administer, one baptism men are commanded to receive. The baptisms of the Holy Spirit, of fire, and of suffering rest wholly with the initiative of others.

One or Three?

When we have learned that the one baptism of Ephesians 4:5 is baptism in water we have still only partially defined Bible baptism. For many years the religious world has practiced at least three distinct and different ceremonies, each of which has been termed "baptism." Some denominations honor one, some another, and some honor all three. If we are to be truly Biblical, we must try to discover which one of the three was the "one baptism" practiced by Paul, which one of the three Christ had in mind when He used the term, which one of the three can be said without doubt to be Bible baptism.

BAPTISM BY BURIAL

Baptism a Symbol of Death

We shall first ask if sprinkling or pouring fit the figure Paul himself uses in Romans 6:1 ff. Here we learned that we are buried with Christ in baptism. Is Paul referring to the mechanics of performing the act? Probably not, but he is saying that baptism signifies the death

(Romans 6:3), the burial (6:4), and the resurrection of Christ (6:4, 5). In immersion there is a picture of death. The eyes are closed as in death. Breathing stops as in death. The candidate is in the hands of the administrator. He not only appears as one dead, he is in fact close to actual death, as the Israelites were when they were baptized in the cloud and in the sea (1 Corinthians 10:1, 2). Is this picture of death seen in sprinkling or pouring? Not at all. Only in immersion is death dramatically portrayed.

A Symbol of Burial and Resurrection

That immersion symbolizes a burial and a resurrection is obvious from the very mechanics of performing it. More than this, baptism resembles a resurrection because the candidate resumes breathing, opens his eyes, and walks away from the place of baptism. Surely none will doubt that the death, burial, and resurrection of Christ are the cardinal points of the gospel. Since it is clear that baptism is to be a symbol of these, there can be no doubt that immersion is the intended portrayal. A symbol must resemble. The Lord's choice of fruit of the vine and unleavened bread as symbols of His body and blood was a natural choice. They resemble flesh and blood. If they did not resemble, they would not be appropriate symbols. That immersion does symbolize these things is noted in a footnote to Romans 6:3 in the official Catholic translation of the New Testament. The footnote reads, "St. Paul alludes to the manner in which Baptism was ordinarily conferred in the primitive Church, by immersion. The descent into the water is suggestive of the descent of the body into the grave, and the ascent is suggestive of the resurrection to a new life. St. Paul obviously sees more than a mere symbol in the rite of Baptism. As a result of it we are incorporated into Christ's mystical body and live a new life."

The Greek Word

The word "baptism" is not a translation of the Greek word at all, but a transliteration. What does *baptidzo* mean? In his book, *That They May Be Won*, F. J. Winder lists fifty-eight Greek lexicons which unanimously define *baptidzo* as "to dip, to plunge, or to immerse." Now, it is true that if we consult an English dictionary we find all three acts are given. But we must remember that the purpose of the dictionary is to give us the current American usage of English words. What we wish to know is the meaning of a Greek word at the time Jesus and the apostles used it. To find this we turn to the lexicons or the encyclopedias. As we have seen, the lexicons of the Greek language are unanimous in affirming that to baptize means to immerse. Winder also lists sixteen religious encyclopedias that agree. Dozens of examples from the Greek literature of the time can be pointed out. Homer so used the word many years before Christ. Poryphyry so used it in A.D. 233. Josephus, the great Jewish historian, used it in this way. The early church fathers declared that immersion was the practice. Quotations from the Epistle of Barnabas, Justin Martyr, Tertullian, Eusebius, Athanasius, and Chrysostom all indicate this to be the case.

Places and Circumstances

More than this, a close look at the very wording in our English New Testament indicates that immersion was the act in view. When it is said that John baptized at Aenon because there was much water there, and that Philip and the eunuch "went down into the water," there is little doubt as to the action that took place. As Alexander Campbell said in *The Christian System*, "Indeed a mere English scholar, who has only heard that baptism is a Greek word, may indubitably ascertain that it means neither sprinkling nor pouring, by substituting the definition of the term, and trying its sense in all places where the ordinance is spoken of. This is an infallible canon of interpretation. The proper definition of a term substituted for it will always make as good sense as the term itself. Now if an English reader will try sprinkling or pouring in those places where he finds the word baptism, he will soon discover that neither of these words can possibly represent it, if the above canon be true. For instance, we are told that all Judea and Jerusalem went out to John and were baptized of him in the Jordan. Sprinkled them in the Jordan! poured them in the Jordan! immersed them in the Jordan! Can any one doubt which of these truly represents the original in such passages? I may sprinkle or pour water upon a person; but to sprinkle or pour them into water is impossible. It is not said he baptized water upon them, but he baptized them in water, in the river."

An Obvious Conclusion

We have seen that only immersion fits the figures in the New Testament of a death, a burial, and resurrection, not to mention those of a planting, a birth, and a washing. We have seen that this is the meaning of the Greek word, as shown by the lexicons, the encyclopedias, and by its use in other Greek literature of the time. We have seen that the early church fathers so understood the term. We have seen that even in our English Bible the very use of the word indicates immersion. Since all these lines of evidence point to immersion, how does it happen that these facts have escaped the attention of the great Bible scholars of Christendom? They have not! In almost every denomination there can be pointed out a scholar who, contrary often to the practice of his own church, declares that baptism in the Bible is immersion. Martin Luther and Melanchton both thought that "baptize" meant "immerse." Dean Alford and Dean Stanley of the Anglican church agreed. So did Methodist scholars like John Wesley, Adam Clarke, and George Whitfield and Presbyterians Philip Schaff and Richard Baxter. Congregationalist scholars like Doddridge and Stuart likewise agreed.

Joining this unanimous verdict of Protestant scholarship is the voice of the Roman Catholic Church. In "A Catechism for Adults," a training booklet for persons who wish to become Roman Catholics, William J. Cogan answers the question, "How is Baptism given?" as follows: "Baptism is given by pouring water over the forehead of the person to be baptized ..." The next question is "Is this the only way Baptism can be given?" In response this text replies, "No, Baptism used to be given also by placing the person to be baptized completely in water; it was done this way in the Catholic Church for 1200 years."[1] Not only do Protestant scholars declare immersion to be the baptism of the Bible, but Roman Catholic scholars say that it continued to be the practice for the first twelve hundred years. If we remember that the church was established in A.D. 30, then we can see that sprinkling and pouring are, historically speaking, recent innovations in the life of the church.

The Testimony of Scholars

The Encyclopedia Britannica says, "The Council of Ravenna, in 1311, was the first council of the church which legalized baptism by sprinkling, by leaving it to the choice of the officiating minister."[2] Alford, the famous Episcopal scholar, says, "The baptism was administered by the immersion of the whole person." Martin Luther's opinion was, "Baptism is a Greek word and may be translated immerse. I would have those who are to be baptized to be altogether dipped." In John Wesley's *Notes on the New Testament* he comments on Romans 6:4, "We are buried with him—alluding to the ancient manner of baptizing by immersion." The comment of Doddridge on the same verse is, "It seems but the part of candor to confess that here is an allusion to the ancient manner of baptizing by immersion." In the face of such testimony surely the person who wishes to do Bible things in Bible ways will insist upon being baptized by immersion.

QUESTIONS

1. What is necessary to prepare a person for baptism?

2. Name four uses of the word "baptism" in the New Testament.

3. What are the two deaths that are involved in baptism?

4. What is the one baptism of Ephesians 4:5? Why?

5. In what ways does immersion symbolize a death? A resurrection?

6. Give at least four lines of proof that the meaning of the Greek word baptidzo is "to dip, plunge, or immerse."

7. Name some denominational scholars that agree.

8. Are ceremonies important?

9. How did Paul say a person came into Christ? Into His death? Into the one body?

10. How is the blood of Christ connected with baptism?

---

[1] Used by permission of William J. Cogan.

[2] Used by permission of Encyclopedia Britannica.

BAPTISM IN THE LIFE OF THE CHRISTIAN

Romans 6:1-7; Titus, 3:4-7; Acts 8:12-24, 26-40

BELIEVER'S BAPTISM

Proper Candidate

Who is a proper candidate for baptism? The Bible plainly teaches believer's baptism, i. e., that a person who does not believe cannot be baptized. Consider in this connection Acts 8:36, 37 where the question, "What doth hinder me to be baptized?" is answered by, "If thou believest, ... thou mayest." Lack of faith then would hinder or prevent one from receiving baptism. You will note also that in Mark 16:16 Jesus placed faith before baptism, as does Acts 16:31-33. That repentance precedes baptism is clearly seen in Acts 2:38. That one must be old enough or intelligent enough to "receive the word" is shown in Acts 2:41. Jesus placed things in the proper order in Matthew 28:19, 20. Here you will note that teaching comes before baptism, as well as after. We see, then, that until a person has been taught, has received the word, believes on Christ with all his heart, and repents, he cannot be Scripturally baptized.

Household Baptisms

Those who practice infant baptism sometimes point to the household baptisms as the Scriptural basis for the practice. There are four of these in the New Testament, yet in not one is there any mention of the baptism of infants. In Acts 16 it is said that Lydia was baptized "and her household." As J. W. McGarvey points out, in order to find infant baptism here one must first assume that Lydia was married. This the Bible nowhere says. Her household could have been made up of servants, nieces, nephews, or cousins. Assuming, though, that Lydia was married, one must next assume that she had children. The Bible does not say that she did. One must further assume that, being married and having children, they were with her at Philippi and not back home in Thyatira (Acts 16:14). Finally, one must assume that if she were married, did have children, and they were with her at Philippi, that at least one of them was too young to believe. There is little proof here for infant baptism. In the other three cases we can be certain that there were no infants in the household. In Acts 10 it is said of the centurion Cornelius that he "feared God with all his house." In the story of the jailer it is said that he rejoiced, "believing in God with all his house." In these cases it is obvious that whoever was included in Cornelius' household was old enough to fear God, and whoever may have been a part of the jailer's family was at least old enough to believe. In the first chapter of 1 Corinthians Paul says he baptized the household of Stephanas, a man about whom we know little. While nothing more is said in that chapter, in the last chapter of the same epistle Paul mentions the family of Stephanas again and notes that they "have addicted themselves to the ministry of the saints." Thus they were old enough to perform some service that could be called a ministry. While we know little about the persons included in these households, they cannot logically be pointed out as examples of infant baptism.

THE PURPOSE OF BAPTISM

Remission of Sins

If we recall that the purpose of baptism is the remission of sins, then it will be seen at once that only a sinner can be baptized. That baptism is indeed for the remission of sins is clearly taught in Acts 2:38; 1 Peter 3:21; Acts 22:16; Romans 6:1-7; and Mark 16 :16. That infants are not sinners is plainly implied by Jesus when He said, "Of such is the kingdom of heaven" (Matthew 19:14; Luke 18:16). In fact, Jesus taught that unless we become like little children we could not expect to go to heaven (Mark 10:15). The Biblical definition of sin as "transgression of the law" (1 John 3:4) exonerates all who are too immature to obey the law.

A Strange Fact

If there is no Scriptural basis for the baptism of infants, why is the practice so widespread in modern Protestantism? Infant baptism stems from the doctrine of original sin. This doctrine teaches that infants are born in sin, that God holds them personally responsible for the collective iniquity of the human race, that they are guilty even though the deeds were done by others and done before they were born. To hold such a position one would have to greatly alter his view of God. The Bible pictures a God of love and of justice. While an innocent child may have to suffer the consequences of others' sins, yet a God of love and justice does not hold an infant eternally responsible for their sins. What parent, having two children, would punish one for the misdemeanors of the other? What sort of God would hold an infant responsible through eternity for things utterly beyond his control?

However, if one believes in original sin, he must also believe in infant baptism, since baptism is for the remission of sins. The strange fact is that many denominations no longer believe in original sin, yet continue to practice infant baptism. The custom lives, though the conviction that prompted it no longer exists!

MORAL RESPONSIBILITY

An Individual Matter

That we bear personal responsibility for our sins is taught throughout the Bible. In Romans 14:12 we read, "Every one of us shall give account of himself to God." Compare also Revelation 20:12, 13, where the dead are judged according to their works. Just as we cannot shift our responsibility to someone else, neither are we held responsible for another's guilt. When God made man in His image, made him morally free, He made him personally responsible for his sins.

The Age of Accountability

At what age does a child become accountable to God? When is he old enough to believe with all his heart and to repent of his sins? When is he old enough to commit sin? Only one person can say exactly when this takes place. That person is the child himself. The parents may have a fair idea of the child's maturity, and the minister's advice and counsel may be sought. In the final analysis, though, it is the child himself who knows. Very early in life a child learns that he is accountable to his parents for his actions. When he enters school, he learns that he is accountable to his teacher and principal. Sometime in the growing-up years he knows in his heart that he is also accountable to God. When a child knows that, he is old enough to choose right and wrong; he has become a responsible individual and has reached the age of moral accountability.

Freedom of the Will

If we keep in mind that baptism is the ceremony of initiation into Christ's body, the church, then it will be quite clear that such an act cannot take place contrary to the will of the individual. If it could, then why could not adults as well as children be inducted against their will? This point is well illustrated in a story that has come down from the early history of the Restoration movement. Years ago the Kentucky hills echoed to the preaching of an evangelist named John Smith. One of the earliest leaders in the movement to restore the New Testament church, he bore the nickname "Raccoon" John Smith. It is said that on one occasion, after an open-air baptismal service, Smith came up from the water's edge and took by the arm one of the ministers in the community. The minister asked Smith what he was doing, and he is said to have replied, "I'm going to baptize you." "But, Brother Smith," he protested, "I don't want to be baptized." Brother Smith kept pulling him toward the water and replied, "I don't care, I'm going to baptize you anyway." The minister cried out, "Brother Smith, you know if you baptize me against my will it won't do me any good." At this point Smith stopped and addressed the crowd. "Ladies and gentlemen, last Sunday this man took a little baby and against its will performed for it an act that he termed baptism. And now, you have heard from his own lips that it really didn't do him any good!"

RECONSECRATION

Sins After Baptism

Since baptism is for the remission of sins, would not one have to be baptized all over again every time he sinned after his conversion? Not at all. Baptism is the crowning act that makes one a Christian, a member of the household of God, one whose citizenship is in heaven. His sins are now seen in a different context. A citizen has certain rights and privileges, even when he breaks the laws of his land. An alien does not have those rights. A member of a family has certain rights and privileges not enjoyed by those outside the family circle. So when a sinner has been adopted into the family of God, he has entered a new situation. He is in fact a new creature. Now when he sins he need only repent and pray and he has an advocate with the Father, Jesus Christ (I John 2:1). This is clearly seen in the eighth chapter of Acts, where Simon the sorcerer falls into grave sin after his baptism. He is not told to be baptized again, but to repent and pray that he may be forgiven. This is one of the privileges of every child of God. He may be reinstated into the family of God by repentance and prayer.

Rebaptism

There is one case of rebaptism in the New Testament. At Ephesus Paul met disciples who had known only the baptism of John the Baptist. John baptized "unto repentance," but Christian baptism is "into Christ." Paul rebaptized these, according to Acts 19:4, 5. Occasionally there are those who feel certain that at the time of their baptism their motives were not pure. Only they are qualified to say. The danger is that we may underestimate the amount of knowledge possessed at that time. Certainly the growing Christian knows more now than when he was baptized, but the fact that he knows more now need not reflect upon his sincerity then. Rebaptism is necessary only in the case of persons who are convinced that they were baptized for the wrong purpose or from the wrong motive.

Rededication

Sometimes in the life of a Christian there comes a time that is something like a second conversion experience. It is a time of great sorrow over one's sins, a time of renewing of allegiance to Christ. Such a reconsecration need not involve rebaptism, though the sin be great. The Lord's Supper is the time of rededication for the Christian. Here he sees again the same dramatic portrayal that attended his baptism. Here he can renew his allegiance to Christ and reconfirm his determination to serve Him.

BAPTISM AND GRACE

Not a Work of Righteousness

A very important text in connection with baptism is Titus 3:5. Study closely this verse. It gives perhaps the best picture of the relationship between baptism and grace. It has sometimes been charged that when we say baptism is for the remission of sins we deny that we are saved by grace. Paul did not feel that there was any conflict here. In writing to Titus he explained that baptism was not a work of righteousness; that by obeying the command to be baptized a person was no more earning his salvation than by obeying the command to repent. Baptism, said Paul, was the washing of regeneration. It was closely involved in the new birth, but this did not mean that Paul believed in salvation by works. Indeed, to Paul baptism was not to be classified as "works" at all. He saw baptism as a channel of God's grace, a part of man's necessary response, if he would receive that grace.

Baptism Saves

How then could baptism be said to save us? How can 1 Peter 3:21 declare that just as Noah was saved during the flood "the like figure whereunto even baptism doth also now save us"? If we study the verse carefully we see that Peter is pointing out that the physical washing is the visible manifestation of an unseen spiritual washing. That is why he calls baptism "the answer of a good conscience toward God" and points out that baptism is not "the putting away of the filth of the flesh." An old illustration fits well here. A farmer could say, "I plowed that field today." He could with equal truth say, "That horse plowed that field today." or "That plow plowed that field today." While man and horse provided the power, the plow was a necessary instrument. In a similar way, it may be said that faith saves, baptism saves, and grace saves, without there being any contradiction. The merit is wholly in the grace of God. Man's necessary response is characterized by faith—faith that finds expression in repentance and baptism. A man may say he has faith, but is he willing to formally and publicly commit and bind himself by that faith? In this way the water separates, just as it separated Noah from those who perished in the flood.

Justification by Faith

There is no conflict between Acts 2:38 and Romans 5:1 or Ephesians 2:8, 9. Years ago J. W. Sweeney published a sermon entitled, "Baptism for Remission of Sins Is Justification by Faith." It is certainly true that man cannot be saved by the works of the law, nor by works of righteousness. Baptism for remission of sins is not in conflict with Luther's dramatic discovery that the Bible says, "The just shall live by faith." Baptism is faith in action, faith made public, faith formalized and ceremonialized. The classic Biblical illustration is Abraham. When he offered up Isaac it was seen as an act of faith, and by that faith he was justified (Romans 4). So baptism procures no merit and purchases no pardon, but only proves one's faith in the grace of God. Indeed, only with the eye of faith could one see blood in baptism. How else could one connect baptism in water in the twentieth century with the blood that dried in the dust of Golgotha in the first century? How else could one connect the washing of the body in pure water with the sprinkling of Christ's blood upon the heart (Hebrews 10:22)?

BAPTISM AND CHRIST

Jesus' Own Baptism

Although Jesus knew no sin (Hebrews 4:15; 1 Peter 2:22), still He walked at least thirty miles to be baptized by John in the river Jordan. When John hesitated, Jesus indicated that it should be done in order to "fulfill all righteousness." God gave His approval in a most dramatic way when He broke the silence of heaven to say, "This is my beloved Son, in whom I am well pleased." Is it not fair to say that, when we follow in Jesus' steps and imitate His baptism, God is well pleased with us as well? There is a hint, too, regarding the mechanics of performing the act itself. Notice in Matthew 3:16 that Jesus, when He was baptized, came up out of the water. Those immersed into Christ are assured that their baptism is like His.

Sometimes it is said that baptism is not important enough to warrant the lengthy discussions of it that have taken place in every age. Baptism was important enough to Jesus for Him to go out of His way to receive it and to insist that it be done. If the sinless Christ went to so much trouble to receive it, surely it is not a matter that we can view lightly or indifferently.

Our Baptism and His Burial

It has been seen that Romans 6 suggests that baptism is, however, much more than a symbol. To see it as mere ceremony or ritual and nothing more is to miss greatly its true import. Note in Romans 6:4 that we are buried with Him. One minister has entitled his sermon on this text: "Two Men in One Grave." Christ lives. He is present when we gather in worship. And when a person is buried in baptism he is not laid beneath the waters alone. There is great significance in the fact that we are buried with Christ.

Baptism, a Solemn Act

If baptism, then, involves the presence of the living Christ, if it is a sacramental as well as a symbolic act, then the ceremony must be regarded as a most solemn one. Baptism is never to be considered lightly. The performing of it should not be made the occasion of crude jokes. The witnessing of it is a high and holy privilege. The minds of the candidates, those assisting, and those witnessing should be carefully prepared, so that all may come to the water's edge in a state of reverence. Let the act be performed with dignity and let it be as meaningful as the Lord's Supper to all present.

QUESTIONS

1. What are the four prerequisites to Bible baptism?

2. Explain the household baptisms of the New Testament.

3. What is the purpose of baptism? Give Scripture for your answer.

4. How did the practice of infant baptism originate?

5. What is the age of accountability? Who knows best when it is attained?

6. Is there a case of rebaptism in the New Testament?

7. How does a person receive forgiveness for sins committed after baptism?

8. Why is baptism not a work of righteousness?

9. Is the doctrine of baptism for remission of sins in conflict with the doctrine of justification by faith? Explain.

10. What differences are there between the baptism of Jesus and our baptism? What similarities?

11. Is baptism a symbolic act or a sacramental act? Give reasons for your answer.

12. What can be done to make the services of baptism reverent and inspiring to both the candidate and those who witness?

THE CHURCH AT WORSHIP

1 Corinthians 11-14; Matthew 18:19, 20; Psalms 95, 100

EARLY BEGINNINGS

An Important and Comprehensive Term. Worship is mentioned in almost the same breath with the gathering of the church. Acts 2:41 says, "The same day there were added unto them about three thousand souls." Acts 2:42 describes briefly their activities: "And they continued steadfastly in the apostles' doctrine and fellowship, and in breaking of bread, and in prayers." These four areas certainly do not exhaust the matter of Christian worship, but they form a convenient summary. The apostles' doctrine was at that time a word-of-mouth proposition. Future generations have been able to continue steadfastly in the apostles' doctrine through the record left us in the New Testament. The term "fellowship" used here is also translated "communion" in 1 Corinthians 10:16; 2 Corinthians 6:14; and 13:14. The word literally means "participation" and could be translated "partnership." It is a very general term and no doubt embraced both the Lord's Supper, giving, and other aspects of fellowship. *The New English Bible* translates it "to share the common life."

Scholars disagree over the meaning in this passage of "breaking of bread." Some hold that here, as in 1 Corinthians 10:16, the term refers to the Lord's Supper. Many others contend that the term means the same thing here that it does in Acts 2:46, i.e., that it refers to the love feasts, the meals that the Christians shared together as a family. Some feel that Luke would not use the term in two different senses in the same chapter without some explanation. Since the Lord's Supper may be included in the term "fellowship" (communion), the better view may be that this was actually the common meal shared together. Such a view does not disassociate the meal from worship, for among the Jews the breaking of bread was that act of blessing that the master of the house pronounced preceding a meal. (See Luke 24:30 and Matthew 14:19.) The act closely corresponded to our modern custom of saying grace before meals.

Prayer was an integral part of both public and private worship from the very beginning. Much profit could be gained by a close study of all the prayers recorded in the Bible. It is interesting to note here that this general summary of four areas of worship may be thought of as including public worship, family worship, and private worship.

Spontaneous Worship

The second mention of worship on the part of the Christians follows closely on the heels of the first. The two final verses of the second chapter of Acts indicate that they continued to worship God in the temple and that they also conducted worship "from house to house." The term "praising God" is to be seen in connection with the preceding verse. These verses suggest a spontaneous sort of worship that kept springing up from within their hearts. Accustomed as they were to the formal worship of the temple and the synagogues, we may imagine that the early Christians did conduct organized worship services. At this early time, however, they were caught up in the fervor and excitement of the hour in a unique way.

Unaffected by Externals

Should the faults, or even the hypocrisies, of other worshipers have any effect upon my worship? Apparently Jesus did not think so, for He went often to the temple, though He knew it to be riddled with hypocrisy. Peter and John went to the temple at the hour of prayer (Acts 3:1) though they were a part of that new covenant that superseded the old. Some of the tragic divisions that have rent the body of Christ have come about because worshipers have felt that they could not worship God sincerely in an unsatisfactory environment. In the Bible, true worship is seen to be a matter of the heart, little affected by matters external.

THE MEANS OF WORSHIP

Worship Through Singing

Christianity is the only great movement among men to give great and lasting prominence to singing. In no other society is there a comparable practice. The Jews enjoyed the singing of choirs, but congregational singing is distinctively Christian. It is not by accident that singing occupies so large a place in Christian worship. Ephesians 5:19, Colossians 3:16, and James 5:13 enjoin the practice. The rendering, "psalms and hymns and spiritual songs," suggests a wide variety of choice in selecting the songs to be used. The New Testament offers us no help in making the selection or in indicating what instruments should accompany the singing. Some few have contended that only inspired songs may be sung, but there is no reason for this extreme position. The use of musical instruments in worship is neither approved nor condemned explicitly in the New Testament. Evidently there was ample room allowed for freedom of choice and for individual taste in these matters.

Worship Through Prayer

Prayer was so much a part of the Hebrew worship that it is inconceivable that it would not occupy a large place in Christian worship. Only a few prayers are recorded in the New Testament, but they reflect a deep sense of the abiding presence of God and a firm conviction that prayer does avail much. Without doubt they followed the example of Jesus and prayed before partaking of the Lord's Supper. All their important decisions were attended by prayer. They prayed at the choosing of Matthias (Acts 1:24), at the setting aside of the first deacons (Acts 6:6), and at the commissioning of Paul and Barnabas (Acts 13:1-3). Emergencies called forth fervent prayer in behalf of Peter and John (Acts 4:23-31), again in behalf of Peter (Acts 12:5, 12), and by Paul and Silas in the Philippian prison (Acts 16:25). In 1 Corinthians 11 and 14 we catch a glimpse of the important position prayer occupied when the church gathered to worship. Prayer for one another is enjoined by James (5:16), and Paul sets the example by mentioning again and again in his epistles that he is praying for the brethren. Ordination of elders was made the occasion of prayer and fasting (Acts 14:23). The disciples spent the ten days between the ascension and Pentecost in prayer (Acts 1:14.) Indeed, it would be impossible to overemphasize the place that prayer held in the life of the early church.

Worship Through Preaching

In the New Testament, preaching is seen as something more than entertainment. While its objective is educational in part, it is also seen to be a way of worshiping God. In declaring the mighty acts of God, both the speaker and the listener are offering praise. While preaching is intended to convict the sinner and to confirm the saint, it is also offered to God as worship.

Worship Through the Lord's Supper

So much needs to be said regarding the Lord's Supper that an entire chapter of this book is devoted to it. The place of the Lord's Supper as an integral part of worship in New Testament times is attested to by Paul, by Luke, and by Jesus himself. While it would be incorrect to say that worshiping God in one way is more important than another, certainly the Lord's Supper was a dramatic focal point of worship. Just as the death, burial, and resurrection of Christ are key points in Christian doctrine, so did the Lord's Supper occupy a key position in Christian worship.

Worship Through Meditation

It was in the Psalms that the Lord said, "Be still, and know that I am God." Surrounded as we are by a noisy, hurried, and harried world, it is essential that Christians find time for meditation. Perhaps that is why we have come to call the house of worship a sanctuary. Surely it is as true in our time as in Isaiah's that "in quietness and in confidence shall be your strength."

Giving as Worship

There can be no doubt that the early Christians regarded the sharing of their material wealth a very real part of their Christian experience. In the beginning, the disciples placed everything they had at the disposal of the church (Acts 2:44, 45). This was a voluntary offering (Acts 5:4), but the bringing of gifts to God they recognized as serious and solemn business. Read in this connection the story with which Acts chapter 5 opens.

Many are like the little boy who was told by his parents that when he got to Sunday school, he must remember to put his nickel in for Jesus. He replied, "I bet that preacher'll get it." Many have no higher view of giving than this. The Biblical view is that one gives to Christ, not to a cause; to a divine Person, not to a dramatic program; to God, not to men.

It is unfortunate that in modern times, in an effort to make the offering seem less of an intrusion into the service, many have treated giving as a light and amusing experience. The effect has been exactly the opposite of that desired. When giving is presented as an act of worship, there is no embarrassment connected with it in any way, and it becomes a meaningful part of the service to the worshipers, a real and vital way for them to express thanksgiving to God.

Was benevolence the only way these gifts were used? In the beginning, this appears to be the case (Acts 6:1). The offering in 1 Corinthians 16:1, 2 is also for benevolence. The taking of that offering seems to have been a part of the program of worship much as it is in the churches today. A careful consideration of 1 Corinthians 9 indicates, however, that contributions were also used to support those who preached the gospel.

Paul argues that those who devote all of their time to service in the church ought to be supported in a similar fashion to the priests, who, under the old covenant, "are partakers with the altar." The preaching and the teaching of the gospel can be underwritten in only one way—through the gifts of those people who love God.

THE DAY OF WORSHIP

First Day of the Week

It is not difficult to show that the first Christians met together on the first day of the week. The very day of the resurrection itself found them together in the evening (John 20:19). If we accept the Jewish method of counting time, they were together again one week later (John 20:26). Paul met with them at Troas on that day (Acts 20:7), and he assumed that the Corinthian church would be together then

THE NEW TESTAMENT CHURCH

(1 Corinthians 16:2). Since the resurrection occupied such a key place in their faith and dominated their preaching, it is logical that Christ would choose for them to meet for worship on that day of the week on which the resurrection had occurred.

The Sabbath

It seems clear from a study of Deuteronomy 5:15 that no Gentile could ever "keep the sabbath day." Only if one's ancestors had been in Egypt would this be possible. Israel could commemorate her deliverance from Egypt by keeping the Sabbath. Christians commemorate their deliverance from the power of sin and death by worshiping on the first day of the week. It is incorrect to call the first day of the week the "Christian Sabbath." Christ did not merely change the day of the week involved. The only relationship between Sabbath worship and Christian worship on the first day is that both involved the setting apart of a certain day for a special purpose. Beyond this the Bible draws no parallels. Hebrews 4:1-11 indicates that the Christian's sabbath awaits him in heaven, when he shall eternally rest from his labors.

The Lord's Day

This term is used only once, in Revelation 1: 10. Some have thought it synonymous with the day of the Lord and have identified it with some future time. However, the two terms have the same difference in the original Greek that they have in English translation. Moreover, a close reading of the text indicates that John was not, at first, transported into some future time. In Revelation 1:19 we see that he must write "the things which are, and the things which shall be hereafter." Revelation 4:1, 2 indicate the transition from the things which are to the things which shall be. Most commentators agree that John uses this term, as early non-Biblical Christian literature used it, to refer to the first day of the week.

Keep It Holy

The interpreters of the Jewish law spelled out exactly what was involved in keeping the Sabbath, even though God had been much less specific. For Christians there are no exact specifications for the keeping of Sunday. It is a matter that must be settled in every Christian's conscience. The person who makes his use of Sunday a matter of prayer, and who tries to make it truly the Lord's Day, will not go far astray. In a complex urban society, there may be more problems than were present in the largely rural and agrarian society of a generation ago. There were problems in early times as well. Many of the Christians in New Testament times were slaves, and could meet for worship only in the evening (cf. Acts 20:7-12). Still, they managed to make it God's day, worshiping at every opportunity.

THE SIGNIFICANCE OF WORSHIP

Regular Worship

The importance of regular private worship was made clear by Jesus and is corroborated by Paul on many occasions (Philippians 4:6, 7). Hebrews 10:24, 25 urges upon every Christian regular attendance at all sessions of public worship. Attending worship is seen to be an important response of man to God, and a mark of consideration for one's fellow man. There seem to be unusual spiritual values attached to corporate worship. Praying together, taking the Lord's Supper together and sharing together seem to be vital to Christianity. The person who chooses to worship alone when he could worship with others is missing a great and special blessing from God. More than this, he is not being considerate of others who need his presence in order to make the fellowship complete.

Meaningful Worship

A careful study of the New Testament leads to the conclusion that worship in the early church avoided two popular extremes of modern times. Their worship was characterized neither by emotional extravagance, nor by stiff and stilted ritualism. With their Jewish background, we may be certain that these first Christians worshiped in an atmosphere of dignity and respect. Still, their meetings were not lacking in warmth, enthusiasm, or vigor. Their worship had an emotional content and an intellectual content. It could meet the needs of men from various backgrounds and with differing cultures without giving false impressions of the nature of God.

First Corinthians 14:15 should be included in any consideration of meaningful worship. To "sing with the spirit" does not mean to sing in a spirited fashion. The reference is to divine and miraculous gifts. However, there can be no mistaking the import of "I will sing with the understanding." All worship must involve an understanding of God and His will.

Decently and in Order

While the New Testament does not give detailed specifications for the conduct of public worship, 1 Corinthians 14:40 lays down a general principle that can help in all such decisions. Whatever allowances one makes for taste in music, for preference in the manner of distributing the Lord's Supper or collecting the offering, for arrangements for a place, time, and order of worship, let all be done with this verse in mind. Worship is too holy and too vital to be hastily and carelessly arranged. It is worthy of thoughtful planning and painstaking preparation.

QUESTIONS

1. What are the four areas of worship mentioned in Acts 2:42?

2. How early is worship mentioned in connection with the church?

3. Can you mention six means of worship?

4. Why do we sing in worship?

5. How important was prayer in the New Testament church? Explain.

6. Why is regular worship important?

7. Are we commanded to worship regularly? Where?

8. What can be done to assure meaningful worship?

9. What do you think Paul meant when he said, "Let all things be done decently and in order?"

10. What is the day set aside for Christian worship? Why?

11. Give Biblical examples of Christians meeting for worship on the day indicated.

12. Compare the Lord's Day and the Sabbath Day.

THE CHURCH
AROUND THE LORD'S TABLE

1 Corinthians 11:18-34; Matthew 26:17-30;
Mark 14:12-26; Luke 22:7-39

ITS INSTITUTION AND MEANING

The Lord's Supper occupied so strategic a position in the worship of the New Testament church that it deserves an entire chapter in this course. Its importance in the history of the church, and the many theological battles fought over it, further warrant an extended treatment of this topic. The solemnity attending its institution, the stern warnings regarding its abuse, and the very time chosen to inaugurate it, all underscore the incalculable significance of the ceremony. The Supper is inseparably related both to the cardinal facts of the gospel and to man's response to the gospel. The Supper is described in Scripture as a time to remember Christ's body and blood, a time to repent of our sins and shortcomings, a time to renew our allegiance to Him, a time to recall His promise to come again. Surely no man can take lightly a ceremony so fraught with historical and spiritual significance.

The Last Supper

The Lord's Supper bears the title "Last Supper" because it occurred just before the awful events of the betrayal, the trials, and the crucifixion. It could as well be called the "First Supper," for on that night Jesus instituted the first of a continuing series of Communion observances. It will never be finally settled as to the exact day of the week on which the event took place. A great many scholars contend that the Lord's Supper was instituted on Thursday evening, with the crucifixion following on Friday. Some disagree. That we cannot fix with accuracy the day of the week does not really matter, since the Christians in Bible times (and ever since) have always kept the observance on the first day of the week. It may have been in anticipation of this that the New Testament does not fix precisely the day. Had it done so, some might have been led to doubt the propriety of observing the Supper on Sunday. Nor can we fix with accuracy the details concerning the Passover supper. Biblical scholars have produced long and involved arguments as to whether this was actually the Passover meal or a substitute for it. It is unlikely that this question will ever be settled, and it did not seem to concern the disciples at all.

The Night of Betrayal

What did concern the disciples was the fact that the Supper was instituted on the night of betrayal. There seemed a strange irony here! Was Judas actually present when the supper was instituted? Here again we can only guess. At any rate, when the Passover meal was finished, Jesus took the unleavened bread (bread without yeast), gave thanks, and distributed it among them. He then took the cup, which was a customary part of the Passover, and gave thanks again, and they all drank of it. What was in the cup? The Bible calls it "fruit of the vine." Since it is never called wine, many believe that this was not fermented wine, but grape juice. Others feel that it may have been wine mixed with water.

Symbol or Sacrament?

What did Jesus mean by "This is my body," and "This is my blood"? Interpretations range all the way from transubstantiation to memorial. There are those who say the elements actually become flesh and blood; others say the Supper is only a symbolic memorial. No doubt Jesus said, "This is my body," in the same way that He said, "I am the door," or "I am the vine." Jesus was never miraculously transformed into either a door or a vine. He was merely speaking in colorful and highly figurative language. The view that the bread actually becomes body and the cup becomes blood will not stand the tests of chemistry and science, nor does it appear to be reasonable. On the other hand, it may be quite correct to say that the supper is simply a symbolic memorial. Christ is alive! One generally erects memorials to people who are dead! Christ promised to be with His followers when they met in worship: "For where two or three are gathered together in my name, there am I in the midst of them" (Matthew 18:20). Consider also Jesus' words, "I will not drink henceforth of this fruit of the vine, until that day when I drink it new with you in my Father's kingdom" (Matthew 26:29). While the meaning of the passage is disputed, some hold that this refers to Christ's presence at the table now. Whether or not the passage applies, the fact remains. Christ is present with His followers when they meet to share the Supper. It is a memorial, but it is much more than a memorial. We not only remember Him; we also commune with Him.

The Supper as Communion

Read carefully Paul's words in 1 Corinthians 10:16: "The cup of blessing which we bless, is it not the communion of the blood of Christ?" If we remember that this word "communion" can be translated "fellowship" we see that Paul had in mind the presence of Christ among His worshipers. Those who gather at the table do not commune with one another. They commune with Him. This principle is quite important when one considers the long quarrel over who is entitled to partake and who is not.

Close or Open Communion?

Since one communes with Christ, the sincerity or hypocrisy of others has no bearing whatever upon the service. Indeed, every other worshiper might not be entitled to partake. That would not ruin the Supper for him who was entitled. Perhaps the best question is not, "Who is entitled?" nor even, "Am I entitled?" but, "Am I prepared?" The fact that it is the "Lord's Supper" is also significant in this regard. I would not think of inviting someone to your home for dinner, nor denying a person that privilege. Neither have I the right to invite anyone to the Lord's Supper or to deny anyone that privilege. If the table is the Lord's, He must invite, He must debar.

THE MANNER OF ITS OBSERVANCE

Partaking Unworthily

Paul's words in 1 Corinthians 11:27, 29 have caused many to fear to partake of the emblems. They have felt that they were not worthy because of some sin or mistake in their lives, and that if they partook, they would be bringing condemnation upon themselves.

It must be kept clearly in mind that the word "unworthily" as used here is an adverb. It modifies the verbs "eat" and "drink." It does not have reference to the bread, the cup, or the worshiper, but to the manner in which the eating and drinking are done. A better translation is that of the Revised Standard Version, "in an unworthy manner." J. B. Phillips phrases it well: "Whoever eats the bread or drinks the wine without due thought is making himself like one of those who allowed the Lord to be put to death.... He that eats and drinks carelessly is eating and drinking a judgment on himself, for he is blind to the presence of the Lord's body."[1]

Proper Reverence

What is a worthy manner? What constitutes proper reverence? Two items are specifically mentioned in the text. The first is "let a man examine himself" (1 Corinthians 11:28). My concern at the table is not whether or not you are qualified to participate, but whether or not I am qualified. It is to the everlasting credit of the eleven that they had this attitude on the very night of the Supper's institution. When Jesus said that one of them should betray Him, not one pointed an accusing finger at Judas, nor at any other of their number. Each asked, "Is it I?" Such must be the attitude of him who partakes. The second essential to partaking in a worthy manner is to "discern the Lord's body." In the symbol must be seen the sacred act itself. Visions of Calvary must fill the mind and the imagination. "Here, O my Lord, I see Thee face to face!"

Who Is Worthy?

We see, then, that it is possible to partake in a worthy manner. It is obvious that it is never possible for any man to be worthy. What man can say that he deserved the sacrifice of Christ? Indeed, the man who comes feeling himself worthy to approach the table has by that pride been rendered most unworthy. Only the man who comes feeling that he is not and can never be worthy of Christ's love is in a position to partake in a worthy manner.

When and How Often?

While the Lord's Supper was instituted during the week, perhaps on Thursday evening, the only recorded times of its celebration among early Christians was on Sunday, the first day of the week. If ever in apostolic times it was observed on any other day, there is no record of it. The question of how often the Supper shall be observed is one that has enjoyed considerable discussion. If we take the term "breaking of bread" in Acts 2:42 to refer to the Lord's Supper, then we must consider the word "steadfastly." The word means either "constantly" or "at regular intervals." A close look at Acts 20:7 reveals a strong implication that meeting for the Supper was a customary occurrence at Troas on the first day of the week. Early church history bears this out. This quotation from Justin Martyr, written about A.D. 140, offers conclusive evidence regarding the practice of the early church. "And on the day called Sunday, all who live in cities or in the country gather together to one place, and the memoirs of the apostles or the writings of the prophets are read, as long as time permits; then, when the reader has ceased, the president verbally instructs, and exhorts to the imitation of these good things. Then we all rise together and pray, and, as we before said, when our prayer is ended, bread and wine and water are brought, and the president in like manner offers prayers and thanksgivings, according to his ability, and the people assent saying, Amen; and there is a distribution to each, and a participation of that over which thanks have been given, and to those who are absent a portion is sent by the deacons."

Objection to Weekly Communion

The only objection ever raised to weekly Communion is that such a practice renders the Supper common and robs it of meaning. It should be noted that this objection is not based upon any passage of Scripture, for what light the Scripture throws on the subject implies weekly observance. Nor is the objection based upon history, for history's unequivocal testimony is that in apostolic times the ceremony was observed every week. Nor is such an objection based upon experience, for it is not raised by those who practice weekly Communion, but by those who have never done so. Who is in the best position to evaluate weekly Communion? Is it the person who has practiced it, or the person who has never tried it? The testimony of those who observe the Supper weekly is that it grows more sacred with every feast.

It should also be noted that no one applies this objection to any other aspect of worship. No one declares that the more you pray the less meaningful prayer will become. No one believes that the less you attend church, the more beneficial attendance will be. No one feels that the fewer sermons one hears, the more blessing he will get from them or that the more seldom he gives, the greater will be his joy in giving. Since in each of these cases the very opposite is true, since the more we pray and worship and give the greater our benefits from them, is it not logical that the more frequently we commune the more meaningful Communion will become?

Some Opinions on Weekly Communion

Charles Spurgeon said, "When we began to break bread on every first day of the week, I heard some say that they thought that the coming so often to the table might take away the impressiveness of the holy feast. Well, I have scarcely missed a Sabbath these twenty years, and I never was so impressed with the solemnity and sweetness of the Master's Supper as I am now. I feel it to be fresher every time. When it was observed once a month, I had not half the enjoyment, and I think that where friends have the communion once a quarter or once a year, as in some churches, they really do not give the ordinance a fair opportunity to edify them. They do not fairly test the value of an ordinance which they so greatly neglect...." John Wesley and John Calvin both advised observing the Supper every Lord's Day. Doddridge said, "It is well known that the primitive Christians administered the Lord's Supper every Lord's Day." Such noted commentators as Scott, Mason, Torrey, and Adam Clark are agreed that in the beginning and throughout the first and second centuries, Communion was observed on the first day of every week.

Matters Left to Human Judgment

Neither the Bible nor church history sheds any light on the mechanics of distributing the emblems. Should all partake in unison, or should each partake as he is served? Should the bread and cup be passed among the worshipers, or should they come to the front and kneel to commune? Who should officiate at the table? Should it be the minister or the elders, or just any member of the congregation? Should the Communion be at the close of the worship period, at the beginning, or in the middle? None of these questions are answered for us, and we may safely assume that God has left these details to the individual taste and preference of the congregation. "Let all things be done decently and in order."

ITS WIDER SIGNIFICANCE

The Lord's Supper and Christian Unity

No treatment of the Lord's Supper would be complete without a consideration of 1 Corinthians 10:17. "For we being many are one bread, and one body: for we are all partakers of that one bread." One great purpose of the Supper is to unite the worshipers and weld them into a single unit.

It is strange that this Supper which Paul sees as the great uniter has often been also the great divider. In interchurch meetings, it has often been seen that churchmen who could pray together, sing together, and fellowship together found that they could not conscientiously commune together. How far we have come from Scriptural things, when divine institutions have exactly the opposite of their intended effect. How tragic the division that plagues Christendom when the separation is so severe that one Christian cannot sit down at the table of the Lord with others who likewise profess Christ.

Till He Comes Again

The Lord's Supper is a sermon, a sermon in symbol. Its mute elements speak persuasively and eloquently to every sincere worshiper. "For as often as ye eat this bread, and drink this cup, ye do shew the Lord's death till he come." When the table has been spread and worshipers have sincerely and reverently partaken, then the hour of worship has been worthwhile. Whether the words of the preacher were eloquent and learned and helpful or not, still the gospel has been effectively preached. No one need go away feeling empty in heart and soul. The death of Christ has been proclaimed in the Supper. The word of the cross has been preached. And the same symbolic finger that pointed backward to Calvary has pointed forward to His return. Alongside the dramatic events of the crucifixion and the resurrection must be placed the return of the Lord. It is a cardinal doctrine of the Christian faith and an impressive aspect of the Lord's Supper.

QUESTIONS

1. Where, when, and by whom was the Lord's Supper instituted?

2. On what day of the week did the apostles and early Christians observe the Lord's Supper?

3. Give the two extreme views regarding Jesus' words, "This is my body" and "This is my blood."

4. What is unleavened bread?

5. Discuss the meaning of "fruit of the vine."

6. Discuss the various views regarding open and closed Communion.

7. What does Paul mean when he speaks of partaking unworthily?

8. What two things must one do in order to partake with proper reverence?

9. What evidence is there for weekly observance of Communion in the Bible? In history?

10. What is the common objection to weekly Communion? Is it a valid objection? Give reasons for your answer.

11. What bearing does the Lord's Supper have on Christian unity?

12. How is the Lord's Supper related to Christ's return?

---

[1] From *The New Testament in Modern English*, © J. B. Phillips 1958. Used by permission of The Macmillan Company.

THE CHURCH AND ITS OFFICERS

Acts 1; Ephesians 4:11-16; Titus 1:1-11; 1 Timothy 3;
Acts 6:1-8

TEMPORARY OFFICES

In the Beginning

At the outset, responsibility for the affairs of the church lay in the hands of men personally chosen by Jesus himself. The term that most correctly identifies them is "the twelve." Not only were they personally chosen by Christ, and designated as His closest associates, they were intensively trained by Him for more than three years. In addition to this, they were promised and given a measure of the Holy Spirit unequaled before or since. That baptism of the Holy Spirit made it possible for them to recall unerringly the words and works of Jesus. More than this, the indwelling Spirit would teach them "all things." Thus divinely inspired, they would logically be the leaders during the formative years of the church's history. It was not until fifteen or twenty years after the church was begun that the first book in the New Testament was written, and it was seventy years before the final one was set down. Without the written word as a guide, the early church had to depend upon men directly led by God.

The Apostles

Generally we refer to "the twelve" and Paul as "apostles." However, this word is also used of Barnabas, Andronicus, Junias, and James, the Lord's brother. Some believe that by implication Silvanus, Timotheus, Aponos, and Epaphroditus are also termed apostles

(1 Corinthians 9:5; 15:7; 4:6, 9; Galatians 1:19; 2:9; Romans 16:7; 1 Thessalonians 1:1; 2:6; Philippians 2:25). The word "apostle" means simply "one sent forth." While some feel that all of these were apostles in the fullest sense of the word, others are of the opinion that the term may have both a specific and a general meaning. That is, it may have been used generally of anyone sent as an envoy or missionary, but when used of Paul or the twelve it had reference to their special position of responsibility in the church.

The Thirteenth Apostle

We have also the problem occasioned by the death of Judas, reducing the twelve to eleven. Jesus did not choose anyone to fill the vacancy, so after His ascension the disciples (numbering about 120) met to select Judas' successor. Two candidates were chosen and then by lot Matthias was selected. Bible scholars are not agreed as to whether the brethren were acting in accord with divine directions, or on their own. It must be remembered that the promised gift of divine inspiration had not yet come. Were they acting on their own initiative? Had Jesus purposely not chosen a successor because He planned for Saul (Paul) to fill the vacancy? That is possible, but the fact that this was recorded in Acts after the Holy Spirit came, and recorded by an inspired man, Luke, without any comment at all, seems to imply that the action was not out of harmony with God's plans.

Successors to the Apostles

The question now arises, who shall succeed the other apostles when they, like Judas, are dead? The New Testament provides no means for appointing additional apostles, lists no qualifications, and records no duties. Acts 1:21, 22 implies that only one who had been personally with the resurrected Christ could be an apostle. Their primary function was to witness to what they had seen and heard, and no man can be a successor to a witness. Further, they were provided with miraculous gifts directly from God, and were enabled to pass those gifts on to others. Those claiming apostleship today possess none of these attributes, and we are safe in assuming that this was a temporary office, that it was designed for the church's formative years, and that once the New Testament had been completed it was needed no longer.

Prophets

Much that has been said of the apostle may also be said of the prophet. In its broadest sense the term refers to anyone who speaks for God. It is used in this way in the Old Testament, but it also carries a narrower meaning, that of one specially chosen for a particular revelation from God. It is in this more specific sense that the word is used in the New Testament. Prophets in the early church were the possessors of special knowledge, and without a written revelation they were indispensable to the work of the infant church. Only a few prophets are mentioned (Acts 21:9-11; 13:1 ff.), though there must have been many (1 Corinthians 12:28, 29; 14:29-32). Once the New Testament was written and circulated among the churches, the prophetic office in its miraculous sense would no longer be needed. It, too, may be regarded as a temporary office without provision for succession.

THE SERVANTS

Deacons

The first officers to be selected by the church itself were the deacons. The word means "servant" or "assistant" and is sometimes translated "minister." Of course, every Christian is a servant of Christ. For special duties, however, special appointments were made, much as any organization appoints committees to efficiently carry on its work. In the sixth chapter of Acts there is recorded the selection of men to care for the distribution of food to the needy. It was felt that the apostles should give their time to more pressing matters and not "leave the word of God, and serve tables." The phrase, "Look ye out among you," indicates that the congregation itself selected the deacons, who were then formally installed by the apostles to work under their direction.

Their Qualifications

Qualifications for those who hold this office are listed in Acts 6 and also in 1 Timothy 3. They were and are to be men of good character and reputation, that the church should not come into disrepute. No polygamist, no dishonest person, no one given to strong drink, and no greedy man was to be placed in such a high office. The deaconship is sometimes thought of as a training ground for the more responsible position of elder. While this may be true, to be elected a deacon is a high honor. To serve is the highest attainment in the church. "Whosoever will be chief among you, let him be your servant." Jesus himself could find no better way to characterize His own work. "Even as the Son of man came not to be ministered unto, but to minister."

Deaconesses

Bible scholars are not agreed on the subject of deaconesses. Since the word may be translated "servant," we have no good ground for assuming that Romans 16:1 means anything more. First Timothy 3:11 is more complex. The King James Version translates the passage, "Even so must their wives be," and leaves the impression that not only the deacon but also his spouse must be qualified before he can hold office. Some other translations, however, render the passage, "Even so must the deaconesses be." Actually, the Greek says, "Women, also." Does Paul mean women deacons, or does he mean their women, that is, the wives of the deacons? Since this verse is the only one on the subject, it would seem unwise to build too strong a case for the office of deaconess on it, particularly in the light of 1 Timothy 2:12.

THE SUPERINTENDENTS

The Need

As the number of churches multiplied it became obvious that the apostles, so few in number, could not possibly give proper oversight to so many widely scattered congregations. There was also the problem of the vacuum that would be left as the apostles died. Someone would be needed to guide the spiritual affairs of the churches. Those who served in this high office were called by at least three names: elder, bishop, and pastor. The term "elder" was borrowed directly from the Jewish synagogue where elders were in charge. The word means "older," and implies a person of maturity to be respected. The word "bishop" means "overseer" or "superintendent." The word "pastor" means simply "shepherd." That congregations were to have both elders and deacons is evident from Philippians 1:1 and 1 Timothy 3. A plurality of elders rather than one superintendent of a congregation is implied in Acts 14:23 and in Titus 1:5.

Manner of Selection

Since the qualifications and duties are carefully outlined, it seems likely that the churches elected their elders just as they did their deacons. The word translated "ordain" in this connection may mean either "elect" or "appoint." The method of selection, then, is not clearly defined and there have been some who contended upon the basis of Titus 1:5 for the right of evangelists to make the selection. There is, however, no more reason to believe this than to believe that they were elected by congregational vote, and certainly the latter is the wiser course. In fact, the root meaning of the word translated "ordain" in Acts 15:3 is to appoint by stretching forth the hand, thus offering good ground for the election of elders by congregational vote. Indicative of the high regard in which elders or bishops were to be held is Paul's admonition in 1 Timothy 5:19: "Against an elder receive not an accusation, but before two or three witnesses." Those who held this high office were not to be made the objects of hasty and thoughtless criticism or victims of careless and unfounded gossip.

Qualifications and Duties

Who is qualified to hold such an office? When we compare 1 Timothy. 3:1-7 and Titus 1:5-9, we have a long list of qualities such a man must possess. They might be summarized by saying that an elder must be qualified by physical, mental, emotional, and spiritual maturity. He must be a man of the highest character. His own life must be an example and above reproach, his home a model of harmonious Christian living. He must be a man trained by experience, capable of exercising good and sound judgment. He must be disciplined in mind, body, emotions, and soul.

As pastors (shepherds) the elders are to feed the flock of God (1 Peter 5:1-3; Acts 20:28). They are held directly responsible for what is taught and preached in the churches. Certainly a thorough knowledge of the Word of God is essential to the carrying out of such a task.

THE SPOKESMEN

In addition to these responsibilities of service and instruction, there were men charged specifically with the responsibility of preaching. Sometimes they shared with the deacons the term "minister." Sometimes they shared with the elders the term "pastor." Sometimes they shared with all Christians the term "evangelist," i. e., "a bringer of good tidings."

Evangelists

Every Christian was an evangelist, in that he told abroad the good news. Some, though, whose talent and training fitted them better than others, devoted all of their time to proclaiming the gospel. Sometimes they were itinerant preachers, moving from place to place. Sometimes they stayed for years in a given locality. (Even Paul stayed three years at Ephesus and two years at Corinth.) In 1 Corinthians 9:1-14 Paul argues strongly that those who thus serve should be paid from the tithes and offerings of the congregation. Israel always had had a supported ministry in the priesthood, and to Paul it was unthinkable that the church should not also have a paid ministry. Even though Paul himself chose to forego any salary, he was careful to point out that he had the right to receive a salary and that others should not be expected to support themselves as he did. Without a family to support, Paul could do what others could not.

Pastors

The word "pastor" appears in Ephesians 4:11, with reference to the church. In 1 Peter 5:2 and Acts 20:28 a verb form of the same word (translated "feed") is used to describe the work of the eldership. The idea is that the elder is one who feeds the flock, the church. However, 1 Timothy 5:17, 18 indicates that full-time workers for the church may be recruited from among the eldership, and so in many cases the preacher would also be regarded as an elder. In modern times the word "pastor" has come to be applied almost exclusively to the preacher. While a congregation in New Testament times recognized each of its overseers as a pastor or shepherd, certainly in that day as in ours the preacher was a pastor in the fullest sense of the word and shared the responsibilities of the church's eldership.

Ministers

The word most often used today to describe the church's preacher is actually the least definitive of all. As we have seen, the word really means "servant" and is transliterated "deacon" (the Greek word is *diakonos*). Remembering that Jesus himself claimed this title saying, "The Son of man came not to be ministered unto, but to minister," preachers have seen in it a mark of the humility that must characterize a leader in the kingdom of God. Certainly it is not an inappropriate term for one who serves as the spokesman of a local church. The qualifications and duties of the preacher are given in great detail in 1 and 2 Timothy and in Titus, but there are no instructions regarding the manner of selection.

A General Framework

It will be noted that the division of responsibility among elders, deacons, and evangelists provides for the adequate discharge of the duties incumbent upon the church; yet there is no clear line of demarcation of responsibilities. By failing to spell out exactly where the authority of elder, deacon, and minister fall there results a kind of check-and-balance similar to that seen in the American political system. Just as the executive, legislative, and judicial branches of government overlap, so do the three functions in the church. This is a great safeguard of liberty. No one man and no group of men can become very dictatorial in a congregation that takes seriously the plan of organization described in the New Testament.

Actually, what we have in the New Testament is a general framework of church organization. Its exact details are not spelled out. This flexibility makes it possible for the church to adjust itself to the particular needs and circumstances of its own time. In a congregation newly established there might be no one qualified to serve as an elder. In such a case the burden of responsibility might rest almost entirely on the minister. When a church is served by a very young minister, he might not in that situation be regarded as one of the elders. God's plan is flexible, allowing diverse approaches to one's own particular situation, as long as that approach is kept within the framework of God's design.

History's Warning

We must never draw the conclusion that the manner of organization in a church is unimportant simply because all the details are not given. It was departure from the divine plan that made possible the rise of the Roman Catholic Church. When congregations came to have but one bishop instead of many, and when voices beyond the local congregation began to dictate its affairs, the seeds of apostasy were sown. The autocratic power of the Roman Church continues today as history's warning to all who would take lightly God's plan for His church.

Areas of Human Judgment

How long does an elder serve? Is a deacon elected for one year, for three years, or for life? Should elders and deacons meet jointly, separately, or both? Should meetings be held regularly, or as the need is seen to arise? What matters should be referred to the congregation? These and many other details are left to the discretion of each congregation. They are to be determined by what has been called "sanctified common sense."

Beyond the Local Church

These officers bore their responsibilities in a single given congregation, with the exception of those who did itinerant preaching. Beyond the local congregation, no plan of organization was provided at all. If we remember that the church is not really an organization at all, but a living organism, a body, then we may think of each local congregation as a cell in that body. Christ is the head and the Bible the constitution of the church. Beyond that, Scriptural organization provides for nothing more above the local level. Christians are thus left free to work together co-operatively as the times, the locale, and the need demand. There is plenty of room for human judgment and initiative. The unfortunate fact is that voluntary co-operation has sometimes been allowed to grow into large, formal, and complex arrangements that often have destroyed Christian freedom. In New Testament times, local churches were dictated to only by the apostles and the sacred Scriptures, but they co-operated whole-heartedly in benevolent and evangelistic enterprises. They may be said to have had local church government, but world-wide responsibility and fellowship.

QUESTIONS

1. What are the two temporary offices in the church?

2. Give two other names for the office of elder.

3. What does the word "bishop" mean? "Elder"? "Pastor"?

4. Give at least two possible translations of the word "deacon."

5. Show how the preacher in a congregation is an evangelist, a pastor, and a minister.

6. Where in the New Testament can the qualifications of elders and deacons be found?

7. How does the flexibility allowed by the New Testament pattern benefit the church?

8. What historical event is a stern warning to those who would depart from God's plan of organization?

THE CHURCH AT WORK IN GOD'S WORLD

Romans 12:10-12

WITNESSING

Commissioned

We customarily quote the great commission from Matthew and sometimes from Mark, but Luke and John record a similar commission, as does the book of Acts. Compare the "go ye" passages in the first two Gospels with Luke's quotation from Jesus: "That repentance and remission of sins should be preached in his name among all nations, beginning at Jerusalem. And ye are witnesses of these things" (Luke 24:47, 48). Consider, too, John 15:16: "Ye have not chosen me, but I have chosen you, and ordained you, that ye should go and bring forth fruit, and that your fruit should remain." After the resurrection, it is recorded in John 20:22 that Jesus said, "Receive ye the Holy Ghost: Whosoever sins ye remit, they are remitted unto them; and whosoever sins ye retain, they are retained." In the final chapter of John's Gospel is recorded Jesus' insistent refrain, "Feed my sheep." Whether we think of it in terms of teaching, preaching, witnessing, or feeding His sheep, each Christian is under an often-repeated commission to engage in the work of the church. Jesus summed it up in Acts 1:8, "Ye shall be witnesses unto me both in Jerusalem, and in all Judaea, and in Samaria, and unto the uttermost part of the earth."

117

Empowered

The first witnesses were directly empowered with a special measure of the Holy Spirit (John 14:16-18; 16:13; Acts 1:7, 8). This miraculous manifestation of power continued for some years (Romans 12:5-8; 1 Corinthians 12:1-11). Even in that age, however, not all Christians possessed these striking gifts, as Christians in our day do not possess them. That does not mean they were without power. The gospel was seen to have power in and of itself. "It is the power of God unto salvation," said Paul. In whatever age and under whatever circumstances the church has preached the gospel, God's power has been felt. The application of that power to men's lives may not always have been accompanied by startling manifestations, but even great physical power is not always attended by noise and fanfare. A tree root breaking a concrete walk goes about its work silently but irresistibly. So God's power is always at work through the gospel, whether its impact is seen and heard at the moment or not.

Channel of Revelation

God expects to use the church to carry the good news of redemption to all men. Through the church He expects to communicate His self-revelation. In *The New English Bible* we read, "Now, through the church, the wisdom of God in all its varied forms might be made known" (Ephesians 3:10)! Until Jesus comes again, this will continue to be the work of the church, bearing witness in every age to the truths that God has revealed in Christ Jesus.

UNITED

The Prayer of Christ

Knowing the great responsibilities soon to rest upon His disciples, and the fierce persecution soon to confront them, Jesus earnestly prayed "that they might be one." Before the church was born, Jesus was concerned that it might not be divided. That prayer, recorded in John 17, is truly "The Lord's Prayer." It was on the way to Gethsemane that Jesus offered this eloquent petition. He longed for a unity among all His followers that was as close and as real as that which He himself shared with the Father. Why did unity so concern our Lord? "That the world may believe," was the reason He gave. In every generation movements for unity must be similarly motivated. Men must never try to unite the followers of Christ from motives of ambition, pride, or lust for power. We must strive for a united church only in order to win a lost world.

Paul's Plea

Christ's fears that His followers would become divided were not unjustified. Paul found it necessary to write to Corinth barely thirty years after Christ's death, censuring the divisions there. His eloquent plea in the first chapter of 1 Corinthians indicates that mere confederate union is not enough. Paul urged that there be no divisions and that all Christians have the same mind and the same judgment. He also relates unity to the preaching of the gospel to lost men. He points out that already men are stumbling at the cross. What if it is held aloft by a divided and warring church?

GROWING

In New Testament Times

How literally shall we take Paul in Colossians 1:6? In *The New English Bible*, the verse is translated, "In the same way it is coming to men the whole world over; everywhere it is growing and bearing fruit as it does among you." Certainly the church was growing very rapidly. While we may be sure that Paul's expression, "the whole world," must be limited to the then-civilized world, or what historians have called "the known world," still, the statement is rather amazing. As Jesus had planned, the Christians had been like leaven and their faith had spread like wildfire over all Roman realm. In the beginning the Roman government had bitterly opposed the new faith and tried to stamp it out. Their able helpers in this were the Jews who regarded Christianity as a Jewish heresy. It soon became obvious, however, that Christianity was here to stay. All persecution from Rome ended in A.D. 313, and it was not long after that the Emperor Constantine gave it special privileges. In less than three hundred years the church had conquered imperial Rome! This recognition by Rome was not an unmixed blessing, however. With the end of persecution and opposition came the beginning of lethargy, self-satisfaction, and self-righteousness. The church had conquered Rome, but now the church herself was about to be swept away in the flood tides of popularity and power.

CHANGING

Decline

As the church increased in popularity, she decreased in purity. Persecution had kept hypocrites out of the church. Now the church became the vehicle for personal gain and aggrandizement. When the church was brought to political power, she began to lose her spiritual power. Not many years passed until the church of the New Testament was hardly recognizable. For her simple local government had been substituted a complex hierarchy headed by the pope of Rome. The political system that had been so successful in governing the Roman empire was adopted by the church. Man no longer turned to the memoirs of the apostles, to the sacred books of the New Testament, but looked instead to the direction of bishops and archbishops. The great institutions of Communion and baptism likewise underwent striking changes and modifications. The church entered the Dark Ages a wholly different institution from that born at Pentecost.

Darkness

Since the written Word was God's intended guide for the church, illiterate men could hardly be expected to know where the church fell short. Through this long period of history, only a privileged few could read or write. Copies of the Bible were expensive and scarce. What an ideal opportunity for the power hungry to establish themselves in positions of authority. What an opportunity for Satan to strike back at Christ and the church! It is true that through the Dark Ages many small groups of Christians tried to stem the tide and attempted to hold fast to Biblical principles and practices. Unfortunately, their number was small and their influence slight. How great was the darkness of those ages for the church of Jesus Christ!

Division

Finally a new day dawned. The Dark Ages came to an end, and soon many were able to read the Word of God for themselves. The invention of movable type made copies of the Bible much less expensive. Reformers, like Luther, began to see the errors in the Roman Catholic Church and cried out against them. All over Europe men rose to call the world back to the Word of God. They were not without influence. It was not long until every country in Europe had its great reformers. To counteract the amazing growth and inroads of these Protestant groups, the Catholic Church launched a reformation of its own!

Unfortunately, the reformers were separated from one another by geographic and linguistic barriers. In many cases the Protestants were soon organized into state churches, and there resulted a sorely divided Christendom. While the reformers brought new life to the church, their work ended in a sadly separated and thus a severely crippled church.

Restoration

While the divisions in Christendom were felt in Europe, the results were most severe in the New World. To America came men from all over Europe. The new land became not only the melting pot of nationalities, but also a steaming cauldron of religious controversy. Certainly Europe had known its religious dissenters, and had been plagued by the divisions among Christians. Still, America brought the situation into sharper focus and showed with greater clarity the need to consider anew the prayer of our Lord.

So it was in America that there sprang up a movement to unite all who believed in Christ. While the movement's roots were in Scotland, it was in America that it gained a real hearing. On the Atlantic seaboard, and especially beyond the mountains on the western frontier, men began calling for a united church—a church that would follow again the pattern laid down in the New Testament, a church that would know again the power of a united and a Scriptural witness. From its great beachhead in the Ohio River valley, the movement spread with the settlers across the plains and the Rockies. Within less than a hundred years, it was the fastest growing religious body on the American continent. It is yet the largest religious body with roots in American soil.

HISTORY AND DESTINY

The Book of Revelation

It may seem at first that much of this chapter has no place in a book on the church of the New Testament. Should not such a study end where the book of Acts ends? No, for God has revealed in the New Testament the history of His church and its ultimate destiny. The book of Revelation chronicles all the events that we have so briefly considered in this chapter. More than this, the Revelation points ahead to the ultimate and eternal destiny of the church.

To be sure, every Bible student finds himself sometimes perplexed in studying the Revelation. Certainly one needs to avoid being dogmatic in asserting that a particular symbol must refer to a certain event, person, or institution. Still, Revelation does present the broad outline of the church's history. The form of the presentation is necessarily vague. Is the book written in symbolic code? Is it a great stylized drama of the church? How much of it is to be taken literally? However one answers these questions, the careful student of Revelation cannot miss the distinct outline of a church that goes through many trials, but that is finally victorious.

The Bridegroom Cometh

That dramatic story in the Bible's final book reaches its climax in chapter nineteen. "Let us be glad and rejoice, and give honour to him: for the marriage of the Lamb is come, and his wife hath made herself ready. And to her was granted that she should be arrayed in fine linen, clean and white: for the fine linen is the righteousness of saints. And he saith unto me, Write, Blessed are they which are called unto the marriage supper of the Lamb. And he saith unto me, These are the true sayings of God."

A glorious destiny, then, awaits the church. All earthly kingdoms will become Christ's. All opposition to Him will forever be put down. Throughout eternity He shall reign supreme ... and reigning with Him will be His bride, the church of the living God!

IN THE MEANTIME

A Continuing Task

The church cannot sit idly by and wait for God to work out His will in human history. It is undoubtedly God's intent to use human instrumentality to bring about His objectives for the church. The great work begun by the Christians of the first century and so nobly carried forward in succeeding centuries must now be continued by our generation.

For everyone who tries to serve Christ there will be temporary setbacks and momentary discouragements. Despite these pressures, the knowledge of ultimate victory will keep determination and enthusiasm high.

The Primary Task

The prime objective of the church is to bear witness to the mighty acts of God. The preaching of the gospel is its main business. While the church must be involved in numerous other important and worthwhile endeavors, none must overshadow this fundamental task. Preaching may be viewed in both a formal and informal sense. The Bible attaches great importance to the public proclamation of the good news. Equally powerful and effective is the witness "from house to house." The church is engaged in the business of communication. She has a story to tell, a message to deliver. It is not a message that the church has had any part in devising. It was delivered to us by others, and we in turn must deliver it to those whom we may influence. God revealed himself to man in Christ Jesus, His Son, and through the Bible, His Word. To communicate that revelation to every creature is the task of the church and of each of its members.

Additional Aims

Certainly the church is interested in every aspect of human betterment. No church that takes seriously the words of Jesus can ignore the naked, the homeless, the hungry. They are to be clothed and housed and fed, not in order to gain a hearing for what we have to say, but simply because of the compassion of our hearts. It is because the church has failed its responsibilities in this field that public charities were created.

Social action is also an area of the church's concern. What men and nations do with respect to racial, economic, and educational problems reflects the degree to which our world knows and understands Christ. The church will want to make its influence felt in these areas. How this shall be done may present some interesting problems. Perhaps the best approach is to carefully and consistently reiterate the basic Biblical principles from which our ideas of freedom and justice have come. Perhaps we can make certain that the church sets before the world an appealing example of what ought to be done. We will not always agree upon the approach to these matters, but one thing is sure: The church must bring its knowledge of Christ to bear upon the social concerns of its world. The church must manage to do this without becoming another pressure group exerting political influence. God intended that His kingdom, like leaven, should permeate and influence all of society.

The Means to Be Used

How will the church accomplish the manifold tasks before her? First, it will be necessary for each individual member to accept personal responsibility. Church members will have to give and witness and serve. They will have to provide themselves the funds for great educational, benevolent, and missionary ventures. They will themselves have to provide the talent to man these enterprises. Each individual Christian will have to witness at work and among his friends and neighbors. Every workbench must become a pulpit and every home a center of evangelism. Only if each member regards this as his individual and personal task, can the work be done!

As essential as it is for every member to do this, there are many aspects of the church's task that only a congregation can accomplish. Thus every member must work both as an individual and as a member of a team. Through the local congregation to which he belongs a member is able to harness his talents and resources to definite goals and projects. The members are a source of mutual encouragement and edification. It becomes possible to do together what could never be accomplished alone.

There remains an even larger area of need. When churches set themselves to bringing into existence institutions of higher learning, homes to care for the orphans and aged, hospitals, far-flung missionary stations, then congregations must work together. Few congregations are large enough to attempt even one of these gigantic tasks. Co-operation among congregations is essential to progress in education, benevolence, and missions. No congregation need yield its autonomy over local affairs. Appropriate safeguards exist to insure faithful adherence of these auxiliary institutions to the purpose of their founders. Without them the church can never hope to meet the needs of the present generation!

My Place in a Working Church

Every child of God must ask, "What is my place in the work of the church?" He must consider in what areas he can best serve what resources of time, energy, and wealth God has given him. Many imagine that they can do little, but they are often wrong. The person who has nothing to offer except influence (and every person has that) may find that the gift of influence is far greater than is sometimes apparent. What talents of leadership, teaching, singing, or serving can be consecrated to God through His church? This is a question for every church member to prayerfully consider. If the church is to become what God intended it to be, every one of its members will have to seriously imitate the example of Him who "went about doing good" and who felt that He must be about His Father's business.

QUESTIONS

1. In how many of the four Gospels is there a commission to Christ's followers?

2. To what was the church to bear witness?

3. Why did Jesus pray that His followers might be united?

4. What changes did the church undergo after persecution ended in A.D. 313?

5. Describe the church in the Dark Ages.

6. Why did the work of the reformers result in a divided Protestantism?

7. Where was the division most acutely felt? Why?

8. Describe briefly the beginnings of the Restoration movement. What motivated its leaders?

9. What is the destiny of the church?

10. What is the church's primary task?

11. What three areas of effort are necessary to accomplish this task?

BIBLIOGRAPHY

BARTH, KARL. *The Teaching of the Church Regarding Baptism*. London: S. C. M. Press, 1954.

DORNETTE, RALPH M. *Bible Answers to Popular Questions* (outlines). Muskogee, Oklahoma: Privately printed, 1954.

FLEW, R. NEWTON. *Jesus and His Church*. Naperville, Illinois: Alec R. Allenson, Inc., 1955.

FORSYTH, P. T. *The Church and the Sacraments*. Naperville, Illinois: Alec R. Allenson, Inc., 1955.

HAYDEN, W. L. *Church Polity*. Kansas City, Missouri: Old Paths Book Club, 1953.

KERSHNER, F.D., and PHILLIPS, WOODROW. *The Restoration Handbook*. 5 vols. San Antonio, Texas: Southern Christian Press, 1960.

MILLER, DONALD G. *The Nature and Mission of the Church*. Richmond, Virginia: John Knox Press, 1957.

MURCH, JAMES DEFOREST. *Christians Only*. Cincinnati: Standard Publishing, 1962.

ORR, JAMES (ed.). *The International Standard Bible Encyclopedia*. (Volumes 1 and III.) Grand Rapids: Wm. B. Eerdmans Publishing Company, 1957.

PHILLIPS, THOMAS W. *The Church of Christ*. Cincinnati: Standard Publishing, 1943.

STEVENSON, DWIGHT E. *The Church—What and Why*. St. Louis: Christian Board of Publication, 1963

TOMLINSON, L. J. *Churches of Today*. Nashville: Gospel Advocate Company, 1957.

WINDER, F. J. *That They May Be Won*. Portland, Oregon: Privately printed, 1950.

THE CHURCH THROUGH THE CENTURIES

by JOHN W. WADE

STUDY COURSE FOR
YOUTH AND ADULTS

TABLE OF CONTENTS

FOREWORD

This book is designed to be no more than a very brief survey of church history. Obviously such a brief treatment of such a vast subject requires a great deal of selectivity. Readers may want to take issue with us over material that is included or omitted. This is to be expected, and even applauded.

What one includes in such a book as this tells a good deal about the frame of reference from which he writes. Even a casual perusal of this book is likely to reveal that we write from a theologically conservative point of view, that we have a passionate concern for Christian unity, that the New Testament provides the only adequate framework for unity, and that we have a firm faith that God's purpose for the church will ultimately be accomplished.

For many persons using this book, this will be their first introduction to church history. Unfortunately, history can be so taught as to be distressingly dull. For this reason, we hope that teachers will study widely in preparing to teach this course. The bibliography included herein suggests only a few of the thousands of works available in the field. Teachers will also find that encouraging students to do some or all of the projects included will stimulate interest.

We owe a word of gratitude to many who in one way or another helped make this book possible. We especially want to thank William E. Blake, Jr., who read the whole manuscript in its early form and made many helpful criticisms and suggestions.

THE COMING OF THE CHURCH

IN THE FULLNESS OF TIME

Just as a lens gathers divergent rays of light and bends them to a brilliant focus, so God reached out with infinite wisdom and gathered the turbulent strands of history and brought them to a focus in the life of Christ. Paul's words in Galatians 4:4, "When the fulness of the time was come, God sent forth his Son," are so laden with meaning that we need to pause and look at some of the things that may be involved.

Preparation Among the Jews

Let us look first of all at how God through revelation and through providence prepared this chosen people, the Jews, for the coming of His Son. In the period that intervened between the time of Malachi, last of the Old Testament writers, and the birth of Christ, many sweeping political changes had enveloped the Jewish nation. During the time of Malachi, the Jews, while a part of the Persian Empire, enjoyed a good measure of religious and even political independence. This arrangement, continuing for about a hundred years after Malachi wrote, was finally altered by the rise of a new leader, Alexander the Great. With surprising ease he swept aside decadent Persia, and in a few years made Greece the master of the ancient world. At his death the political unity he had imposed upon his world was lost as his generals became rivals in a struggle for power. Out of this struggle Egypt and Syria emerged as separate powers, and the Jewish nation suffered the fate so common to lesser powers caught between two major powers.

Finally, about 200 B.C., Palestine fell under the control of Syria. One of the Syrian rulers, Antiochus Epiphanes, became so oppressive that the Jews, led by the Maccabees, revolted in 167 B.C. After years of bitter fighting, the Jews gained their independence under Maccabean leadership. But the Maccabean period did not bring with it the blessings many had anticipated. Before long the throne was surrounded by plots, intrigue, and murder. This situation continued for almost a hundred years until it was interrupted by the Romans, led by Pompey, who took Jerusalem in 63 B.C.

The Romans often found it practical to rule the provinces through local leaders. Thus it was that Herod became king over the Jews. Cruel and arbitrary, Herod was in addition possessed of an insane jealousy. The slaughter of the babies of Bethlehem is a tragic commentary on his jealousy.

One might reasonably ask what all this has to do with preparing God's people to receive the Messiah. The many disappointments and defeats of the Jewish people were a negative kind of preparation. It served to convince them that God's Messianic kingdom was not to be a physical kingdom. Many, of course, even after several hundred years of this kind of discipline, did not learn this lesson. Even those whom Jesus chose as His disciples expected Him to usher in a physical kingdom.

When one shifts from the Old Testament period to the time of Christ, he finds that a number of important changes have occurred in the religion of Israel. Prominent in the religious life of the Jews in Jesus' day were the synagogues, local places of worship and study that developed during the intertestamental period. The Sanhedrin (usually translated "council") was the nation's highest religious tribunal.

Religious parties were conspicuous in the life and ministry of Jesus. In control of the temple in Jerusalem were the Sadducees. Rejecting a belief in life after death, they devoted their energies toward making this life more pleasant for themselves. To the dismay of their bitter enemies, the Pharisees, the Sadducees succeeded in maintaining a profitable co-existence with the Roman rulers.

By contrast, the Pharisees, the custodians of orthodoxy, held foreigners in disdain. They professed a great loyalty to the law, but this loyalty was often surpassed by their loyalty to traditional interpretations of the law. The Pharisees' concern about the minutia of the law readily led to legalistic quibbling, formalism, and hypocrisy. But certainly not all Pharisees fell into this trap, for some—Nicodemus, Gamaliel, and Paul, for example— displayed commendable integrity and piety.

A third sect or party among the Jews was the Essenes. This group, numbering only a few thousand at most, lived a simple, monastic life in the area around the Dead Sea. The discovery of the Dead Sea Scrolls has shed a good deal of light on this sect, for many scholars now identify the Essenes with the members of the Qumran Community, whose members wrote the Scrolls. These Essenes, however, are nowhere mentioned in the New Testament.

The Judaism of Jesus' day was not confined to Palestine. Jews were found in large numbers in almost all parts of the empire. Many who had been carried to Babylonia preferred to remain there, rather than to return to Palestine. Others had found refuge in Egypt during the troublous times before and during the captivity. The Jewish community at Alexandria, Egypt, was a very substantial and influential one. To the Alexandrian Jews we owe the Septuagint, a Greek translation of the Hebrew Old Testament. Made about 250 B.C., this translation enjoyed a wide circulation among the Jews of Jesus' day. New Testament writers show a familiarity with this version.

Wherever the Jews went, they carried their religion with them. Synagogues, where faithful Jews met to pray and to hear and study the law, were found in almost all the important cities of the Empire. Many persons had turned from their pagan religions, becoming proselytes to the Jewish faith. On his missionary journeys Paul customarily visited these synagogues. Often his message was received favorably by these Jews of the dispersion and even more favorably by Jewish proselytes. There is little doubt that Christianity spread more rapidly because of the presence of these Jewish outposts across the Empire.

Preparation in the Non-Jewish World

Many things had happened in the non-Jewish world to help prepare the way for the coming of the church. The whole Mediterranean basin was under the political control of Rome. Contrary to what we may believe today, Rome was not, by the standards of its day, a cruel instrument of oppression. Rome brought a high degree of order and justice to the vast area she ruled.

The Greeks had made important contributions too, perhaps none more important than their language. From Alexander's time on, the Greek language became increasingly the second language of much of the population of the Empire. Its marvelous flexibility allowed it to serve both as a language of literature and a language of business, enjoying the status that English does in our modern world. Because a common language was spoken by so many persons, early Christian missionaries were able to get a wide hearing for their message. Nor is it any accident that the New Testament and most of the writings of the early Christian scholars were written in Greek.

The bankruptcy of pagan religions and philosophies prepared the non-Jewish world to receive the gospel. The masses were perhaps still enthralled by the old familiar deities. Especially popular were those whose worship involved unspeakable sexual activities. The intellectuals of the first century had long since abandoned their beliefs in the deities of classical Greek and Roman mythology. They had turned instead to such philosophies as Stoicism and Epicureanism. Others found comfort in Gnosticism or the esoteric cults or mystery religions. But among many there was growing dissatisfaction with the immoralities of the popular religions on the one hand and the pessimism of the philosophies on the other hand. In many ways it was evident that the world of the first century was hungry for a religion that could answer man's highest moral longings and at the same time give him a hope of immortality. Christianity—and Christianity alone—was exactly the religion to meet these needs.

Thus in both the Jewish world and the pagan world, God had providentially brought to pass the preparation hinted at in Paul's classic statement: "When the fulness of the time was come."

"GOD SENT FORTH HIS SON"

The Birth of Jesus

No first-century secular historian has recorded for us the birth of Jesus. For that reason, we have to rely exclusively upon the Scriptures for our knowledge of Jesus' birth and ministry. After telling us of Jesus' birth, the Gospels pass over the next thirty years of His life in almost complete silence. We are told that Joseph and Mary fled with the babe to Egypt (Matthew 2:13, 14), and then returned to Nazareth after the death of Herod (Matthew 2:19-23). Luke records Jesus' experience in the temple, when He was twelve years old (Luke 2:42-50).

The Ministry of John and Jesus

When Jesus was about thirty years old, His kinsman, John the Baptist, began a dramatic ministry in the wilderness near the northern end of the Dead Sea. The burden of his message was much like that of the Old Testament prophets: "Repent ye!" But it was also strikingly different: "The kingdom of heaven is at hand!"

John's preaching prepared the way for the coming of Jesus the Christ. Jesus' message continued John's emphasis upon the kingdom. When one examines Jesus' teaching, he is impressed with how much Jesus has to say about the kingdom and how little He has to say about the church. In the Sermon on the Mount Jesus set the guidelines for the moral conduct of citizens of the kingdom. In numerous parables Jesus described the nature of the kingdom. In all of this, Jesus was preparing His listeners and especially the apostles for the coming of the church. But even the apostles had difficulty understanding the nature of the kingdom Jesus described to them.

THE BIRTH AND EARLY GROWTH OF THE CHURCH

Pentecost; A.D. 30

Sent back to Jerusalem to await power from on high, the apostles spent ten days waiting and praying. Then on Pentecost the Holy Spirit was poured out upon the apostles, and, speaking in tongues, the apostles proclaimed the gospel so effectively that 3,000 persons were converted. Whatever shortcomings the apostles may have had, this one thing they knew: Jesus was the Christ, raised from the grave with power. These converts, having heard the gospel, believed that Jesus Christ is the Son of God, repented of their sins, and were baptized for the remission of sins (Acts 2:38). They "continued steadfastly in the apostles' doctrine and fellowship, and in breaking of bread, and in prayers" (Acts 2:42).

The church continued to grow, but as it did, it attracted attention, attention that soon led to persecution. Apparently the enemies of the church resorted first to economic pressures. Many Christians responded by selling their possessions and turning the money over to the apostles. It would seem that this was a temporary measure to meet the crisis, for the New Testament gives no indication that this practice was repeated in other churches.

Saul of Tarsus Becomes Paul the Apostle

When economic pressures failed to halt the growth of the church, its enemies turned to violent forms of persecution. This early persecution gave the church its first in a great host of martyrs, Stephen (Acts 7). Witnessing and giving assent to the murder of Stephen was a brilliant young rabbi, Saul of Tarsus. Enraged by the rapid spread of Christianity, Saul received permission from the religious leaders in Jerusalem to travel to Damascus to seek out and destroy Christians. But Saul the persecutor was never to reach Damascus—at least, not as Saul the persecutor.

On the road to Damascus the persecutor was brought face to face with the persecuted—Jesus Christ. "Saul, Saul, why persecutest thou me?" came the voice from heaven as Saul fell to the ground, overwhelmed by a brilliant light from above. When the speaker revealed that He was Jesus, Saul, humbly seeking His will, was told to go into Damascus and await further instructions. Stricken blind by this experience, Saul spent the next three days in fasting. At the end of this period, Ananias, "a certain disciple at Damascus," was sent to Saul by God in order that Saul might be restored. As soon as he had received his sight, Saul was baptized. In a short time this former persecutor of

Christians was himself a proclaimer of the message he had once despised.

Saul witnessed so effectively for the Lord that he aroused antagonism among Jews in Damascus. Returning to Jerusalem, Saul sought to find fellowship with the Christians there, but his former antagonism against the church made him suspect. Finally, under the sponsorship of Barnabas, he was received into the Christian community. But once again his preaching aroused the Jews, and safety required that he leave Jerusalem. This time he went to his hometown of Tarsus.

Later, Barnabas was ministering at Antioch, and, needing help, enlisted Saul. The two labored together effectively with the great church at Antioch. It was during this period that the disciples were first called Christians (Acts 11:26). After a time Barnabas and Saul were set apart for missionary service by the Holy Spirit. Taking with them John Mark, the nephew of Barnabas, they sailed for Cyprus. From this time on, Saul was referred to as Paul.

From Cyprus the company journeyed to southern Asia Minor. As they prepared to move into the hazardous interior, young John Mark, for reasons that Paul deemed less than commendable, left and returned to Jerusalem. Undaunted, Paul and Barnabas continued their journey through Pisidia and Lycaonia, and in the face of strong Jewish opposition succeeded in establishing churches in Antioch, Iconium, Lystra, and Derbe. Once this work was done, the faithful pair returned to Antioch where they reported their activities, especially the fact that God "had opened the door of faith unto the Gentiles" (Acts 14:27).

The Judaizers Object

The spread of the gospel to the Gentiles was not to go unchallenged. Jewish Christians from Judea arrived in Antioch and began to teach that one must first be circumcised before he could become a Christian. In Antioch, where many of the Christians had come from pagan backgrounds either directly or as Jewish proselytes, this doctrine caused "no small dissension and disputation" (Acts 15:2). Finally, Paul and Barnabas and certain others were sent to Jerusalem to confer with the apostles and elders about the matter. In the discussion that followed, Peter told how the Lord had sent him to preach to Cornelius (Acts 10:1-48), and Paul and Barnabas related the miracles and wonders that had accompanied their work among the Gentiles. With this evidence before them and led by the Holy Spirit, the apostles and elders with James, the brother of the Lord, serving as spokesman, declared that circumcision was not necessary for Gentiles who became Christians. This should have settled the issue, but prejudice and tradition die slowly. Judaizers continued to trouble the church, as several of Paul's letters indicate. Even Peter, on a visit to Antioch, failed to live up to his understanding in the matter (Galatians 2: 11, 12).

Paul Continues His Missionary Efforts

Soon after his return from the Jerusalem conference Paul proposed that he and Barnabas visit the churches they had established. But, as a result of a controversy over taking John Mark with them, the two separated: Barnabas took Mark with him to Cyprus, and Paul took Silas with him on a trip that led through Asia Minor, Macedonia, and Greece. The details of this trip, usually referred to as Paul's second missionary journey, are reported in Acts 16-18. Paul's third missionary journey, recorded in Acts 18-20, took him back over the same area. At its conclusion Paul went up to Jerusalem. Here he was attacked by the Jews and barely escaped with his life. As a result of this controversy Paul spent the next two years (A.D. 59-61) in prison (Acts 21-26). Because he had exercised his rights as a Roman citizen and appealed to Caesar, Paul was sent to Rome for trial (Acts 27, 28). After another two years spent under house arrest in Rome (A.D. 61-63), Paul was apparently released. We do not have a detailed account of Paul's activities after his release, but we know that he traveled in the East and possibly even visited Spain. Tradition has it that Paul suffered martyrdom in Rome during the persecutions of Nero in A.D. 67 or 68.

THE ORGANIZATION, DOCTRINE, AND PRACTICES OF THE EARLY CHURCH

Organization of the Church

The organization of the early church was simple. Each congregation, while concerned about the welfare of other congregations, enjoyed local autonomy. There is no evidence in the New Testament of the extra-congregational structure and the elaborate hierarchy that later were to play such a prominent part in the life of the church. Each congregation apparently had elders (or bishops) and deacons who were responsible for its leadership and oversight. It is true that the apostles exercised certain authority over the congregations, but the Scriptures give no hint that either their office or their authority was passed on to others. In addition to the apostles, we read of prophets, evangelists, pastors, and teachers (Ephesians 4:11).

Modern Christians, conditioned to accept the necessity for complicated ecclesiastical organization, have difficulty understanding how the church of the first century survived, let alone thrived. Several things need to be noted. First of all, early Christians were possessed of a faith that expressed itself in a consuming zeal. Even if organizational structures had existed, such zeal could hardly have been contained within them. Further, the lack of organization gave the church a flexibility that it needed to meet the various challenges that it faced. The lack of organization was also an advantage when persecutions arose. Persecutors to this day find it more difficult to seek out and destroy individual Christians than to attack less mobile but more visible church hierarchies.

To suggest a return to the simplicity of the church of the first century may seem hopelessly idealistic to our organizationally minded age. Yet the success of the early Christians, bound together by little more than a common faith in Christ, should lead us to some serious second thoughts in the matter.

The Creed of the Church

The creed of the apostolic church, like its organization, was simple: "I believe that Jesus Christ is the Son of God" (Acts 8:37).

While some manuscripts do not contain this verse, its inclusion in others indicates its early origin. This creed did not consist of an elaborately worked-out system of theology, but was centered instead in a living and reigning Person. Whatever valid reasons may be given for the later formulation of complicated creedal statements, few today will challenge the necessity of restoring this simple creed of the New Testament to a place of primacy.

Worship in the Church

Worship in the early church was also befittingly simple. Few, if any, church buildings were built in the first century, and so the disciples met in homes or elsewhere if convenient. Nowhere in the New Testament do we find a description of a complete worship service, although we do get occasional hints of how Christians in the first century worshiped. In the very beginning it seems that Christians met daily for worship (Acts 2:46), but as time went on, the common practice was to meet on the first day of each week. The church in Jerusalem "continued steadfastly in the apostles' doctrine and fellowship, and in breaking of bread, and in prayers." In addition, the worship services included reading from the Old Testament and later from the writings that became the New Testament. Singing, preaching, and extemporaneous speaking were also often included. The Lord's Supper, observed as a simple memorial feast, was often accompanied by a love feast, the agape. Abuses of the love feast at Corinth prompted Paul to write about the matter (1 Corinthians 11:20-22), but in spite of some abuse, the practice continued for many years.

Along with the Lord's Supper, baptism was the only ordinance observed by the apostolic church. Persons who believed in Jesus Christ as the Son of God and who repented of their sins were admitted to the church by baptism. The evidence indicates that New Testament practice was by immersion. This outer act, in obedience to the command of Christ, symbolized a death to the old life, a burial, and a resurrection to a new life (Romans 6:4-11). In the New Testament, baptism is linked with the new birth (John 3:5) and the remission of sins (Acts 2:38).

The Christian Life

The lives of the early disciples reflected their simple but vigorous faith. Their love of Christ knit them together in a brotherhood of love. They provided for the needy and those who suffered as a result of their faith. As a tiny minority in a sea of paganism, they had little opportunity to influence by direct action the social and cultural patterns of their age. Yet Christians penetrated every level of their society, working like leaven to change that society for the better.

CONCLUSION

For nearly a generation the church at Jerusalem, in spite of persecution, provided leadership for the whole of Christendom. But even before the destruction of Jerusalem in A.D. 70, other great churches were beginning to be looked to for leadership. By that date, or perhaps even before, the majority of the church membership was drawn from Gentile rather than Jewish origins. Across the Empire this reduced the friction between Jews and Christians. It also meant that Gentile churches began to loom more and more important. It was natural enough that the church at Antioch would become such a church. It was the first great church outside of Palestine and it was blessed with such leaders as Paul and Barnabas.

Before the end of the century the church at Ephesus also became prominent. Very early traditions tell us that the apostle John spent his final years here, thus further enhancing the reputation of the Ephesian church. By the end of the apostolic period there were also prominent churches at Corinth, Rome, and Alexandria. In the next period the latter two were to assume even greater importance.

The church faced persecutions during this period. Christians suffered first at the hands of the Jews and later under emperors Nero and Domitian. But these persecutions were relatively mild and brief and in no way comparable to the trial of suffering the church had to undergo later.

In the first century the church had been transformed from scattered and misunderstood prophecies into a thriving reality. From a band of twelve it had become a "sect everywhere spoken against," numbering countless thousands. The message of salvation, spoken first by simple peasants, had been heard gladly both by slaves and by their masters as well. The parable of the mustard seed did indeed exemplify the growth of the church of the first century.

QUESTIONS

1. What idea is conveyed by Paul's expression, "the fulness of time"?

2. Discuss some of the ways in which both the Jewish world and the pagan world were prepared for the coming of Christ.

3. Discuss some of the problems faced by the early church. How did the church meet these problems?

4. Discuss the organization of the church of the first century. How did it differ from modern church organization?

5. Describe the creed of the early church. Contrast it with modern church creeds.

EXPANSION AND PERSECUTION 100-313

THE CHURCH FACES PERSECUTION

By A.D. 100 the church had so outgrown its Jewish origins that it was no longer mistaken for just another Jewish sect. Christianity had now become a separate sect. This new status meant that Christians no longer need fear persecution from the Jewish community. But it meant that they now had to face persecution from Rome.

Causes for Persecution

Actually Roman persecutions had begun before 100, but these (the most serious were under Nero and Domitian) were brief and more the result of whimsy than concerted effort. But this was to change as the second century unfolded. There were several reasons for these recurring persecutions, which increased in violence until they reached a terrible crescendo about A.D. 300 under Emperor Diocletian.

Perhaps the most important reason Rome had for persecuting Christians was political. For Rome, the state was all-important. So long as one was willing to participate in the state religious ceremonies, Rome was inclined to be rather tolerant. But Christians refused to divide their loyalties. For them, devotion to God required that no other person or thing—emperor or state—be elevated to the place that God rightfully occupied. Romans had difficulty understanding the Christians' devotion to a God who could not be seen and to whom no idols were dedicated. As a result, they came to believe that Christians were disloyal to the state. As far as the Romans were concerned, Christians were persecuted more as subversives than because they followed a different religion.

There were, of course, religious reasons for much of the persecution that Christians suffered. Christians had no idols, no elaborate priesthood, and no impressive ceremonies and processionals. People who were not prepared to appreciate a spiritual religion often felt that Christians had no religion—thus giving rise to the charge that Christians were atheists. Because Christians often met secretly as a safety measure, they were accused of many vile practices. Pagans heard rumors of the Lord's Supper and, not understanding its spiritual nature, interpreted expressions like "drinking blood" and "eating flesh" to mean that Christians were practicing some sort of ritualistic cannibalism.

Christians were also persecuted for social and economic reasons. Christians refused to participate in pagan religious ceremonies or attend the theater or the games. Their non-conformity left them open to the charge that they were "haters of mankind," and as such were considered a threat to society. Since Christians insisted upon the equality of all men, aristocrat or slave, many, especially the aristocracy, feared the effect their teaching would have on the class-ridden Roman society.

At Ephesus, Paul faced an early form of economic antagonism from the silversmiths, whose business had been crippled by the teachings of Christianity (Acts 19:27). Throughout the Empire, priests in the established religions felt the results when persons became Christians and no longer patronized pagan temples. It is not surprising that pagan religious leaders banded together against Christianity. When plagues, famines, earthquakes, or other natural disasters struck, Roman leaders naturally looked for a scapegoat, and more often than not, Christians became the innocent victims of their wrath.

The Course of These Persecutions

The earliest persecutions of the church by the Roman government were local and sporadic. The first-century attacks of the emperors Nero and Domitian have already been mentioned. The attacks of later emperors followed this same general pattern until about 250. Until that time they were generally of brief duration and confined to limited areas.

During the period from 100 to 250 some areas felt scarcely any persecution. In these areas the church grew in numbers and influence, built substantial buildings, and carried on its general educational and benevolent programs with little interference.

Other areas during this period, however, did feel the wrath of Rome. One such persecution occurred in Bithynia during the reign of Emperor Trajan. We have some of the interesting correspondence (dated about 112) between the emperor and the governor of Bithynia, Pliny the Younger. In writing to the emperor, Pliny told how the pagan temples were being deserted. He also gave a rather accurate description of a Christian worship service and candidly acknowledged that Christians were honest, upright people. When Christians were brought before him, he gave them a chance to deny their faith, thereby saving their lives. Trajan approved this method of dealing with Christians. Christians were not to be hunted down, but if any were charged, they were to be punished unless they recanted and worshiped pagan gods. One of the early church fathers, Ignatius, lost his life during this persecution.

In the middle of the second century, a persecution broke out at Smyrna that took the life of the aged saint, Polycarp. Given a chance to recant and save his life, he affirmed his faith in words that exemplify the spirit that caused the church to grow in the face of persecution: "Eighty and six years have I served Him and He hath done me no wrong. How then can I speak evil of my King who saved me?"

Christians in Rome suffered under Emperor Antoninus Pius (138-161). Persecutions also occurred during the reign of his successor, Marcus Aurelius (161-180). Aurelius, a Stoic philosopher, was one of the ablest and most conscientious rulers Rome ever had. These very qualities caused him to attack Christianity, which he believed was undermining the structure of civilization and the unity of the Empire he was laboring so diligently to preserve. Justin Martyr, many of whose writings in defense of Christianity are available to us today, suffered death during the reign of Aurelius.

Persecutions also occurred under Septimius Severus (193-211), especially in North Africa. But for 40 years following his reign, the church enjoyed a general respite from violent attack. During this breathing spell, countless thousands were drawn to the church.

But all of this changed abruptly in 250 under Emperor Decius, who had come to the throne the year before. By imperial edict, the most severe persecutions yet swept across the whole Empire. All citizens were required to sacrifice to the gods. To comply would be apostasy, a sin that many Christians then believed was unpardonable. Some, preferring this present life, complied. Others avoided compliance by purchasing certificates that falsely stated that they had offered the required sacrifice. Some fled, seeking safety in remote corners of the Empire or even beyond the borders of the Empire. Still others suffered imprisonment, banishment, or outright martyrdom.

Fortunately for Christians, Decius was killed in battle in 251. But even more violent persecutions arose in 257 under Valerian. The bishops and other church officers, along with leading citizens, were singled out for attack. Many suffered martyrdom, including the bishop of Rome and the famous Cyprian, bishop of Carthage. Once again these persecutions were cut short when Valerian was captured in a war against the Persians.

Relative peace followed for nearly a generation. But this peace was shattered in 303, when Emperor Diocletian unleashed the most violent and systematic attack the church had yet experienced. Churches were destroyed, copies of the Scriptures were burned, Christian leaders were tortured and executed. On occasion Christians were slaughtered outright. This all-out campaign lasted for a decade.

During this period a bitter struggle was going on among rival claimants to the imperial throne. Constantine finally emerged victorious, and in the process attributed much of his success to Christianity. He is reported to have seen a vision of a flaming cross with the inscription, "In this sign conquer." Inspired by this, he went forth under the sign of the cross to defeat a rival in a crucial battle. The following year, 313, the imperial edict of Milan was issued that granted complete toleration to Christians. Constantine did not make Christianity the sole official religion of the Empire, but he did become increasingly friendly to Christianity, granting many privileges to it.

Results of Persecution

The church was born in the midst of persecution and for the first 300 years never escaped its palling shadow. Yet in spite of, and perhaps often because of, persecution the church continued to grow. The fires of persecution purged the church of those whose commitment was only lukewarm, thus keeping the church from an easy accommodation with the world about it.

Yet we must be careful lest we look upon these persecutions as a rich blessing in disguise. Those who faced persecution rarely took such an optimistic view. Viewed objectively, it must be frankly acknowledged that persecutions did hinder the spread of the faith. They also left in their wake severe controversies about the status of those who had recanted and then desired to be reinstated in the church. These controversies eventually even led to schisms.

Even though we cannot today properly evaluate the effects, good and bad, that persecution had on the early church, we can find inspiration in the courageous way that so many followed their faith into the fires of martyrdom.

THE CHURCH FACES ATTACK FROM WITHIN

The drama involved in the persecutions and the thrilling stories of martyrdom often have obscured other important developments in the first three centuries of the life of the church. One vital activity of the period was the church's struggle to keep the doctrine pure.

Legalism

This struggle began almost as soon as the church was born. We have seen already how the Judaizers attempted to fasten the yoke of the law upon all who became Christians, Jew and Gentile alike. Even though the Jerusalem conference ruled against the Judaizers, the church still had a struggle in its insistence that salvation is by faith in Christ rather than by works. By the beginning of the second century this particular form of legalism was no longer a serious threat to the church, but legalism kept appearing in other forms.

Gnosticism

One of the most serious internal threats to the church during this period was that posed by Gnosticism, which appeared even during the New Testament period, but reached its peak about 150. Gnosticism took many different forms, but basically it was an attempt to fasten a pagan philosophy onto Christianity. Gnostics taught that matter was evil, and since Jehovah of the Old Testament had created matter, it was obvious that Jehovah was inferior to the God of the New Testament. The incarnation raised a similar problem. Christ could not be associated with a physical body because it (matter) was evil. Gnostics therefore argued that Christ's body was either a phantom or was occupied by Christ for only a brief time during His ministry.

Gnosticism had an elite following because it catered to human pride. The word *gnosticism* comes from a Greek word meaning "to know." Gnostics took pride in the fact that they had knowledge denied other Christians.

Marcion, a native of Pontus, is considered by many to have been a gnostic, and a very able defender of it at that. Marcion hated Judaism and rejected the Old Testament. He even rejected New Testament books that seemed too Jewish. He was eventually expelled from the church, but not before he had gathered a number of followers about him. Other prominent gnostics were Basilides and Valentinus.

Montanism

Arising in Phyrgia about 140 was a teacher, Montanus, who protested the rising formalism and the increasing power of the bishop in the church. These were both valid points of protest, but unfortunately, as so often is the case, he went to the opposite extreme. In addition to extravagant claims he made for himself, he insisted that his followers adhere to ascetic diet and living habits. This movement had its greatest strength in North Africa and the East. Among its most capable advocates was Tertullian, one of the outstanding church fathers. Montanism, like so many reform movements in the long history of the church, allowed itself to become fanatical about a few issues and neglected many others just as important.

Results of These Struggles

These, and many other serious internal struggles, came at a time when the church was caught up in a life-and-death combat with the Roman Empire. There is no doubt that the church was weakened by these doctrinal controversies. Yet it is a mistake to suppose that their effects were entirely evil. For one thing, the church responded to Marcion's canon of the Scripture by giving earlier recognition to the canonical books than they might otherwise have received. As a result of these attacks upon their faith, Christians were forced to give considerable thought to theology, an exercise that was certainly beneficial. The office of bishop was greatly strengthened since bishops often became rallying points against error or heresy.

CHURCH ORGANIZATIONS DEVELOP

In the New Testament the officers of elder and bishop (overseer) were the same (Acts 20:17-38). As time went on the two became distinct offices. Each church came to have one bishop and several elders or presbyters. This process whereby one bishop was elevated was a gradual one, and it did not occur everywhere at the same time. The presence of a strong bishop seemed at the time to be the best defense against persecution and heresy, and apparently few saw any danger in this departure from the simplicity of New Testament polity.

At the same time that the bishops were being elevated, the relationship between congregations, loose and informal in the New Testament period, began to take more definite and eventually more rigid form. Churches in the more important cities carried on aggressive evangelistic programs, resulting in many smaller congregations in the villages and countryside surrounding the cities. It seemed quite proper that the larger churches should maintain some supervision over these newer churches to protect them. Gradually this oversight fell to the bishops in the larger churches. In the course of time, these smaller churches no longer had bishops, their chief officers being elders.

In the second century, bishops, and perhaps other church leaders, began meeting together for consultation and common action. At first the pronouncements of these gatherings or "synods" were not authoritative, but gradually they came to be more generally accepted and carry more weight. Originally these consultations were convened to deal with serious problems facing the church. For example, one of the first that we know anything about was held in Asia Minor (A.D. 160) to meet the problem of Montanism. After the passage of many years, these meetings that started out as consultations became official and their pronouncements became binding. Thus gradually and without any apparent conscious intent to do so, leaders of the early church forged an ecclesiastical organization that eventually became authoritative. This organization soon began to bear a striking resemblance to the governmental organization and territorial subdivisions of the Roman Empire.

To strengthen the hands of the bishops, the doctrine of apostolic succession gradually developed. This doctrine affirms that the bishops' authority has been transmitted in a direct line from the apostles. They are looked upon as successors of the apostles and as such have the right to exercise many of the prerogatives of the apostles in setting in order and defending the church. Eventually many came to believe that ordination to any church office must come through this line of succession and that any other ministry was invalid.

DOCTRINAL DEVELOPMENT

One important development of this period was the formation of the canon of the New Testament (a listing of the books recognized as being inspired by the Holy Spirit). The writings of the apostles were certainly recognized as inspired as soon as they were written, but even by the end of the first century it is quite unlikely that every congregation had a copy of every apostolic writing. Since these manuscripts had to be laboriously copied by hand, it was many years before all the inspired writings had circulated throughout the church. In the meantime, other writings were also being circulated. Some of these were inspiring and beneficial; others were the products of heretics. Providentially the wheat was separated from the chaff; the inspired Scriptures came to be distinguished from other literature in the thinking of the church. This process was not accomplished without some conflict, but eventually truth triumphed. By the end of this period, synods and other church bodies were issuing official lists of the inspired canonical books.

This period also saw the beginning of the first creeds. It is generally held that the early creeds grew out of the simple statements of faith used in the baptismal service. Usually these were no more than paraphrases of the good confession, such as, "Jesus is Lord."

But as the doctrinal attacks upon the faith grew, these creedal statements became more elaborate, seeking thereby to define the faith in such a way as to keep heretics out of the church. The Apostles' Creed arose in this period, although in its present form it probably did not come into existence until many years later.

As a result of the great doctrinal controversies from the fourth century on, later creeds came to embody involved theological and philosophical speculation. They also became divisive with serious schisms occurring in the church over the turn of a few phrases. It is tragic indeed that the first steps toward creed-making, necessary as they seemed at the time, should lead to so much controversy later. As with the rise of the strong bishop and the development of ecclesiastical organizations, these seemingly inconsequential departures from the simplicity of the New Testament had serious repercussions.

In this period baptism and the rites associated with it underwent change. As we have seen, baptism in the New Testament period was a simple ceremony: a believer in Christ, upon the confession of his faith, was immersed in water. Presumably any Christian could administer baptism to a candidate. But evidences of change appear early in the second century. The *Didache*, a Christian writing dated about A.D. 120 or even earlier, indicates that baptism by pouring water over the head of the candidate was permitted in some instances. Other sources indicate that sprinkling of water upon the candidate was acceptable in cases of serious illness, although the person so sprinkled was expected to be immersed if he recovered. By the end of this period there is evidence that some were baptizing infants, although many opposed this practice.

In similar fashion a more involved ritual was growing up about the Lord's Supper. It came to be called the Eucharist, from a Greek word meaning "to give thanks." As in the New Testament period, the church observed the Lord's Supper on the first day of each week. The Lord's Supper came to be looked upon with increasing awe and reverence, so much so that non-Christians were often not even allowed to observe the service. Gradually only the clergy, emerging as a distinct group from the laity, could preside over a Communion service.

The church also came to give more attention to the observance of various holy days. Easter was the most prominent Christian holy day, and as time went by the Easter season was lengthened, becoming eventually the Lenten season. One serious controversy that threatened to divide the church was over the date for Easter. By the end of this period several other holy days, or fast days, were being observed in various parts of the church.

CONCLUSION

What concluding observations can we make about this period, A.D. 100 to 313? First we note that the church was under severe pressures both from within and from without. The church reacted to these pressures by elevating the bishops, taking more definite organizational form, collecting the Scriptures into a definite canon, and by forming creedal statements. Each of these actions had far-reaching results in the later history of the church. This fact should remind all Christians that actions have consequences. For this reason, every action taken should be viewed not only in terms of its immediate results, but in terms of long-range results as well.

QUESTIONS

1. Discuss some of the reasons that the church was persecuted in the period 100-313.

2. How did some members of the church escape persecution or martyrdom?

3. What effects did persecution have on the church?

4. Discuss some of the doctrinal controversies and developments of this period.

5. What kind of church organization began to develop during this period? What factors contributed to this rise of organization?

THE CHURCH IN THE EMPIRE
313-590

The rise of Constantine to power as Roman emperor brought a dramatic change in the status of the church. From a persecuted minority, the church became a tolerated sect, then a favored religion, and finally, long before the end of this period, the official religion of the Roman Empire. During this period the organizational structure of the church began to assume a definite form, some of the great doctrinal issues that have ever since troubled the church were raised, and the seeds that later sundered the church into East and West were sown. Let us now look at some of these matters.

CHURCH-STATE RELATIONS

Contrary to popular belief, Constantine did not make Christianity the sole religion of the Empire. His policy was one of toleration. As the years passed, he became more favorable to Christianity and granted the church more privileges. Under the three sons of Constantine, who ruled after his death in 337, Christianity was granted additional rights and some restrictions were placed upon pagan religions.

With this kind of encouragement thousands turned to Christianity. Unfortunately not everyone who embraced Christianity did so for the highest motives. Now that Christianity was a favored religion, church membership brought with it prestige, opportunity for political advancement, and even wealth.

A brief interlude occurred in Christianity's favored position from 361 to 363, during the reign of Julian, often referred to as the "Apostate." A nephew of Constantine, Julian had been reared as a Christian, but some unhappy incidents in his life and the study of pagan philosophy turned him against the church. Once he became emperor, he sought to restore the old pagan religions and to deprive the church of some of its privileges. But his efforts were cut short when he was killed in battle.

Following his death the church quickly regained its lost privileges and added new ones. Emperor Theodosius I issued an edict in 380 that made Christianity the exclusive religion of the state and threatened punishment to any who followed another religion. By 395 Christianity had become recognized as the official religion of the Empire and its promulgation was carried out in the name of patriotism. Pagan temples were often seized and converted into churches, and devotees of pagan religions were on occasion the victims of angry mobs led by Christian priests. It is one of the distressing ironies in the history of the church that Christians should in less than a century change from persecuted to persecutor, forgetting so readily the lessons learned in the catacombs and the arenas. Unfortunately, the next fifteen centuries furnish additional examples of the dangers of wedding the church to the power of the state.

THE DEVELOPMENT OF THE HIERARCHY

We have already seen in the previous chapter how the office of bishop became distinguished from that of the elder. We also saw how that gradually only the larger churches were allowed to have bishops, who became responsible for the oversight of the smaller churches about them. In this period the process was continued as the bishops of the great churches became more influential. Finally, by the end of this period, the bishop of Rome had gained wide recognition as the leader among the bishops.

Let us look more carefully at this process and see how all this came about. At first all the bishops of the larger churches began to exercise more and more authority over the surrounding bishops. In 341 a council declared that in each province the bishop of the most important city was to be accorded special authority. These bishops came to be known as archbishops or metropolitans. Eventually the metropolitans of Jerusalem, Alexandria, Antioch, Constantinople, and Rome achieved even greater prominence. The bishops of these cities came to be called "patriarchs."

The patriarchs theoretically were equal in authority, but a series of circumstances arose that enabled the patriarch of Rome to gain pre-eminence. One obvious reason that the Roman patriarch became so prominent was that he enjoyed the prestige attached to the city of Rome. Even though Constantine moved the seat of his government to Constantinople, Rome was still looked upon as the center of the Roman Empire. From all over the Empire persons traveled to Rome. When they returned to their native lands, these persons carried with them tales of the glory of Rome.

But there were other reasons for Rome's ascendancy. The Roman church took a great interest in missions. Missionaries from Rome went into every province in the West, winning converts and establishing churches. It was only natural for these churches to look to Rome for leadership. Several bishops of Rome distinguished themselves for courage in time of crisis. The most notable example was Leo the Great, who was bishop of Rome from 440 to 461. When Attila the Hun swept down Italy and poised ready to attack Rome in 452, it was Leo who persuaded him to spare the city. Three years later, when the Vandals attacked Rome from North Africa, Leo again spoke in defense of his city.

As the Roman Empire began to fall into two major divisions, the temporal ruler in the West rapidly lost his power. These rulers became incapable of holding their portion of the Empire together and warding off the invading barbarians. In this power vacuum it was only natural the people of the West should look to someone to provide stability. More often than not, the bishop of Rome provided this stability. By contrast, the emperors in the East remained powerful through this whole period and into the Middle Ages. As a result, the bishop of Constantinople was not in a position to accumulate a great deal of power and was, in fact, thoroughly subordinated to the Emperor.

It is difficult to say when the bishop of Rome became in fact the pope. Roman Catholics assert that Peter was the first pope, and since the bishops of Rome were his successors, they were all popes also. But this dogma does not square with the historical facts. While the bishops of Rome were accumulating power and considerable recognition, this recognition was far from universal. While the patriarchs of the East came to recognize the patriarch of Rome as the first among equals, their concessions did not go beyond this. And even at the end of this period and well beyond, the patriarch of Constantinople claimed priority over the Roman patriarch. As a result of this lack of clear evidence, historians are divided in their opinions as to who actually was the first pope: some say Leo the Great; many prefer Gregory the Great, who was bishop of Rome from 590 to 604.

DOCTRINAL DISPUTES

This period in church history produced some of the most serious doctrinal controversies in the whole history of the church. The church has from its beginning been faced with doctrinal disputes, but until the church became a legal religion, these controversies did not threaten to engulf the whole of the church.

Dispute Over Christ's Relationship to God

The first of the great disputes of this period arose over the relationship of Christ the Son to God the Father. The Eastern church leaders especially became concerned about this issue. Steeped as they were in Hellenistic philosophy that reveled in hair-splitting, many of the Eastern theologians sought to probe the mystery of the Trinity. The controversy began in Alexandria and centered about two presbyters there—Arius and Athanasius. Arius was troubled because it seemed to him that Christians were teaching that there were three distinct Gods— God, Christ, and the Holy Spirit. He took the position that Christ was of different essence from the Father and was thus inferior. Athanasius, on the other hand, asserted that Christ and the Father were of the same essence and thus equal. The argument spread and theologians all over the East began to take sides. Eventually the controversy so threatened the unity of the church and possibly the Empire, that Constantine became alarmed. His solution was to call a great conference or council at which the bishops and theologians would settle the issue. The bishops were so concerned about settling the controversy that they did not stop to consider the implications of allowing the state to intervene in religious matters. In the centuries that followed, the state often intervened in the affairs of the church, especially in the affairs of the Eastern church.

In 325 the council convened at Nicea, a small city in Asia Minor, and discussed the issue. The Western bishops showed little interest in this controversy and only a few attended. After much bitter discussion the view of Athanasius—that the Father and the Son are equal and have existed from eternity—officially prevailed. From that day to this, this view has been accepted as the orthodox view. But orthodoxy did not win so easily. Although Athanasius' position won at the Council of Nicea, the tide of public opinion began to run against it, and Athanasius suffered persecution and banishment. But at later councils (Constantinople in 381 and Chalcedon in 451) the orthodox view was vindicated. Arianism, however, did not die quickly and quietly. Many Arians were active missionaries and carried their Arian faith to the Gothic tribes that were just beginning to put pressure on the northern rim of the Roman Empire. Later, when the Goths and other barbarians broke into the Empire, they carried with them Arian Christianity. In the intervening centuries Arianism, or views very similar to Arianism, have arisen again and again to challenge the orthodox view of Christ.

Dispute Over Christ's Nature

A second great controversy, in some ways a continuation of the first, dealt with the incarnation—the relationship of the human and the divine in Christ. One position stressed the deity of Christ almost to the exclusion of His humanity. The opposite view emphasized Christ's humanity so strongly that His deity was seriously compromised. Nestorius, who became patriarch of Constantinople in 428, championed this latter view. The Nestorian view was condemned by the church leaders who met at the Council of Ephesus in 431. But the followers of Nestorius refused to surrender their position so easily. In spite of persecution, many of them persisted in the eastern provinces of the Empire. Others migrated to Persia, India, and even China. After centuries of persecution a few Nestorians still exist in widely scattered areas, especially in the Middle East.

But even though the Council of Ephesus condemned the Nestorian position, the controversy was far from settled. Advocates of the view that stressed Christ's humanity soon went to such extremes that they too were criticized. For a time, however, it appeared they were going to have their way. In a council meeting at Ephesus in 449 they even resorted to intimidation and physical violence to gain a favorable vote. Even though this council had been convened by the emperor, it was soon repudiated and is often referred to as the "Robber Council." In 451 the fourth Ecumenical Council was called at Chalcedon, just across the Bosporus from Constantinople. This council decreed that the divine and the human were united in Christ "inconfusedly, immutably, indivisibly, inseparately."

In other forms this controversy continued into the sixth century and later. Many of those who opposed the decree of the Council of Chalcedon lived in Syria, Egypt, and Ethiopia. In those areas today churches still exist that find the Chalcedonic formula unacceptable.

Dispute Over How Man Is Saved

The third major controversy, unlike the first two, drew its chief protagonists from the West. Since this controversy dealt with the practical issue of how men are saved, it was understandably of greater concern to the more practical Roman mind. Pelagius, an austere British monk who came to Rome about 400, expounded the view that salvation is essentially a matter of making the right choices. He repudiated the doctrine of original sin and held, in effect, that each man is as free as was Adam to choose good or evil. Since this position seemed to deny the need for God's grace, it was vigorously opposed by Augustine, the great bishop of Hippo in North Africa. Augustine held that man's nature was completely corrupted by Adam's fall, so corrupted that man could not even will to do good. According to Augustine, a man can be saved only if God wills to save him. Since not all are saved, it is obvious that God has through His grace elected only a part of mankind to salvation. This led to the doctrine of predestination, a doctrine that was to be taken up by several leaders in the Protestant Reformation, especially Calvin.

Pelagius was banished from Rome in 418, but he made his way to the East, where the controversy continued. In 431 the Council of Ephesus condemned Pelagius and attempted to silence him and his followers. But in one form or another the controversy about the part both God and man play in human redemption persists to this day.

Results of These Great Controversies

It is difficult to overestimate the effect these great controversies had on the succeeding history of the church. While the unity of the church was preserved, it was preserved at the expense of the freedom of spirit that characterized the early church. These controversies led to the formulation of three great creeds: the Apostles', the Nicene, and the Athanasian. These creeds gave the church authoritative standards by which future controversies could be settled. But to gain this advantage the church had allowed the state to intervene, and as a result the Eastern Church has never been able to free itself of some measure of state control. Further, the theologians who wrought these creeds helped create the impression that doctrinal orthodoxy is more important than a vital faith that seeks to fulfill itself in a life of commitment.

MISSIONARY ACTIVITIES

The vigor that expressed itself in theological controversy was by no means exhausted in controversy. It also expressed itself in an impressive missionary outreach. Through this whole period, Christianity continued to gain adherents from among the inhabitants of the Roman Empire. Christianity never became the universal religion in the Empire, but by the end of this period an overwhelming majority of the population were professing Christians.

Moreover, Christianity was not to be contained within the borders of the Empire. The Goths to the north, because they had many contacts with the Empire, were among the first to be reached. The most famous missionary among these people was Ulfilas, who himself was a Goth. As a young man he was converted in Constantinople to the Arian form of Christianity, and he eventually returned to his own people as a spokesman for this faith. Ulfilas reduced Gothic to a written language so that the Goths could have the Bible in their own language—a practice that later missionaries were to duplicate around the world.

In the fifth century, Clovis, a powerful leader of the Franks, was converted through the -efforts of his wife. The Franks, who were settled in northern Gaul and along the Rhine, soon conquered surrounding territories, thus spreading the faith into Germany.

It was also in the fifth century that Christianity established a strong foothold in Ireland. The famous missionary to the Emerald Isle was Patrick, a native of Britain which was then still under Roman control. Patrick as a youth was taken to Ireland as a slave. Apparently he escaped, wandered in Europe, and spent some time in a monastery before he returned to Britain. By this time he was determined to go to Ireland as a missionary. The stories about Patrick are so numerous that it is difficult to divide history from legend, but we do know that the island was won for Christianity.

Other missionaries carried the faith to Armenia, Mesopotamia, and even into central Asia. In the fourth and fifth centuries churches were to be found in Arabia and perhaps even in India and Ceylon. Christianity had also found its way into Ethiopia where a strong church was to develop.

Thus in less than 600 years Christianity had swept across the Roman Empire and spilled beyond its borders. This it had accomplished in the face of persecution and the barriers of distance, differences in language and customs, and opposition from pagan religions.

SOME OUTSTANDING INDIVIDUALS OF THIS PERIOD

In every period of the history of the church outstanding leaders have contributed to its growth and development. The church during this period produced an abundance of such leaders, and in some respects their contributions are disproportionately important because they helped create the molds that were to shape the whole future of the church. Space will prevent anything but brief mention of a few of these men.

Augustine (354-430)

Perhaps no man since the apostle Paul has so influenced the church as Augustine, the scholarly bishop of Hippo in North Africa. Augustine was born of a devout Christian mother, but in spite of her influence, he wasted much of his youth in worldly living. But he was not satisfied with this kind of life, and turned to Manichaeism and later to Neoplatonism to satisfy his religious hunger. But these failed to free him from his fleshly lusts. Eventually he made his way to Italy where he heard the preaching of Ambrose, the brilliant bishop of Milan. The message struck a responsive chord in Augustine's heart and he was converted. With all his talents dedicated to the church, Augustine soon rose to prominence, eventually becoming bishop of Hippo in his native North Africa. His controversy with Pelagius already has been noted. His *Confessions,* an autobiographical account of his spiritual struggles, has become a devotional classic. His *City of God* still stands as one of the greatest Christian interpretations of history.

Jerome (340?-420)

Jerome was born in northern Italy, of devout Christian parents. As a young man he went to Rome where he was attracted to the ascetic life. Later he traveled in the East where he was ordained a priest. Then he returned to Rome to serve for a time as secretary to the bishop of Rome. During this time he was encouraged to pursue scholarly studies and writing, and while in Rome he began a translation of the Scriptures into Latin. Eventually he left Rome and lived most of the remainder of his life in a cave in Bethlehem close to the supposed site of Jesus' birth. Here he wrote commentaries and other theological works, but his most notable literary effort was completing his translation of the Bible. This translation was done so effectively that it became the basis for the Vulgate, which is the official Bible of the Roman Catholic Church.

John Chrysostom (345-407)

Born in Antioch, Chrysostom was baptized when he was about 25 years old. After his baptism he spent 10 years in ascetic study and retirement, after which he was ordained a priest. Chrysostom was perhaps the most eloquent preacher that the church of his time produced. (The name Chrysostom, which comes from a Greek word meaning "golden-mouthed," was given to him in recognition of his oratorical powers.) Eventually he became bishop of Constantinople, but his life as a leader was never easy. His insistence upon purity in Christian living and the orthodoxy of his theology often led to conflict and even to his exile. But today he is recognized, especially in the Eastern churches, as one of this period's most able leaders.

Other Leaders

Even a brief list of leaders from this period would have to include such men as Eusebius (c. 260-c. 340), the greatest historian of the early church; Ambrose (c. 340-397), the able bishop of Milan whose integrity and courage led him on occasion to defy even the powerful Emperor Theodosius; and Benedict of Nursia (c. 480-c. 453), who gave great impetus to the monastic movement and whose rules became a standard for Western monasteries.

CONCLUSION

As has been pointed out, this period (313-590) is a crucial one in the study of church history. During this period the ecclesiastical structure of the church took definite shape and what came to be the orthodox theology was hammered out in the fires of controversy. By the time this period ended, the lengthening shadows of the future were already casting their ominous pall across the Roman Empire. The barbarians from the north had breached the defenses of the Roman Empire in the West, and soon they would sweep the culture of Rome before them. The eastern portion of the Roman Empire, the Byzantine Empire, warded off the barbarians and maintained a high level of culture throughout the Middle Ages. But the subordination of the church to the emperor led to a sterility that was almost as disastrous to simple, New Testament Christianity as was barbarianism in the West.

QUESTIONS

1. Discuss the process whereby Christianity became the official state religion of the Roman Empire.

2. What advantages did Christianity enjoy as a state religion? What disadvantages did it suffer?

3. Discuss some of the factors that contributed to the prominence of the Roman bishop.

4. Discuss some of the major doctrinal disputes of this period. How were these disputes settled?

5. Describe the missionary activity during this period.

THE CHURCH IN THE EARLY MIDDLE AGES 590-1054

History does not fall into the neat compartments that labels like "ancient," "medieval," and "modern" seem to imply. Recognizing that any divisions one makes in the history of the church are arbitrary, we have in this work chosen to make the break between ancient and medieval church history at 590, the date that Gregory I became the bishop of Rome. The nearly 500 years that followed were difficult ones for the church. Through this period the church faced numerous foes: barbarians and Mohammedans from without and corruption and power struggles from within. The amazing thing is not that the message and influence of the church were often perverted and even almost lost; the truly amazing fact is that the church survived in spite of all these things.

THE CONTINUED DEVELOPMENT OF THE PAPACY

Gregory the Great

The ecclesiastical organization, originating in an early period, continued its development that led to a further concentration of power in Rome. Gregory I (540-604), often called "The Great," was the son of a wealthy and noble Roman family. Born in troublous times when Italy knew both the pillaging bands of Teutonic tribesmen and the invading armies of the Eastern emperor, Gregory prepared for legal and governmental service. But while still in his thirties, he gave up his wealth and position and became a monk. His devotion, asceticism, and obvious talents soon won him prominence in the church. When the bishop of Rome died in 590, Gregory was named as his successor. As has been indicated, historians are not agreed as to who really deserves to be called the first pope. But few indeed question the fact that Gregory exercised the many prerogatives of a pope, while at the same time refusing to be called pope.

Gregory had a vital concern about missions. On one occasion he happened to be in the marketplace and saw some blond, blue-eyed slaves up for sale. When he inquired about them, he was told that they were "Angles from Britain." "They are not Angles but angels," was his reply, and soon commissioned a monk to carry the gospel to the portions of Britain that had been overrun by pagan Angles and Saxons.

Gregory was a capable administrator, and under his leadership the secular affairs of the Roman Church were handled profitably. He was also a good preacher, stressing piety, humility, and practical Christian living in his sermons. Under his influence the liturgy of the worship was revised. Perhaps his best-known contribution to the worship service was the Gregorian chant, which came to have an important place in Roman Catholic worship.

As a theologian, Gregory must be ranked with Jerome, Ambrose, and Augustine. His position provided the basic guidelines for the theological discussions for the next 500 years in the Western church. Generally speaking, he followed the theology of Augustine, although he seemed to give less emphasis to predestination and more to man's own activity in redemption.

Additional Factors in the Development of the Papacy

Other strong popes arose in the 500 years following Gregory, but none influenced the strengthening of the papacy so much. Much more important in enhancing the reputation of the papacy were two documents, both of which are now considered to be spurious. One of these was the Donation of Constantine. Purporting to be written by Constantine, this document told of his being healed of leprosy by the bishop of Rome. In gratitude, Constantine assigned to the bishop and his successors the city of Rome and all the provinces of the West. The second document (really a collection of documents), the Decretals of Isidore, asserted the popes' supreme authority from Peter on, subordinated the archbishops to the pope, and regarded the bishops and the pope immune from secular control. In an uncritical age these false documents were not seriously challenged, and as a result were used to reinforce the claims of the popes.

In the tenth and early eleventh centuries, the papacy sank to such depths of degradation that it lost much of its authority and prestige. On occasion the papacy was bought and sold like any other political office. At times more than one man claimed to be the official pope. The Roman Catholic Church denotes these rival claimants as anti-popes. Many of the popes of this period kept concubines and engaged in other gross immoralities. Yet before the period closed, a serious effort to reform the papacy had begun. This reform movement was so successful that in the later Middle Ages many of the popes were without serious question the most powerful men in the West.

THE CHURCH AND SECULAR RULERS OF THE WEST

In the wake of the barbarian invasions of the West, secular Roman authority weakened and finally disappeared entirely. As the Roman roads fell into disrepair and travel became dangerous, Western Europe was broken up into numerous small states. Only gradually did some order begin to emerge out of this chaos.

The Franks

Through the influence of his wife, Clovis (Frank king mentioned in the previous chapter) was led, along with his army, to embrace Christianity. Fortunately for Clovis, he had accepted Catholic Christianity rather than its Arian form, held by most of the Goths who had invaded Gaul (now modern France). The Gauls, of course, were Catholics, and when Clovis began to expand his kingdom into Gaul, they helped him against the Arian Goths.

The successors of Clovis continued his career of conquest for half a century or more, until practically all of what is now France had come under the control of the Franks. The power of the Frankish kingdom was often weakened by civil war and the debauchery of its rulers. Yet it survived and provided a bulwark for orthodox Christianity. By the middle of the seventh century the Frankish kings were so weak that they were mere puppets. The real power was wielded by a line of administrative officers known as "mayors of the palace."

In the meantime the papacy was in trouble. About 568 a new group of barbarian invaders, the Lombards, had broken into northern Italy and were soon threatening Rome. Although Italy was at this time nominally under the control of the Byzantine Empire, the Eastern emperors were unable to stem the Lombard invaders. Pope Gregory was able to stave them off, but under weaker popes the Lombards renewed their pressure upon the papacy and its Roman possessions. Finally in desperation the popes turned to the Franks for help.

By this time the weak descendants of Clovis had been replaced by the mayors of the palace. One of the most able of these was Charles, later called Martel (the Hammer). By 720 he was the effective ruler of all of the Frankish kingdom. His son, Pepin the Short, desired the title as well as the power, and so he proclaimed himself king of the Franks with the approval of the pope. To repay the pope, Pepin sent his armies in a successful campaign against the Lombards. The land he seized from them in central Italy he returned to the pope. Known as the "Donation of Pepin," this area became the Papal States, which remained under the control of the Roman Catholic Church until 1870, when it became a part of reunited Italy.

The Carolingians

The new dynasty founded by Pepin is known in history as the "Carolingian dynasty," named after its most illustrious member, Charlemagne (Charles the Great). Charlemagne succeeded Pepin to the throne in 768 and ruled for 46 years. He continued his father's alliance with the papacy by shattering the Lombard power in Italy and declaring himself king of the Lombards in 774.

Charlemagne carried on vigorous military campaigns against several of his non-Christian neighbors. He fought the Moors in Spain, the Saxons to the north, and the Asiatic invaders who had settled in Hungary. His victorious armies were often accompanied by missionaries who endeavored to win the conquered people to Christianity. His most notable success in this respect was among the Saxons, who came to accept Christianity.

By the year 800 the figure of Charlemagne dominated the West. It was only natural that people should begin to compare him with the great Roman emperors of the past. Further, the papacy had kept alive the memory of a united Roman Empire in partnership with a strong Roman Catholic Church. Thus it was that on Christmas Day in the year 800 Pope Leo III crowned Charlemagne as emperor. An empire had been recreated, an empire that was Roman in name but German in fact, and, more significantly, was inseparably linked to the papacy, a fact that was to play an important part in the years to follow.

The Holy Roman Empire

The empire that Charlemagne built was too large and too diverse to be held together by anyone but an administrative genius. These administrative skills Charlemagne could not pass on to his descendants, and thus almost as soon as he died his empire began to disintegrate. Under his grandson it was split into three portions: France, Germany, and a strip between stretching nearly a thousand miles from the mouth of the Rhine into Italy. Even these areas soon broke up into smaller states as the power of the kings weakened.

Finally out of this chaos of competing kings and nobles arose a new ruling house, the Franconians, and a new political entity, the Holy Roman Empire. Otto, Duke of Franconia, was able to establish his authority over several of the duchies in the central and eastern portions of what had been Charlemagne's empire. Eventually this control was extended to Italy, where in 962 he was crowned emperor of the Holy Roman Empire. This was a revival of Charlemagne's dream just as Charlemagne's empire had been a revival of the dream of a Roman Empire.

The Holy Roman Empire tied the church and the secular authority ever more closely together. The concerns of the Empire became those of the church and vice versa. This arrangement later led to a long series of struggles between the emperors and the popes for ultimate supremacy. Unfortunately the spiritual level of the church was not enhanced by these struggles.

THE RISE OF MOHAMMEDANISM

As the fortunes of the church in the West ebbed and flowed with the political tides, some apparently insignificant events were happening in the distant Arabian desert. But these events, as it turned out, were to have a profound influence upon the church, both East and West.

The Religion of Islam

Mohammed was born about 570, apparently of humble origin. For a number of years he worked for an uncle as a camel driver. This work brought him some contact with both Jews and Christians, whose faiths were so different from the idolatrous paganism of his own Arabia. Eventually he married a wealthy widow, and, with time for meditation, he began to have visions, which he thought to be revelations from God. Among other things, these revelations led him to oppose the idolatry so prevalent in Mecca. Opposition forced him to flee Mecca in 622 and he found refuge in Medina. This flight from Mecca to Medina, called the Hegira, marks the beginning of the Mohammedan calendar. Mohammed called his religion *Islam*, meaning "surrender," i.e., to the will of God, whom he called Allah. The sacred book of Islam was called the Koran.

Expansion of Mohammedanism

Islam enjoyed an amazingly rapid expansion. Its Arabic devotees, driven by religious fanaticism and a desire for booty, streamed out of the desert in invincible waves. Damascus fell in 635, Jerusalem in 638, and by 642 Egypt had also fallen. In the century following Mohammed's death (632-732) Islam had swept across North Africa and Spain, and far into France, where the Saracen armies were finally stopped by Charles Martel in the famous battle of Tours. In the East the Byzantine Empire had lost all but Asia Minor to the Arabs.

At first the Arabs were quite intolerant of Christianity. Christians whose territory fell to the Arabs often had but two choices presented them: the Koran or the sword. Under such pressures many Christians defected or practiced their faith secretly. Bibles were destroyed, Christian schools were closed, and churches were converted into mosques. The influence of the great patriarchates of Alexandria, Antioch, and Jerusalem, so prominent in the earlier chapters of this history, were practically eliminated. The Arabs, however, were apt students of the higher culture they had overrun, and as they acquired culture, they also acquired tolerance. Christians now were often given the choice of the Koran, the sword, or tribute. Thus many Christians were able to keep their faith by paying tribute. But they were reduced to second-class citizens, and the church in these areas was permanently crippled.

THE GREAT SCHISM

This period from 590 to 1054 subjected the church not only to political strife and pressures from barbarians and Mohammedans it also saw the church torn by its first great division, a rent that even today has not been repaired.

Causes of the Division Between the East and the West

Church historians have often emphasized the theological differences that led to the division of the church. It may be more enlightening, however, to look first at the political and cultural differences between the East and the West that helped produce the theological differences.

In the East the Grecian language and culture predominated. The Grecian mind had a flair for philosophy and the fine shadings of thought that theologians must have. It was no accident that most of the great theological controversies of the fourth and fifth centuries began and were continued in the East. At the same time, the predominance of the emperor over the church tended to stagnate the church, and eventually much of this theological discussion was stifled.

In the West, on the other hand, the practical-minded Roman way of looking at life prevailed. The church in the West was more inclined to face its problems in a practical fashion whether these problems be political, theological, missionary, or church administration. These differing outlooks on life, along with a growing political and cultural isolation as this period wore on, made a schism within the church almost certain.

The Final Break

The break between the East and the West occurred only gradually and took several hundred years to be accomplished. Over the years many differences arose; many of these were quite minor, but through the centuries they mounted up. As early as the second century differences had arisen about the date for observing Easter. Marriage was forbidden to clergymen in the West, while in the East clergymen below the rank of bishop could marry. Priests in the West shaved, while those in the East grew beards. The Western version of the Nicene Creed had the Holy Spirit proceeding from both the Father and the Son. The East disagreed. At times the East rigidly forbade images, whereas they were increasingly used in the West.

The traditional date for the final break came in 1054. Just prior to this a new line of vigorous popes intent upon reform had begun to occupy the chair of Peter. At the same time an able and ambitious man served as Patriarch of Constantinople. A petty quarrel in which neither side was especially conciliatory led the pope and the patriarch to excommunicate each other. Within a few years came the Crusades, which might have reunited the church, but instead only drove the sections further apart. Several serious attempts have been made to bring the two together, but separate they still remain—the Roman Catholic Church and the Eastern Orthodox Church.

MISSIONS

In spite of the fact that Christendom suffered a serious decline in its moral level, in spite of the church's compromising involvement in secular politics, and in spite of the serious loss of territory to Islam, the church showed an amazing vitality in its missionary efforts. One such bright spot was Ireland. This island, which in the fifth century had itself been a mission field, became in the early Middle Ages a great missionary sender. Irish missionaries invaded England, which had lapsed into paganism due to the Anglo-Saxon invasions. A few Irish monks built a monastery on Iona, a rocky island off the coast of Scotland. From this little island came a steady stream of missionaries. Gregory the Great's interest in sending missionaries to England has already been mentioned.

Soon missionaries were crossing the English Channel to the continent. Two of these were especially outstanding: Willibrord, who labored in what is now Holland; and Winfrith (better known as Boniface), whose great work was in Germany. Receiving papal approval, Boniface began his labors among the Germans early in the eighth century. His most notable success was in Hesse. On one occasion he began to chop down a tree dedicated to the Teutonic god, Thor. A superstitious crowd gathered, expecting any moment to see Thor strike down the impertinent missionary. Instead, a strong wind arose just as he had about finished his task, and the tree went crashing down. The pagans were immediately convinced of the power of this new faith.

Many Scandinavians had first come into contact with Christianity as they had engaged in raids on western Europe and even into the Mediterranean. Perhaps some of these fierce Northmen had picked up glimpses of the gospel on these raids. In any event, before the end of this period, missionaries had begun to work in Scandinavia. Also by the end of this period missionaries were actively at work in Russia. Kiev became the first great center of Russian Christianity. Since the missionaries to Russia came from Constantinople, their allegiance was to Eastern Orthodoxy rather than to Roman Catholic Christianity. By contrast, other Slavic peoples in Bohemia and Poland were won to Roman Catholicism. In Spain, which had been overrun by Arabs in the seventh century, Christianity slowly began to replace Mohammedanism as the Spanish peninsula was regained by military action.

Even though Christendom had lost much territory to Islam, Christianity could still claim more territory in 1054 than it had in 590. This gain had been achieved both by military action of Christian princes and by the sacrificial labor of untold thousands of missionaries. Sometimes whole areas were won by mass conversions. We may entertain serious doubts about the sincerity of such conversions, especially when the converts displayed little change in their lives or beliefs. Yet the power of the gospel is such that even in these areas a solid Christian faith eventually took root.

DOCTRINE, LIFE, AND WORSHIP

Doctrine

While theological controversy did not hold the center of the stage as it had in the previous period, several controversies of note did arise in this period. Augustine's doctrine of predestination continued to be discussed especially in the West. Gradually Augustinianism was so modified that it came to resemble Pelagianism, at least to the extent that it granted man greater freedom of will.

A definite development in the doctrine of the Lord's Supper also took place during this period. One view, which was to become more popular and even be adopted as the official view of the Roman church, was that the bread and wine in the Lord's Supper actually become the body and blood of Christ. This doctrine is called transubstantiation.

Perhaps the most serious controversy in the East revolved around the use of images. The West, of course, had long accepted the use of images as aids in worship and devotion. The controversy became serious in the East early in the eighth century and lasted for more than a hundred years. Several Byzantine emperors attempted to eliminate the use of images, or icons. They became known as iconoclasts (image-breakers), and this is often referred to as the "iconoclastic controversy." These efforts to eliminate images failed, but to this day the Eastern Orthodox churches use pictures or low reliefs rather than statues.

Life and Worship

Pagans who came into the church often brought with them many of their superstitions and much of their pagan religion. Too often it seemed that the worship of pagan gods was simply transferred to Mary and the saints. The cult of Mary grew rapidly in popularity. New festivals were added. The penance system continued to develop, and masses for the dead were accepted as standard practice. In an age that was ignorant as well as superstitious, it is not surprising that such things as trial by ordeal were practiced. With such ignorance were connected immorality and crime. Unfortunately, these conditions persisted through most of this period, for the priests, to whom the people looked for leadership, were often as ignorant as the people.

One of the very important aspects of the religious life of the Middle Ages was the growth of monasticism. Even in the early periods of the history of the church, some had forsaken society and sought a deeper spiritual life by living alone in the desert or other isolated places. Soon groups of these hermits began to live together, forming the basis of monastic life. Benedict of Nursia, who founded the famous monastery of Monte Cassino in central Italy, established the rules that became the pattern for monastic life in the West. During the Middle Ages hundreds of monasteries and nunneries (for monasticism was by no means confined to men) sprang up all over Europe.

The idea of the monastic life is that if one withdraws from the evils of the world, he can give himself without reservation to service for God. Unfortunately, however, these temptations sometimes only changed forms and followed the monks into the monasteries. Yet, even though monasteries lost their ideals and became corrupt, reforming forces frequently arose from within to purge them. In spite of their weaknesses it must be acknowledged that the monasteries often performed a valuable service in holding up to the world outside the ideal of a completely dedicated life. The monasteries also rendered a great service in preserving and passing on the learning that remained in the West.

CONCLUSION

The period from 590 to 1054 was a difficult one for the church. One historian speaks of this period as the "Great Recession"; others refer to it as the Dark Ages. Certainly many aspects of the church's life did suffer a serious decline. Yet before the period closed, signs of a revival were evident. The gates of hell still had not prevailed against the church.

QUESTIONS

1. Discuss church-state relations during the early Middle Ages. What problems were posed by the nature of these relations?

2. Who was probably the most important pope during this period? Tell of some of his work.

3. What effects did the rise of Mohammedanism have on Christianity?

4. What factors contributed to the great division of the church?

5. Mention and discuss some of the changes that occurred in the doctrine, life, and worship of the church. Contrast these with the doctrine, life, and work of the apostolic church.

6. Tell of the missionary activity of the church during this period.

THE CHURCH IN THE LATER MIDDLE AGES 1054-1517

The later Middle Ages was a period of stark contrasts. Side-by-side existed the extremes of dire poverty and great wealth, deep piety and gross immorality, acts of self-giving love and vicious religious intolerance, the drab peasant existence and the pageantry of tournaments. As this period opened, a great tide of spiritual revival was beginning to sweep across the church; as the period closed, this tide was not only spent but had so receded that a spiritual depression plagued the church.

THE PAPACY'S STRUGGLE WITH SECULAR POWERS

In the tenth and early eleventh centuries the papacy had become so corrupt that it commanded little respect or authority. At the same time, the secular powers of Western Europe, divided by feudalism and torn by dynastic struggles, were quite weak. Where there were no great powers—spiritual or secular—there could be no great power struggles. But this was already changing by the time the later Middle Ages began. Thus the stage was being set for a showdown between the claims of a revived papacy and those of the reviving secular powers.

Papal Reform

It is ironical that the papal reform, which made the pope a serious challenge to the emperor of the Holy Roman Empire, was begun by an emperor. The first great stride toward reform was begun by Emperor Henry III, when he had Leo IX elevated to the papacy in 1048. During the twenty-five years that followed, Leo was succeeded by other reforming popes. Working quietly but effectively behind the scenes during this period was Hildebrand, an Italian monk who was committed to reform. In 1073 Hildebrand himself was made pope, taking the name Gregory VII. The papal reign of Gregory VII, like that of Gregory I, is one of the highwater marks of the papacy.

Gregory VII

Gregory's view of the papal office was far from modest. He believed that since the spiritual realm is superior to the physical, the pope should be superior to any secular ruler. Ordinarily the two realms would be kept separate with no chance of conflict, but should any conflict arise, the pope was superior. This was not an idle theory as far as Gregory was concerned, and when the proper occasion arose, he attempted to enforce it with courage and determination. Secular rulers might have armies at their disposal, but the pope was not without weapons. A rebellious ruler could be excommunicated, which was often an open invitation for his assassination. Or, in extreme cases, the pope might use the interdict whereby all public religious services would be withdrawn from a city or larger area. These services were considered so important to people of the Middle Ages that, denied them, they would bring pressure to bear upon their ruler to submit to the pope.

The first great challenge to Gregory's views of papal authority came in the person of Henry IV, son and successor of Henry III, emperor of the Holy Roman Empire. The quarrel arose over the matter of investiture. At that time many of the bishops exercised secular as well as spiritual rule over sizable territories. Henry contended that, since they were secular rulers, he should have the right to choose them and install them in office. Gregory strongly disagreed, insisting that the bishops were spiritual rulers first of all. The upshot of the controversy was that Gregory deposed Henry, releasing all his subjects from allegiance to him. To save his throne, Henry crossed the Alps in the winter of 1077 to visit the papal court at Canossa. Gregory humbled the proud emperor by letting him stand barefoot in the snow on three successive days before giving him an audience. But Henry had his revenge. Later he deposed the pope, and Gregory died in exile in 1085, apparently frustrated in his efforts to make the papacy superior to secular powers. But history has a way of delaying its final decisions. People in Western Europe soon forgot Gregory's defeat, but for many years they remembered vividly Henry's humiliation at Canossa.

Innocent III

By all odds the greatest of the medieval popes was Innocent III, who was pope from 1198 to 1216. He came closer than any other to putting into practice the sweeping view of papal authority that Gregory VII had advocated. Just before Innocent became pope, the emperor of the Holy Roman Empire had died, leaving his infant son as nominal ruler. Thus the pope faced no serious challenge from the Empire, and was able to turn his attention to other rulers. Philip Augustus, king of France, had divorced his wife and remarried. Innocent forced him to take back his first wife. When King John of England refused to accept the pope's nominee for the Archbishopric of Canterbury, Innocent brought him to heel by excommunicating him and placing England under the interdict. To save his throne John surrendered his kingdom to the pope and then received it back as a fief, becoming in effect a vassal of the pope. During Innocent's pontificate the Fourth Crusade was launched, which resulted in the capture of Constantinople. Another important event of Innocent's reign was the Fourth Lateran Council, the most important church council of the Middle Ages. Convened in 1215 by Innocent and influenced strongly by him, this council defined a number of important Roman Catholic dogmas.

The Decline of Papal Power

The thirteenth century saw several strong popes, but none ever again scaled the pinnacle of power reached by Innocent. The decline of the papacy became pronounced during the reign of Boniface VIII, pope from 1294 to 1303. Boniface made even more exaggerated claims for the papacy than had his predecessors. In his bull (an official papal pronouncement) *Unam Sanctam* he affirmed that "it is altogether necessary to salvation for every human creature to be subject to the

Roman Pontiff." But Boniface had neither the power nor the ability to make such sweeping claims stick.

The decline of the papacy became even more obvious during the so-called Babylonian Captivity. For nearly seventy years beginning in 1309, the popes resided in Avignon (in what is now modern France) rather than in Rome. The popes were weak and were often dominated by the king of France. But the prestige of the papacy was to sink even lower in the Great Schism that followed. In 1378 a new pope was elected in Rome and he chose to remain in Rome. But many of the cardinals, preferring the luxuries of Avignon, returned to the papal court there and selected another pope. Thus Europe was treated to the spectacle of two rival claimants to the papal chair. (The Roman Catholic Church recognizes the Roman popes, declaring the others to be "anti-popes.") Motivated largely by politics, the rulers of Europe began to support one or the other of the two. This situation continued for about fifty years and was settled only after several church councils.

The later Middle Ages saw the papacy emerge from its corruption and rise in prestige until the pope was the most powerful man in the West. By the end of the Middle Ages the papacy had been so reduced in power that the pope was little more than a petty Italian ruler. Several things account for this sharp decline in power. First of all, feudalism declined, paving the way for the rise of nationalism, which laid the foundations for the modem states of Western Europe. In the second place, the spirit of the Renaissance swept across the West, turning, men's thoughts from things of heaven to things of the earth. A third important reason for the papal decline was the behavior of the popes. The Babylonian Captivity, the Great Schism, and the lives of some of the popes all took their toll of papal prestige. But after all this is said, perhaps the amazing thing is not that the papacy, declined; the truly surprising thing is that it gained so much power and retained it so long.

THE CRUSADES

Pilgrimages had become big business by the later Middle Ages. Every Christian land was dotted with holy places that attracted pilgrims by the thousands. Rome, with its famous churches and other sacred sites, was high on the pilgrimage list. But Palestine was the Holy Land, the most cherished destination of pilgrims. Many years before, Palestine had fallen into the hands of the Moslems. At first, the Arabs had banned pilgrimages and had persecuted those who violated the bans. But in time the Arabs had found it profitable to permit pilgrimages, and as a result these had grown in popularity through the years. Then in the eleventh century the Seljuk Turks swept out of Asia and took over the crumbling Arab empire. The Turks, who only recently had been converted to Mohammedanism, pursued their newfound faith with a zeal that led them to begin persecuting Christian pilgrims. Thus the stage was set for the Crusades.

Motives of the Crusades

In 1095 Pope Urban II, in a council of church leaders and nobles, issued a stirring call to arms against the infidels. Many inducements were held out to those who would participate: remission of sins, indulgences, the hope of plunder. The audience responded, "God wills it."

No doubt Urban hoped to enhance his office and unite the church, East and West, in this one great effort. But why should feudal barons, merchants, and peasants respond to the pope's call? First and foremost was the religious motive. The Crusades were but one expression of the deepening religious concern that swept across Western Europe in the eleventh, twelfth, and thirteenth centuries. Beyond the religious motives, economic considerations led many to participate in the Crusades. Others, no doubt, were drawn to Palestine in the hope of military venture.

The March to the Holy Land

Enthusiasm for the Crusades was not confined to the warrior class. Thousands of peasants and artisans, aroused by the preaching of Peter the Hermit and Walter the Penniless, started across Europe to Palestine. Many died along the way and others who managed to reach Turkish soil were massacred or sold into slavery.

Later the organized Crusaders arrived, and after many months of hard fighting were able to capture much of Palestine. Finally in 1099 their goal was reached—Jerusalem was taken.

While the First Crusade was the most successful, several others followed. In all, the Crusading fervor lasted nearly 200 years. The Second Crusade was necessitated when Edessa, a key to the defense of the Crusaders' kingdom, fell in 1144. Bernard of Clairvaux, a great leader in monastic reform, preached this Crusade. In spite of the success of Bernard in arousing enthusiasm for the venture, the Crusade itself failed. The Third Crusade, launched in 1189 after the Turks had retaken Jerusalem, called forth the most illustrious leadership of any of the Crusades. At its head was the eminent Holy Roman Emperor Frederick Barbarossa, King Philip Augustus of France, and King Richard the Lionhearted of England. The emperor drowned on his way to Palestine and the two kings spent more time quarreling between themselves than they did fighting the Turks, who at this time were led by the brilliant and generous Saladin. As a result, this Crusade failed in its purpose of retaking Jerusalem.

The Fourth Crusade, launched in 1202, was directed against Constantinople rather than against the Turks. The Crusaders succeeded in capturing the Byzantine capital and installing one of their own number as ruler. An attempt was also made to place the Eastern Church under the authority of Rome, but this effort to unite the church by force was doomed to failure. The most tragic of all was the Children's Crusade. It was argued that the earlier Crusades had failed because the Crusaders did not have clean hands or pure hearts. As a result of this reasoning, thousands of children left their homes in 1212 to wander across Europe toward the Holy Land. Untold thousands died along the way and the few who did manage to reach Turkish territory were immediately seized and sold into slavery.

Results of the Crusades

The Crusades did, at least for brief periods, open the Holy Land for pilgrimages. But other results were more far-reaching. Feudalism was weakened, for many of the nobles never returned, thus allowing the kings to centralize their authority. During the Crusades the papacy was enhanced, although the ultimate result may have been to undermine the papacy by strengthening the kings of Western Europe. Italian cities were strengthened economically, and the provincialism of the West was partially dissipated. Unfortunately, the crusading spirit left a heritage of bitterness between the Turks and the West, and between the Eastern and Western branches of the church. Another tragic aspect of the Crusades was that the religious zeal it generated was later directed toward the Cathari and others who were considered heretics.

MONASTICISM AND SCHOLASTICISM

Renewal Within the Monastic Movement

One of the most important indications of a spiritual renewal in the West was the increased activity within monastic communities. Toward the end of the previous period signs of this were seen in the monastic reforms begun under the leadership of the monastery at Cluny, France, and its great abbot, Odo. This reforming zeal was carried on by the Cistercians, a new movement that had its beginnings in France about 1100. The best-known of the Cistercians was Bernard of Clairvaux, one of the most fervent preachers of the Middle Ages. His reforming efforts will be noted in greater detail in a later chapter.

In the thirteenth century an important new form of monasticism emerged—the mendicant orders. The older orders, following the example of Benedict of Nursia, placed a premium upon withdrawal and quiet devotion. The mendicants, so called because they begged for their subsistence, believed, on the other hand, that their mission was to preach and serve in the world. Because of their obvious concern for their fellow men, the mendicant monks became known as Friars, derived from the Latin word for brother.

The two most important mendicant orders were the Franciscans and the Dominicans, although many similar orders arose during this period. The Franciscans will be discussed in the next chapter. The Dominicans owe their origin to Dominic (c. 1170-1221), a Spanish priest who became concerned about the defections from the Catholic church in southern France. In 1215 he journeyed to Rome to get permission from Pope Innocent III to found an order dedicated to winning back the heretics. The Dominicans later became connected with the Inquisition, that infamous effort to win back heretics by torture and persecution.

While the Dominicans and the Franciscans were similar in many ways, they also differed in important respects. The Franciscans sought to win men by the example of good deeds; the Dominicans stressed learning and logic in their approach. We might say that the Franciscans appealed to men's hearts; the Dominicans to men's heads. Both of these orders contributed greatly to the Scholastic movement of this period, and often the two were vigorous rivals in some of the great theological controversies of the period. Both orders were quite missionary, and have been responsible for much of the missionary growth of the Roman Catholic Church even to this day.

Scholasticism

In addition to a great spiritual revival, the later Middle Ages witnessed a great revival of learning. This movement, often referred to as Scholasticism, was an effort to support the faith by the use of reason. The Scholastics tended to approach theology from the viewpoint of philosophy rather than from the viewpoint of the Bible. The Scholastics relied heavily upon the writings of the Greek philosophers Plato and Aristotle, especially the works of the latter.

The first of the great Scholastics was Anselm (c. 1033-1109), a native of Italy who eventually became Archbishop of Canterbury in England. Anselm's efforts to combine faith and reason may be summed up in the statement, "I believe in order that I may understand." In other words, faith, which came first with him, was a basis for knowledge.

In contrast to the approach of Anselm was that of Abelard (1079-1142), who lectured in theology at the University of Paris. Abelard's position may be summarized in the motto, "I understand in order that I may believe." He believed that doubt led to inquiry, inquiry to truth, and truth to the dogmas of the church. Thus Abelard emphasized reason more than faith. In regard to the atonement, he held that Christ died to set an example, to exert a moral influence upon man. A view similar to this is held today by many who take a liberal theological position. Abelard also challenged those in his day who appealed to the

Church Fathers for authority. In a book called Yes and No he showed that on many issues the Fathers contradicted themselves.

The greatest of all the Scholastics was Thomas Aquinas (c. 1225-1274). Born of a noble Italian family, he was educated at Monte Cassino and the University of Naples before he became a Dominican monk. In his greatest work, *Summa Theologica* (or Summary of Theology), Thomas used reason to provide arguments for the existence of God. Some of these arguments still have compelling force today. Although he relied upon reason to prove the existence of God, Thomas felt that it was necessary to turn to Scripture to learn of God's loving concern for man. Thomas' greatness lay, not in the fact that he was an innovator, but rather that he was so successful in synthesizing faith and reason. Thomas believed that since God was the author of both reason and revelation, there could be no conflict between the two. Thomas' thinking was so thorough and systematic that it has had an appeal to scholars, both within and without the Roman Catholic Church, ever since.

Thomas was not without his critics, however. The sharpest critics of his position arose from among the Franciscans, rivals of the Dominicans. Noteworthy is John Duns Scotus (c. 1265-1308), a native of Scotland. In contrast to the view of Thomas that the truth of doctrines can be demonstrated by reason, Duns Scotus felt that reason had definite limitations. Franciscan scholars who came after him, notably William of Occam, or Ockham (c. 1300-c. 1349), went so far as to deny that dogma could be demonstrated by rational arguments. Occam, a native of England, held that even the basic tenents of Christianity must be accepted by faith. In effect, he abandoned any hope of reconciling the wisdom of God and the wisdom of man. For several reasons Scholasticism began to decline after the time of Occam.

LIFE, DOCTRINE, AND WORSHIP

During the Middle Ages a new culture emerged in the West. Deeply rooted in the classical heritage of Greece and Rome, this new culture owed not a little to the culture imported by the invading barbarians from the north and the east. The church had played an important part in taming some of the wilder barbarian passions, yet had been affected in the process. To appreciate just how much the church had changed, one need but compare the apostle Peter to one of his "successors"—take Innocent III, for example. Or compare the simple faith and worship of the New Testament with the superstition-laden worship of the Middle Ages.

Important to the religious life of the laity were the sacraments. Only two ordinances are mentioned in the New Testament— baptism and the Lord's Supper. But gradually the church had added to these until in the fifteenth century the number was fixed at seven: baptism, confirmation, penance, the Eucharist, extreme unction, marriage, and ordination.

Infant baptism had become the universal practice of the church. It was believed that an infant dying unbaptized could not, because of the taint of original sin, enjoy the presence of God. Baptism was by immersion or by affusion (pouring).

Private confession of sins to a priest had become a standard practice, as was the performance of good deeds commanded by the priest, who had the power to remit sins. The Fourth Lateran Council required every Christian to attend confession at least once a year. As a part of this system, the practice of indulgences had grown up. By doing certain good deeds one could receive an indulgence that would remove from him the temporal penalty of sins. Urban II, for example, granted a plenary indulgence to any who went on the First Crusade. By the end of the Middle Ages it was popularly believed that the living could obtain indulgences that would help those supposedly in purgatory.

At the heart of public worship was the Eucharist, or the Mass. By the later Middle Ages the cup had been withdrawn from the laity, who got only the bread. The Fourth Lateran Council declared the doctrine of transubstantiation to be an official dogma of the church. This doctrine affirmed that the bread and the wine became actually the body and blood of Christ in the ceremony of the Mass. The Mass was said in Latin, and since fewer and fewer of the laity could understand Latin, the ceremony tended to lose its original significance.

To persons of the Middle Ages the world of the unseen was very real. Satan and his demons were considered the source of many kinds of evils. Since Christ had overcome Satan, the cross and other symbols were extensively used as fetishes to ward off the evil spirits. Since the saints had also triumphed over evil, they were revered. The virgin Mary was especially honored. Mary and the saints were thought to be already in the presence of God, and thus to pray through them was to have readier access to God's ear.

Pilgrimages were quite popular. Travel of any kind was often quite hazardous in the Middle Ages; yet in spite of this a constant stream of pilgrims made their way to Rome, and hardier souls even ventured to the Holy Land. The veneration of sacred things and places found another outlet in the use of relics. These relics were bits of clothing, bones, personal effects, or other items connected with a saint or some hallowed event. The heavy demand made the traffic in relics a profitable one.

A word must be said about the church architecture of this period. Scattered across Western Europe are the great Romanesque and Gothic cathedrals, a tribute to the devotion and patience of this age. These cathedrals tower over their surroundings, giving silent but eloquent testimony to the central place religion had in the lives of the people.

CONCLUSION

As we have seen, the later Middle Ages was a period of contrasts, even contradictions. Thus any generalizations we make about the period must always be made with some reservations. The church of this period had in so many respects departed so far from the simple church of the New Testament that Christians of the first century would not have recognized it. Yet in spite of corruption, this church was able to provide a light, flickering and feeble though it was, that challenged some men to keep reaching higher. Earthen vessel though it was, yet this church contained a great treasure.

QUESTIONS

1. Tell of some of the struggles between the popes and the secular rulers. Name some of the outstanding popes of this period.

2. What factors contributed to the decline of the papacy near the end of this period?

3. Discuss some of the motives that led to the Crusades.

4. What were some of the results of the Crusades?

5. What two important monastic orders arose during this period?

6. What is meant by Scholasticism? Who was probably the greatest of the Scholastics?

7. Discuss some aspects of the doctrine, life, and worship of this period.

8. The later Middle Ages have been described as a time of great contrasts. Discuss this.

PRE-REFORMATION REFORMERS

In spite of Rome's pretensions to and her actual acquisition of power, the pope has never controlled the whole of Christendom. The Orthodox patriarchs, while at times recognizing the pope as the "first among equals," were never willing to place themselves under the authority of Rome. Other Eastern Churches (e.g., Coptic, Syriac, Ethiopic, Nestorian) that did not belong to the Orthodox family of churches were also independent of Rome. Some of these, called "Uniate Churches" later acknowledged the authority of the pope, but in so doing were granted several concessions by Rome (services in their native tongues and a married clergy, for example).

But even in Western Europe the Roman Church has never held complete and unchallenged religious sway. The vision of a church that is holy and Biblical has never been entirely lost in the long sweep of the centuries; and men, catching that vision, have arisen from within the church to challenge the violations of this vision.

Unfortunately we know little about these men. The names of most of them have never been inscribed in any records. Many were, no doubt, secret rebels against the established religious order —the 7000 who never bowed to Baal and at the same time, never made public their profession of faith. Perhaps others—a rude swineherd, a simple serving maid, an unlettered priest—raised their protests, but were ignored or tolerated. Still others, more vocal or less fortunate, were martyred by the hundreds or the thousands. We cannot even hazard a guess as to who these people were, how many of them there were, when or where they all lived, or what their specific doctrines were. Yet we do know about a few of them.

In this chapter we will discuss a few of these people. They are important because some of them definitely helped pave the way for the coming of the great reformers of the Protestant Reformation. They are also significant because they remind us that even in our times we need a vision of a church that is holy and apostolic.

Some of these reformers emphasized the necessity for spiritual and moral improvement. Others protested against what they considered doctrinal errors of Rome. Still others added to these objections a voice of protest against the monolithic ecclesiastical organization that had evolved in the West.

MONASTIC REFORMERS

Bernard of Clairvaux (1090-1153)

Very often in the long history of the church, movements and organizations have, after a generation or two, turned aside from their original purpose. We should not be surprised then to find that the monastic movement, begun originally as a protest against worldliness, had by the Middle Ages fallen victim to the same worldliness it had once opposed. The rule of Benedict, which had once been the code of conduct for many of the monastic movements, was almost forgotten.

Many men sought to restore monasticism to its original purposes and purity. But none were more effective than Bernard of Clairvaux. When only twenty-two he took charge of the Benedictine monastery at Citeaux, in what is now France. Soon this monastery became a center for monastic reform and out of this grew the Cistercian order. Bernard was such an eloquent preacher that when he arrived at an area to preach, women hid their husbands and sons lest they renounce all and follow Bernard into the monastic life.

Bernard's emphasis was mainly upon spiritual and moral reform, and as a result he showed little interest in reforming the church hierarchy. Nor was he concerned about doctrinal reform. Indeed, Bernard was an outstanding champion of the orthodox Catholic theology, and led the attack against some of the unorthodox views of Peter Abelard. But regardless of how far short Bernard fell of seeking a thorough reformation of the church, we must credit him with seeing beyond the corruptions of the church of his day. This intense devotion to Christ is no better illustrated than in one of the great hymns that came from his pen: "Jesus, the Very Thought of Thee."

Francis of Assisi (1182-1226)

Another effort to reform the religious life of the twelfth and thirteenth centuries led to the development of a whole series of new monastic orders, referred to as "mendicant orders," that differed in several important respects from the older Benedictine orders. The Franciscans, founded by Francis of Assisi (a town in central Italy), was one of the most famous of the mendicant orders. Francis, a fun-loving and none too serious son of a wealthy merchant, experienced a decisive change of heart during a serious illness. As a result he pledged himself to a life of sacrificial service and devotion to God. Refusing gifts of money as he went about preaching, Francis would accept only the food, clothing, and shelter he needed for the day. He was, he said, wedded to "Lady Poverty." Hundreds were attracted to the simple life of service advocated by Francis; and the Franciscan order, recognized by Pope Innocent III in 1210, became a prominent one in the further history of the Roman Church.

The reforms and manner of life advocated by Francis were not embodied by the majority of either the people or the clergy of the Western church. His reforms were too austere, too demanding, ever to be widely popular. But in a society that was putting an ever-increasing emphasis upon wealth and power, his voice sounded out a reminder that this pomp and pageantry were a far cry from the simple Christianity of the first century.

REFORMING SECTS

The reform movements instigated by Bernard and Francis, while important to any study of the history of the church, could scarcely be called precursors of the Protestant Reformation. Both were carried out within the framework of the church and, in fact, with the official blessing of the papacy. But arising about the same time were other movements that in their search for a purified church challenged not only the immorality but the very ecclesiastical structure of the church. Unfortunately we know less about these groups than we would like to know. Most of the existent references to them come from the pens of their enemies, whose zeal for orthodoxy led to distortions and propaganda-making.

The Cathari

One of these groups, the Cathari, sought to purify the church by returning to the church of the New Testament. But unfortunately their doctrines were often a curious mixture of the teaching of the New Testament and the dualistic and ascetic ideas of the Gnostic and Manichean movements mentioned in an earlier chapter. For example, many of the Cathari, often referred to as Albigenses because many of them lived about Albi, France, believed that Christ and Satan were both sons of God. Christ was the good son who made the souls of man, while Satan, the bad son, made their bodies. As a result the physical bodies were looked upon as evil, leading them to shun anything having to do with reproduction. Many did not marry, and they refused to eat meat, milk, or eggs, all of which were considered to be fruits of reproduction. They rejected the authority of the Roman Catholic Church, and as a result were the subjects of persecution.

But in spite of their unorthodoxy, even their critics often admitted that the Cathari were of high moral character. In the face of persecution, they carried on missionary activities, winning converts as far away as northern France. The Cathari were most numerous in northern Italy, southern France, and northern Spain.

Under Pope Innocent III the Cathari were the victims of a bloody crusade that all but eliminated them. Although the Cathari disappeared as a reforming force in Western Christianity, some of their emphases lived on. The Cathari had translated the Scriptures into their own language, making it available to the people. This practice was employed by later reformers, and became one of the major factors in the success of the Protestant Reformation.

The Waldenses

Another reforming group, the Waldenses, also arose in France about the same time as the Cathari. It is generally believed that the Waldenses were founded by Peter Waldo, a rich merchant of Lyons. In 1176 Waldo, heeding Jesus' injunction to the rich young ruler, distributed his possessions to the poor and began to preach in the city and countryside, begging his daily bread as he went. Soon others, attracted to Waldo and inspired by his example, began to preach. Calling themselves the "Poor Men of Lyons," these men went about preaching and doing good in much the same manner that Francis of Assisi and his followers were to employ some three decades later.

The Waldenses made the New Testament central in their beliefs and practices. They had access to vernacular translations of the New Testament and committed large portions of it to memory. Their adherence to the New Testament led them to repudiate many beliefs and practices of the Roman Catholic Church. They looked upon the Roman Church as corrupt, and rejected the authority of all clergy except those who lived as the apostles had lived. They also rejected masses for the dead and the use of Latin in the worship services. While they observed the Lord's Supper and practiced baptism, they held that these might be administered by a layman as well as by a priest.

Waldensian membership was for the most part drawn from the common people, although on occasion wealthy and influential persons became Waldensians. The movement spread more widely than did the Cathari, and were soon to be found in Italy, Germany, Spain, and Bohemia, as well as in their native France. Pope Innocent III tried to win them back into the Roman fold, and some did respond to the pope's efforts. Later, however, the Waldenses were branded as heretics and subjected to vicious persecution. As a result, they were practically eliminated except in some of the remote valleys of the Italian Alps. Here, in spite of sporadic persecution (John Milton's bitter sonnet, "On the Recent Slaughter of the Piedmontese," was written to denounce one such persecution), they have persisted to the present day.

The Waldenses, more than any of the other groups mentioned thus far in this chapter, resemble the Protestant Reformers who arose in protest against Rome in the sixteenth century. Their emphasis upon the

Bible as the ultimate authority was a fundamental tenet of the Reformation. Their stress upon the priesthood of believers and their repudiation of many Catholic practices was also echoed in the teachings of the Reformers. But in spite of these resemblances, the Waldenses did not spark a major revolt against Rome. The reason for this lies not so much in the religious realm as in the political. Unlike the Reformers of northern Europe, the Waldenses were unable to enlist any powerful princes or dukes to their cause. Thus they had no political shield against the persecutions aimed at them. But the very fact that they arose and have persisted to the present time is testimony to the fact that God sometimes chooses the weak and humble to do His work.

INDIVIDUAL REFORMERS

John Wycliffe

Eventually protests against Rome began to rise in central and northern Europe. One of these, led by John Wycliffe (or Wiclif), was important in preparing the way for the Reformation in England. The exact date of his birth is unknown, but it was probably about 1320. Wycliffe attended Oxford University, where he later became an outstanding scholar and teacher. There was in England at this time a growing resentment of the power of the pope. Even though a clergyman himself, Wycliffe approved these sentiments and thus won for himself the support of many English noblemen, who were quite willing to protect him from the disfavor of Rome.

Until 1378 Wycliffe's attacks upon the church were mild. He sought only to eliminate the immorality of the clergy and strip the church of much of its property, which he thought was a source of corruption. But beginning at this date and continuing for the remaining half dozen years of his life, Wycliffe carried on a more revolutionary attack against the Roman Church and its teachings. He repudiated the authority of the pope and insisted that Christ rather than any human being was the head of the church. He insisted that the Bible instead of the church councils or tradition was the supreme authority for Christians. Making the Bible the Christians' authority required making the Bible available to all Christians. This Wycliffe did by translating the

New Testament into the English of his day. Others were inspired to translate the Old Testament, and by 1384, the year of Wycliffe's death, the whole Bible was available in English.

Wycliffe became critical of monks and friars and later held that every Christian is a priest. He condemned the practice of praying to saints and the reverencing of relics. He questioned the spiritual value of pilgrimages that had come to be so important in the practice of the church. Eventually he even called into question the doctrine of transubstantiation, which teaches that the bread and the wine in the Communion become the actual body and blood of Christ. Along with this he repudiated indulgences and masses for the dead.

As Wycliffe became more radical in his attacks upon the Roman Church, he lost much of the support of the noblemen. Finally he was forced to retire from Oxford to a country parish. Here Wycliffe continued and spread his work by sending out traveling preachers. They were to live simply and preach wherever they could get a hearing. In their preaching they were to stress the Bible rather than dwell upon fables and lives of the saints that characterized much of the preaching of that day. As they traveled, these preachers also distributed portions of Wycliffe's translation of the Bible.

The writings of Wycliffe and the efforts of these preachers won many followers, who came to be known as Lollards. At first many scholars as well as the landed gentry were attracted to Wycliffe's views, but later the movement became almost exclusively made up of the poor.

Wycliffe himself died in peace in 1384, but his followers were soon facing persecution. Several years after his death a church council declared Wycliffe's views heretical, ordered his writings burned, and demanded that his remains be removed from consecrated soil. At papal command his bones were dug up and burned and the ashes cast into a stream.

But neither persecution nor papal action could eliminate the movement Wycliffe had started. In spite of persecution, the Lollards persisted. When the seeds of the Reformation finally did come to England, they found a ready soil in which to take root. This explains in part why the Reformation was so readily received in England.

John Hus

The influence of Wycliffe was not confined to England. Students from Bohemia, studying at Oxford, came into contact with some of Wycliffe's teachings and carried them back to their native land, where they were widely disseminated, especially at the University of Prague. It was here that as a student John Hus first came into contact with them. In 1402, when he was only about thirty years old, Hus was appointed rector of the university. Through his eloquence and moral earnestness Hus soon attracted quite a following.

Hus did not slavishly copy Wycliffe's teachings. For one thing, Hus was more conservative than Wycliffe. But the positions of the two men were similar in many respects. Both stressed the importance of the Scriptures. Both wanted the Bible available in the language of the people. It was Hus's practice to teach and preach in Czech, his native tongue. This emphasis coincided with a rising tide of nationalism that was sweeping across Bohemia, and it no doubt contributed to Hus's popularity with the people.

While Hus had the support of many of the people and even the aristocracy, including the queen, he also soon aroused strong opposition. His attacks upon the immoral lives of the clergy were hardly designed to win their friendship, and his doctrinal position eventually led to his excommunication by the Archbishop of Prague. Finally the pope placed Hus under severe excommunication and the city of Prague under the interdict. (Placing a city under the interdict meant that its priests would refuse to perform any religious services for the people.)

Eventually Hus was called before a great church council, the Council of Constance, to answer for his reputed heresies. This was the same council that condemned the teachings of Wycliffe. Sigismund, emperor of the Holy Roman Empire, assured Hus safe conduct for him to attend the council and present his views. But the council was in no mood to debate theological differences with Hus. Without being given a fair chance to present his position, Hus was condemned to be burned at the stake. Sigismund, who apparently had some qualms about his promise of safe conduct, was assured by the church leaders that he had no moral obligation to a heretic, as Hus was now proclaimed to be. Even as he was being tied to the stake, Hus is reported to have said,

"You may burn the goose [Hus was nicknamed "the Goose], but a swan shall arise to take his place." A bit over a century later, Hus's prophetic words were fulfilled several times over in the persons of Luther, Zwingli, Calvin, and others.

But Hus's death did not end the movement that bears his name. His followers continued the reforming efforts he had begun, and some even went further, demanding even more sweeping reforms. Unfortunately his followers divided, and even carried on a bloody civil war among themselves. Some of the more conservative Hussites, after gaining some concessions from the Roman Church, were nominally received back into it. But others, demanding more radical reforms, could find no means of reconciliation with Rome, and so continued their separate existence. These served as the spiritual ancestors of such groups as the Moravian Brethren of our own time.

CONCLUSION

The men and movements discussed in this chapter are only a few of the dozens that might have been named. These were chosen because they typify some of the various reforming currents in the great stream of Western Christianity. Some of these currents remained within the Roman Church to purify it. Others were branded as heretical and were persecuted to extinction. Others blazed a trail for subsequent reformers. Still others persist, perhaps in modified form, to the present day. The activities of these reformers should remind us that God's Word has been a potent force in every age, calling men back to God and Christ.

QUESTIONS

1. Discuss the work of two of the monastic reformers.

2. How did the reforms advocated by the reforming sects differ from those advocated by the monastic reformers?

3. Which of the reforming sects still exist? In your opinion which of the reforming sects mentioned in this chapter most resembled the church of the New Testament? Why?

4. What reformer carried on a successful work in England? What was perhaps his greatest contribution to future reform efforts?

5. Discuss the trial and execution of John Hus.

CONTINENTAL REFORMATION 1517-1650

By the year 1500 the foundations of the old medieval society had been shaken. Soon thereafter these foundations began to crumble. Protestant historians laud the sixteenth century as one of the most important periods in the history of the church, and rightly so. But this period is no less important for Roman Catholics, for the sixteenth century saw lasting changes effected in the organization and doctrine of the Roman Catholic Church.

PRELUDE TO THE REFORMATION

The Protestant Reformation did not suddenly spring into existence without any antecedents. In the preceding chapter we noted a long history of reforming impulses that reached far back into the Middle Ages. In addition to these individual reformers and the movements they helped launch, many other factors were at work to help bring about changes within the church.

The Reforming Councils

A series of church councils in the first half of the fifteenth century sought to reform the church "root and branch" from within. The first of these met at Pisa in 1409. Seeking to heal the Great Schism, the council deposed the two conflicting popes and appointed a third in their place. But both of these popes refused to recognize the actions of the council and the new pope, and so the Roman Church was left with three men all claiming to be the legal successors of Peter.

The Council of Constance (1414-1418) finally succeeded in removing all three and appointing still another pope who soon gained wide recognition as the legitimate pope. This council attempted to combat heresy and carry out more thorough reforms in organization and doctrine. A serious effort was made to strengthen the power of the council and weaken the authority of the pope by providing frequent and regular council meetings. This council is best known for its condemnation and execution of John Hus. The other so-called reforming councils—Basel, Ferrara, and Florence —were not able to reform the church nor were they able to assert their authority over the pope. In fact, the irony of the reforming councils was that by healing the papal schism they succeeded in so strengthening the papacy that the conciliar movement for reform was weakened.

The Renaissance

Beginning about 1350, southern Europe began to experience a new concern for cultural and literary activities. We often refer to this as the Renaissance, a rebirth. Popularly we are likely to think of the Renaissance as a period during which the learning lost in the Dark Ages was regained. We have already seen that the later Middle Ages was a period of relatively high culture, and so it is not correct to think that the Renaissance brought a revival of learning. But it did bring a definite shift in the direction of man's interests. The Middle Ages were oriented toward religion; God was the measure of all things. But in the Renaissance men began to turn from God to man for his standards. The Renaissance view of man was individualistic and secular. We often speak of this as a humanistic view of life and the leaders of this movement are commonly referred to as humanists.

Beginning in Italy, this movement gradually spread northward. In Italy the movement was strongly secular. Among its leading figures were Petrarch and Boccacio. North of the Alps humanism took on a strong religious coloration, especially in the persons of such leaders as Desiderius Erasmus, John Colet, and Thomas More. An important factor in spreading humanism was the invention of movable type about 1450.

Nationalism

As the Middle Ages waned, the feudalism associated with the period began to break down. In Italy, never very completely feudalized anyway, powerful city-states emerged. But these were so jealous of their independence that Italy was not finally united until the latter part of the nineteenth century. In northwestern Europe a different political structure was developing—the nation-state. Binding together all people who spoke a common language or shared common traditions, the nation-states built strong central governments that were able to rule effectively over large areas. England, France, Spain, and Portugal had all succeeded in building strong central governments by 1500. These new nations were soon so powerful that they paid little heed to the pope—a far cry from the Middle Ages.

CAUSES OF THE REFORMATION

It is a serious misunderstanding of history to suppose that the Reformation sprang entirely from religious motives. But even though social, economic, and political causes played an important part in the origin and progress of the Reformation, one can still believe that its ultimate cause was God's providence.

The Roman Catholic View

Roman Catholics frequently refer to the Reformation as the Protestant "revolt." They look upon it as a revolt against the authority of the pope and the church and thus a revolt against God. Certainly it was a revolt against Rome, but it was a turning to God from the evils and corruption of the Roman system.

The Secularists' View

Secularists are likely to look upon the Reformation as a freeing of men's minds from domination by superstitions and religious authority. But they are quick to point out that the Reformation was but one step in this process.

Political motivation is likely to be strong in any movement as large as the Reformation. The rising power of the new nations in Western Europe and the many small German states caused them to seek independence from the international power of Rome. It is quite clear that several rulers of England and the various German states gave their backing to reformers as much out of political as out of religious motives. It is worth noting that the Reformation was initially successful only in those areas that were on the fringes of or beyond the borders of the old Roman Empire. This has led some to suggest that the Reformation was a revolt of Teutonic political thinking against Latin political thinking.

The current interest in economics will certainly require that we look at some of the economic motives back of the Reformation. By the time of the Reformation the church had acquired large holdings in land. Rulers and members of the rising middle class began to cast covetous eyes upon these holdings, and so we need not be surprised that much church property was confiscated in the early stages of the Reformation. Further, northern Europe resented the steady flow of gold from their lands to the coffers of the papacy.

Moral and Religious Motives

As learning became more prevalent across Europe and as the Bible and other religious matter became more available, men could see more clearly the glaring discrepancies between the church revealed in the Scriptures and the Roman Catholic Church. Many reformers before the sixteenth century had sought to bring these needed reforms. Some had attempted to bring moral reforms, others organizational reforms, still others theological reforms. But most of these attempts had been made within the framework of the Roman Church. It is conceivable that Luther's efforts might also have been contained within the church had not these other causes—political, economic, social—been operative.

The Immediate Cause of the Reformation

The spark that finally ignited the Reformation was the glaring abuse in the sale of indulgences in Germany. Pope Leo X, a member of the famous de Medici family, had embarked upon an elaborate building program in Rome, including St. Peter's. Since this program was quite expensive, the pope had authorized the sale of indulgences as a means of income. The practice of granting indulgences went far back into the

Middle Ages and was completely accepted in the church. But when Tetzel, a Dominican monk, came into Germany with a clever sales campaign in which he made exaggerated claims about indulgences, this was more than Martin Luther could stand. Thus on October 31, 1517, Luther posted on the door of the church at Wittenberg his famous Ninety-five Theses, challenging Tetzel.

THE REFORMATION IN GERMANY

Martin Luther

Behind every great movement in history stands at least one great personality. Certainly there were many leaders in the Reformation, but none occupies quite the place deserved by Luther. Born in Eisleben, Germany, in 1483, Luther was reared in a rather typical hard-working peasant home. After his early education, he attended the university at Erfurt. Here he earned the Master of Arts degree in 1505 and then turned to the study of law. But within a short time he entered a monastery and pledged himself to become an Augustinian monk.

It is clear that Luther was searching for an assurance that he was acceptable to God. His ordination as a priest in 1507 and his prayer, fasting, and mortification of his body still did not bring him the assurance he sought. He was sent on a trip to Rome on business for his order, but there the corruption of the clergy only further distressed him.

Not until he had been assigned to teach theology in the University of Wittenberg did the light finally begin to break upon him. His studies and lectures in Romans and Galatians led him to catch a new meaning in Romans 1:17: "The just shall live by faith." He began to realize that man cannot be saved by good works, but must trust God and find justification by faith. Armed with this conviction, Luther was certain to begin to oppose the use of indulgences and relics, which suggested that man could in some way earn salvation.

Luther's Break With Rome

Just as Luther was coming to these conclusions, Tetzel appeared in Germany with his indulgences. The Ninety-five Theses, which were propositions for discussion or debate, challenged the whole indulgence system. When word of the Theses reached Rome, the pope dismissed them as simply a debate among monks. But the Theses were printed and widely distributed and soon became a matter of public discussions. By this time the pope became concerned about the situation and demanded that Luther come to Rome to answer charges of heresy. Fortunately for Luther, he had the support of the Elector Frederick of Saxony, who was powerful enough to keep the pope from harming Luther.

By the force of circumstances and the nature of his opposition, Luther was gradually led to become ever more critical of the Roman Church. In 1520 he issued five tracts that stated his position and brought Rome under thorough indictment. As a result the pope issued a bull (official pronouncement) condemning many of Luther's teachings and demanding that he recant under threat of excommunication. Luther showed his contempt for the bull by burning it publicly in December 1520.

Cut off from the church and branded as a "wild boar," Luther, along with his followers who by this time were quite numerous, posed an increasingly serious problem to the secular rulers. In order to settle the question, Luther was summoned to the imperial Diet, which met in Worms in 1521. Supported by Frederick and several other German princes, Luther was encouraged to stand firmly before the Diet. When the Diet demanded that he recant his teachings, Luther affirmed that since his conscience was captive to the Word of God he would only recant if these teachings were proved false by the Word of God. He concluded his defense by affirming, "Here I stand. I cannot do otherwise. God help me."

Luther's actions led the Diet to condemn him as an outlaw and prohibit the circulation of his works. But in the meantime Luther had left Worms. On the way back to Wittenberg he was kidnapped by friendly hands and taken to the castle of Wartburg, where he remained in disguise for several months. These months in seclusion, however, were not wasted, for while at Wartburg he wrote several books and translated the New Testament into German. While this was not the first translation into German, it remains today as perhaps the most powerful and dignified German translation. During Luther's absence from Wittenberg, the revolution went on apace.

Upon his return Luther assumed the leadership of the movement and turned at once to the practical problems that beset the movement that was becoming a church. Abolishing the Mass, he made provisions for a worship service. He prepared a hymnal, himself writing some of the hymns ("A Mighty Fortress" is the best known of these). He also took steps to provide education for the people. Luther's concern about education was a logical corollary of his insistence upon the priesthood of all believers. If Christians could not read the Bible for themselves, their priesthood would be seriously compromised.

In many ways Luther was a conservative reformer who soon became impatient with those who carried his teachings to more radical conclusions. One example of this is seen in the Peasant's Revolt in 1525. Many of the peasants, applying revolutionary principles to the social order, began to make demands upon the nobles. When these demands were not met, the peasants rose in violent rebellion. They would not be placated, and as a result Luther turned against them. Yet Luther himself was considered too radical by many who at first sympathized with his efforts. Erasmus, for example, at first approved of Luther's criticism of Rome, but Luther's violent and abusive language soon proved offensive to Erasmus. Luther's uncompromising position in regard to the Lord's Supper also prevented any sort of united action between Lutherans and the Swiss reformers. General agreement between the two groups was reached at a colloquy at Marburg in 1529, but Luther's insistence on Christ's real presence in the Lord's Supper kept the two groups apart. Unity between the German and Swiss reformers at this time might have allowed them to present a united front against Rome.

From the Diet of Augsburg to the Peace of Augsburg

The growing tensions in Germany in the 1520's seemed a certain prelude to violence. Fortunately for the reformers, the Empire was being threatened by the Turks who were invading from the east. But by 1529 the Catholic forces in the Empire were able to use their majority in the imperial Diet to hamper the growth of Lutheranism. This Diet, meeting in Speyer, ordered that no further changes be made in the religious status. Catholics in Lutheran territories were to be granted freedom of worship, while the same privilege was denied Lutherans in Catholic territories in the Empire. The Lutheran princes, finding this order unacceptable, filed a formal protest against it. From this came the name "Protestant," which eventually was applied to all those in the West who broke with Rome.

The following year the Diet met at Augsburg. At this meeting Charles V, who had only recently been crowned emperor, attempted to seek a means of restoring religious liberty to his empire. The Lutheran position was defended very ably by Philip Melancthon, a young colleague of Luther. This document, known as the Augsburg Confession, remains to this day an important creedal statement among Lutherans. Other Protestant groups were present and set forth their positions separately. But the Protestant position was unacceptable to the Catholics and no agreement could be reached. As a result, for the next twenty-five years hostilities, intrigues, and even open warfare continued between Protestants and Catholics in Germany. Before this period of bitterness ended, Luther died (1546) and the leadership of the movement he had started fell to others.

In 1555 the Diet, again meeting at Augsburg, came to a settlement that allowed Germany to have a long but uneasy truce from these religious wars. The so-called Peace of Augsburg provided that the princes of Germany would determine the religion of their realms. No prince was to disturb the religion of another territory. If on religious grounds a person wanted to move from one area to another, he was to be allowed to sell his property and move. This agreement pretty well set the religious geography of Germany, and its effects are ones evident even today. Northern Germany is largely Lutheran; southern Germany is Catholic. But this Peace of Augsburg made no provision for anything but Lutheran Protestantism. Calvinism, which soon became an aggressive force, threatened to upset the agreement, especially in the Rhineland.

Lutheranism in the Rest of Europe

Lutheranism spread rapidly northward from Germany into Scandinavia. In most cases the rulers accepted the new faith and then it spread among the people. Within a generation or so Denmark, Norway, and Sweden, along with Iceland, Finland, and the eastern Baltic regions, had become Lutheran.

Lutheranism made some inroads in Poland, but it was more successful in Bohemia and Hungary. However, the Counter-Reformation and later religious wars decimated Protestantism in these areas. The writings of Luther circulated widely and influenced thinking even where they did not win large numbers of converts. Luther's writings were popular in the Low Countries and in Great Britain, in France, and some places in Italy, especially Venice.

THE REFORMATION IN SWITZERLAND

Zwingli and Zurich

About the same time that Luther was beginning his attacks on the abuses of Rome, a Swiss contemporary, Huldreich Zwingli (1484-1531), was beginning to raise similar protests in Switzerland. Educated at the University of Basel, Zwingli became a parish priest. Apparently he soon began to have misgivings about some of the religious practices of his day, but his real work as a reformer did not begin until he had been called to be pastor at Zurich in 1519. Using the Bible as his guide, he began to challenge openly many of the teachings of Rome. The people seemed ready to follow him and by 1525 the reforming process in Zurich was practically completed.

Luther, as we have noted, was a conservative reformer who retained many Roman practices that were not specifically condemned by Scripture. Zwingli, however, was more thoroughgoing. While he was far from consistent in his practices, he was much more concerned about returning to the pristine apostolic church. Luther, for example, took a view of the Lord's Supper that stressed Christ's presence in an almost Roman Catholic fashion. For Zwingli the Lord's Supper was essentially a memorial.

The reforms begun at Zurich spread to other cities in Switzerland, and soon much of the mountainous little country was in revolt against Rome. However, not every canton accepted the new faith, and violence broke out. While serving as a chaplain in one of these wars, Zwingli was killed; but several other leaders were ready to take his place.

Calvin and Geneva

The outstanding leader of Swiss Protestantism after the death of Zwingli was John Calvin. Born in France in 1509, he was a precocious lad, and was so able in his studies that he entered the University of Paris when only fourteen. Like Luther before him, he began the study of law, but his earnest religious convictions turned him toward religion. He soon found himself at variance with Roman Catholic authorities. Leaving France, he found refuge in Basel, Switzerland. Here at the age of twenty-six he published what was the most scholarly and perhaps influential book of the whole Reformation period—*The Institutes of the Christian Religion.*

Calvin was soon invited to Geneva to lead the Reformation there. Along with Farel he worked to make the city a model community, but his unwillingness to compromise many practical issues led to his banishment. This time he found a haven in Strassburg, where he ministered to a French-speaking Protestant church. Then the political climate of Geneva changed and Calvin was invited to return, which he did in 1541. For nearly twenty-five years Calvin was the dominant figure in that city, which became a virtual theocracy, patterned after the Old Testament theocracy.

Geneva under Calvin became a stern and strait-laced community. Excess in food and drink and frivolity in speech and habit were punishable by law. Nor were significant differences in doctrine tolerated. Michael Servetus, for instance, who refused to accept the doctrine of the Trinity, was burned at the stake, and several others were burned as witches.

But Calvinism was far more than a series of stern negatives. It had within it a dynamic force that soon made it a challenge to all of Europe. Luther stressed God's grace and salvation by faith only. Calvin, who borrowed heavily from the theology of Augustine, stressed God's sovereignty and man's election. Going beyond Augustine, Calvin taught double predestination: the elect have been predestined to salvation, and the non-elect to damnation.

Students from all over Western Europe came to Geneva to sit at Calvin's feet; then, inspired by his teaching, they returned to their native lands to spread Calvinism. Thus it was that Calvinistic churches (often referred to as Reformed churches) appeared in Germany, the Netherlands, France, and central Europe. Through John Knox and others, Calvinism spread to Scotland, where it was embodied in the Presbyterian Church. Calvinism also appeared in England where it gave rise to Puritanism. From England and Scotland Calvinism was transplanted to the New World where it has played a very important part in the development of America.

OTHER ASPECTS OF THE REFORMATION

France and the Low Countries

A further word must be said about the spread of Protestantism into these countries. While the teachings of Luther were circulated in France, it vas Calvinism that took root there. The strategic location of Geneva, along with the fact that Calvin was French, no doubt contributed greatly to the success of Calvinism in France. During the second half of the sixteenth century French Protestants (called Huguenots) fought a series of bloody civil wars with the Catholics. Perhaps the most notorious event of these Wars of Religion, as they are called, was the infamous St. Bartholomew's Day Massacre in 1572. As many as two thousand Huguenots who were gathered in Paris were treacherously slain by Roman Catholics, and perhaps twenty thousand more were killed as the slaughter spread to the provinces. Yet Protestantism was not wiped out. In 1594 Henry of Navarre, who had been reared a Protestant, became king of France. In order to receive the throne he became a nominal Catholic, but he brought an end to the bloody wars and granted many rights to the Huguenots.

If anything, the Reformed faith had an even more severe test in the Netherlands. Lutheranism spread early into the Low Countries, which included what is now Belgium and the Netherlands. While this area was controlled by Emperor Charles V, he was so busy fighting Protestantism in Germany that he tended to be lenient toward the Low Countries. When Charles V retired, his realm was divided and the Netherlands fell under the control of his son, Philip II, who also ruled Spain. Philip was not inclined to be tolerant and he sent strong Spanish forces into the Netherlands to crush Protestantism. Thousands were slain, but Dutch Protestantism (now in the form of Calvinism) continued to grow. William of Orange became the famous leader of the Dutch resistance. He was eventually assassinated by a Jesuit priest, but the Dutch continued their struggle until in 1609 their independence was recognized. The "Dutch Reformed Church," Calvinistic in doctrine, became the state church in the Netherlands.

The "Radical" Reformers

In addition to the three major wings of the Reformation—Lutheran, Reformed, and Anglican (which we will study in the next chapter)—there were other reformers often collectively referred to as radical reformers or "left-wing" reformers.

The Anabaptists were the most numerous of these radical reformers. The Anabaptists received their name from the fact that since they insisted on the baptism of believers only, they re-baptized those whose only baptism had been in infancy. The Anabaptists were a varied lot, and because of the excesses of a few of them, they early got a bad name and were persecuted by Protestant and Catholic alike. Anabaptists practiced believers' baptism and often they practiced baptism by immersion. They believed in the separation of church and state and ordinarily refused to bear arms or serve in public office.

The largest group of Anabaptists to survive persecutions was the Mennonites. Their leader was Menno Simons, who had been a Catholic priest in the Low Countries. In 1536 he renounced his priesthood and cast his lot with the Anabaptists. Through his teaching and writing the movement spread widely. Anabaptists were also numerous in Switzerland, where they were vigorously opposed by Zwingli, in the German Rhineland, and in Moravia. Many later groups such as Baptists, English Separatists, Quakers, and German Brethren were no doubt influenced by these simple, pious people.

The Catholic Counter Reformation

Not everyone who sought to reform the Roman Catholic Church in the sixteenth century broke with Rome. Many remained in the church to try to purify it from within. The Council of Trent was called in 1545, and held sessions for the next eighteen years. In part this council took measures to counter Protestantism, but it also took steps to bring about reform. Unfortunately, the Council of Trent so defined many dogmas that the rift between Catholicism and Protestantism was widened and made permanent.

This period also gave birth to a Catholic order that soon became the most powerful in the church—the Society of Jesus, or the Jesuits. Its founder was Ignatius Loyola, a Spaniard, whose conversion led him to obedience to the Church rather than reform. Interestingly, both Calvin and Loyola were students at the University of Paris at the same time, but apparently never knew each other. The Jesuit order was given official papal approval in 1540 and it grew very rapidly. Its influence was strongly felt in the closing sessions of the Council of Trent and upon the papacy itself. As a missionary order the Jesuits rivaled the zeal of the Franciscans. Francis Xavier, the most famous missionary of this period, did missionary work in India, Japan, and other areas of the Far East. The Jesuits also soon challenged the Dominicans as scholars. But they rendered their greatest service to Rome as shock troops of the pope. In many areas, notably Poland and central Europe, they succeeded in rolling back the Reformation. In later centuries they became so powerful that they were finally curbed by the papacy, but that is another story.

CONCLUSION

The Protestant Reformation is so important in the history of the church that one has difficulty summarizing a chapter covering this period. Perhaps we can best do this by stating three fundamental principles of the Reformation: (1) Justification is by faith and not by works; (2) The Bible is the ultimate source of authority; (3) Every believer is a priest.

QUESTIONS

1. Discuss some of the factors that contributed to the rise of the Protestant Reformation. Do these factors help explain why Luther succeeded where Hus failed?

2. What was the immediate occasion that sparked Luther's opposition to the Roman Church?

3. Compare and contrast the reforming efforts of Luther and Zwingli.

4. Why did the German and Swiss reformers not unite against Rome?

5. From Germany into what other areas did Lutheranism spread?

6. After the death of Zwingli, who became the great leader of the Swiss Reformation?

7. Discuss the response of Roman Catholicism to the Protestant Reformation.

8. Who were the "radical" reformers? What groups today are among their spiritual descendants?

ENGLISH REFORMATION

As important as was the continental Reformation, the Reformation in the British Isles has even greater significance for most American Protestants. Indeed, it is impossible to understand American Protestantism without some knowledge of the English Reformation. Although the English Reformation procceded along lines peculiar to itself, yet it shared many things in common with the continental Reformation.

CAUSES OF THE BRITISH REFORMATION

Pre-Reformation Activity

We have seen that the Reformation did not suddenly appear on the continent without any preparation or warning. Nor, for that matter, did it in Britain. In an earlier chapter we have mentioned the work of Wycliffe and his followers, the Lollards. Although the Lollards were opposed and even persecuted, their emphasis upon the Bible and personal religion was never lost.

The Intellectual Preparation

As the sixteenth century opened, a good deal of intellectual ferment was taking place in the English universities, Cambridge and especially Oxford. John Colet and Thomas More, along with Erasmus, who had been invited to England, were prominent leaders in this movement. William Tyndale and Miles Coverdale were active in translating the Bible into English and distributing it. Tyndale was later martyred for his efforts, but the work of the Scriptures in arousing men against the corruptions of Rome went on.

Henry VIII

The immediate occasion for the beginning of the English Reformation, but by no means the basic cause, was the desire of Henry VIII to divorce his wife, Catherine. She had been married first to Arthur, Henry's brother, but Arthur had died a few months after the marriage. For political reasons Henry had then been betrothed to her. Since it was a violation of canon law for a man to marry his brother's widow, Henry needed a papal dispensation in order to marry her. The dispensation was granted and Henry was eventually married to Catherine. Several children were born to this union, but only one of them, a daughter, survived. Henry, who desperately desired a male heir, began to feel that God disapproved of his marriage. This feeling was intensified, no doubt, by his growing attraction to Anne Boleyn.

Thus after twenty years of marriage to Catherine, Henry appealed to the pope for an annulment. Had the political situation been different, Henry probably would have gained his desired annulment. But the pope could scarcely afford to offend Catherine's nephew, the powerful Emperor Charles V, and so no annulment was granted. Henry then turned to Parliament, which in 1533 declared that the Church of England was competent to judge the case itself. Henry was immediately granted the divorce by Archbishop Cranmer. As a result of this action the pope excommunicated Henry. To complete the breach between the Church of England and Rome, Parliament took steps to make Henry the head of the English Church.

THE ENGLISH REFORMATION UNDER HENRY

Response to Henry's Action

Some protested against Henry's action, a few so strenuously that Henry had them executed. Among those executed were Thomas More, the humanist scholar whose work in some ways had anticipated the

English Reformation. Many accepted the break with Rome with enthusiasm, and the rest acquiesced with little protest.

A Conservative Reformation

Under Henry a violent theological reaction against Rome did not occur. For one thing, Henry was shrewd enough politically to avoid radical actions that would prove offensive to any large number of his subjects. In 1536 a theological statement, the Ten Articles, was issued. It was certainly not a radically Protestant document, for it retained such things as masses for the dead, the use of images, and the invocation of the saints. Three years later Parliament passed the Six Articles, which were even more conservative, for they advocated transubstantiation. During this period the Church of England was so conservative that some advocating the more radical ideals of Zwingli and Luther were persecuted.

But in spite of this very conservative approach to reform, Henry did take two actions that looked more distinctly Protestant. First of all, the monasteries were dissolved. Henry's motives were definitely open to question in this action, for most of the wealth of the monasteries was confiscated and went to the royal coffers or to Henry's favorites. At the same time, it should be noted that this action was not at all unpopular with the people, who had grown resentful of the monasteries. The other distinctly Protestant action during Henry's reign was the publication of the Bible in English. Just a few years before, Tyndale's translation was smuggled into England and circulated secretly. Tyndale was eventually martyred on the continent, but, ironically, his translation, which had been so much opposed by the authorities, became the basis, in part at least, for the Coverdale Bible and the Great Bible that were approved by the authorities.

CONTINUED REFORMATION AND REACTION

The Reformation Continues Under Edward I

Henry did not solve his marital problems by disposing of Catherine and marrying Anne Boleyn. Anne bore him a daughter,

Elizabeth, but Henry soon tired of Anne and she was executed for infidelity, in all likelihood a trumped-up charge. Henry's third wife, Jane Seymour, bore him the son he had so desperately wanted. It was this son, Edward, who came to the throne at Henry's death in 1547. A precocious but physically frail lad, Edward was less than ten years old at the time. Since he was a minor, the actual decisions of state were made by a series of regents.

These regents reflected Edward's Protestant sympathies, and as a result England moved toward a more definitely Protestant position. The Catholic-flavored Six Articles were rescinded, images were removed from the churches, and restrictions on circulating the Bible were removed. Under Archbishop Cranmer the Book of Common Prayer was issued. The Prayer Book and its later revisions, which turned definitely away from many Roman practices and terms, remains today as the guide to worship in the Church of England. Cranmer was also largely responsible for formulating the Forty-two Articles (later to become the Thirty-nine Articles) which set forth the doctrinal position of the Church of England. All of these actions served to bring the English Reformation closer to the position occupied by the continental reformers. On the whole, the English people seemed ready to follow their monarch in these moves.

The Reaction Under Mary

Edward, who was never strong, died before he reached his sixteenth birthday. This brought Mary, the daughter of Catherine of Aragon, to the throne in 1553. Rigidly Catholic in her convictions, Mary soon made efforts to return England to the Roman fold. This was accomplished in 1554 when the realm was received back into the communion of the Roman Catholic Church. Mary was in the meantime married to her cousin, Philip, who was soon to become Philip II of Spain. This union with Catholic Spain seemed certain to ensure that England would remain Catholic.

Many opposed this return to Catholicism. In order to break the opposition, about 300 were executed. Although Mary was not personally cruel, these executions earned her the nickname "Bloody Mary." Among the most famous of the victims were the theologians

Latimer and Ridley and Archbishop Cranmer, all of whom were executed at Oxford. Latimer is reputed to have said at the stake, "Be of good cheer, Master Ridley, we shall this day light such a candle by God's grace in England as, I trust, shall never be put out."

Protestantism Returns Under Elizabeth

Fortunately for the Protestant cause in England, Mary's reign lasted only five years. She was succeeded in 1558 by her half-sister, the famous Elizabeth I, whose long reign lasted until 1603. Under Elizabeth the church in England once more turned toward Protestantism. It must be acknowledged, however, that in her actions Elizabeth was motivated more by political concern than by deep religious motives. By the Act of Supremacy in 1559 the authority of the pope in the Church of England was denied and Elizabeth was made "Supreme Governor" of the realm, which included spiritual as well as secular things. Later the Thirty-nine Articles were issued as a definition of the doctrinal position of the Anglican Church.

Elizabeth's middle way between vigorous Protestantism on the one hand and Roman Catholicism on the other was generally acceptable to the English people. As a result, during her long reign England was spared the bitter religious wars that plagued the continent during much of this period. Elizabeth had problems, however. Some Roman Catholics, unwilling to accept this arrangement, plotted against Elizabeth. Aided by Jesuits, they hoped to put the Catholic Mary Stuart, "Queen of Scots," on the English throne. This led Elizabeth to imprison Mary in the Tower of London and eventually execute her.

Elizabeth had foreign problems too. Philip II of Spain had hoped that Elizabeth would marry him and thus keep England closely tied to Spain. Elizabeth skillfully postponed the fulfillment of these hopes without destroying them. She knew that if England were to become powerful, she could not be kept tied to Spain; yet Elizabeth also knew that England was not yet strong enough to challenge Spain. When Philip finally realized that Elizabeth was not going to marry him, he sent his famous Armada against England.

Long before the end of Elizabeth's reign those who sought to make the Church of England more Protestant became numerous.

Because they sought to purify the church from all traces of Romanism, they became known as Puritans. They objected to the vestments required for the clergy and to any acts in the observance of the Lord's Supper that might suggest the bodily presence of Christ. Many also felt that the episcopal form of church government was foreign to the Bible and desired the presbyterian form instead. On the whole, the Puritans were more influenced by the theology of Calvin and the Rhineland cities than by the theology of Luther. Still more radical were the Separatists or Independents. They broke completely with the Church of England and formed independent congregations. The famous Pilgrims of the early seventeenth century were Separatists. The origins of the English Baptists and Congregationalists may be found among some of these Separatists.

THE REFORMATION IN SCOTLAND

We will do well at this point to interrupt the account of the English Reformation and look northward to what was happening in Scotland, which until 1603 was a separate realm. Although Scotland was independent, it had, because of marriages between the French and Scottish royal families, become connected with France. Many Scots had come to resent and fear this alliance with France.

The Beginnings of Reform in Scotland

At the beginning of the sixteenth century Scotland was torn by political strife, and immorality and lawlessness were commonplace. Although the nation was nominally Catholic, most of its people could hardly be called devout. With the advent of the continental Reformation, the writings of Luther began to circulate in Scotland. Soon a few men began to preach some of the doctrines of the Reformation.

John Knox and the Scottish Reformation

John Knox was to the Scottish Reformation what Luther was to the German Reformation. Born sometime between 1505 and 1515, Knox was educated in a Scottish university and was ordained a priest. He became a disciple of George Wishart, and in the turmoil that followed the murder of Cardinal Beaton, he was seized by the French. He spent a year and a half as a galley prisoner before he was finally released. Unable to return to Scotland, he went to England where the Reformation was gaining ground under the reign of Edward I. But when Mary came to the throne, he fled to the continent. Eventually he made his way to Geneva, where he came under the influence of Calvin.

In the meantime, the Reformation in Scotland was making progress. The nominal ruler of Scotland was Mary Stuart, "Queen of Scots," but she was only a few days old when her father died leaving the throne to her. During her childhood she was sent to France for her education while her mother served as regent. In 1558 Mary, when sixteen, was married to a French prince. The unpopularity of Mary's mother, along with the prospect of Scotland being tied more closely than ever to France, made the people more willing to listen to the reformers.

Knox returned to Scotland for a few months in 1555, and even though he was forced to leave again, he was looked to for leadership by Scottish reformers. In 1557 some of the nobility banded themselves together in a covenant to carry out reform and oust the French. In the civil war that followed, the Scottish reformers were given aid by Elizabeth of England. By the end of 1560 it seemed that the reformers had won.

But in the meantime Mary's husband, Francis II of France, died and Mary returned to Scotland. Staunchly Catholic, she was determined to return her realm to the Catholic fold. Some of the most dramatic moments of the Scottish Reformation came in a series of confrontations between the stern and rugged Knox and the determined and attractive young queen. Mary might have been able to carry the day, or at least work out a compromise, had she conducted herself well. But her private love life was so scandalous that she lost the support of the people. Eventually (1567) she was forced to flee to England for refuge, leaving her infant son who became James VI of Scotland.

Under John Knox the Scottish Reformation continued apace, becoming much more Protestant than the Reformation going on in England at the same time. For one thing, the influence of Calvin was strong. The Scottish Church, although it was an established church (that is, supported by the state), enjoyed much greater freedom from the state than did the English church. In its form of church government the Scottish church became presbyterian. As important as all this was, the influence of John Knox, who died in 1572, reached far beyond Scotland. American Presbyterianism, one of the major Protestant families in this country, owes in part its origins to John Knox and his stalwart band of followers.

THE ENGLISH REFORMATION
UNDER THE STUARTS

With Elizabeth's death in 1603 the English house of Tudor came to an end. Since a daughter of the Tudor Henry VII had married into the Stuarts (the ruling dynasty of Scotland), James VI, the king of Scotland, had a tenuous claim to the throne of England. Thus it was that James VI of Scotland became James I of England. The two countries were not united at this time; they simply shared the same ruler.

England Under James I

The Puritans in England anticipated that the coming of James would benefit their cause, for James had been reared as a Scottish Presbyterian. But they were doomed to disappointment, for James favored the episcopal form of church government, since it seemed more in keeping with the theory of the divine right of kings, which he cherished. In 1603 as James was on his way to London he was presented with the Millenary Petition, which asked for further reforms in the English Church. Early in 1604 a conference of bishops and Puritans met with James at Hampton Court. He made it quite clear that he had no truck with the Puritans by threatening to "harry them out of the land or worse" if they did not conform. The most important thing to come out of this conference was James's consent for a new translation of the Bible into English. This new translation, published in 1611, and known as the Authorized or King James Version, became the most widely circulated English Bible in history.

Roman Catholics did not fare any better than the Puritans under James. Restrictions against Roman Catholics led to the infamous

Gunpowder Plot in 1605. A few fanatical Roman Catholics placed several barrels of gunpowder under the Parliament building, hoping to destroy James and Parliament with him. Authorities were warned just in time to prevent the disaster. This plot led to further restrictions against Catholics.

England Under Charles I

James's successor on the thrones of England and Scotland was Charles I, who became king in 1625. Under James the Puritans had grown in strength until they were a major power in Parliament. Charles, who believed even more strongly than did his father in the divine right of kings, simply could not cope with this hostile Parliament. Finally in 1629 he dismissed Parliament and attempted to rule without it until 1640. to further enrage the Puritans he appointed William Laud to be Archbishop of Canterbury. Laud was a high-handed Anglican who insisted that the Puritans conform to the Prayer Book. During this period as many as twenty thousand Puritans emigrated to America.

Perhaps Charles's most serious error was in attempting to force the episcopal form of church government and the Prayer Book on Presbyterian Scotland. The Scots rebelled, and in order to raise money to carry on the war against them, Charles was forced to call Parliament back into session. By this time Parliament had become even more strongly Puritan, and soon civil war broke between the forces of the king (called Cavaliers) and the forces of Parliament (called Roundheads).

England Under the Protestant Radicals

The Parliamentary forces, ably led by Oliver Cromwell, finally defeated the king's forces. The triumph of Parliament led to a power vacuum into which Cromwell stepped as virtual dictator. In 1649 Charles was condemned and beheaded. This action sent a shock of horror through Europe and caused the Cromwellian forces to be considered more radical than they really were. As a matter of fact, England enjoyed greater religious freedom under Cromwell than it had ever known before. Almost all religious groups, including Roman Catholics, were permitted to worship according to their consciences so long as they did not disturb the public peace. One exception was the Friends or Quakers, a group that had been founded by George Fox in 1647.

Once in power Cromwell and the Puritans attempted to reform the moral life of the realm. The theater, which had become terribly corrupt, was abolished, and many worldly sports, encouraged under James and Charles, were banned. Some, perhaps, hoped to convert England into a theocracy much as Calvin had done at Geneva. But such was not to be. England was so politically and religiously divided that it needed a firm hand to prevent chaos. When Cromwell died in 1658, that firm hand was lost. His son attempted to carry on, but he was no match for the problem. Finally in 1660 the son of Charles I was returned from exile and crowned Charles II. The return of a Stuart to the throne of England meant a return to Anglicanism and an end, at least temporarily, of many of the freedoms granted under Cromwell.

CONCLUSION

As we have seen, the Reformation in England and Scotland proceeded differently than it did on the continent. The Reformation came to Scotland late, but when it finally arrived, it came quickly and rather completely. In England, on the other hand, the reforming efforts swung back and forth like a pendulum. Under Henry the Reformation was very conservative; it became more decisively Protestant under Edward I; then came the return to Catholicism under Mary. Under Elizabeth, Protestantism returned, with Puritanism becoming quite pronounced by the end of her reign. The Stuarts, James I and Charles I, had little sympathy with the Puritans and finally drove them to open rebellion. This led to the brief triumph of radical Protestantism under Cromwell, but the unpopularity of the Cromwellian regime led to the return of the Stuarts and the reinstatement of Anglicanism.

QUESTIONS

1. Discuss the immediate occasion that brought on the English Reformation.

2. Discuss how the changing of monarchs in England led to changing emphases in reform.

3. Who was the great leader of the Scottish Reformation? Under what great Reformer did he study?

4. Who were the Puritans? Distinguish between the Puritans and the Separatists.

5. Discuss religion under the rule of the Stuarts.

6. Who was Oliver Cromwell?

CHRISTIANITY IN THE SEVENTEENTH AND EIGHTEENTH CENTURIES

The great religious upheavals of the sixteenth century have proved to be a watershed in the history of the church. The religious unity that Western Europe had known through the Middle Ages was shattered by the Protestant Reformation. One church had become many churches. The history of the church in the seventeenth and eighteenth centuries must deal in a large part with the struggles of these many churches (or denominations) to adjust themselves to the situation in which no one church could assert its predominance.

THE THIRTY YEARS' WAR

Unfortunately the efforts of the churches to establish some sort of balance of power led to wholesale bloodshed. Even the fratricidal religious wars of the sixteenth century did not equal the violence of the religious struggles of the first half of the seventeenth century. In the previous chapter we have already told about the civil war that convulsed England. Now we turn to the series of conflicts on the continent that is referred to as the Thirty Years' War.

The Background of the War

The Peace of Augsburg of 1555 had brought an uneasy truce to the religious wars in Germany that came in the wake of the Reformation. But the Peace of Augsburg was a truce between Catholicism and Lutheranism, not a permanent settlement. It established the principle that the religion of the ruler was to be the religion of the people. But this arrangement did not make adequate provision for the consciences of the people. Nor did it consider the rise of Calvinism. Calvinism had spread into areas covered by the agreement, but under the terms of the agreement Calvinists had no legal status. A further unsettling factor was the aggressive effort of the Jesuits to win Protestants back to the Catholic faith. Through intrigue and behind-the-scenes maneuvers, the Jesuits had by 1600 come to exercise considerable influence on the political scene.

The Thirty Years' War was really a series of conflicts: the Bohemian phase, 1618-1624; the Danish phase, 1625-1629; the Swedish phase, 1630-1635; and the French phase, 1635-1648. While religion was certainly an important motive in the Thirty Years' War, it was not the only motive involved. Other motives were the desire of the Hapsburgs, rulers of the Holy Roman Empire, to achieve political unity within their domains, and the desire of Denmark, Sweden, and France to enlarge their territory at the expense of the Empire.

As it became increasingly apparent that the Peace of Augsburg could not be maintained indefinitely, both Protestants and Catholics formed defensive alliances. In 1608 Protestant rulers formed the Evangelical Union, and the following year the followers of the pope created the Catholic League. As the lines hardened, the situation became increasingly tense until only a spark was needed to set off the explosive forces of war.

The Course of the War

The spark was provided when Protestants of Bohemia refused to accept a Catholic ruler and chose instead a Protestant. Emperor Ferdinand, determined to maintain a Catholic ruler on the Bohemian throne, sent his forces against the Bohemian Protestants. Once the Protestants were defeated, he began a ruthless effort to eradicate Protestantism from Bohemia. He also directed an attack against some of the Protestant states in the Rhineland that had supported the Bohemian Protestants.

The success of the Catholics alarmed northern Germany and Denmark, which was outside the Empire. As a result, King Christian

IV of Denmark and Norway entered the war on the Protestant side. But the Danish forces were soon overwhelmed and much of northern Germany was overrun or threatened by the victorious Catholic armies. In the wake of their victory the Catholics made stringent demands upon the Protestants.

The Catholics might have made their victory almost complete had they not been divided among themselves and had not other forces entered the picture. In 1630, Gustavus Adolphus, the staunchly Lutheran king of Sweden, invaded northern Germany and drove out the Hapsburgs. But many Protestants in Germany were unenthusiastic about this help from Sweden, for they rightly feared that Adolphus wanted to make the Baltic Sea a Swedish lake. Adolphus won several victories over the Catholics, but he was killed in battle in 1632. Without his able leadership, the Swedes were unable to make further gains, and a stalemate followed.

The fourth and final stage of the war came when France broke the stalemate in 1635. France, motivated by a desire for territory and a desire to protect herself against the Empire, entered the fray on the Protestant side. The fact that France was Catholic illustrates as well as anything that motives other than religious often prevailed. The long struggle was finally concluded in 1648 by the Peace of Westphalia, one of the great peace settlements in modern European history.

Results of the War

Since neither side won a clear-cut victory, the Peace of Westphalia was a compromise settlement. It was agreed that the areas that were Catholic in 1624 would remain Catholic and the areas that were Protestant as of that date would remain Protestant. The independence of the Netherlands and Switzerland was finally given formal recognition. Brandenburg, which later emerged as an important power in Germany, gained some important territories. Calvinists were finally granted recognition.

The compromise thus worked out seemed to be a fairly successful one, for the boundaries fixed between Protestantism and Catholicism have with some minor exceptions prevailed until today. But the war was a terribly costly one, not only in the loss of lives and property, but in lowered morality and vigor. Some German states, across which the contending armies marched for thirty years, lost half or more of their population. The war so demoralized the people that it took some areas perhaps a hundred years to recover from its effects. Whatever else the results of the Thirty Years' War may have been, it did teach one dreadful lesson: religious differences within Christendom ought not to be settled by physical violence. And apparently this lesson has been learned, for since the Peace of Westphalia, nations have not been willing to go to war over religion.

RATIONALISM AND REVIVALISM

The growing religious toleration that has marked the course of modern church history is not the result of brotherly love and respect for individual integrity alone. In a large measure this toleration is the result of religious indifference. As the fervor of one's convictions diminish, so also does the zeal to impress those convictions upon others.

The Changing Intellectual Climate

In the modern age man has grown ever more confident of his own abilities. As a result he feels that he has less need for God and less need for religion. This changing attitude really began in the Renaissance, long before the Reformation. The Renaissance humanists turned their emphasis from the things of God to the things of man, and most of them did so without consciously feeling that they were repudiating religion. But they were sowing the seeds that in later centuries did lead to this.

The Deists

Modern science had some of its important roots in the seventeenth and eighteenth centuries. Francis Bacon and Descartes laid the philosophical groundwork for the empirical, or scientific, method. Galileo, building upon the earlier work of Copernicus, challenged the dogma that the earth is the center of the universe. Later Isaac Newton worked out careful formulas that seemed to indicate that the universe was a complicated machine that operated in accordance with certain unchanging laws.

It was not long before some men began to assert that one could apply reason and the empirical method to work out a natural religion that had no need for revelation. The god envisioned by these rationalists was often likened to a watchmaker who had made a wonderfully complicated watch, made the laws that governed its workings, wound the watch up and set it in motion, and left it to run and eventually run down. Persons who held this view of religion came to be called "deists."

Since, according to the deists, God had left His creation once He had created it, there could be no such things as miracles or revelation. To them Christ was no more than a great teacher and an example of morality. On the whole, persons attracted to deism were of the educated, urbane classes. Their faith lacked the glowing fervor of dedicated Christians, but this lack of fervor was in part balanced by a spirit of toleration that was often lacking among evangelical Christians of that period. In fairness to the deists it must be acknowledged that their opposition to intolerance and bigotry helped cool the fires of bitter religious antagonism. Deists were often active in reform movements of that period. Many deists were also active in creating and implementing the new political philosophies that were arising in the seventeenth and eighteenth centuries. It is perhaps no accident that three of the outstanding spokesmen of the American Revolution—Thomas Jefferson, Thomas Paine, and Benjamin Franklin—all held to some form of deism.

Deism left a definite mark on the thinking of Christians of this period. Many who retained their faith in Christianity, including some of the prominent theologians of the period, reflected something of the same rationalistic approach to religion seen in the deists. Joseph Butler, for example, in his famous *Analogy of Religion* (1736) showed that the rational arguments used to disprove the existence of God could also be used to prove His existence. The unfortunate thing was that this rationalistic approach to Christianity, as helpful as it may have been to some, often robbed the faithful of their zeal. Religious persecution and intolerance were on the wane, but unfortunately, so was the living, pulsating faith that warmed the hearts of men.

The Revival in Great Britain

If you have read this far in this book, you are well aware by now that a lifeless or immoral church is the seedbed for revival. Such was the case in the eighteenth century. Many men labored in Great Britain to fan into flame the dying embers of faith, but no man played a more important part in this revival than did John Wesley. Born into the home of an Anglican minister in 1709, John was the fifteenth child in a family of nineteen. He was educated for the Anglican ministry at Oxford University, where he, along with his brother Charles, was active in a student group that sought a more spiritual life. This group was sometimes referred to by others as the "Holy Club" or the "Bible moths." Because of their methodical prayer life and Bible study they became known as "Methodists," a name that eventually stuck.

John Wesley was ordained to the Anglican ministry and came in 1735 to serve in the newly founded colony of Georgia. But his strictness and rigidity proved unacceptable to many of the colonists, and he returned to England in 1738. This trip to the New World was a memorable one, for on the voyage to Georgia his ship was caught in a severe storm. Wesley, in spite of his deep faith, was frightened, but a group of Moravian Brethren, coming to America as colonists, calmly sang hymns in the midst of the gale. This left such an impression on Wesley that he had many other contacts with these simple, pious people.

Soon after his return to England, Wesley was in a meeting where the preface to Luther's *Commentary on Romans* was being read. Wesley later reported that during the meeting his heart was "strangely warmed," and from that time on he trusted in Christ alone for his salvation. Other important influences bore upon Wesley's life. George Whitefield, a great English evangelist of the period, often preached to men on street corners or in fields. Wesley, who still held strongly to the importance of proper ritual in worship, was hesitant about such methods of preaching to men. But eventually he was led to follow Whitefield's example, and the results, of course, are well known. It is reported that Wesley traveled nearly 250,000 miles on horseback, preached nearly 42,000 sermons, and wrote more than fifty books.

Wherever he went, Wesley established Methodist societies— groups that met together to study and worship. Wesley himself lived and died within the Anglican Church, and he had no intention of starting a new church. His aim was to revitalize the faith of his church by revival from within. But like so many reforming movements in the past, these Methodist societies eventually became Methodist churches, separate from the Anglican Church.

Today the Methodist Church is one of the largest churches in Protestantism. It has made a major contribution to Western Christianity by helping to rekindle the fires of evangelism that had almost burned out in England. Methodists also became leaders in many of the reform movements that were especially prominent in the nineteenth century. Christendom also owes Methodism at least one other debt—the precious hymns of Charles Wesley. About six thousand hymns flowed from his lyrical pen, and almost any hymnal published today will contain several. Among the best known are such favorites as "Oh, for a Thousand Tongues!" "Love Divine," "Jesus, Lover of My Soul," "Hark, the Herald Angels Sing," "Christ the Lord Is Risen Today," "A Charge to Keep I Have."

The Revival on the Continent

The Wesleyan revival in England was not an isolated affair. During the same period a revival swept across the American colonies, and the continent was affected by similar religious stirrings. In Germany this movement is known as the Pietist Movement. It arose as a reaction to the cold orthodoxy of seventeenth-century Lutheranism. Pietism, perhaps because it lacked the guidance of an organizational genius like Wesley, did not find its greatest expression in the founding of a separate church. Pietism, in rejecting the lifeless creedalism of Lutheranism, emphasized the subjective elements of one's faith. Great stress was placed upon Bible study, prayer, pious living, and the work of the Holy Spirit in the life of the Christian.

The University of Halle, largely through the efforts of August Francke (1663-1727), became a Pietist center. From it went forth a steady stream of evangelists and missionaries. Some of the pioneer missionaries in Africa and the Pacific islands were from Halle.

German Pietism had other far-reaching effects. Count Nicholaus Ludwig von Zinzendorf (1700-1760) received part of his education at Halle, which helped give to him a zeal to spread the gospel throughout the world. On his estates he provided a sanctuary for refugees from religious persecutions in Bohemia and Moravia. Out of this grew the Moravian Brethren, from whose village, Herrnhut, went forth a steady stream of missionaries. It was a group of these devout people who so influenced John Wesley on his trip to Georgia. Wesley later visited Herrnhut, and held the Moravians in such high regard that he translated several of their hymns into English.

Religion of the Inner Light

The seventeenth and eighteenth centuries put increasing emphasis upon reason. Yet in contrast to this general intellectual trend, this period also saw a flowering of mysticism. Mystics believe that they can, by contemplation and devotion, have more or less direct communion with God. Mystics usually feel no need to justify their position by an appeal to reason or revelation. By its very nature mysticism takes many different forms, and so we can look at only two or three varieties that developed during the seventeenth and eighteenth centuries.

Perhaps the best known of these groups are the Quakers, or Friends. The Quakers came into existence during the Civil War in England. Their founder was George Fox (1624-1691), who in 1647 had a religious experience that gave him deep personal satisfaction and led him into strange new paths. Submitting himself to the direction of the "Inner Light," he looked to it rather than to the Bible or creeds for direction. He insisted upon simplicity and honesty in every phase of life. He renounced the taking of oaths and participation in war.

In spite of persecution Fox's appeal found a response in the hearts of many, and the number of Quakers grew. Several prominent persons, including William Penn, were won to this position. While the Quakers never became numerous, they soon began to exercise an influence quite out of proportion to their numbers. They were, and have continued to be, active workers for many social reforms.

Another example of Protestant mysticism is that of Emanuel Swedenborg (1688-1772). He believed that he had communication with heavenly beings who brought information about a spiritual world that lay beyond this physical world. Among his voluminous writings were spiritualized interpretations. Eventually a sect, the Church of the New Jerusalem, resulted from his writings.

Through the centuries Roman Catholicism has produced many mystics, and the seventeenth and eighteenth centuries proved to be no exceptions. During this period one form of Catholic mysticism was Quietism. One of the leaders of this movement, Michael Molinos (1640-1690), emphasized the importance of making the soul passive so as to open one's heart to the divine light from God. A later disciple of this movement, Francis Fenelon (1651-1715), wrote *Christian Perfection*, which has been an aid to the devotional life of Catholics and Protestants alike.

CONCLUSION

It is impossible in a few sentences to make anything like an adequate summary of Christianity in the seventeenth and eighteenth centuries. We can make only a few pointed observations: (1) The religious wars of the period demonstrated the futility of trying to settle spiritual matters by physical warfare. (2) The changing intellectual climate that put emphasis upon reason and science was forcing Christianity more and more on the defensive. (3) The growth of toleration provided the opportunity for the rise of many new sects and denominations, paving the way for a period of complacent denominationalism. (4) By the end of the period the state-supported church was being challenged by some. In the French Revolution, the church lost its state support and became the object of persecution.

QUESTIONS

1. Why did the Peace of Augsburg fail?

2. Discuss some of the results of the Thirty Years' War. What evidence is there that the Peace of Westphalia, ending this war, was a rather fair compromise?

3. What were some of the beliefs of the deists?

4. Discuss some of the responses to the spiritual decline of the seventeenth and eighteenth centuries.

5. Who was the founder of the Society of Friends?

THE CHURCH IN AMERICA
1600-1800

EARLY SETTLERS IN AMERICA

Religion played an important part in the lives of sixteenth and seventeenth-century Europeans. It should not be surprising, then, that religion played an important part in the settlement of the New World. Early Spanish settlers were accompanied by priests, usually Jesuits or Franciscans, who went everywhere with their teachings. Virtually all of Central and South America were covered by their missionary efforts and their missions penetrated far into what later became the southwestern part of the United States. Their heroic, and often sacrificial efforts left a durable imprint, for even to this day Central and South America are nominally Roman Catholic.

In Canada, French missionaries displayed a similar concern for converting the Indians. The exploits of priests like Father Marquette, a Jesuit priest, are legendary.

The early English settlers expressed a similar concern for the souls of the Indians. Many of the charters of the English colonies in North America give missionary work as one of the motives for colonization. In practice, however, the English were never able to match the missionary successes of the Spanish and the French. Apparently several things contributed to this failure. Among other factors the English Protestants had no religious orders such as the Jesuits or the Franciscans, both of which had great missionary zeal. Further, the English, because they came as farmers who destroyed the Indian's

111

hunting grounds, never enjoyed the happy relations with the Indians as did the French, who came as trappers and traders.

But if the English did not succeed in converting the Indians, they did enjoy a great success in transplanting their religion to the New World. They also succeeded in transplanting their religious differences to America, where some of them have persisted to the present day.

THE VIRGINIA COLONY

After earlier efforts financed by individuals to establish colonies in the New World, the London Company, operating under a charter granted by the throne, succeeded in planting a permanent settlement on the James River in 1607. One of the petitioners for the charter of the London Company was an Anglican (Episcopalian) clergyman. He also was among the first group of settlers to land, and in the spring of 1607 led the group in celebrating Holy Communion in an improvised chapel under the trees.

Since the church and state were united in England, it was perfectly normal for the settlers to create a similar arrangement in the new colony. Church attendance was required by law, and persons guilty of blasphemy and Sabbath-breaking were punished. As it turned out, the laws were not rigidly enforced and were soon modified. The ministry was supported by the income from glebe lands (a common practice in the Middle Ages) set aside for that purpose, and a tithe levied against the citizens.

Persons who were not members of the Church of England (nonconformists) were received with reluctance. Roman Catholics and Quakers were especially unpopular. During the English Civil War, Virginia was sympathetic to the cause of the king, and even after the Puritans gained control of Parliament, Anglican worship in the colony was not interfered with.

The Anglican Church remained the established (that is, state-supported) church during the whole of the colonial period. But as time went on, the influx of population reduced the Anglicans to a minority in the colony. As a result, religious restrictions on nonconformists were gradually eliminated. During the Revolutionary War and the period immediately after, the Anglican (now the Protestant Episcopal Church) lost even their status as the established church.

The religious experiences of the Carolinas and Georgia paralleled, with some differences, the experiences of Virginia. In each of these the Anglican Church was established, but in the course of the colonial period the Anglicans in each state became a minority and eventually lost their preferred position.

THE NEW ENGLAND COLONIES

Religion played a far more important part in the founding and early history of the New England colonies than it did in Virginia. Religion was the prime motive that brought many to New England, and it was religion that sustained them during difficult times. The Pilgrims came first, landing in the fall of 1620. They were religious dissenters who had withdrawn from the Church of England, forming independent congregations. A dozen years before coming to the New World they had left England for the Netherlands, hoping to find there a religious sanctuary. For several reasons this arrangement proved unsatisfactory, and with almost unbelievable courage and meager resources they set out for America.

Within a few years they were joined by an ever-increasing stream of Puritans. Unlike the Pilgrims, the Puritans had not broken with the Church of England. They desired to remain within the Anglican Church and purify it of what they considered to be worldly and Roman Catholic influences. But under Charles I this became increasingly difficult, thus many turned to the New World, hoping there to create a theocracy where God's will would be supreme. It has been estimated that twenty thousand or more came during the "Great Migration," from 1628 to 1640. As a result, the Puritans soon outnumbered the Pilgrims. But an interesting thing happened.

The Puritans who arrived as members of the Church of England soon found it expedient to adopt the congregational form of church polity, and soon they no longer considered themselves members of the Anglican Church. They were instead Congregationalists. The Puritans came to gain religious freedom, but it must be understood that they were interested only in religious freedom for themselves. Persons who took exception to Puritan doctrine or practice were soon invited to leave the colony or suffered persecution. Religious freedom as we understand it today was to endure many growing pains before it came of age.

Contrary to popular belief, the Puritans were probably always a minority group, even in Massachusetts. But it was a powerful minority, controlling the government and setting the standards for much of the colonial period. Yet for all of their sternness and narrowness, there is something commendable about these Puritans. Their intense passion for God helped them meet and overcome the difficulties of establishing a colony on the inhospitable New England shore. Their devotion to hard work and their frugality made them astute businessmen, and helped them accumulate the capital needed to build a new nation. Their concern for learning made New England the intellectual center of the rising American nation.

Roger Williams, one of the founders of Rhode Island, suffered some of the growing pains exacted of those who sought to bring religious liberty along the road to maturity. Arriving in Massachusetts in 1631, Williams soon found himself at odds with the orthodox leadership in the colony. Eventually he was ordered banished from the colony, but to escape being deported, he fled into the frozen wilderness. Here he was given refuge by the Narragansett Indians among whom he had done missionary work. The following spring (1836), Williams and some other exiles founded Providence on Narragansett Bay. Here Williams founded what many regard as the first Baptist church in America. Because of the religious toleration granted by this colony, other dissenters were soon attracted to it. But during the whole of the colonial period, orthodox New England looked askance at what they considered a dangerous experiment in religious liberty.

THE MIDDLE COLONIES

The religious life of the middle colonies was as varied as it is interesting. In New York, originally settled by the Dutch, the Dutch Reformed Church was the established church. But by the time the British took over the colony, New York City was well on its way to becoming a cosmopolitan city with' a population claiming membership in several different churches.

Pennsylvania became a stronghold for minority groups who were elsewhere persecuted. Granted a charter in 1681, William Penn, a wealthy Quaker, began his "Holy Experiment" as a refuge for Quakers who flocked to the colonies in large numbers. But Penn encouraged other groups to migrate to Pennsylvania and many came, especially Germans—Lutherans, Reformed, Brethren, Mennonites, Amish, Baptists. Because many of these retained their German ways for many generations, they became known as the "Pennsylvania Dutch." Later they were joined by even larger numbers of Scotch-Irish Presbyterians.

Cecil Calvert, the second Lord Baltimore, founded Maryland to provide a refuge for Roman Catholics. But Protestants were not excluded, and they were generally allowed to practice their religion without restriction. The English Civil War brought friction in the colony, and out of it came a legislative act that provided toleration for all Christians. Although Roman Catholics were the large landowners and for a time controlled the government, they eventually lost control of the government. Before the end of the colonial period, ironically enough, Anglicanism became the established religion. Thus during the latter part of the colonial period the Anglican Church was the established church in all the colonies from Maryland to Georgia.

THE GREAT AWAKENING

Religious Decline

The religious fervor that motivated the Puritans (and other groups, for that matter) lost its intense heat within a generation. This was no new experience in the history of the church, for often before this, reforming zeal had swept through the church, cleansing and purifying as it went. Yet within a few years such movements had become institutionalized and eventually fossilized.

It would not be fair to say that religion in America in the early eighteenth century had become fossilized, but it had lost much of its penetrating vitality. Many things contributed to this. The difficulty of transmitting zeal from one generation to the next is well known.

Conditions had changed too. Puritans were no longer a persecuted minority seeking refuge in a forbidding land. By the eighteenth century they were the ruling oligarchy in New England. The rigors of the early days, during which the first settlers had been forced constantly to look to God for help, had now melted away. Puritans in the eighteenth century had attained a level of living that their grandfathers would have branded as unspeakable luxury. Few things can extinguish the flame of fervor more quickly than material wealth.

These factors together and in combination worked to bring a religious recession. But, as so often has been the case, religious recession is the soil from which springs religious revival. Such was the case in colonial America. Beginning in the 1730's in several colonies and in a number of denominations were a number of revivals that together constitute the Great Awakening.

Jonathan Edwards

Perhaps the best known of the leaders of the Great Awakening was Jonathan Edwards of Massachusetts. The son and grandson of Congregational ministers, Edwards graduated from Yale when only 17, and before long had acquired a reputation for scholarship and piety. In 1727 he became assistant to his grandfather, who ministered to the church at Northampton, Massachusetts. At the death of his grandfather he became the minister of the congregation. While Edwards' sermons can hardly be called sensational, they began to have sensational effects on his hearers. By 1734 his preaching had so instilled the fear of the wrath of God in the community that 300 were converted within 6 months.

Edwards was soon in wide demand as a speaker, and as he visited up and down the Connecticut River valley; the revival followed in his wake. Edwards' message was taken up by other ministers, and the revival began to reach toward eastern Massachusetts and southward toward the middle colonies. In the middle colonies William Tennant and his sons stirred the Presbyterians while Theodorus Jacobus Frelinghuysen preached similar sentiments among the Dutch Reformed. In 1740 the efforts of American evangelists were reinforced by the arrival of George Whitefield from England. Whitefield played a part in the Wesleyan revival in Britain, and his renown, along with his unusual abilities, soon won him a large following in America.

Results of the Great Awakening

Within a few years the more obvious aspects of the Great Awakening began to wane. In the second half of the eighteenth century, many men were giving more and more attention to politics, with the result that religion was relegated to the background. But the Awakening left behind a permanent heritage. For one thing, it stirred interest in education. Several colleges were started as a result of the revival spirit: Princeton, Rutgers, Brown, Columbia, Dartmouth, and Washington and Lee. The Awakening led to new concern about Indian missions. David Brainerd worked courageously among the Indians, dying of tuberculosis, which he contracted in these labors. Since Brainerd was engaged to a daughter of Jonathan Edwards, Edwards took a particular interest in his work and later published the young man's diary. This aroused great interest in missions, first in missions among the Indians and later among foreign missions. Philanthropic enterprises were encouraged as a result of the revival, George Whitefield's orphanage in Georgia being but one example. Revivalism also wrought a change in the prevailing theology. The rigid Calvinism of earlier Puritanism was tempered; God's love came to receive greater emphasis and His sovereignty and justice less.

RELIGION IN THE NEW NATION

The decade or more preceding the American Revolution saw the interest of the colonists shifting from religion to politics. This decline in religion was accelerated in the war period, which brought with it the dislocations and immorality that so often accompany a war. When independence came with the peace in 1783, American churches found themselves in a weakened condition. At the same time, they were forced to make decisions that would eventually lead greatly to their strengthening.

Many of the American denominations, such as the Anglicans, had organizational ties with the Old World. Now that America was independent, these denominations felt it expedient to lay aside these ties and create their own American organizations. Other denominations, such as the Baptists, that had no such connections, began to move in the direction of national organizations that would serve to unite them. During this period the Methodists, whose first members had arrived in America only a few years before the Revolutionary War, separated themselves from the Anglican Church to form their own organization. Francis Asbury, who became a bishop of the Methodist Church, played a prominent part in this organization and in the Methodists' rapid rise to prominence.

The Roman Catholics, a relatively small minority at the close of the American Revolution, were concentrated mainly in Maryland and Pennsylvania. The Roman Church suffered from a shortage of priests, and because there was no bishop in America, the ecclesiastical authority was challenged both by priests and laity. In 1790 the able and energetic John Carroll, a Jesuit, was consecrated Bishop of Baltimore. Under his leadership Roman Catholicism was soon organized to begin to meet the challenge of an expanding America.

CONCLUSION

The colonial period imparted to America a strongly religious heritage. Puritanism left a lasting imprint on the whole American outlook. The colonial period also gave to America a tradition of religious pluralism; that is, many churches, with no one church numerically strong enough to be dominant. The foundations of religious liberty were laid during the colonial period, as was begun our esteemed principle of separation of church and state. For some groups, such as Quakers and Baptists, separation of church and state was advocated as a matter of principle. By the end of the Revolutionary War many others were driven to accept this position as the only possible one, granted our religious pluralism.

The religious picture in America at the close of the eighteenth century was not especially promising. The strong religious motivation that was so conspicuous in the early colonial days had long since disappeared. Even the Great Awakening had not for long stemmed the tide running against religion. It has been estimated that less than ten per cent of the population belonged to any church by 1800. The

Episcopal Church, which had been the established church in several of the Southern colonies, had lost these privileges, to its dismay. The Congregational Church was, before long, to lose similar privileges in New England. Most would agree that separation of church and state has proved beneficial in the long run to both church and state, but at the time that the established churches lost these privileges, few of their leaders were able to foresee the advantages that separation would bring.

The Revolutionary War left in its wake a good deal of religious indifference and a rather general decline in the moral tone of the nation. Further, the popularity of Tom Paine, avowed deist and outspoken critic of the church, had no slight influence in turning the young intellectuals against Christianity. At Yale, for example, a school originally founded to prepare men for the ministry, only a handful of professing Christians could be found in the student body in 1795 when Timothy Dwight, grandson of Jonathan Edwards, became its president.

Many believe that organized religion reached its lowest level of influence in the generation following the Revolutionary War. Nor were there many factors in American society to lend much optimism to the situation. And prophets of gloom could readily be found who predicted an early demise to organized religion in America. Yet these prophets were wrong, as they have been so often wrong about the church in the past. In this case their limited vision did not permit them to see that even at this darkest moment forces were at work that would soon give the church a new burst of vigor.

QUESTIONS

1. Of the Spanish, French, and British, which was the least successful in converting the Indians? Why?

2. Were the religious motives for colonization stronger in the southern colonies or in New England?

3. The Puritans of New England, who came seeking religious freedom, willingly granted it to others. True or false? Discuss.

4. In what respects did the settlers in the middle colonies differ religiously from the settlers in New England and the southern colonies?

5. Discuss the Great Awakening. Who was its greatest leader?

6. What effect did the Revolutionary War have on religion in America?

THE CHURCH IN THE NINETEENTH CENTURY

Historians do not find the nineteenth century an easy one, either to evaluate or to write about. The very bulk of the historical data available is overwhelming. But more serious yet, the nineteenth century is complicated. The intellectual and political winds that blow over this period are complex, and we should not be surprised that the history of the church that attempts to meet these challenges is also complex. At best, we can in this chapter indicate only a few of the major events and trace only a few of the trends of the times.

THE INTELLECTUAL FERMENT OF THE NINETEENTH CENTURY

Quite appropriately, the nineteenth century had been termed the "age of ideologies." Many things were wrong with the society of this century. The Industrial Revolution had arrived in force, bringing with it both bane and blessing. The blessings were numerous—more rapid and dependable transportation and communication, an increase in both the quantity and quality of goods available to purchasers at lower prices than ever. For a few, industrialization brought handsome rewards, but often these rewards were exacted from the sweat and suffering of the masses.

Political Ideologies

Reformers, religious and secular, turned their attentions to the evils accompanying industrialization and urbanization. Let us look briefly at the efforts of some of the political reformers. We should note, first of all, that these reformers were optimists. As heirs of the eighteenth-century rationalists, they believed that man was inherently good and thus capable of almost unlimited improvement. Even the terror of the French Revolution, in which the ideas of the rationalists had gone to seed, did not seriously dampen their enthusiasm.

Many of these reformers believed that the unequal distribution of property was the main source of evil in society. To improve society, so they felt, all that was needed was a fair distribution of goods. Men who held such views came to be called "socialists."

The most important of all socialistic advocates of reform was Karl Marx (1818-1883), whose book, *Das Kapital,* proved to be a revolutionary timebomb. His importance was not immediately evident in the nineteenth century, and it was not until the twentieth that his pre-eminence was universally recognized. Marx is especially important to Christianity, for his system is militantly atheistic, and wherever his teachings have been put into practice the church has suffered.

All these political theories posed some threat to Christianity because they all suggested that the source of man's troubles lay in his environment rather than in the spiritual realm. The result was that Western man came to look more and more for his salvation in political and economic panaceas rather than in religion. But the church was in part to blame for the rise of these threatening ideologies. The teachings of Christ had stirred within many a vital concern for human welfare. But in the nineteenth century the church as an institution showed little concern about applying these teachings to the evils of the day. As a result, men sought other avenues through which to exert their altruistic impulses.

Organic Evolution and the Church

When Charles Darwin's book, *The Origin of the Species,* in which he set forth the hypothesis of evolution, was published in 1859, probably few persons realized what an impact it would have on religion. The Darwinian theory, which holds that the higher forms of life descended from simpler forms, seemed to flatly contradict the Genesis account of special creation. Darwin's theory, popularized by Thomas Huxley and

Herbert Spencer, provided for some what seemed to be a scientific basis for rejecting special creation, and even belief, in God. Others found a way of accepting evolution while still holding on to a belief in God by reducing the Genesis account of creation to a myth.

The evolutionary hypothesis had application beyond the biological realm. The idea of the "survival of the fittest" was applied to human society to give a philosophical undergirding to business competition and to rising nationalism. Since, according to evolution, higher forms of life had developed through competition for a limited food supply, it was held that similar competition would in the business realm produce a superior level of mankind. The result of this kind of thinking led, in the closing decades of the nineteenth century, to probably the fiercest dog-eat-dog competition in economic history. Many applied the same kind of thinking to the various races. The fact that the Germanic and Anglo-Saxon peoples enjoyed economic and military domination over much of the world seemed to indicate that these races were superior on the evolutionary scale.

The acceptance of evolution also challenged the Biblical basis of morality. If, after all, man is but the product of a long evolutionary process, then any ethical system he might have is also a product of evolution. Since one of man's basic concerns is survival, then any actions he takes to protect his survival can be justified (regardless of how immoral these actions may be). Fortunately not many persons followed this line of reasoning to its bitter conclusions.

Biblical Criticism

Christianity in the nineteenth century had to fight a war on many fronts. Even as it was defending itself against radical political theories and evolution, it also had to fight off a violent attack upon the Scriptures from within its own ranks. Those who thus attacked the Scriptures are often referred to as "higher" critics.

Perhaps we ought to define some terms before we go any further. "Lower" criticism deals with problems of the text itself. It is concerned with trying to prepare the most accurate Bible text possible. Lower critics have rendered a valuable service in giving to us a text that is, for all practical purposes, almost identical with the originals. Higher criticism, on the other hand, deals with such things as authorship and date of the Biblical writings. These are certainly legitimate areas of study, and every serious Bible student must give some attention to the matters of date and authorship if he is to understand the Scriptures. The trouble arises when men come to the Bible with presuppositions that are antagonistic to the very idea of divine revelation. Because many of the higher critics approached the Bible in this way, higher criticism has had a bad name among conservatives.

Well before the nineteenth century, a few men had begun to question the generally accepted views of the authorship of the Pentateuch. By the end of the nineteenth century some scholars had become convinced that the first five books of the Bible had been written by several authors over a long period of time. They also held that these had been written much later than the time in which Moses had lived. One such elaborate theory, the Graf-Welhausen theory, was widely adopted by the higher critics. Modifications of this theory are still held by many scholars. Later critics attributed Isaiah to two or more authors living many years apart, dated Daniel quite late, and denied Jonah's historicity.

The New Testament did not escape the attacks of the higher critics. In the nineteenth century Baur, Strauss, and Renan were prominently associated with these attacks. Some scholars undermined faith in the historicity of the Gospel accounts by asserting that they were written much later than the dates usually assigned them and that they were based upon earlier documents or sources. Some held that a conflict existed between the teachings of Christ and the teachings of Paul. Some of the critics expressed a preference for what they said were the moral teachings of Jesus rather than the later theologizings about Jesus. Later critics have, of course, demonstrated the difficulty of trying to separate Jesus from the theological teachings about Him.

Secularism

Still another enemy posed a serious threat to Christianity—secularism. Perhaps in some ways it was (and still is) a more serious threat than any of the others we have discussed. Secularism—the substitution of worldly values for Christian values—is so dangerous because it is all-pervasive, penetrating almost every facet of the work of the church, and because it is so difficult to recognize.

The Industrial Revolution that began in England in the eighteenth century touched every nation in the West before the nineteenth century was over. It brought with it a rising standard of living, which soon became accepted as a positive Christian value, rivaling the status that poverty had enjoyed among some in the Middle Ages. The Industrial Revolution brought rapid urbanization. Millions of people swarmed to the cities, leaving their religion behind them in far too many instances. Urban life with its sophistication and culture offered numerous opportunities for the further secularization of society. On the whole, the response of the church to urbanization was quite inadequate. The result was that the great industrial and commercial centers, which by the end of the nineteenth century were beginning to dominate Western culture, were not being effectively reached by the gospel.

THE RETREAT OF ROMANISM

Political Events Adversely Affecting Catholicism

Even before the nineteenth century began, Romanism was having its difficulties in France. Many of the leaders of the French Revolution, which began in 1789, were openly anti-Christian. As soon as they came to power they began to strip the Catholic Church of many of the privileges it had long enjoyed in France.

When Napoleon came to power in 1799, he sought to use the church for his own ends. While he restored some of the church's privileges, he made it very clear that the church was subordinate to him. Rome enjoyed better relations with France after the fall of Napoleon in 1815, but Catholicism was never again to enjoy the privileges she had known prior to the Revolution. When Louis Napoleon came to power in 1848, he sought better relations with Rome and even sent troops to Rome to defend the pope. But after Louis' fall in 1870, relations between France and the Roman Catholic Church deteriorated.

The winds of political liberalism that swept across nineteenth-century Europe looked upon the Roman Church as an enemy. Nor was this feeling without some justification, for in many countries the

Roman Church worked closely with reactionary regimes to maintain the status quo. The rising nationalism in Germany and Italy also looked upon Romanism as a foe. In Germany, Bismarck, the architect of German unity, considered the Roman Catholic Church as a dangerous adversary in his efforts to unify Germany. The Kulturkampf he launched against the Roman Church, while it met with only partial success, did cripple the Church for a time. By contrast, Roman Catholicism in Poland was a rallying point for Polish nationalism, and as a result came under serious restrictions by Russia, which controlled most of Poland in the nineteenth century.

The Papacy in the Nineteenth Century

The activities of some of the nineteenth-century popes gave solid ground for the fears of advocates of nationalism and democracy. The most noteworthy of these popes was Pius IX, whose rule extended from 1846 to 1878. It was he who proclaimed the dogma of the Immaculate Conception in 1854. This dogma, which asserted that Mary from the moment of her conception was preserved from any taint of original sin, did much to advance the cause of Mariolatry and thus increase antagonism between Catholics and Protestants. In 1864 he issued the famous encyclical, *Syllabus of Errors*. In it he attacked liberalism, communism, democracy, and separation of church and state. This encyclical also challenged the powers of the state in such matters as education, marriage, and morals. There is no question that the rising power of the state in the West posed a threat to Rome's traditional claims to authority. But neither is there any question that the pope's stubborn refusal to accommodate himself to some of these political changes hurt the church in the long run.

This fact was apparently recognized by Leo XIII, Pius IX's successor who retreated considerably from some of Pius' extreme positions. Leo took a more friendly attitude toward the rising secular powers, thus easing some of the tensions that had built up. He also took up the cause of labor against the rising industrialism. Pius X, pope from 1903 to 1914, drew back somewhat from the liberal position of Leo. Perhaps his most notable action was to curb "modernism," which was beginning to be felt by the turn of the century among a few Catholic scholars.

The Vatican Council

No discussion of nineteenth-century Catholicism could be complete without a mention of the Vatican Council, which convened in late 1869 and continued into 1870. This was the first such council since the conclusion of the Council of Trent in 1563, a period of more than 300 years. Perhaps the most important action of the Vatican Council was to declare as dogma the doctrine of papal infallibility. In brief this dogma asserts that the words of the pope are infallible when he speaks *ex cathedra* (literally, "from the chair," or officially) in matters of faith or morals. Many bishops were opposed to making this doctrine official dogma and refused to vote in favor of it at the council. A few Roman Catholics, refusing to accept this dogma, formed the Old Catholic Church.

Signs of Continuing Life

Even though the Roman Catholic Church suffered serious losses during the course of the nineteenth century, it was far from being dead. By the end of this period, Rome had, with reluctance, begun to accommodate herself to the changing political and intellectual scene. The action of the Vatican Council in giving the pope greater authority served to give Rome greater organizational unity. There was also considerable evidence of spiritual renewal within the church. Many new orders were formed, and the missionary outreach of Rome exceeded its previous efforts. While Rome had lost many of her privileges during the course of the nineteenth century, she was still at the beginning of the twentieth a vigorous force that could not be easily blinked away.

THE PROBLEMS OF PROTESTANTISM

As difficult as were the problems facing Roman Catholicism during the nineteenth century, those confronted by Protestantism were, if anything, even more trying. The Industrial Revolution, which remade Europe politically, socially, and economically, advanced more rapidly in Great Britain and northern Europe—the areas where Protestantism was strongest. Protestantism also felt more sharply than did Romanism the impact of the new intellectual currents. Rome found security from many of these currents by walling herself off from them. Protestantism, on the other hand, was so involved in some of these trends that she could not escape being affected. In fact some of these trends (such as destructive Biblical criticism) had their origins within and were nurtured by Protestantism.

Protestantism in Great Britain

At the beginning of the nineteenth century conditions left much to be desired in the Church of England, the only established church in England. While the revivals of the previous century had a beneficial effect on the Church of England, many of these benefits had waned. All too often clerics were perfunctory in performing their duties, services were empty and ritualistic, and members habitual but unenthusiastic. But there were exceptions to this pessimistic picture. The Evangelicals, though a small minority, kept alive within the church some of the glowing embers of revivalism from the eighteenth century. Perhaps the most permanent contribution of the Evangelicals was the great number of hymns they gave to the church. Many of these, such as Henry Alford's "Come, Ye Thankful People, Come," Arabella Katherine Hankey's "I Love to Tell the Story," and Francis Ridley Havergal's "Take My Life, and Let It Be Consecrated, Lord, to Thee," are still widely sung.

Another effort to revive the Church of England took a strikingly different form. Known as the Tractarian movement or the Oxford movement, this effort sought revival by looking back into the past. It emphasized the value of ritual and stressed many doctrines, such as apostolic succession, that seemed more Roman Catholic than Protestant. Indeed, many refer to this as the Anglo-Catholic movement. Some of the leaders of the Oxford movement, including John Henry Newman and Henry Edward Manning, became so pro-Catholic in their views that they eventually left the Church of England to join the Roman Catholic Church.

The Nonconformists—the Methodists, Baptists, Congregationalists, Presbyterians, and others outside the Church of

England—enjoyed a remarkable growth in numbers and prestige during the nineteenth century. Nonconformists had their greatest strength among the thrifty farmers, artisans, merchants, and manufacturers—groups that became increasingly prominent in Great Britain after 1815. During the nineteenth century most of the laws restricting Nonconformists were removed, and for all practical purposes they came to enjoy complete religious freedom. Perhaps the greatest preacher in nineteenth-century England was Charles H. Spurgeon, a Nonconformist.

Through the lives of committed individuals, Christianity made itself felt in Great Britain. A great deal of the social legislation in England sprang from Christian motivation. William Wilberforce headed a movement that eventually abolished slavery in the British Empire. Others worked for laws to improve conditions for mine and factory workers. Many other benevolent and philanthropic works resulted from Christian influences. Many government officials were motivated to make their religion meaningful in public office. William Gladstone, prime minister four times, was perhaps the outstanding example of a Christian in politics.

Protestantism on the Continent

Only a few brief generalizations can be made about Protestantism on the continent. In Germany the church was greatly affected by the unification of the numerous German states into one Germany in 1870. This led in some respects to less state control over the affairs of the church. German scholars, such as Schleiermacher, Kant, and Ritschl, were leaders in the negative criticism and speculative theology previously mentioned. Yet most Germans remained staunchly loyal to their church and were more likely to be influenced by Pietism than by the attacks of the scholars.

Liberalism became strong in the state church in the Netherlands, leading to more than one secession during the nineteenth century. In the Scandinavian countries Protestantism, predominantly Lutheranism, enjoyed a revival. Pietism was on the upsurge and missions were advanced. Danish Lutheranism produced Soren Kierkegaard, practically unrecognized in his own time, but now regarded as one of the century's outstanding theologians.

THE MISSIONARY AWAKENING

Beset as she was by strong and numerous enemies, one might have expected the church to assume a defensive stance as the nineteenth century wore on. Yet just the opposite was true. Not since the first century has the world witnessed such an immense outpouring of missionary energy. The result was that even though the church may have lost ground on some fronts, it still enjoyed the greatest geographical extension in its history.

Causes of the Missionary Expansion

Many things contributed to the growing interest in and support of missions. Man's growing control over his environment helped. The greater ease and speed with which man could travel opened up previously inaccessible areas to the gospel. The advance of medical knowledge gave missionaries new and effective avenues of service. The Industrial Revolution brought a vast increase in wealth. And though only a small percentage went for missions, this still was, by earlier standards, a vast sum.

Nationalism, which was often a foe of the faith, also served to spread the faith. In the mad race for colonies, missionaries with the gospel were not far behind the soldiers with the flag in entering new areas. The nineteenth century, in spite of growing national rivalries, was a period of relative peace. The *Pax Britannia* of the nineteenth century in some ways paralleled the *Pax Romana* of the first century, in which Christianity was born and spread so rapidly. This period was a time of great optimism. There is little question that this bounding optimism carried trade, culture, and Christianity over many a formidable barrier.

But none of these reasons alone or together are adequate to explain what happened. In part the missionary enthusiasm was no doubt a continuation of the momentum of the eighteenth-century revivals. Yet there is more involved. Apparently the Holy Spirit used these many external factors to focus Christians' attention once more on the divine imperative to "Go ... make disciples ... baptize."

Some Outstanding Missionary Personalities

Space allows us to do little more than mention a few of the outstanding missionaries of this period. William Carey, the English cobbler, is often credited with being the pioneer of the modern missionary movement. Catching the vision of great need, Carey in 1792 went to India. Even though the British East India Company discouraged his efforts, he was able eventually to do a great work there. Other missionaries soon followed. Robert Morrison went to China. Robert Moffat and his more famous son-in-law, David Livingstone, labored in the heart of the Dark Continent. Adoniram Judson, an American, pioneered in Burma. During the early part of the nineteenth century several missionary societies were formed, many of them being interdenominational and independent of denominational control. Roman Catholic missionary endeavor enjoyed a similar revival around the world, and their efforts often rivaled or surpassed the efforts of Protestants.

CONCLUSION

The intellectual ferment of the preceding centuries began to make a serious impact upon the church. Surging philosophical and political currents beat incessantly upon the foundations of the church. Secularism and growing industrialism took their toll. A glance at the forces the church faced in the nineteenth century is enough to make one pessimistic about her future. Yet in spite of many defeats suffered by Christendom, vigorous life was evident within the church. Concern about social reform and the new surge of missionary zeal are but two evidences of this life. By the end of this century it was clear that the gates of Hades still had not prevailed against the church.

QUESTIONS

1. In what ways did the increasing emphasis on politics affect religion in the nineteenth century?

2. How was Christianity affected by Darwin's book, *The Origin of the Species*?

3. What other factors posed a threat to orthodox Christianity during the nineteenth century?

4. How did Roman Catholicism respond to these threats?

5. Discuss the missionary activity of the church during the nineteenth century.

RELIGION IN NINETEENTH-CENTURY AMERICA

In a previous chapter we have noted that the nineteenth century has been termed the "Great Century" in missions. In some respects this same title would not be inappropriate for religion in nineteenth-century America. The hundred-year period from 1800 to 1900 saw a great increase in church membership, both in the total number of church members and in the percentage of the population that was church members. Church membership rose from a scant ten per cent of the population in 1800 to nearly forty per cent in 1900. The nineteenth century saw significant changes in the relative numerical strength of the major denominations. These changes came about because of immigration, the birth of new religious bodies, and the greater adaptability of some groups to the conditions of the frontier that moved relentlessly across the continent.

The nineteenth century also witnessed an unprecedented participation of Christians in numerous social reform movements. Christians were active in the anti-slavery crusade that convulsed the nation until 1860. But they were also active in women's rights movements, prison reform movements, temperance movements, peace movements, and numerous other reforming ventures. This century was also a time of revivals. From the preaching in the brush arbors of the Second Awakening to the great urban revivals of Dwight L. Moody, the nineteenth century witnessed one surge of revivalism after another.

THE SLAVERY ISSUE

Perhaps no other issue in American history had produced more strife, both political and religious, than the slavery issue. Even before the United States became an independent nation, some antislavery sentiment had existed. This feeling was most conspicuous among the Quakers, but by 1800 it was beginning to spread widely. Many solutions to the problem were proposed from 1800 to 1830. Among the most widely discussed was the colonization plan, which called for the emancipation or purchase of slaves and resettling them in Africa. As a result of these efforts, Liberia, in west Africa came into existence. But considering the large number of slaves involved, this was not a very practical solution to the problem.

About 1830 the antislavery movement took a more radical turn. From all across the North came a rising chorus of voices demanding action—the immediate abolition of slavery rather than gradual emancipation or resettlement. The motivation for this new antislavery sentiment was varied. Some were motivated by politics, some by liberal humanitarianism, and some by religion. During the next three decades this cry for the abolition of slavery came to dominate the nation's political discussions and many of its religious discussions, as well.

Finally, in 1861, words were replaced by swords and ballots by bullets as the nation blundered its way into the terrible Civil War. But long before the political bonds that held the states together had been severed, the religious bonds had begun to unravel. In 1844 the Methodist Episcopal Church split into Methodist Episcopal North and South. The split was occasioned by the fact that a bishop had, through marriage, acquired some slaves. Northern Methodists insisted that he either rid himself of the slaves or cease to function as a bishop. Southern Methodists, on the other hand, insisted that the bishop had a right to own slaves.

Slavery also separated the Baptists. The issue came to a head in 1844 and 1845 over whether or not a man who owned slaves could be sent out as a missionary. Southerners supported the slave owner while Northerners refused to support him. The result was two churches: Northern Baptists and Southern Baptists.

The slavery issue arose among the Presbyterians as early as the middle 1830's. While one split occurred in 1837, leading to the formation of the New School Presbyterians, the issues were mainly theological, with the slavery issue appearing only in the background. But in 1857 the New School Presbyterians, under the influence of abolitionists, took a strong stand against slavery. As a result the Southerners in the New School wing withdrew. Moderates among the Old School Presbyterians managed to keep the slavery issue in the background until the eve of the Civil War. But then the Presbyterians, like the Baptists and the Methodists, were sundered.

The slavery issue thus divided three of the largest and most influential religious groups in the nation. In other groups the issue was often warmly debated, but it did not lead to open division. Long after the slavery issue was settled, the divisions it caused lived to plague the American religious scene. In 1939 Northern and Southern Methodists reunited, but as yet neither the Baptists nor the Presbyterians have had effected a reunion.

Even in denominations not sundered by the slavery issue, serious tensions developed in the years before the Civil War. These tensions, along with racial feelings, helped produce a number of separate Negro denominations, both before and after the war. Among the largest of these were the African Methodist Episcopal Church; the African Methodist Episcopal Church, Zion; National Baptist Convention of America; and National Baptist Convention, U.S.A.

The churches, as we have seen, were actively involved in the slavery controversy. It is indeed tragic that the churches were not able to prevent or even significantly ameliorate the terrible fratricidal war that slavery helped precipitate. If one seeks evidence to demonstrate that the church reflects rather than shapes society, one can find it in this controversy. With equal eloquence proslavery and antislavery advocates quoted the Bible to substantiate their positions. One's position was much more likely to reflect the section of the country from which he came than it was to reflect scholarly Biblical insights.

REVIVALISM

The nineteenth century was a century of religious revivals. It opened with the Second Awakening and closed with the great urban revivals of Moody and his successors. As we have indicated in the previous chapter, religion had reached a low ebb by the end of the eighteenth century. Such times are ripe for revival, and a revival indeed did come. It began in the east, notably at Yale, where Timothy Dwight, grandson of Jonathan Edwards, led an offensive against deism and infidelity. Awakenings were felt at other eastern colleges.

But the eastern phase of the Second Awakening was mild compared with what happened on the frontier. Beginning about 1800 a series of camp meetings began to stir the west. These culminated in a great camp meeting at Cane Ridge meeting house near Paris, Kentucky. From ten to twenty thousand persons attended this great meeting, and numerous preachers of several denominations were kept busy preaching to the throngs. Great excitement attended this and other camp meetings, and this excitement often led to the display of unusual religious "exercises."

Sentiment in regard to these camp meetings was not unanimously favorable, with the result that divisions arose in some of the frontier religious bodies. Although the excitement of these meetings died down, some results were more permanent. The general moral tone of frontier life was raised, and there was a general ingathering of souls into the churches. The frontier played an important part in altering the relative strength of several of the religious bodies. On the frontier the Methodists and Baptists fared better than did the older, more respected churches, such as the Congregationalists, Presbyterians, and Episcopalians. So successful were the Methodists and the Baptists that they had by 1850 become the two largest denominations in the land.

As the frontier moved ever westward, camp meetings gradually became less important, but revivals in other forms continued. Among the outstanding revivalists were men like Lyman Beecher, who ably defended the orthodox position against the growing Unitarianism in New England. In the 1830's and 1840's perhaps no revivalist was better known than Charles G. Finney. Revolting against the rigid Calvinism in which he had been reared, Finney preached a message of "free and full salvation." He enjoyed many outstanding successes in the cities of the east. Later he became president of the new Oberlin College in Ohio, which became a center of revivalism and antislavery sentiment.

Just before the Civil War, revivalism took a new turn. In the summer of 1857 a financial panic struck in several northern cities. This panic was largely responsible for a revival movement that was unusual because it was confined largely to the cities and because its leadership was drawn almost entirely from the laymen. It began in New York City when a janitor left the door of a downtown church open for noonday prayer services. The prayer meeting grew and soon spread to other churches and to other cities. The Young Men's Christian Association, which had just recently started in the United States, played a significant part in the revival. It has been estimated that as many as a million persons were eventually won to Christ as a result of this revival. But perhaps even more important, this revival raised up a number of able Christian leaders (among them Dwight L. Moody) whose efforts won countless thousands of others.

Perhaps the greatest of all the nineteenth-century evangelists was Dwight L. Moody. In 1860, on the eve of the Civil War, he left the business world, where he had been a successful shoe salesman, and turned to religious service. For the next four decades Moody's voice was heard across the land and even across the sea in Britain, where he held a number of successful campaigns. Teamed with Ira D. Sankey, a gifted song leader, Moody was without question the most effective mass evangelist of the nineteenth century.

RELIGION AND THE RISE OF THE CITY

The nineteenth century saw the United States change from a nation of farmers to an increasingly urban nation. This shift in population to the cities brought sweeping social and religious changes in the American people. These changes were all the more pronounced because most of them came in the last three decades of the century.

Immigration

Perhaps the most significant factor in bringing changes in the religious structure of the nation was the rising tide of immigration, occurring in the last two or three decades of the nineteenth century. America is, of course, a nation of immigrants, but for the first 250 years of her existence immigrants came at such a rate that the predominantly Anglo-Saxon, Protestant culture was not seriously challenged. But this changed after 1870, for from that time on more and more of the immigrants came from eastern and southern Europe. The result was a substantial increase in membership in Roman Catholic and orthodox churches and in Jewish congregations.

As a result of immigration these religious groups, once numerically insignificant, now became sizable minorities in the population as a whole and even majorities, in some areas. In the long run the presence of these minority groups served to dilute the predominant Protestant culture, paving the way in the twentieth century for a pluralistic society.

The Changing Urban Society

The Industrial Revolution brought with it teeming cities too rapidly built, crowded slum tenements, and a dog-eat-dog competitive spirit. Thus the city brought new challenges to the church, challenges that all too often passed unmet. The patterns of evangelism and nurture that seemed adequate in a rural society failed to reach or hold the millions who flocked to the city. One effort to meet the needs of the city was the "institutional" church. The institutional church, in addition to the conventional worship services, sponsored many educational and social activities to minister to people living in the congested city. Perhaps the most famous of these was Philadelphia's Baptist Temple, ministered to by Russell H. Conwell. Eventually this grew into Temple University. In 1880 the Salvation Army, founded in England, made its way to America, where it rendered a commendable service in ministering to the cities' down-and-outers.

The tremendous growth in industry and business burst upon a nation that was ill-prepared to meet the new ethical demands that this growth brought with it. The individual pietism that worked reasonably well in a society of farms and small businesses could not cope with these changes. The business ethics of many of the leaders of this period are shocking to us. Yet in their private lives their morals were above reproach, and many of them were even outstanding church leaders. It was this situation, along with the social evils accompanying the Industrial Revolution, that helped give rise to the social gospel movement.

THE RISE OF NEW RELIGIOUS GROUPS

The rapidly changing social conditions of the nineteenth century combined with religious freedom to produce a fertile soil for the germination of new religious groups. During the course of the century there were dozens of these, but we can mention only a few that because of size or peculiar emphasis became outstanding.

Religious Bodies Arising on the Frontier

At least three groups that were later to become sizable religious bodies had their origins during this period. One of these, the United Brethren in Christ, came into being in 1800. Philip William Otterbein, a German Reformed minister and a close friend of Francis Asbury, was one of the leaders of this new group. Martin Boehm, a Mennonite, was the other. These two, along with their followers, were united in 1800 to form the United Brethren Church, which in doctrine closely resembled the Methodists.

The second of these, also a German group in its origin, was the Evangelical Association, formed by Jacob Albright. This denomination also closely resembled the Methodists in polity and doctrine. These two churches, much alike in polity and doctrine and concentrated in the same general part of the country, eventually merged in 1946 to form the Evangelical United Brethren Church.

The third frontier group is variously known today as churches of Christ, Christian churches, or Disciples of Christ. The Second Awakening, or Great Western Revival, struck Kentucky with full force in 1801, climaxing in a great camp meeting at Cane Ridge where Barton Stone ministered. Stone, a Presbyterian minister, was soon in difficulty with the synod because of some of his views, and eventually he and others were excluded. Eventually Stone and his followers came to call themselves simply "Christians." They abandoned man-made creeds and turned to the Bible alone as their authority, seeking thus to find unity for a divided Christendom.

A few years later in western Pennsylvania, Thomas Campbell, a Scotch-Irish Presbyterian minister, also had differences with his presbytery and was excluded. In a historic document, issued in 1809, *The Declaration and Address*, Campbell pleaded for Christian unity upon the basis of the Bible alone. He was joined at this time by his son, Alexander, who had just arrived from Scotland. In their search of the Scriptures the Campbells came to believe that baptism was by immersion only and were immersed. As a result, they were soon accepted by the Baptists. For nearly twenty years the Campbells and their followers worked among the Baptists, but eventually doctrinal differences arose, and the Baptists gradually withdrew from the Campbells and their followers.

In the meantime the followers of Stone and of Campbell had met in Kentucky. The two groups soon found that they shared a common concern: a desire to bring together divided Christians by the restoration of the church revealed in the New Testament. Beginning in 1832 the two groups chose to unite, a process that could be achieved only gradually because both groups were congregational in polity.

The Adventist Bodies

Around 1830 William Miller, a New Englander of Baptist background, began to preach earnestly about the return of Christ. A wave of interest and enthusiasm swept across the land, engulfing thousands. As time went on, Miller became more definite in his predictions. The second coming was to be in March 1843. When this date passed without unusual incident, Miller was disappointed. But soon other dates were set—with similar disappointing results. As a result of this enthusiasm several adventist groups were formed, but the strongest of these was the Seventh-day Adventists.

The Cults

The nineteenth century produced its share of bizarre and unusual cults and sects. Many of these, because of their anti-Scriptural teachings of crucial doctrines, cannot fairly be called Christian. Yet these groups had their origins in Christian teachings. Among the largest of these are the Church of Jesus Christ of Latter-day Saints (better known as the Mormon Church), founded by Joseph Smith; the Church of Christ, Scientist (Christian Science Church), founded by Mrs. Mary Baker Eddy; and the Watch Tower Bible and Tract Society (now known as Jehovah's Witnesses), founded by Charles Taze Russell.

CONCLUSION

In many ways the nineteenth century in America was a great century. It was a century of great social change—from a rural to an urban society. It was a century of great revivals—from the frontier camp meetings, to Finney, to Moody. It was a century of great preachers—from Lyman Beecher, to Henry Ward Beecher, to Phillips Brooks. It was a century of great challenge, great achievement, and great disappointments. And, as great as it was, it was but the prelude to an even greater century.

QUESTIONS

1. What social and political issue divided several American denominations during the nineteenth century? What major groups divided over this issue?

2. Discuss the changing aspects of revivalism in America during the course of the nineteenth century.

3. What effects did immigration have on religion in America?

4. Name and discuss some of the religious groups that arose in nineteenth-century America. What explanation can you give to account for this phenomenon?

INTO THE TWENTIETH CENTURY

"ADVANCE THROUGH STORM"

In his great history of the expansion of Christianity, Dr. Kenneth Scott Latourette appropriately uses the above title for the concluding volume, which deals with the church in the twentieth century. In the more than nineteen hundred years of its history, the church has been no stranger to difficulties and dangerous new challenges. But at no time have these challenges come so frequently, nor in such varied form. Nor in any age have the stakes been quite so high, for today the very existence of the race hangs in the balance.

Challenges to Christianity

Perhaps the most persistent challenges to Christianity, especially Christianity in the West, is that posed by secularism. Since the Renaissance, man has increasingly looked to himself as the source of his values. In the process he has turned his back upon God. Secularists are not likely to subject Christianity to persecution. In fact, a standard trademark of secularism is tolerance, a bland indifference that puts a premium on a stance of noncommitment.

Secularism assumes that Christianity is irrelevant in the twentieth century. Men no longer need to look to God for help, for science can provide all of his needs. Science seems to work, and to men who possess a pragmatic mind, no further argument is needed. Young people often find a greater challenge in science than they do in a call to Christian service. In the United States the study of science in the public

143

schools is vigorously pushed; at the same time religion has been all but squeezed out by public apathy and a series of Supreme Court decisions.

Secularism sets the values for our age. It is still appropriate to pay public lip service to the values long associated with Christianity — integrity, love, frugality, virtue, sexual purity—but in practice these values have been supplanted by secular values. The pervasive nature of secularism allows it to insinuate its values even into the church, where men all too readily accept quantitative, materialistic standards to evaluate its progress.

A more obvious foe of the church in the twentieth century is communism. This nineteenth-century ideology, largely the product of the thinking of Karl Marx, first became a real threat when communists swept to power in the Bolshevik Revolution in Russia in 1917. Communism is avowedly atheistic and antireligious. Marx believed that Christianity was an "opiate of the masses" used by the ruling class to help keep the working class under control. Almost as soon as they came to power in Russia, the communists did their best to eliminate the church, which in this case was the Russian Orthodox Church. Churches and seminaries were closed, priests were executed or exiled, religious festivals were abolished. Further, the communists began a concerted effort to indoctrinate their people in atheism. In part this violent reaction against the church stemmed from the fact that the church in Czarist Russia often worked hand in glove with the Czars' oppressive policies.

The amazing thing is that this campaign against religion, while it greatly hampered and weakened the church, failed to stamp out religion in Russia. The Orthodox Church still claims as many as fifty million members, and there are perhaps as many as five million members in the Baptist or Evangelical churches scattered across Russia.

Wherever communism has gone, the story has been pretty much the same. In central and eastern Europe, the church, whether Protestant, Roman Catholic, or Orthodox, has been persecuted and has suffered restrictions. In China the church has suffered even more severely. Almost as soon as the communists took over, all foreign missionaries were executed, imprisoned, or expelled. Chinese

Christians suffered untold hardships, and perhaps little remains of the church in China, which once numbered three million adherents.

A third important challenge to the church in the twentieth century, especially in the West, is that posed by the rapid changes in the fundamental nature of our society. These changes have come so rapidly that we have learned to accept them as a part of life; in the process we have lost sight of the danger these pose to the faith. First of all, most nations have become or are becoming urbanized. It is readily observable that cities are not as conducive to the growth of Christianity as are the towns, villages, and open countryside. (It is worth noting here that the reverse was true in the first century when Christianity was a new faith. Then the great cities became centers for evangelizing the surrounding area.) Urbanization has brought with it a high level of mobility to our people. In the Middle Ages most men probably lived and died within ten miles of their birthplaces. Rare indeed are such persons in our society. This transiency makes for rootlessness; it makes it easy for persons to avoid commitments to a local congregation; and it makes it difficult for a congregation to build leadership. Our society is rapidly becoming mechanized. In the process it is becoming dehumanized. Our mass society tends to reduce man to a number, thus in effect denying his personality and essential kinship to God.

One further threat to Christianity in our times is that presented by nationalism. This threat is more obvious among the new nations, those that have only recently won their independence. These Asian and African nations have been the recipients of much of the missionary effort of the West in the past 150 years, yet in many of them the doors have closed or are being closed to missionaries. In some the doors have been closed by official government action, in others by raising native hostility against anything that even resembles Western imperialism. Nationalism has in many cases created antagonism toward Christianity; it has also served to revive non-Christian religions. Hinduism, Buddhism, and Mohammedanism are notable examples of religions that have been stimulated by rising nationalism.

Christianity's Response to Challenge

One who believes that God works in history has no difficulty believing that God can use adversity to chasten and revive His people. Many see in the challenges of the twentieth century God's chastening hand; many believe that the church has been purged and often made stronger by these. Let us look at some of the signs that indicate that the church still has a source of power to meet these new challenges.

In the West, especially in the United States, we have witnessed a spiritual revival since World War II. Some critics feel that this revival has been superficial, that it is broader than it is deep. Yet all will agree that we have experienced a revival rather than a spiritual depression, which usually follows great wars. Whether he has been a producer or a product of this revival, Billy Graham stands out among its leaders. Even if this revival spirit has reached its crest, as some say, already it has left a permanent mark in the pages of church history.

The continued missionary activity of the contemporary church gives further evidence of its vitality. If the nineteenth century was the "great" century in missions, we must acknowledge that the twentieth century is even greater. In 1960 more than 42,000 Protestant foreign missionaries were at work, a figure that has increased steadily since World War II. Another encouraging aspect of missionary work is the growing maturity of the churches on the missionary fields. Many missionaries have increasingly stressed the importance of creating an "indigenous" church, a church made up of nationals that is able to stand on its own when foreign support is withdrawn.

Another important indication of vigor in the contemporary church is the renewed interest in the Bible and Biblical theology. This interest in the Scriptures is evident among liberals, conservatives, and even Roman Catholics. Several modern language translations have become best-sellers, and the market seemingly is still far from saturated. Bible societies are printing and distributing the Bible in record quantities, and each year sees the Scriptures being translated into new languages. Of course, critics have pointed out weaknesses in this return to the Bible, but persons who believe that the Bible has the power to touch men's hearts can still rejoice at its wider circulation.

WINDS OF DOCTRINE

A key to understanding the twentieth century is change, rapid change. This is just as true of religion as it is of politics, economics, or sociology. Probably no similar period of history has seen so many significant theological changes. In earlier periods changes in doctrine came about slowly, with generations or even centuries passing before important changes were evident.

Theological Liberalism

As the twentieth century opened, liberalism was in the ascendancy. As we have noted in an earlier chapter, liberalism is largely the product of several nineteenth-century developments. Liberals were optimistic; thus they shared the general feeling at the beginning of the twentieth century. Rejecting any form of the doctrine of human depravity and taking a rather light view of sin, liberals could believe in the ultimate perfectibility of the human race. Social and personal evils were not, so they said, the result of sin but of ignorance. The obvious conclusion from their reasoning was that education would alleviate most of these evils.

Liberals gave themselves unstintingly to programs of social reform. In America this program became known as the "Social Gospel" and numbered among its ablest advocates men such as Walter Rauschenbush, Washington Gladden, and Shailer Matthews. In Great Britain a somewhat similar movement was known as "Christian Socialism." The Social Gospelers differed from earlier social reformers. Earlier reformers usually had limited goals: the abolition of slavery, the abolition of liquor, etc. By contrast, the advocates of the Social Gospel wanted to reform the whole structure of society. Many of them felt that this could best be achieved along socialistic lines. Since these liberals felt that the reforms they sought could not be achieved by personal piety, they turned more and more to legislative means to reach them.

Advocates of the Social Gospel rendered an important service in calling attention to the numerous social ills affecting modern society. They led or gave support to numerous social reforms that had become a crying necessity in an increasingly industrial and urban nation. But as the century wore on, it became ever more evident that the easy

147

optimism of the liberals was no match for the demonic forces being unleashed all over the world. Today, a generation or so later, the optimism of these reformers seems shallow and naive. Rarely in the history of the church has a theology so widely espoused become so quickly out of date.

But in other respects liberalism has made a more lasting impact on the twentieth century, especially in the organized activities of the major American denominations. Liberals infiltrated denominational structures and soon controlled many of them. Educational boards, benevolent enterprises, publishing houses, mission boards, and colleges were before long firmly in the hands of men of liberal persuasion. From the beginning, liberals were in positions of leadership in the Federal Council of Churches of Christ in America, which began to operate in 1908.

Liberals were not able to achieve these victories without strong opposition from conservatives. Serious struggles developed in several major denominations, leading to bitterness and even division. The Conservative Baptists have separated themselves from the American (Northern) Baptists; a similar division is in progress among the Christian churches; and a sizable minority of the Congregational Christian churches has refused to become a part of the United Church of Christ.

The conservative cause was strengthened by the publication of twelve paper-bound books, *The Fundamentals*. Financed by two California millionaires, these books were circulated among ministers, teachers, and students. Conservatives who vigorously defended what they considered the fundamentals of the gospel—an infallible Bible, the deity, virgin birth, and bodily resurrection of Christ, the substitutionary atonement, and the second coming of Christ—became known as "fundamentalists." Unfortunately this term soon began to carry overtones of reproach that suggested that fundamentalists were obscurantists, opposed to all progress.

Neo-Orthodoxy

The First World War came as a decided shock to liberals, who had just about convinced themselves that man had evolved to the point where he would no longer stoop to war. Even before the war was over, a new voice was being raised that was to undermine some of the most cherished liberal views. Karl Barth, a Swiss theologian, was this new voice, first heard in 1918 when he published his *Commentary on the Epistle to the Romans*. This new theological stance, variously known as "neo-orthodoxy," "theology of crisis," or "dialectical theology," soon attracted a substantial and enthusiastic following. Outstanding among these are Emil Brunner, another Swiss theologian, and Reinhold Niebuhr, the leading American spokesman of this school.

The very nature of neo-orthodoxy makes it difficult to define with precision. Its name suggests a return to orthodoxy, but this is misleading in many ways. While Barth is indebted to Calvin, his system falls far short of a return to Calvinism. We may observe, however, that it shares with liberalism an acceptance of the results of higher criticism. For neo-orthodoxy the Bible is not an infallible, objective revelation of God. Barth, for example, holds that the Bible is merely another book until in a moment of crisis God speaks to one through its words. Neo-orthodox theologians differ with liberals about the nature of God. Liberals made God almost entirely immanent, that is, confined within man and nature; the neo-orthodox, by contrast, make Him transcendent, "wholly other." Neo-orthodox theologians also take a serious view of sin and repudiate the liberals' optimistic view of man. Chastened by two terrible wars and the threat of atomic destruction, these theologians look upon man's predicament as stemming from a radical flaw in his nature, not from some minor skin blemish.

Conservative Christians find neo-orthodoxy unacceptable at several points, especially its rejection of Biblical inerrancy and its ambiguous statements about the historicity of such things as the virgin birth and bodily resurrection of Christ. Yet it must be acknowledged that neo-orthodoxy has provided an antidote to some of the extreme liberal positions, and has helped revive interest in the study of the Bible. Conservatives can be appreciative of these correctives without approving the whole neo-orthodox position.

The New Evangelicalism

During the first three decades of the twentieth century, modernism seemed to sweep everything before it. A human prophet might have predicted the withering away and eventual disappearance of the conservative forces. But such limited foresight would have been doomed to failure, for in the years since, conservatism (variously termed "orthodoxy," "evangelicalism," and "neo-evangelicalism") has enjoyed a tremendous resurgence. Several important factors have contributed to this revival, which has swept across denominational lines with relative ease. The Bible colleges, now numbering about 250 in the United States and Canada, are pouring forth a steady stream of capable leaders. Most of the schools have been started since 1930. Several publishing houses provide volumes of literature that lends support to the conservative position. At one time much of this literature was reprints of nineteenth-century conservative scholars, but now young conservative scholars are producing literature that commands wide respect. Christian camps, a revived interest in Sunday schools, and evangelistic zeal have all contributed to the vigor of the conservative revival.

THE ECUMENICAL MOVEMENT

No history of the church in the twentieth century could be complete without some reference to the many forces and organizations working toward union. Several things have contributed to this increased concern for unity. Rapid communications have broken down geographical isolation, making this globe of ours indeed one world. Recurring international tragedies and the shadow of nuclear destruction have caused many theological differences, once important enough to divide brothers, to pale into insignificance. The strength of Christianity's foes has caused many to cry, "Unite or perish!" The impotence of a divided church in evangelism, and especially missions, has led others to seek unity. But beyond these reasons is a growing conviction that God desires a united church, that division is a sin. In other words, men have become convinced that the "church is essentially, intentionally, and constitutionally one" and are now seeking means to implement this unity.

Beginnings of the Ecumenical Movement

The roots of the modern Ecumenical Movement reach far back into the nineteenth century. Such organizations as the Evangelical Alliance (founded in 1846), the Young Men's Christian Association (begun in 1844), the Student Volunteer Movement (begun in 1886), and the Student Christian Movement were interdenominational and international in membership. Bringing together persons of many religious backgrounds, these organizations helped break down sectarian attitudes. In the United States the Federal Council of Churches (founded in 1908) brought denominations together as these earlier organizations had brought individuals together.

Many feel that the modern Ecumenical Movement had its real beginning in the World Missionary Conference in Edinburgh in 1910. World War I temporarily delayed the development that this meeting seemed to predict, but following the war came a series of similar meetings that gave a great boost to the ecumenical effort. Meetings at Lausanne (1927), and Edinburgh (1937), dealt with faith and order. Meetings dealing with life and work were held at Stockholm (1925) and Oxford (1937). The International Missionary Council, also growing out of the great meeting at Edinburgh (1910), held important meetings at Jerusalem (1928) and Madras (1938).

The World Council of Churches

As a result of these meetings, many felt the need for a more comprehensive organization to encompass larger areas of co-operation. Plans for such an organization were laid, but these had to await the end of World War II before they were consummated. The World Council of Churches came into being at Amsterdam in 1948 and numbered at that time more than 100 religious bodies. Among these were included most of the major Protestant bodies of Europe and North America, several of the orthodox churches, and most of the "younger churches" of Asia and Africa.

Subsequent meetings of the World Council were held in Evanston (1954) and New Delhi (1961). At the New Delhi meeting the Russian Orthodox Church was admitted to membership and the International

Missionary Council was incorporated into the World Council. By the New Delhi meeting the number of constituent bodies had reached 200.

Other Unitive Efforts

In addition to these organizations, the concern about Christian unity has been manifested in various other ways. One of these ways has been through church mergers. Most of these have been within denominational families. In the United States the most conspicuous of these are the union of the Evangelical and United Brethren Churches in 1946 to form the Evangelical United Brethren Church; of the Southern Methodists, Northern Methodists, and Methodist Protestants in 1939 to form the Methodist Church; of several Lutheran bodies to form the American Lutheran Church and the United Lutheran Church in America; and the United Presbyterian Church and the Presbyterian Church, U.S.A., to form the United Presbyterian Church, U.S.A.

Some mergers have drawn members from different denominational families, involving these groups in the additional difficulty of making provisions for differing theologies and polities. Among these are the United Church of Canada, formed in 1925 of Methodist, Congregational, and Presbyterian Churches; the Church of South India formed in 1947 of churches from Presbyterian, Congregational, Reformed, Methodist, and Anglican backgrounds; and in the United States, the United Church of Christ, formed in 1957 from the Evangelical and Reformed Church and the Congregational-Christian Church, each of which was the product of an earlier merger. Currently being debated in the United States is the proposal of Eugene Carson Blake to merge the Protestant Episcopal, Methodist, Presbyterian Churches, and the United Church of Christ. The Disciples and United Brethren have joined these discussions.

The concern for Christian unity is expressed in other ways. Among conservatives the National Association of Evangelicals, without any interest in promoting mergers, has provided a meeting ground for denominations and individuals who have not felt at ease in the liberal atmosphere of the World Council and the Federal Council (which became the National Council of Churches in 1950). The National

Sunday School Association has provided a similar platform for conservatives who have an interest in promoting the Sunday school.

A word must be said about the Roman Catholic approach to Christian unity. Since Roman Catholics believe that theirs is the only true church, the solution is relatively simple—erring non-Catholics can enjoy unity any time they want by returning to the Roman Church. Obviously, this approach is unacceptable to Protestant and Orthodox Christians. But there are indications that some Roman Catholics have taken a more conciliatory attitude. Many public statements of Pope John XXIII and Pope Paul VI and other Roman prelates along with some of the actions of the Second Vatican Council, which first convened late in 1962, clearly show a sympathetic concern for unity.

What final assessment can be made of all of these unitive efforts? Some have hailed the World Council as the beginning of a movement that will lead to one great world church. Others, viewing the diverse theologies represented by the constituent bodies, feel that real unity is still far in the future. These theologies range from extreme liberalism to fundamentalism. As a result, many feel that the World Council has a concern for organization and bureaucracy that precludes the possibility of real unity based on a solid Biblical faith. Critics of the World Council also see in it the danger of a super-church that might be a threat to Christian liberty.

There is a real danger that mergers, especially those that cross denominational family lines, will result in reducing the basis of unity to the lowest common denominator. Such a unity, lacking a solid Biblical basis, would be a caricature upon Jesus' prayer for the unity of His followers.

In a religious world that has become increasingly concerned about a divided church, there is a growing need to emphasize that real unity must be in Christ and must be based upon the Scriptures. Any such plea for unity is not likely to make a sensational impact upon a world that is becoming constantly more organizationally minded. Thus those who espouse such a position must do so with consummate patience. Since it took Protestantism more than 400 years to reach its present divided state, one must be unduly optimistic to suppose that all the scars of these divisions can be erased in less than a generation.

QUESTIONS

1. List and discuss some of the challenges that Christianity faces in the twentieth century. In your opinion, which of these poses the most serious threat to Christianity?

2. Is there any evidence that Christianity is meeting any of these challenges with any degree of success? Discuss.

3. Discuss neo-orthodoxy and new evangelicalism. How is each of these a reaction against liberalism?

4. What is meant by the Social Gospel?

5. What is meant by the Ecumenical Movement?

6. What dangers are posed by an organization such as the World Council of Churches?

7. Discuss the traditional Roman Catholic attitude toward unity. Note some recent changes in this attitude.

PROJECTS

1. Prior to the beginning of the first-class period, appoint several students to prepare a map of the Mediterranean Basin, using cardboard or newsprint. Then lesson by lesson color in the areas into which Christianity spread, using a different color for each period. Color in black the Christian area that was overrun by the Moslems in the seventh and eighth centuries.

2. Prepare a time chart across the front of the classroom. This may be a band of paper or cardboard a foot or more wide. Mark the dates and events as they come up in the lessons. A class member with artistic skill could illustrate these events with cartoons or symbols.

3. Use a telephone directory or a city directory to compile a list of the different denominations in your community. Have each member of the class select one of these and report on the doctrines peculiar to it.

4. Creeds have been important in reflecting and shaping the history of the church. Assign several representative creeds for class reports by the students. Schaff's *Creeds of Christendom* is a convenient source for this information.

5. Have selected students prepare a world missionary map, locating the areas served by missionaries that your congregation supports.

BIBLIOGRAPHY

BAINTON, ROLAND. *The Reformation of the Sixteenth Century.* Boston: Beacon Press, 1951

CAIRNS, EARLE E *Christianity Through the Centuries.* Grand Rapids: Zondervan, 1954.

LATOURETTE, KENNETH S. *A History of Christianity.* New York: Harper and Brothers, 1953.

MARTY, MARTIN E. *A Short History of Christianity.* Cleveland: World Publishing Co., Meridian Books, 1959.

NICHOLS, JAMES H. *A History of Christianity*, 1650-/950. New York: Ronald Press, 1956.

SCHAFF, PHILIP. *Creeds of Christendom.* New York: Charles Scribner's Sons. 3 vols. (6th ed.), 1890.

SWEET, WILLIAM W. *The Story of Religion in America.* New York: Harper and Brothers (revised ed.), 1950.

WALKER, WILLISTON. *History of the Christian Church.* New York: Charles Scribner's Sons (revised ed.), 1959.

THE RESTORATION MOVEMENT

by ENOS E. DOWLING

STUDY COURSE FOR YOUTH AND ADULTS

TABLE OF CONTENTS

FOREWORD

The Restoration Movement is a religious movement that began about 1800, the purpose being to restore the church to its original state in doctrine, polity, and life. The standard for this restoration is the Word of God, or, more specifically, the New Testament.

From the beginning this movement has been rooted in the conviction that the restoration of the church according to this standard is possible and desirable; that it is the only way to effect genuine Christian unity; and that the unity of the church is essential to and will eventuate in the evangelization of the world. Thus the prayer of Jesus, as recorded in the seventeenth chapter of the Gospel of John, will be fulfilled.

Leaders have spoken of restoring primitive Christianity, Bible Christianity, New Testament Christianity, apostolic Christianity, gospel order. The movement has been called the Restoration Movement, the Nineteenth Century Reformation, the Current Reformation; the body of people: Christians, Christian Church, Church of Christ, Disciples, Disciples of Christ, Reformers. Campbellites and Stoneites have been two of the milder epithets freely used by those not in sympathy with its principles and activities.

Analysis of the conversions recorded in the book of Acts led to the acceptance and proclamation of the following order in conversion: faith (that faith which "cometh by hearing, and hearing by the word of God"), repentance, confession ("Jesus is the Christ, the Son of the living God"), baptism (immersion), forgiveness of sins, gift of the Holy Spirit (Romans 10:17; Acts 16:31; 17:30; 8:37; Matthew 16:16; Acts 2:38). Further examination of the New Testament resulted in an

5

insistence on the autonomy of the local church, each congregation being responsible for choosing its own leaders to guide in its program of worship and service. Human creeds were rejected as bonds of fellowship and tests of orthodoxy. Acceptance of the New Testament as the all-sufficient rule of faith and practice for Christians was urged upon all.

Limitations of space make it impossible to include in these studies of this important segment of American church history many important items that would be helpful in arriving at a more comprehensive knowledge and better understanding of the rise and development of this movement. Therefore, it is recommended that a copy of James DeForest Murch's Christians Only (Standard Publishing, 1962) be provided for the use of the teacher in preparing to teach these lessons; it will be extremely valuable for collateral or supplementary reading. Mr. Murch's analysis of developments in the Restoration Movement found in Chapters 15-23 of Christians Only is particularly recommended for study in connection with Chapters 11, 12, and 13 of this work. If possible, a few copies of Mr. Murch's well-written and definitive history should be added to the church library and made available to the students for individual reference and study.

It is recommended that each student have a notebook in which to record basic facts relative to the history of the movement as well as additional information and insights supplied by the teacher or others during the class sessions. Information gained through individual reading and study may also be included in this notebook. In each case be sure to indicate the source of the information for future reference.

It is hoped that through these studies each student will be challenged and inspired by the faith and devotion of the early leaders in the Restoration Movement and by the principles that have been advocated, and that a continuing interest will lead to further study and to the application of these principles to present day situations, both within the movement and without.

It is also hoped that the conviction of Alexander Campbell may be shared by each teacher and student: "The ground assumed in the proposed reformation is the highest ground which can be assumed at any time or under any circumstances, and it is the only rational and lawful ground which human ingenuity and Christian integrity can propose" (*Millennial Harbinger*, 1831, p. 417).

AMERICAN BACKGROUNDS

Reformatory movements in religion, like movements for reform in social, economic, and political life, are sensitive to the environment of which they are a part and out of which they rise.

It is often pointed out that Christianity itself began at a time when a number of factors were favorable for the rapid spread of the gospel. Philosophers had failed to answer satisfactorily the vital questions about life and its meaning, or to provide men with adequate incentives for a significant moral life. Christ answered the questions and supplied the incentives. Greek, a language suited to clear and forceful expression of thought, was in widespread use by the peoples of the Mediterranean world. While other languages were also known and used, Greek provided the common medium through which the gospel could be made known to all. A splendid network of roads facilitated communication and travel. Free access was provided to all nations, and the gospel was soon carried throughout the Roman Empire. And it was a time of peace; no major war impeded the progress of the messengers of the Prince of Peace.

Some consideration, then, of those environmental factors prevalent in America at the close of the eighteenth century— political, economic, moral, and religious—should contribute to a better understanding of the rise and development of the Restoration Movement.

POLITICAL AND ECONOMIC CONDITIONS

Americans were involved in three wars during the latter part of the eighteenth century and the early years of the nineteenth. The American phase of the struggle for power between England and France in the latter half of the eighteenth century is known as the French and Indian War (1754-1763). A few years of uneasy peace and mounting tension were followed by the Revolutionary War (1775-1783). British interference with American trade, including the impressment of sailors from American ships for service on British vessels, and intrigue in American political affairs, resulted in the War of 1812 (1812-1814).

The Revolutionary War was a struggle by the colonies for independence and self-determination. The defeat of the British brought political freedom to the colonies. This newfound freedom marked every phase of the development of American life, including the religious life. Those who had hazarded their lives for the sake of conscience and liberty would be little inclined to surrender either in religious matters. A rugged individualism based upon the right to worship without interference from others was to mark American Christianity. Freedom under rightful authority, an appeal to the ultimate truth as found in Jesus and the New Testament, with individual freedom in matters not revealed, was to be a basic principle of the Restoration Movement.

The Louisiana Purchase in 1803 greatly enlarged the borders of the United States. The stream of immigrants from the East poured into the older sections of the West and on into this new territory. The Restoration Movement accompanied this westward expansion and was so identified with it that the movement is often characterized as a frontier movement.

MORAL CONDITIONS

The era following the Revolutionary War saw the loss of moral sensitivity, resulting in the practical repudiation of moral obligations and responsibilities. Liberty too often was construed as license; debauchery was widespread. College students generally shared the temper of the times. Many of them, while preparing for places as leaders in the nation, failed to exhibit or to develop that moral integrity which is so vital to effective leadership. Drinking was common, even among the clergy.

Perhaps some of the blame may justly be laid to the influence of the British and French soldiers in America. But moral decay is always a part of the general demoralization accompanying war. Men incited to hatred against an enemy do not lose their ability to hate when the last shot has been fired. War's carnage and destruction tend to make life cheap and uncertain; and when life is so considered, men live primarily for the present, giving the physical appetites and passions priority over everything else.

Another factor that contributed to the low moral tone in the nation was the breakdown in religion. Lack of spirituality, quite often in the pulpit as well as in the pew, made the church ineffective. The skepticism that was prevalent in America, resulting from drinking at the fountains of English deism and French atheism, removed religious restraints and lessened moral stability.

RELIGIOUS CONDITIONS

Spiritual Life at a Low Ebb

It is generally conceded by historians that the period under consideration was one of the lowest eras spiritually in the history of America. We have already noted the impact of English philosophic deism and French atheism, both of which took their toll from among the members of the churches. The universities, such as Harvard and Yale, were openly atheistic. The works of Thomas Paine and Voltaire were read and their views adopted. It was difficult to find a Christian in these universities, and those who were willing to take their stand for Christ were subjected to ridicule and persecution.

Interest in religion was lagging, church membership declining. There were some, of course, who by voice and deportment manifested an abiding faith in the living Lord; but, generally speaking, vital Christianity was at a very low ebb. In fact, the religious conditions were so bad that some were convinced that the "light of the world" would soon be extinguished and the church become merely a relic of the past. Or, if this did not happen, Christianity would at least assume a comparatively unimportant and minor role in the lives of Americans. The outlook was dark indeed.

Desire for Religious Freedom

Religious freedom was closely associated with political freedom. Establishment was on its way out in the colonies. Nine states had established (state supported) churches at the beginning of the Revolutionary War: Massachusetts, New Hampshire, and Connecticut were Congregational; Maryland, New York, Virginia, North Carolina, South Carolina, and Georgia were Anglican, or Episcopal. The Anglican establishment was rejected by all these states except Virginia in the early period of the war, and Virginia followed their example in 1786. Congregational establishment was abolished in the New England states somewhat later: New Hampshire in 1817, Connecticut in 1818, and Massachusetts in 1833.

The new political freedom was not conducive to religious subjection. Even John Wesley, whose sympathies and prayers were with England during the Revolutionary War, and who lived and died a member of the Anglican Church, sent the following word to the Methodist Societies in America at the time of their organization as the Methodist Episcopal Church in America at Baltimore in 1784:

> As our American brethren are now totally disentangled both from the State and from the English hierarchy, we dare not entangle them again either with one or the other. They are now at full liberty simply to follow the Scriptures and the primitive church. And we judge it best that they should stand fast in the liberty wherewith God has so strangely made them free.[1]

All was not to remain dark, however; there were some evidences of a revival of religious interest. History was about to repeat itself.

Religious Awakening

A spiritual drought near the beginning of the eighteenth century had been relieved by the period of refreshing religious revival known as the Great Awakening. It began about 1733 under the preaching of such men as Gilbert Tennant, Jonathan Edwards, and George Whitefield. It revitalized both the ministry and the church, giving great impetus to education and missions. However, the Great Awakening was followed by another period of spiritual apathy, as noted above. But the call for a return to faith in God and to a vital religious practice in harmony with this faith was again to reverberate throughout the nation.

The second religious awakening in America during the eighteenth century came during the latter part of this century. It was most pronounced in the South and West, but was not confined to these areas. The colleges had a rebirth of religious interest and commitment under the preaching and teaching of such men as Timothy Dwight, president of Yale. Dwight was an excellent preacher and an able apologist for Christianity. He refuted the arguments of the deists and atheists and called for a return to Christ and His Word.

We shall note later the development of the great camp meetings, fostered by the dramatic and soul-searching preaching of men like James McGready (Presbyterian) and the McGee brothers, John and William, one a Presbyterian and the other a Methodist. The Cane Ridge Revival, in which Barton Stone and other members of presbyteries associated with the Presbyterian Synod of Kentucky were involved, was a part of this revivalistic movement. The participation of Stone and others in these meetings was to be one factor in their trial and expulsion by presbytery and synod, although the charges against them were primarily charges of violating the doctrines set forth in the *Westminster Confession*.

Creeds as Religious Standards

The Protestant Reformation of the sixteenth century had promulgated the following principles: the all-sufficiency of the Bible, the priesthood of all believers, and the right and duty of private judgment. It is with the second and third principles that we are here concerned. Since each Christian is a priest (Revelation 1:6), the Bible could no longer be considered the sole property of the ecclesiastically constituted priests, such as those made by the Roman Church, to be interpreted by them for the people. As a priest, according to the New Testament, each Christian was to read and apply the Word for himself.

In practice, however, these principles were nullified by the adoption of human creeds as standards of orthodoxy and the basis for Christian fellowship. Each Christian might read and apply Biblical truths as he saw them, but he could have fellowship with others only by accepting the statement of their understanding of the Bible as incorporated in a creed. In one breath the Christian was told, "You have the right and the duty to use your own judgment in interpreting the Bible"; in the next, "If you expect to have fellowship with us your interpretation must agree with ours." Alexander Campbell caricatured this use of creeds in his "Parable of the Iron Bedstead."[2] The Restoration Movement was to seek abandonment of creeds as tests of fellowship.

A Divided Church

Creeds were the seeds of sectarianism. They served as the basis for inclusion and exclusion, for unity and excommunication. They divided the church into denominational camps.

Not only were the Christian forces divided, they were also engaged in civil war. Jealousies, party spirit, striving for supremacy: these marred the peace of Zion. The broader implications of Jesus' statement found in Matthew 12:25 had been overlooked or ignored: "Every kingdom divided against itself is brought to desolation; and every city or house divided against itself shall not stand." The Restoration Movement was to point out the evils of division, call for the cessation of civil war, and plead for the unity of Christian forces through a return to the Word of God as the only standard.

Calvinistic Theology

Calvinism was the dominant theological system in America as well as in Europe. The Methodists were Arminian, but the Presbyterians and Baptists, from whose ranks came many of the early leaders of the Restoration Movement, were Calvinistic in theology.

Calvinism is essentially the theology of Augustine carefully systematized and logically applied. Calvin's basic foundation or starting point for his doctrinal system was the absolute sovereignty of God. His system has been summarized in five points: total depravity, or human inability; election and predestination; limited atonement; irresistibility of grace; and perseverance of the saints. Let us look briefly at these doctrines as taught at that time.

Total Depravity. As the consequence of transgression in the Garden of Eden all the descendants of Adam became totally depraved, incapable of response to God. So deranged is the nature of man that "he could not do good if he would, and would not if he could." He must, therefore, depend solely upon God's grace for salvation.

Election and Predestination. God, by divine decree, chose (elected) certain individuals to salvation. Those whom He elected He predestined to eternal life; all others are predestined to eternal damnation or everlasting punishment. Some believed that this election took place before the fall; others, that it followed Adam's sin.

Limited Atonement. Christ died only for the elect. The blood He shed has meaning only for the chosen one. His death in no way affects the lives or destiny of the non-elect; for them there is no hope, no salvation.

Irresistibility of Grace. Election is a manifestation of the grace (unmerited favor) of God. Since He is absolute sovereign, no one can resist or reject the expression of His mercy and goodness.

Perseverance of the Saints. God's decree of election must stand. One of His elect cannot be lost; or, in terms familiar to us today, "once in grace always in grace."

Conversion

The doctrine of conversion was determined by this Calvinistic theology. Salvation is by faith—"only believe." But all human nature is totally depraved and incapable of any good or response to God, and no man can do anything to merit or achieve salvation, so the sinner *cannot* believe. Therefore, saving faith is imparted to the elect through the direct and miraculous operation of the Holy Spirit, and the blood of Christ cleanses from all sin. God's grace continues to provide for every need and insures the Christian's faithfulness until death, when he will receive "the crown of life" which has been secured by the election of God.

Both Calvinists and Arminians invited sinners under "conviction" to the "mourner's bench" to pray and to be prayed for. By "praying through," either at the "mourner's bench" or elsewhere, sinners received assurance that God had pardoned and accepted them. This assurance brought peace of mind and soul and great joy. It was often associated with a vision or some other "sign" from God.

To many who were accustomed to Calvinism and the mourner's bench" conversions, the preaching and practice of those associated in the Restoration Movement must have seemed cold and mechanical. They presented a rational and Scriptural program of conversion, preaching that faith was the belief of testimony, that all men can believe, that Christ died for all men; therefore, all may come to Christ and all can turn to Him and be saved through His blood. Inquiring sinners who asked, "What shall we do to be saved?" were often answered with the words of Peter on the Day of Pentecost (Acts 2:38). Sinners were not invited to a "mourner's bench" to pray, but to a public confession of their faith, followed by baptism into Christ for the remission of sins.

Neglect and Misuse of the Bible

Nominally, the Bible was the standard for all Christians. But we have already seen that in practice the authority of the Bible was limited by the use of creeds. Thomas Campbell was judged worthy of censure and excommunication by the Seceders for holding doctrines not in harmony with the *Westminster Confession,* and a few years later his son faced charges of heresy for teaching doctrines contrary to the Baptist standard, the *Philadelphia Confession.*

In using the Bible, no distinctions were made between the Old and New Testaments, or the covenants that they represented. Both were considered binding upon Christians; the words of Moses being considered equally authoritative with the words of Christ and His apostles. Thomas Campbell, in the *Declaration and Address,* emphasized the unity of the Bible, but insisted that the New Testament is "a perfect constitution for the worship, discipline, and government of the New Testament Church." Alexander Campbell, in his *Sermon on the Law,* given before the Redstone Baptist Association in 1816, made a distinction between the law and the gospel as set forth in the Old and New Testaments. This, he says, precipitated a "seven years' war" with the Baptists, particularly certain of the clergy.

THE CLERGY

While there were many consecrated ministers conscientiously serving God during the period under consideration, generally the "clergy" were deemed an ambitious and arrogant lot. Alexander Campbell believed the clergy to be responsible for much, if not all, that was evil, unwanted, unscriptural, and unnecessary in the church. He regarded them as "hirelings" or "hireling priests" more concerned about money than men, certain that they were one of the greatest enemies of reform. He carried on an almost incessant war against them. The early issues of the *Christian Baptist* are literally filled with castigations of the clergy. The editor's "Sermon Upon Goats"[3] and "The Third Epistle of Peter"[4] are stinging satires on the ambitions, claims, and work of the clergy.

Such, then, were the conditions in America about the beginning of the nineteenth century. It is against this background that we must see and interpret the activities of the early leaders of the Restoration Movement.

QUESTIONS

1. What part does environment play in religious movements?

2. What effect did the Revolutionary War have upon the moral and religious conditions in America?

3. What political conditions in America were significant for the beginning of the Restoration Movement?

4. Describe the prevalent type of religious conversion in America at the beginning of the nineteenth century.

5. What was the relative importance of the Bible and creeds as religious standards at this time?

---

[1] W. E. MacClenny, *Life of Rev. James O'Kelly*, p. 48.

[2] *Christian Baptist*, Burnet edition, pp. 277, 278.

[3] *Ibid.*, Vol. I, pp. 26-28. Omitted from the Burnet edition.

[4] *Ibid.*, Burnet edition, pp. 166-168.

CONTEMPORARY MOVEMENTS PART I — JAMES O'KELLY, ABNER JONES, ELIAS SMITH

Nineteenth-century America provided fertile soil for the planting and growth of religious reformation. Both need and opportunity were present. Spiritual life was exceedingly low, desperately in need of renewed vitality. Long-established religious traditions and practices present in the Old World had lost much of their awesome power over the lives of men in the atmosphere of freedom which enveloped the new nation.

In the South, East, and West, almost simultaneously, movements sprang up for repudiation of ecclesiastical authority and doctrines imbedded in traditions and human creeds. These movements advocated a return to the New Testament as the all-sufficient guide for Christians. Even Great Britain was affected by similar movements. To the naturalistic interpreter of history the circumstances that occasioned and furthered these movements may seem accidental, but the student having a different philosophy of history sees in them the hand of God.

Three things should be kept in mind as we consider the contributions of the early leaders in these reformatory movements in America: (1) although living in a new country, they did not break from the established religious order without a struggle; (2) a full understanding and concise statement of restoration principles were not arrived at immediately; and (3) these leaders did not foresee the ultimate place to which their actions would bring them.

Habit, sentiment, doctrine, and personal elements are involved in such movements. There is a religious habit, that familiar religious pattern in which the Christian worships, serves, and lives; and it is as difficult to break as habits in other areas of life, probably even more difficult. The religion to which our ancestors are or have been committed acquires a certain sacredness. If living, the presence of these loved ones makes any defection from their religion difficult; if dead, the ties may be even stronger. Doctrinal concepts have a way of remaining in the memory once they have been taught, received, and associated with religious practice. In some instances these may be modified, but it is difficult to forsake them entirely. Warm friendships and fellowship incline one to be more tolerant of differences. Only under the power of conviction too great to be denied and circumstances that can no longer be tolerated does the break finally occur.

In a sense these men "saw through a glass, darkly." It is doubtful that they foresaw the cherished doctrines that had to be abandoned if the restoration they proposed was to be consistent and meaningful. Fellowship would be completely broken or denied; they would be subjected to bitterness, misunderstanding, and misrepresentations. Thomas Campbell, for example, was slow to perceive that it was one thing to announce the slogan, "Where the Scriptures speak, we speak; where the Scriptures are silent, we are silent," and quite another to put it fully and completely into practice. Others actually saw some of its implications more clearly than Campbell. Certainly the determined opposition of the Chartiers Presbytery was not anticipated.

THE MOVEMENT IN NORTH CAROLINA AND VIRGINIA

The beginning of the movement for a return to primitive Christianity in North Carolina and Virginia is attributed largely to the influence and activities of James O'Kelly. Little is known of his birth and early life. He was probably born in 1735; he died in 1826. W. E. MacClenny, in *The Life of Rev. James O'Kelly* (1919), concludes that he was born and educated in Ireland and came to America rather early in his life, settling first in Virginia and later in North Carolina.

O'Kelly was converted by the Methodists at the age of thirty-nine and soon began laboring among them as a lay (unordained) preacher. He was not ordained until some ten years later. As a preacher he developed quite rapidly and soon became a man of influence and power, being favorably received by the people and by his fellow ministers.

Methodists in America

The Methodists in America were a part of the movement launched by John Wesley in England. This Anglican divine, repelled by the coldness and formality in the life and worship of the Church of England, became the leading spirit in a movement to revitalize this body. Societies for developing genuine piety and a deeper devotional life were organized. The members followed a carefully outlined program, which included self-interrogation in religious matters, prayer, and reading the Bible and selected devotional literature. They communed frequently and visited almshouses and prisons. They were called "Methodists" because they lived by rule or method.

Methodist societies were organized in America, following the same general pattern and purposes as those in England. While the members of these societies worshiped together, they lacked ministers who were qualified by ordination to administer the ordinances of baptism and the Lord's Supper, to solemnize marriage, and to bury the dead. For these important functions ministers of the Anglican Church had to be sought out. But the people had little desire or inclination to call upon these ministers, for they were generally considered to be lacking in piety and morality, spiritually unqualified to perform such sacred tasks.

The Revolutionary War wrought havoc in the Anglican Church in America. Many of the ministers in American churches were Englishmen who forsook their people and returned to their native land. Many of those who did not go home favored and worked for the British during the war. O'Kelly served on the side of the colonies.

Following the Revolutionary War, John Wesley chose Thomas Coke and Francis Asbury to be joint superintendents of the Methodists in America. Richard Whatcoat and Thomas Vasey were ordained and sent to administer the ordinances. In 1784, at the suggestion and with the blessing of Wesley, the Methodists organized their own religious body, calling it the Methodist Episcopal Church in America. Asbury was ordained, in succession, Deacon, Elder, and Superintendent. James O'Kelly was one of thirteen ordained as Elders.

Some, however, were not satisfied with a strict episcopacy, but were unable to prevent the setting up of this type of church government. Leading the opposition was O'Kelly. He argued that a sacrifice of freedom was being demanded, a freedom as vital in religion as in the state; that there was no New Testament precedent for such an organization. Had not Mr. Wesley written the Methodists in America that they were "at full liberty simply to follow the Scriptures and the primitive church"? The system practically ignored the people and their wishes, and placed all power in the hands of the clergy.

"The Right of Appeal"

Asbury's autocratic demands and growing power greatly alarmed O'Kelly. Tension increased between the "Bishop" and the "Elder" as the latter continued to oppose the governmental developments in the Methodist body.

The General Conference for 1792 was held in Baltimore. Both Asbury and O'Kelly recognized the importance of this meeting and labored to have those in favor of their particular positions in readiness at the conference. It was here that O'Kelly presented his "Right of Appeal" motion in an attempt to apply some check on the power of Asbury: "After the Bishop appoints the preachers to their several circuits, if any one thinks himself injured by the appointment, he shall have the liberty to appeal to the Conference and state his objection, and if the Conference approve his objection, the Bishop shall appoint him to another circuit."

After some discussion this motion was divided into two parts: (1) should the bishop appoint the preachers to their circuits? and (2) should any preacher be allowed the right of appeal? Little or no opposition was offered to the first part, and it was accepted. Debate on the latter part, however, was prolonged, being "kept a full week upon the anvil of discussion, and was beaten out of all shape."[1] When the vote was finally taken the motion was lost.

O'Kelly may have "out-argued" his opponents, but they "outgeneraled" him. He was accused of trying to "impeach the Bishop" and was otherwise placed in a bad light. The harsh and belligerent attitude of O'Kelly and his friends proved so distasteful to many who favored his position in the beginning that they voted against O'Kelly's motion. As a result, O'Kelly and several other ministers withdrew from the conference.

The Republican Methodist Church

Those who withdrew from the conference still maintained their status as Methodists. They were permitted to preach and work among the Methodist churches wherever and whenever possible. But this proved unsatisfactory. A reconciliation was possible on the part of the O'Kellyites only by a change in the attitude of Asbury. When further discussion removed all hope of reconciliation, the O'Kelly group met in Manakintown, Virginia (1793), and organized the Republican Methodist Church. Almost a year later an "open door" conference, including laity as well as clergy, was held at the Lebanon Church, Surry County, Virginia, to consider matters relating to this religious body.

The "Republicans" Become "Christians"

Progress during the first day of this conference proved so unsatisfactory that a committee of seven was appointed to draft a plan of government for presentation to the conference. This committee also experienced difficulty in coming to an agreement. Finally, they agreed to examine the Word of God and be governed by what they found there. Rice Haggard suggested the name "Christians" (Acts 11:26) as a more suitable name for the body than "Republican Methodists." A. Hafferty, from North Carolina, moved that the Bible be recommended as their only creed. When the committee made its report, their recommendations were immediately accepted. O'Kelly writes:

> The people rejoiced at the consolation, and gave glory to God for the light received. Thus the blessed Jesus was proclaimed King, and the Head of the people, without one dissenting voice, cordially renouncing all human institutions in the church, as being a species of popery, and not fit to govern souls. Then as free citizens in the land of Columbia (America), and servants of the great King, we proceeded according to divine order, to ordain elders.[2]

Division and Reunion

But the peace of the new Zion was soon disturbed over the proper "mode" of baptism. O'Kelly was a firm and unmovable advocate of infant baptism and sprinkling. William Guirey had become convinced that immersion was the Scriptural baptism and he and some others had been immersed. During a heated discussion of /this matter, O'Kelly is said to have asked Guirey: "Who rules this body, you or I?" To which Guirey replied: "Neither of us, brother; Christ rules here."[3] As a result of this controversy the Christians divided, the immersionists continuing to use the name Christians, while the others were known as "O'Kellyites."

The immersionists organized the Virginia Christian Conference. Correspondence between representatives of this conference and the New England Christians led to a union of these two groups in 1811. This union continued until the slavery issue divided them in 1854. At this time there was a reunion of the forces of Guirey and O'Kelly. This united body of southern Christians joined with the New England group in 1890.

THE NEW ENGLAND MOVEMENT

While the movement was developing in Virginia and North Carolina, a similar movement was beginning in the New England States under the influence of Abner Jones and Elias Smith.

Abner Jones (1772-1841)

Abner Jones, the more stable of these two leaders, was a native of Massachusetts. He later made his home in Vermont. He was a schoolteacher, a doctor, and a preacher.

Jones led a rather dissolute and irreligious life until his conversion. He manifested an interest in religion earlier in life, but it was not until he reached the age of twenty that he was fully converted and baptized into the Baptist Church. He immediately instituted an individual study of the Bible. Within a short time he began preaching. His continued study of the Bible led him to break from the Calvinistic system held by the Baptists and to proclaim himself a Christian only. He emphasized Christian character as the only and all-sufficient test for Christian fellowship.

He was ordained by the Free Will Baptists in 1802. His preaching of the Bible had been well received by this particular group of Baptists, with whom he found himself more nearly in agreement than any other religious group. They asked Jones to affiliate with them. While he expressed a willingness to fellowship with them as Christians and to unite with them in the work of the Lord, he declared his determination to be nothing but a Christian. He wanted it clearly understood that he was not "joining" the "Free-Willers," for he would not be subject to any of their rules and regulations. He desired Christian fellowship and willingly associated with them on his own terms; that is, as long as he could remain a free man in Christ.

Among the Christian churches established by Jones were those at Lyndon, Vermont (1801); Hanover, New Hampshire (1802); Piermont, New Hampshire (1803); and Boston, Massachusetts (1804). He was associated with Elias Smith in evangelistic work for a short time.

Elias Smith (1769-1846)

Elias Smith, schoolteacher, doctor, preacher, author, and editor, was born at Lyme, Connecticut, and died at Lynn, Massachusetts. His education began at the age of four and continued in a limited way until he was thirteen. Later, according to his autobiography, he spent thirteen days in learning grammar, devoted ten days to arithmetic, and gave eight evenings to the study of music.

Smith's father was a Baptist and his mother a Congregationalist. When he was eight years old, his mother determined to have him sprinkled. The time arrived but Smith ran. He was caught and forced to submit. He manifested interest in religion at the age of 20 five and again at sixteen. One day he slipped in the snow while carrying a log and was knocked unconscious and pinned beneath the log. When he regained consciousness, and while still held in the snow by the log, he "experienced regeneration" through the grace of God. He dated the beginning of his Christian life with this experience.

Smith found neither command nor example for infant baptism or sprinkling in the Bible, so he determined to be immersed. He was baptized into the Baptist Church. He preached his first sermon when twenty-one, and was ordained about two years later (1792). He was too restless for a located ministry, but succeeded as an evangelist.

Continued reading of the Bible made Smith dissatisfied with the Baptist doctrines. Under the influence of his brother, Uriah, he embraced Universalism for fifteen days in 1801. But he was uncertain and unsettled. He finally resolved to lay aside Calvinism and

Universalism, to search and follow the Bible. By 1805 he had discarded all other books for the New Testament and was using the name Christian to the exclusion of all other names. He was an independent, an advocate of religious freedom; he refused to be a party man.

Elias Smith was rather unstable and moody at times. His religious uncertainty was to cause him great concern and lead to difficulty with the Christians. Five times he accepted and then repudiated Universalism. His Christian brethren feared to trust a man who was blown about by every wind of doctrine." Smith was the author of a number of religious and medical books. His editorial career began in 1805 with the publication of a quarterly entitled *The Christian's Magazine, Reviewer and Religious Intelligencer*. He later edited *The Morning Star and City Watchman* (1827-1829). Perhaps his most important contribution to the movement for a return to New Testament Christianity was the publication of the first religious newspaper in America, *The Herald of Gospel Liberty* (1808-1817). *The Herald* publicized and defended the principles of the Christians. It also served as a medium through which the Christians in the north, south, and west became acquainted with each other.

We have already noted that the southern Christians finally united with this northern group. Some of those associated with the Stone movement in Kentucky and Ohio refused to join with Stone in union with the Reformers and cast their lot with these Christians. Thus emerged the Christian Church, or the Christian denomination in America. This denomination united with the Congregationalists in 1931 to form the Congregational-Christian Church. In 1957 the Congregational-Christian Church merged with the Evangelical and Reformed Church to form the United Church of Christ.

In theology the Christians were basically unitarian. Their "plea" may be outlined in six points: the Lord Jesus Christ as the head of the church; Christian the only name; the Bible as the only rule of faith and practice; individual interpretation of the Scriptures; Christian character the only test of fellowship; union of all the followers of Christ, that the world may believe.

QUESTIONS

1. Where did the Restoration Movement begin in America?

2. Name three factors affecting the early leaders of the movement.

3. What was the "right of appeal"? What was its significance?

4. What church did O'Kelly organize when he left the Methodists?

5. How did this church cease and most of its members become "Christians only"?

6. What contribution did Abner Jones make to the movement?

7. What was the contribution of Elias Smith?

8. Name the six points of the "Christians."

---

[1] MacClenny, Life of Rev. James O'Kelly, p. 96.

[2] *Ibid.*, p. 117.

[3] *Ibid.*, p. 158.

CONTEMPORARY MOVEMENTS PART II — B. W. STONE

A movement for return to the Bible as the only authoritative standard for Christians was inaugurated also in Kentucky near the beginning of the nineteenth century by Barton W. Stone and others. Although he was not primarily responsible for the break from Presbyterianism in which he was involved, Stone later became the acknowledged leader of the movement for reform in Kentucky and adjoining states.

Barton Stone was born near Port Tobacco, Maryland, on the day before Christmas, 1772. He died in Hannibal, Missouri, at the home of his daughter, Amanda Bowen, November 9, 1844. He was buried first in a locust grove on his farm near Jacksonville, Illinois. When the farm was sold in 1846 the body was moved to the cemetery at the Antioch Christian Church east of the city. The following year his remains were taken to Cane Ridge.

Stone has been characterized as benevolent, given to hospitality, pious, gentle, loving peace, humble, not self-seeking, fair, and yet firm in religious matters. At the time of his death A. G. Comings wrote: "I regarded him as the greatest of the Christian reformers of this century, because he was great as a Christian." Another spoke of him as "the moderator of this whole reformation."[1]

EARLY LIFE AND EDUCATION

Stone's first teacher was a firm believer in the use of the rod as an educational stimulus and perfecter of discipline. The young lad, although eager to learn, remained so frightened that he could not recite.

Within a few days he was transferred to another school where he responded to kindness and developed rapidly.

The inheritance left by the father was divided by mutual agreement of all concerned when Barton Stone was sixteen. About a month after reaching the age of seventeen, young Stone entered the school of David Caldwell, which was located in North Carolina about thirty miles from his home. This school had been established some twenty-three years before. It enrolled about fifty students. Caldwell, the only teacher, was an ordained Presbyterian minister and a most thorough and competent teacher. Many graduates of his school later attained prominence in the ministry, politics, and other professions. Stone completed the classical course in 1793.

RELIGIOUS STRUGGLES

Stone's parents were members of the established church in Maryland, the Church of England. His mother later left this body and affiliated with the Methodists. Barton was sprinkled in infancy and became a member of his parents' church.

Even as a child Stone felt the need for a more vital relationship with God. He often listened to the preaching of the Baptists and Methodists. But their preaching was radically different in many respects from that of the Anglican preachers and he became confused. Years later, analyzing his religious perplexity at this period, he wrote:

> My mind was much agitated, and was vacillating between these two parties. For some time I had been in the habit of retiring in secret, morning and evening, for prayer, with an earnest desire for religion; but being ignorant of what I ought to do, I became discouraged, and quit praying, and engaged in the youthful sports of the day.[2]

But Stone's religious longings were not permitted to remain dormant. The school at Guilford had been affected by the religious awakening occasioned by the fiery preaching of James McGready, a prominent Presbyterian revivalist. Many of the students had professed religion and affiliated with the Presbyterian Church. These students engaged in a period of devotions each day before morning classes. Although Stone was impressed by their piety and Christian deportment, he joined with the opposers of religion in the school. This proved unsatisfactory, however, and he became very unhappy. He had too much inborn respect for religion to be comfortable among the impious, yet was afflicted with too much uncertainty and confusion to be happy with the pious.

Stone was so unhappy and unsettled that he resolved to transfer to another school, but was prevented from doing so by "a very stonily day." He later wrote, "I remained in my room during that day, and came to the firm resolution to pursue my studies there, attend to my own business, and let every one pursue his own way."[3]

The course thus determined was not to be followed, however. He was invited by his roommate to hear James McGready again. McGready's sermon focused Stone's attention upon his perilous, unsaved condition and made him resolve to "seek first the kingdom of God and his righteousness" regardless of cost. But even then his problem was not to be easily resolved. He heard other preachers, then listened again to McGready, but failed to find what he was seeking. "For one year," he wrote later, "I was tossed on the waves of uncertainty—laboring, praying, and striving to obtain saving faith— sometimes desponding, and almost despairing of ever getting it."[4]

At last he heard a young Presbyterian preacher named William Hodge preach on the text, "God is love." What the fearful preaching of McGready could not do, the love of God revealed by Hodge accomplished. Stone read his Bible and prayed, and, finally convinced that God loved all men and that salvation was offered to all and not just the elect, he surrendered his life to God and found the peace of soul for which he had sought so long.

LICENSED BY THE ORANGE PRESBYTERY

Stone decided to give his life to the ministry. In 1793, with others from Caldwell's school, he applied to the Orange Presbytery for a license to preach. William Hodge was assigned to supervise his preparation for this event.

One of the areas of study assigned by the Presbytery was "the being and attributes of God and the Trinity." Stone was soon lost in the complexities of his problem and almost gave up his study for the ministry. Fortunately, however, a copy of Isaac Watts's *Glories of Christ* was read and the author's views accepted. The examiner appointed by the Presbytery was Henry Pattillo, who also favored Watts's explanation of this doctrine. Stone successfully passed the examination.

But he was wearied and still confused by his study of Calvinistic doctrines. Again he was almost ready to forsake his chosen work before he had really begun it. He set out for Georgia, but was taken ill on the way. He arrived at his brother Matthew's home in Georgia, where he spent some months in recovering from his illness.

Hope Hull, a Methodist preacher who had been sympathetic with O'Kelly in his battle for modification of the episcopal government as set up by the Methodists, had established a school near Washington, Georgia. He offered Stone the job of teaching languages in this institution and Stone accepted. About seventy students were enrolled. Stone proved to be a popular and successful teacher.

After a period of indecision about his future, Stone decided to fulfill his commitment to the ministry. He returned to North Carolina to receive his license from the Orange Presbytery (1796). On this occasion he was handed a Bible by the venerable Pattillo and given this Scriptural charge: "Go ye into all the world, and preach the gospel to every creature."

Stone made a short visit with his mother in Virginia and then set out with Robert Foster to preach in the southern portion of North Carolina. His companion soon decided to give up the ministry. Stone, beset with doubts of his own fitness for the work, determined to go to Florida. He was turned from his purpose by a lady who suspected that he was "running away" and accused him of being another Jonah.

The West became the Macedonia calling for Stone's labors. He tarried for a few weeks of preaching in Virginia; then, passing through Tennessee and stopping for a short time at Knoxville and Nashville, he went into Kentucky. He soon began preaching for the Presbyterian congregations at Cane Ridge and Concord.

ORDINATION BY THE TRANSYLVANIA PRESBYTERY

Stone preached regularly for the churches at Cane Ridge and Concord as a licensed preacher. When these congregations issued a call through the Transylvania Presbytery for their preacher to locate with them, he became a candidate for ordination. An examination by the Presbytery would precede the ordination.

The standard for Presbyterians was the *Westminster Confession*, a thoroughly Calvinistic document. In his preaching Stone had carefully avoided those doctrines that had given him trouble in his early preparation for the ministry. He now faced an examination while having doubts concerning such doctrines as Trinitarianism and predestination.

October 4, 1798 was the day set for the ordination at Cane Ridge. Stone sought out two prominent members of the Presbytery, James Blythe and Robert Marshall, and explained his difficulties to them. They were unable to explain these doctrines to Stone's satisfaction. Efforts to have his ordination postponed were also unsuccessful.

During the course of the examination the candidates were asked, "Do you receive and adopt the Confession of Faith as containing the system of doctrine taught in the Bible?" To this question Stone replied in a loud voice so that all might hear, "I do, as far as I see it consistent with the word of God." No objection being offered, Stone was ordained to the Presbyterian ministry.

The mind of the newly-ordained preacher continued to be so agitated by Calvinistic doctrines that he could not reconcile with reason or the Scriptures. His study of the Bible convinced Stone that God loved and desired the salvation of all; that Christ died to make this salvation possible; that the testimony in the Word was sufficient for faith; that faith would lead to repentance, and repentance to obedience. Faith and obedience would bring remission of sins, the gift of the Holy Spirit, and eternal life. Reasoning thus, Stone escaped from the "labyrinth of Calvinism and error."

THE CANE RIDGE REVIVAL

Kentucky shared in the religious revival that swept the nation at the close of the eighteenth and beginning of the nineteenth centuries. James McGready, whom Stone heard in North Carolina while attending the school of David Caldwell, was largely responsible for bringing the revival to Kentucky. He had settled in Logan County, Kentucky, in 1796.

Oppressed by the religious unconcern, the infidelity and dissipation of the people, this revivalist set aside one day of each month for fasting and prayer and an hour weekly in which to beseech God for a revival of religion and plead for the souls of men. Associated with McGready in revival efforts were the McGee brothers: William, a Presbyterian, and John, a Methodist.

Stone was also oppressed by the lack of spirituality and interest in religion by members of his congregations and those in the surrounding community. Hearing of the revival which had "broken out" in Logan County, Stone resolved to visit one of the camp meetings in the spring of 1801. He was greatly impressed by what he saw. Although many were repelled by the "religious exercises" associated with these meetings, Stone felt them to be the work of God. He returned to preach with new earnestness and enthusiasm.

The preaching of Stone at Cane Ridge and Concord were increasingly attended with manifestations of the same "religious exercises" as witnessed in Logan County. A meeting at Concord drew a large multitude of people. It lasted five days. Announcements were made for a meeting at Cane Ridge, probably during the first part of August, although opinions differ as to the exact date.

The number present at this memorable meeting has been variously estimated at ten to thirty thousand. Methodists, Baptists, and Presbyterians joined together in this revival, temporarily ignoring the doctrinal standards that divided them into opposing forces in a religious civil war.

A description and discussion of the "religious exercises" manifested in the Cane Ridge revival may be found in Part I, Chapter VI, and Part II, Chapter VI of Roger's biography of Stone. These "exercises" included falling, jerks, dancing, barking, running, laughing, and singing. The number affected was estimated from three hundred to as many as three thousand. While others have explained these as emotional or psychological phenomena, Stone believed them to be the work of God, although not necessary complements to the preaching of the gospel and conversion.

The most common was the "falling exercise," which affected both the converted and the unconverted. Some lay for as long as an hour or more in what appeared to be almost a lifeless state. When they "came to" they praised God, told of their wonderful experiences while unconscious, and exhorted sinners to repent and forsake their wicked ways.

The "jerks" also affected both saints and sinners. There was an exceedingly rapid backward and forward motion of the head or of the entire body when seized by the "jerks." The saved afterward spoke of their great ecstasy and exhilaration during the period of this "exercise," but the wicked often cursed the agitation to which they had been subjected.

Among professing Christians, and only among such, a season of the "jerks" frequently was a prelude to the "dancing exercise." Stone gives the following description of this "exercise":

> Such dancing was indeed heavenly to the spectators; there was nothing in it like levity, nor calculated to excite levity in the beholders. The smile of heaven shone on the countenance of the subject, and assimilated to angels appeared the whole person. Sometimes the motion was quick and sometimes slow. Thus they continued to move forward and backward in the same track or alley till nature seemed exhausted, and they would fall prostrate on the floor or earth, unless caught by those standing by. While thus exercised, I have heard their solemn praises and prayers ascending to God.[5]

Stone associated the "barking exercise" with the "jerks," and did not consider it a genuine religious "exercise" at all. A Presbyterian preacher subjected to the "jerks" seized a sapling to prevent him from falling. As his head was jerked rapidly back and forth he emitted a noise somewhat like a bark. Someone reported that he was "barking up a tree."

The "laughing exercise" was prevalent among the religious. Instead of inducing laughter in others, it was attended with great solemnity.

The "singing exercise" was not ordinary singing. In the words of Stone:

> The subject in a very happy state of mind would sing most melodiously, not from the mouth or nose, but entirely in the breast,

the sounds issuing thence. Such music silenced everything and attracted the attention of all. It was most heavenly. None could ever be tired of bearing it.[6]

Judgments differed as to the significance of the Cane Ridge revival and, in fact, the whole revivalistic movement. Some saw the working of Satan; others, a marvelous outpouring of the Spirit and power of God. Some saw fanaticism and disorder; others, a miraculous transformation of lives. The revivalists themselves laid aside their denominational differences to lift a united voice in proclaiming the love and mercy of God for the penitent sinner.

JURISDICTION OF THE SYNOD OF KENTUCKY RENOUNCED

Many Presbyterian preachers were alarmed by what they saw and heard. Revivals, such as the Cane Ridge revival, were opposed for at least three reasons. The "religious exercises" so evident in the camp meetings were repugnant, violating good religious taste and order. The Presbyterian preachers were associating with uneducated and uncouth Baptist and Methodist ministers lacking proper ordination. And the *Westminster Confession* was being flouted: its doctrine of election was set aside, and an invitation extended to all to come to Christ; the death of Christ for all and not just the elect was proclaimed; and the ability and responsibility of each individual to believe and obey the gospel was emphasized.

The attitude and activities of the Presbyterian ministers who opposed the revival and their brethren who participated in it touched off a war between Presbyterians, Methodists, and Baptists. "The spirit of partyism soon expelled the spirit of love and union— peace fled before discord and strife, and religion was stifled and banished in the unhallowed struggle for pre-eminence."[7]

Trouble was also brewing within the Presbyterian ranks. Among the Presbyterian preachers associated with the revivalistic movement in Kentucky were Barton Stone and Robert Marshall of the West Lexington Presbytery, and Richard McNemar, John Dunlavy, and John Thompson of the Washington Presbytery. The "orthodox" were determined that the revivalists' heresies in doctrine and practice should not go unnoticed; they must be rebuked and disciplined.

Attention was first focused on Richard McNemar at a special session of the Washington Presbytery, which was held in November 1801, at Springfield, Ohio, to ordain John Thompson. (This town is not to be confused with the present Springfield. It was located about eleven miles north of Cincinnati.) A letter of complaint in six points, signed by three elders of the Cabin Creek Church, was presented at this meeting. McNemar was charged with holding and preaching doctrines contrary to the Bible and the *Westminster Confession*, doctrines Arminian in character rather than Calvinistic. No official action was taken since a quorum was not present. By shrewd planning, his opponents succeeded in having a condemnation of McNemar entered on the minutes at the next regular meeting of the Presbytery at Cincinnati in October 1802. In spite of this condemnation, however, McNemar was returned to Turtle Creek as pastor. At the next meeting of the Presbytery—Springfield, April 1803—charges were made against McNemar and John Thompson. The revival men were in the majority and their opponents were voted down.

The larger Presbyterian body, the Synod of Kentucky, met at Lexington in September 1803. Twenty-three preachers and eighteen elders were present. The committee examining the minutes of the Washington Presbytery censured the Presbytery for their handling of the charges against McNemar and Thompson, and especially for permitting McNexnar to continue preaching while under condemnation. The Synod voted to sustain the action of the Presbytery against McNemar at Cincinnati.

The revivalists clearly saw that any action against McNemar would eventually be extended to them. So Stone, Dunlavy, Marshall, Thompson, and McNemar presented a statement protesting the decisions concerning McNemar and Thompson and declining all further jurisdiction of the synod. Attempts by the synod to reconcile and restore these men failed; so they were suspended, their churches declared vacant, and messengers sent to the churches with letters explaining the synod's action. Some time later they were deposed from the ministry and cut off from the Presbyterian body.

Following their renunciation of the jurisdiction of the synod, Marshall, Stone, Thompson, McNemar, and Dunlavy organized their own presbytery, calling it the Springfield Presbytery. In January 1804, they issued An Apology for *Renouncing the Jurisdiction of the Synod of Kentucky*. Marshall, Stone, and Thompson each wrote a section. The document contains the revivalists' version of the separation from the synod, objections against making the *Westminster Confession* a standard of orthodoxy and fellowship, repudiation of the authority of all human creeds, and the all-sufficiency of the Bible as a rule of faith and practice for all Christians.

LAST WILL AND TESTAMENT OF THE SPRINGFIELD PRESBYTERY

In spite of strong opposition this new presbytery grew rapidly and soon numbered fifteen churches. Having repudiated the right of human creeds to govern in religious matters, they were led to question the place of such organized bodies as presbyteries in the church. Within a few months—June 28, 1804—*The Last Will and Testament of the Springfield Presbytery* was given to the public. It was signed by Stone, Marshall, Thompson, McNemar, Dunlavy, and David Purviance. Authorship of this document is usually attributed to Stone, but some believe that McNemar was responsible for it.

The Last Will and Testament is probably the most unusual document produced by the Restoration Movement. It may be analyzed as proclamation, propaganda, and plea. It *proclaims* the dissolution of the Springfield Presbytery as an unscriptural body and inclined to produce a party spirit. It is a cleverly and carefully arranged piece of *propaganda* against the validity of human creeds as tests of fellowship and authoritative religious organizations outside the local congregation. It is a plea for Christians to forsake all human standards and to hold the Bible alone as the standard for faith and conduct, to practice mutual forbearance and love, and to work for the unity of the people of God.

Of the six men who signed the *Last Will and Testament*, only Stone and Purviance remained faithful to the principles set forth in the historic document. In 1805 Shaker missionaries from New York made converts of McNemar and Dunlavy. In 1811 Marshall and Thompson returned to the Presbyterians.

CHRISTIANS ONLY

The Kentucky reformers were often referred to as "Marshallites" and "Stoneites." They were also called "Newlights." In the final choice of a name they were influenced by Rice Haggard, who had been responsible for the adoption of the name Christian by the O'Kelly group in North Carolina and Virginia. Haggard suggested the use of the name Christian by this group, and for a second time his suggestion bore fruit; they became "Christians only," committed to following the Bible only.

In 1807 continued study of the divine standard led to the practice of immersion for the remission of sins. Although it was not made a test of fellowship, within a short time immersion became the common practice of the Christians in Kentucky, and their congregations were composed almost entirely of immersed believers.

Stone made an important contribution to the rise and early development of the Christians in Kentucky. His periodical, *The Christian Messenger* (1826-1845), was to be a significant force in later years.

The stone shaft marking Stone's final resting place at Cane Ridge bears this inscription: "The Church of Christ at Caneridge & other generous friends in Kentucky, have caused this monument to be erected as a tribute of affection & gratitude to BARTON W. STONE, Minister of the gospel of Christ and the distinguished reformer of the 19. Century."

QUESTIONS

1. Outline B. W. Stone's struggle in becoming a Christian.

2. What question was asked Stone at his ordination and what was his answer?

3. What was the Cane Ridge revival?

4. Describe some of the "religious exercises" associated with the Cane Ridge revival.

5. What significance did the Cane Ridge revival have for Stone and his co-laborers?

6. What was the Springfield Presbytery?

7. Who signed The Last Will and Testament of the Springfield Presbytery? What reasons did they give for dissolving this presbytery?

8. Describe the later actions of the six men who signed this document.

---

[1] Cf. John Rogers, Biography of EU. Barton Warren Stone, Chapter III.

[2] Rogers, Biography of ELL Barton Warren Stone, pp. 5, 6.

[3] *Ibid.* p. 7.

[4] *Ibid.* p. 9.

[5] *Ibid.* p. 40.

[6] *Ibid.*, pp. 41, 42.

[7] *Ibid.* p. 46.

THE CAMPBELL MOVEMENT THOMAS CAMPBELL

The Restoration Movement in America is indebted to the Old Light Anti-Burgher Seceder Presbyterians in Ireland for its creative personality, Thomas Campbell. He was born in County Down, Ireland, February 1, 1763. His father, Archibald Campbell, served with the British army and participated in the capture of Quebec. A member of the Roman Catholic Church in his early life, he returned to Great Britain after the war to renounce Catholicism and become a member of the Church of England. He remained a faithful member of this church until his death.

EARLY RELIGIOUS STRUGGLES

The home life maintained by Archibald Campbell and his wife manifested the parental interest in the religious welfare of their family. The Bible was read and studied daily, and a portion of it was committed to memory. The father sought to rear his family in the traditions of the Anglican Church. But the formal worship of the Church of England lacked warmth and genuine concern, and desire on the part of its members to make Christianity a vital and meaningful part of life. Repelled, Thomas Campbell sought elsewhere for more complete satisfaction of his spiritual needs. He availed himself of opportunities to hear and associate with the Covenanters and Seceders.

Thomas Campbell was influenced by the Calvinistic doctrines of hereditary total depravity and election, held and taught by the Seceder Presbyterians. He longed for the peace which would come from the assurance that he was among God's elect. He prayed diligently and

41

sought help from friends, but this assurance was slow in coming. He became greatly disturbed by his failure to reach God and God's failure to touch and transform his life. Finally, however, assurance came. In his *Memoirs of Alexander Campbell*, R. Richardson describes Thomas Campbell's distress, inner struggle, and eventual conversion as follows:

> While in this state, and when his mental distress had reached its highest point, he was one day walking alone in the fields, when, in the midst of his prayerful anxieties and longings, he felt a divine peace suddenly diffuse itself throughout his soul, and the love of God seemed to be shed abroad in his heart as he had never realized it. His doubts, anxieties and fears were at once dissipated, as if by enchantment. He was enabled to see and to trust in the merits of a crucified Christ, and to enjoy a divine sense of reconciliation that filled him with rapture and seemed to determine his destiny for ever. From this moment he recognized himself as consecrated to God, and thought only how he might best appropriate his time and his abilities to his service.[1]

From the time of this religious experience, which he accepted as evidence of divine favor, he resolved to give himself to the ministry. This ministry he desired to fulfill among the Seceder Presbyterians. However, his father, unhappy because of his son's apparent change of religious affections, insisted that he devote his talents to a ministry among the Anglicans. The son was underage at the time of this conflict with his father and subject to his father's authority. Temporarily prevented from pursuing his own course by the attitude of his father, Thomas postponed a final decision.

Meanwhile, he was made aware of the need for teachers in the south of Ireland. He had received a good education in a military school near his home, so was prepared to teach. He determined to answer the call for teachers. He went to southern Ireland and established an academy in the province of Connaught. Although his teaching was greatly needed and well received, his father, still exercising his parental authority, called his son home. He soon began teaching in a school at Sheepbridge, near Newry.

John Kinley, a Seceder Presbyterian, was instrumental in obtaining this teaching appointment for Campbell. He was greatly impressed by the attitude and ability of this young teacher. Knowing of his desire to become a Seceder minister, he offered to supply the funds necessary for his ministerial education. The father, although still somewhat reluctant, finally gave his permission, and Thomas Campbell enrolled in the University of Glasgow. He pursued the three-year course prescribed for ministerial students and at the same time took advantage of the opportunity to form a limited acquaintance with the field of medicine. He desired to be able to help the poor members of his congregation who might need medical attention but were unable to afford it.

Having completed his course at Glasgow, Campbell entered the school maintained by the Anti-Burghers for further study. This school usually enrolled about twenty-five students and was taught by one man, the pastor of the church in the community where the classes were held. The course consisted of five annual sessions of eight weeks each, or an academic year of specialized study devoted to lectures and examinations in systematic theology and the *Confession of Faith*. Practical problems faced by the minister in his work were also discussed.

Campbell completed the required course of study, passed the final examinations, and was licensed as a "probationer" by the Seceder Presbyterians. He was authorized to preach the gospel in needy fields, under the supervision of the synod.

MINISTRY IN IRELAND

Thomas Campbell and Jane Corneigle were married in 1787. Mrs. Campbell was a descendant of the French Huguenots who had located in the area of Ballymena, Ireland, when they fled from France because of persecution. In 1798 the husband became the pastor of the church at Ahorey and settled with his family on a farm near Rich Hill and Newry. He also conducted an academy in order to supplement his income and provide for the needs of his family.

The new minister was welcomed because of his ability and his dedication to his work. He placed great emphasis upon the Bible in his preaching, in teaching the people of the congregation, and in his own family circle. Catechetical examinations of the children in his parish were based largely on the Bible and couched in Biblical terms rather than the words and phrases of the catechism assigned for this purpose.

As already noted, Thomas Campbell was a member of the Old Light Anti-Burgher Seceder Presbyterian Church. Presbyterianism was the established religion in Scotland. Because of efforts to enforce a law denying congregations the privilege of choosing their own ministers, in 1733 four preachers, led by Alexander Erskine, seceded from the Church of Scotland and formed the Associate Presbytery. This group was known as Seceders or the Secession Church. In 1747 the Seceders divided into Burghers and Anti-Burghers over the taking of certain oaths required of burgesses. Both the Burghers and the Anti-Burghers later divided into New Lights and Old Lights. The dispute was over the power of civil magistrates in religious affairs and the perpetuity of the *Solemn League and Covenant*, which was an agreement between the English and Scottish Parliaments. The Scots agreed to assist the English Parliament in the war against Charles I, and in return Presbyterianism was to be introduced into England and Ireland.

This divided Presbyterianism had been transplanted into Ireland. Thomas Campbell was oppressed by these useless and senseless divisions. Some of the matters responsible for divisions in Scotland were never issues in Ireland. He attempted to bring about a reunion of the Seceder Presbyterian forces. Many were sympathetic with his efforts, and he was permitted to present his proposals for union at a meeting of the Synod of Belfast. Sentiment for union grew, but the General Associate Synod of Scotland opposed the union and was able to block it for a time. However, the union for which Campbell pleaded in 1805 was finally consummated in 1820, after he had left Ireland.

EMIGRATES TO AMERICA

Thomas Campbell's labors as minister of the church at Ahorey, his teaching in the academy at Rich Hill, and his efforts to effect a reunion of the Seceders combined to break his health. Upon the recommendation of his physician, and probably in keeping with desires expressed in the family circles (his son, Alexander, had indicated a desire to go to America someday) he set sail for America in April 1807, and arrived in Philadelphia some five weeks later.

The young Seceder preacher found the Associate Synod of North America in session upon his arrival. This synod was a Seceder ecclesiastical body; actually, it was Anti-Burgher, for the Burghers had not organized a separate body in America. The credentials which had been issued by the Presbytery at Market Hill were presented to this body, examined, and accepted. Campbell was received into the synod and assigned to labor in the bounds of the Chartiers Presbytery in southwestern Pennsylvania. This presbytery, meeting on June 30 and July 1, gave the new member appointments through October in Allegheny, Beaver, Indiana, and Washington Counties.

TROUBLE IN PRESBYTERY AND SYNOD

Within five months Campbell was in trouble with the Chartiers Presbytery. At their meeting on October 27, 1807, John Anderson informed the presbytery of his failure to keep an appointment to assist Thomas Campbell in administering the Lord's Supper at Buffaloe because he had learned of statements made by him which were not in harmony with the *Westminster Confession*. William Wilson testified that he had heard Campbell make such statements. His testimony was accepted, and Anderson was excused for not keeping this appointment. A long period of controversy was thus touched off between this preacher from Ireland and the Chartiers Presbytery.

Campbell Suspended From Presbytery

A committee consisting of four preachers (John Anderson, William Wilson, Thomas Allison, James Ramsay) and a ruling elder (John Hay) was appointed to investigate the reports made to the presbytery and to bring a libel suit against Campbell if the evidence justified it. Wilson, Allison, and Ramsay were former students of Anderson. Verbal protests and a formal letter of protest by the accused were rejected by the presbytery, and he was given no preaching appointments during November and December pending the committee's investigation.

The Chartiers Presbytery met again in January 1808. A libel charge in several counts was presented by the committee. Campbell was charged with false teaching concerning the nature of saving faith; rejecting creeds as lawful terms of fellowship; urging ruling elders to pray and exhort in public meetings when no minister was present; that it was permissible for Seceders to hear ministers of other communions when there were no services in their own churches; repudiating the substitutionary concept of the atonement; that it is possible for one to live a sinless life; and preaching in congregations assigned to other ministers.

The libel was read and discussed item by item. Campbell was heard on each point. A copy of the libel was given to the accused, and further discussion was delayed until the next meeting of the presbytery. At the next meeting Campbell sought to defend himself against the charges, but was judged guilty on practically every count. The presbytery voted his suspension on February 12, 1808. His request for reconsideration of his case at the March meeting was voted down. After the presbytery had adjourned and many had gone home, it was again called into session with only three members present (Anderson, Wilson, and Allison), and the suspension of Campbell was made permanent.

Appeals to Synod

He appealed his case to the Associate Synod of North America. Minutes of the synod reveal that the case was discussed on May 19-21 and 23-27. The synod declared the procedure of the presbytery irregular in certain particulars and revoked their suspension of Campbell. They then proceeded to their own investigation of the case. A committee instructed to make a draft of the synod's judgment concluded their report as follows:

> Upon the whole, the committee are of opinion that Mr. Campbell's answer to the two first articles of charge, are so evasive and unsatisfactory, and highly equivocal upon great and important articles of revealed religion, as to give ground to conclude that he has expressed sentiments very different upon these articles, and from the sentiments held and professed by this Church, and are sufficient grounds to infer censure.[2]

Motion was made and carried to "rebuke and admonish" Campbell. A motion to reduce the sentence to admonition only was lost. Campbell then asked a delay in the execution of the judgment until the following day, and his request was granted. At the evening session he filed a protest against the judgment of the synod, stating his unwillingness to submit to censure on the grounds that his answers were "evasive, unsatisfactory and highly equivocal." He would, however, submit to admonition on the ground of having acted imprudently.

The following day, before the discussion of his case was resumed, Campbell sent a letter accusing the synod of "partiality and injustice" and declining their authority. He was summoned before the tribunal and the new development was discussed. Campbell finally admitted that he had acted hastily and agreed to take back the letter and withdraw his charges against the synod.

Further discussion of the case resulted in striking the word "evasive" from the charges. Campbell stated "that his submission should be understood to mean no more, on his part, than an act of deference to the judgment of the court, that, by so doing, he might not give offence to his brethren by manifesting a refractory spirit." Following prayer by a member of the synod, Campbell was "rebuked and admonished" by the moderator. The chastened preacher was sent to Philadelphia to preach during June and July, afterward to report to the Chartiers Presbytery for further appointments.

But the leading spirits of the Chartiers Presbytery were determined that the case should not be resolved so easily. They protested the decisions of the synod, and when Campbell returned for his appointments by the presbytery, he found that none had been made. He learned that he was neither wanted nor welcome in the presbytery, and tolerated only because of the synod's order.

Campbell Withdraws From Presbytery and Synod

Campbell was irked and disgusted by the relentless and vindictive spirit of his opponents, who sought to discredit and annoy him in every possible way. Spies were selected to observe and report on his preaching and other activities; he was subjected to misrepresentations and lies. Finally, convinced that there was no hope of reconciliation with the Seceders and that no avenue of effective service was open to him within their body, Campbell presented a statement to the presbytery on September 13, 1808, renouncing the jurisdiction of the Chartiers Presbytery and the Associate Synod of North America and declaring his withdrawal from their fellowship.

Still the Chartiers Presbytery was not satisfied. It suspended Campbell from all ministerial functions. He was repeatedly called to appear before the presbytery "to be further dealt with," but he refused to appear. In May 1809, his case was again brought before the synod. The leaders of the presbytery were determined to have the synod reverse its condemnation of the presbytery's handling of the case before it was first brought to the attention of the synod. They charged the synod with arrogance, weakness, and folly. At one point the representatives of the presbytery, John Anderson and James Ramsay, became so abusive and intolerable that the synod refused to listen to their complaints.

Campbell Censured by Presbytery

The Chartiers Presbytery continued to summon Campbell to appear, and he continued to ignore their calls. Finally, for reasons already assigned in the suspension of Campbell and "for contumacy in not appearing to answer the citations that have been sent to him," the highest censure which the presbytery could impose was executed. The records for April 18, 1810, show their disposition of the case of the troublesome Campbell:

> Accordingly the Presbytery did and hereby do depose Mr. Campbell from the office of the Holy Ministry, and from sealing ordinances for the reasons above mentioned. Agreed to send an extract of this deposition of Mr. Campbell to the Synod and to intimate it to the congregations under our inspection.[3]

CHRISTIAN ASSOCIATION OF WASHINGTON

Thomas Campbell was not idle following his withdrawal from the presbytery and synod. He preached in groves and in the homes of the community which were opened to him. The inadequacy of creeds as a basis for Christian fellowship, the unique character and supremacy of the Bible, and the desirability and necessity for the union of Christians were emphasized in his preaching.

A group composed of Christians and non-Christians, more or less sympathetic with these principles associated with Campbell, listened to his sermons, and gave him encouragement. He made no attempt to separate these people from the churches to which they belonged; he did not propose the formation of another religious party. The group had no organization of any kind. Richardson says they "were held together by a vague sentiment of Christian union, and by the personal influence and character of Thomas Campbell."[4]

The need for a more formal type of fellowship and organization was apparent. Campbell conceived the idea for a society committed to the promotion of Biblical Christianity and Christian union. The Christian Association of Washington was organized in the home of Abraham Altars on August 17, 1809.

It was at this meeting that Thomas Campbell announced the now famous slogan which was to serve as the rule or guide in all religious matters: "Where the Scriptures speak, we speak; where the Scriptures are silent, we are silent." This principle—so simple, so clear, so concise—was to become the watchword of the Restoration Movement. Richardson makes the following estimate of its importance:

> It was from the moment when these significant words were uttered and accepted that the more intelligent ever afterward dated the *formal and actual commencement of the Reformation* which was subsequently carried on with so much success, and which has already produced such important changes in religious society over a large portion of the world.[5]

In theory this rule was readily accepted; it was to prove much more difficult to apply in every case. In fact, when first announced, it was pointed out that a strict application of this principle would put an end to infant baptism, a practice which even Thomas Campbell was slow to relinquish. Foreseeing the necessity for giving up doctrines and religious practices that had hallowed memories and associations, within a short period of time those unwilling to commit themselves completely to this radical religious movement dropped out.

THE *DECLARATION AND ADDRESS*

A committee of twenty-one was selected at the organizational meeting to join with Campbell "to determine upon the proper means to carry into effect the important ends of their Association." At the next meeting of the Association in September 1809, a document bearing the unmistakable marks of the sentiments and genius of Thomas Campbell and entitled *Declaration and Address* was presented to the Association for approval. It was accepted and ordered to be printed.

49

The *Declaration and Address* set forth the purpose, policy, and program of this new religious society. It consisted of four sections: "Declaration," "Address," "Appendix," and "Postscript."

The sole purpose of the Christian Association—merely a voluntary association of individuals for religious purposes and in no sense to be considered a church—as stated in the "Declaration" was to promote "simple evangelical Christianity, free from all mixture of human opinions and inventions of men." Financial commitments to be paid semiannually were to provide for the support of a "pure Gospel Ministry" and "supplying the poor with the Holy Scriptures." Two meetings were to be held each year, with a committee of twenty-one to act for the Association between the stated meetings.

A divided church was mourned as detrimental to the cause of Christ. The evils of division were pointed out.

> What awful and distressing effects have those sad divisions produced! what aversions, what reproaches, what backbitings, what evil surmisings, what angry contentions, what enmities, what excommunications, and even persecution! ... Thus, while professing Christians bite and devour one another, they are consumed one of another, or fall a prey to the righteous judgments of God; meantime, the truly religious of all parties are grieved, the weak stumbled, the graceless and profane hardened, the mouths of infidels opened to blaspheme religion ... the Gospel of the blessed Jesus, is reduced to contempt, while multitudes, deprived of a Gospel ministry ... fall an easy prey to seducers, and so become the dupes of almost unheard-of delusions.[6]

The core of the "Address" is a series of thirteen propositions. (It is suggested that these propositions be read and discussed in class.) These center in three basic concepts: (1) division and schism in the body of Christ is sin, being anti-Christian, anti-Scriptural, and anti-natural; (2) the Bible is all-sufficient as God's ultimate revelation and is the only adequate standard for doctrine, polity, and life; a truly Christian spirit is manifested through mutual love and forbearance.

The "Appendix" is explanatory and defensive. It seeks to clarify further the Association's attitude toward and relation to the religious world, and, as far as possible, to prevent misunderstandings of its purpose. Objections are anticipated and answered. It is clearly shown that the position taken by the Association is not latitudinarian; in fact, to accept the Word of God as the only standard for faith and practice is the only guard against being too broad—or too narrow. The folly of making opinions tests of fellowship or the ground for discipline is pointed out.

Two projects designed to aid the work of the Association are suggested in the "Postscript": the preparation of a "Christian Catechism" and the launching of a religious periodical. The catechism would be "an exhibition of that complete system of faith and duty expressly contained in the sacred oracles; respecting the doctrine, worship, discipline, and government of the Christian church" (Centennial edition, p. 55). The periodical, to bear the name *Christian Monitor*, would be used "in detecting and exposing the various anti-Christian enormities, innovations and corruptions, which infect the Christian church" (p. 55). The Christian Association did not live long enough to implement these proposals, but they were later objectified by Alexander Campbell in the *Christian System* and the *Christian Baptist*.

QUESTIONS

1. How did Thomas Campbell come to be a preacher in the Seceder Presbyterian Church?

2. How was he affected by the divisions among the Seceders and what did he do about them?

3. When and why did he emigrate to America?

4. Why did the Chartiers Presbytery oppose Thomas Campbell?

5. What action did the Presbyterian Synod take against him?

6. What was the purpose and program of the Christian Association of Washington?

7. What is the *Declaration and Address*? What now-famous slogan was set forth in it?

8. What basic principles of the Restoration Movement are found in the *Declaration and Address?*

[1] R. Richardson, *Memoirs of Alexander Campbell*, Vol. I, p. 23.

[2] *Ibid.*, p. 229.

[3] *Ibid.*, p. 229.

[4] *Ibid.*, p. 232.

[5] *Ibid.*, p. 237.

[6] C. A. Young, *Historical Documents Advocating Christian Union*, pp. 80, 85.

THE CAMPBELL MOVEMENT ALEXANDER CAMPBELL

Alexander Campbell—farmer, teacher, preacher, statesman, postmaster, author, editor, debater—is undoubtedly the dominant figure in the history of the Restoration Movement. So great was his influence and fame that those who disagreed with and opposed him gave the name "Campbellism" to the system of doctrine that he and others taught, and they dubbed his associates "Campbellites."

EARLY LIFE AND EDUCATION

Alexander Campbell, son of Thomas and Jane Corneigle Campbell, was born near Ballymena, County Antrim, Ireland, September 12, 1788. As already noted, his mother was a descendant of the French Huguenots who fled their home country when the Edict of Nantes, the "great charter of Huguenot rights" made by Henry IV in 1598, was revoked by Louis XIV in 1685.

Campbell's boyhood was spent on a farm near Rich Hill, some ten miles from the town of Newry, where his father located and lived while serving the Seceder Presbyterian Church at Ahorey. His education began in an elementary school at Market Hill and was continued in an academy taught by his uncles, Archibald and Enos Campbell. His father, a very successful teacher as well as a Seceder preacher, personally supervised a considerable portion of his son's education.

In this early period young Campbell manifested little of that devotion to study and learning that was to mark his later life and make him an outstanding leader in many areas. He was interested in games and in hunting and fishing. Because of his lack of interest in educational pursuits, his father set him to labor with those hired to do the fanning, hoping that he might be benefited both physically and mentally.

This decision of the father proved to be a wise one. The physical labor helped Alexander to develop a good, strong body, which served him so well in the rigorous schedule that he later followed in America. And within a few years he lost much of his interest in former pastimes and turned his attention to study. He vowed to become "one of the best scholars in the kingdom." Under his father's guidance he read extensively in literature, philosophy, and religion. Having a ready memory, he stored many choice passages from the poets and other literature in his mind for instant recall when needed. He was introduced to the works of the philosopher John Locke, such as his *Essay on the Human Understanding*, and was greatly influenced by the Lockeian philosophical system. He also studied French, Latin, and Greek under his father's tutelage.

Thomas and Jane Campbell were both greatly concerned about their own and their children's spiritual life. The Bible occupied a prominent place in their home. Family worship was conducted daily. Each member of the family memorized a selection from the Bible each day, recited it during the period of worship in the evening, and discussed it afterward. These verses were given again in the family worship conducted during the evening of the Lord's Day.

Alexander was seventeen years of age when his father opened an academy in Rich Hill, only a short distance from where the family was living. The house into which they moved in Rich Hill served a double purpose, providing a home for the family and rooms for the classes. The son served as an assistant in the academy and also continued to study under the direction of his father.

About this time he became more concerned about religious matters, especially his own spiritual condition. The Seceders were Calvinistic in doctrine. Salvation, according to their teaching, involved the sinner's search for God and receiving His assurance that the promise of redemption applied to him personally. Campbell has left the following record of his "religious experience":

> From the time that I could read the Scriptures, I became convinced that Jesus was the Son of God. I was also fully persuaded that I was

a sinner, and must obtain pardon through the merits of Christ or be lost for ever. This caused me great distress of soul, and I had much exercise of mind under the awakenings of a guilty conscience. Finally, after many strugglings, I was enabled to put my trust in the Saviour, and to feel my reliance on him as the only Saviour of sinners. From the moment that I was able to feel this reliance on the Lord Jesus Christ, I obtained and enjoyed peace of mind.[1]

The new convert was received into the Seceder Church at Ahorey, the congregation to which his father ministered.

Thomas Campbell soon made known his desire for his son to become a minister. Alexander was not fully persuaded that this was the work to which his life should be given; nevertheless, he turned his attention to the reading of theology and church history.

A review of the historical record of the Roman Catholic Church, with her arrogant claims of supremacy and power, gross immorality, and persecution of other religious groups, repelled him. Personal observation only substantiated what he read. He was scarcely more favorably impressed by the cold, worldly activities of the Anglicans. Divisions in the church, which were accompanied by bickering, strife, and efforts for advancement of party, greatly perturbed him. He watched with sympathetic interest his father's efforts for reunion among the Seceders.

SHIPWRECK...AND DECISION

The excessive labors of Thomas Campbell as he worked at three jobs—preaching, teaching, farming—impaired his health. His physician recommended a sea voyage as an aid to the restoration of his health. He resolved to go to America and, when settled, have his family join him there. Alexander already had expressed a desire to go to this new country some day. Accordingly, in 1807 the father, leaving the academy and the family in the hands of his eldest son, set sail for America. When the session of the academy was finished, Alexander joined the teaching staff of his uncle Archibald in the school he was conducting at Newry.

In March 1808, the long-awaited letter from the father was received, informing the family that all things were now ready and they should join him. An epidemic of smallpox, which affected the children of the family, delayed preparations for leaving. Finally, arrangements were completed, and on October 1, 1808, the family set sail on the Hibernia from Londonderry.

Their trip was again interrupted, however, when the Hibernia was blown off its course. The ship was brought into a bay of the island of Islay, where it lay anchored for almost three days. On the night of October 7 the winds became so strong that the anchors would not hold, and the ship was blown upon a rock and began to fill with water. For a time it seemed that all would be lost, but when the masts were cut down the ship righted itself and was able to ride out the storm.

This was a significant experience for Alexander Campbell. Having done all that he could for the safety and comfort of his family, he sat down upon the stump of one of the masts and gave serious thought to his life: past, present, and future. This was his hour of decision. He solemnly vowed that if God spared his life he would dedicate it completely to His service.

Help came with the dawning of the new day. The inhabitants of the island perceived the plight of the ship, and by heroic efforts succeeded in saving all the passengers. The islanders proved most hospitable, caring for the needs and comfort of these strangers to their isle. The family settled on the island, Alexander returned to the ship to salvage as much of their personal belongings as possible, including the books that he valued greatly. Since the journey could not be continued immediately, the Campbell family decided to spend the time of waiting in the city of Glasgow. Here the son would have an opportunity to study at the university which his father had attended.

GLASGOW—GENERAL AND RELIGIOUS EDUCATION

Alexander took some letters of introduction with him. to Glasgow. The letters were written by those on the island who had become acquainted with this young man and were impressed by his talents and personality. He presented one of these letters to Greville Ewing, head of the Haldanean theological institute in Glasgow and minister in an Independent Church. Ewing proved to be a most courteous and kindly gentleman and a warm and considerate friend.

The few months spent in Glasgow were to prove very significant for Alexander Campbell. He enrolled in the university for study in Greek, French, logic, and philosophy. He read widely in poetry, ethics, natural history, philosophy, and theology, copying many passages from the books he read into notebooks for future use. In addition to pursuing his own program of study he found time to teach classes in Latin, grammar, and arithmetic, thus helping to take care of the expenses for his education.

Knowledge gained through study in those branches of learning related to the arts and sciences were important to the eager student. But they were secondary in importance to the impact made on his life through association and discussion with leaders, especially Greville Ewing, in the Scottish movement for a return to primitive Christianity as revealed in the New Testament. Since Campbell was later accused of being a Haldanean and a Sandemanian, perhaps a brief outline of the rise and development of their reformatory movements will be helpful.

John Glas was a minister in the Church of Scotland. About 1730, while serving as the minister at Tealing, his connection with the established church was severed and he formed an Independent Church. Within four years congregations had been established in Dundee, Perth, and Edinburgh. Robert Sandeman, the son-in-law of Glas, was associated with him. The churches established by these men were congregational in government. The Old and New Testaments were accepted as the complete revelation of the will of God for man and the perfect rule of conduct for Christians. They taught that "bishop" and "elder" referred to the same office or person. Elders were the overseers of the congregation and deacons ministered in material things. Apostolic succession, as well as all spiritual or religious distinctions between "clergy" and "laity," were denied. Sprinkling was accepted as the "mode" of baptism and was administered to believers and their children. They emphasized the memorial character of the Lord's Supper, communed weekly, and practiced closed Communion. The holy kiss and feet washing were made part of the congregational life. Members were subject to a ready and exacting discipline. For some reason, the Glasites, or Sandemanians, never became a popular or numerous group.

Archibald McLean and Robert Carmichael were founders of the Scotch Baptists. McLean left the Church of Scotland to join the Glasites in 1761, and Carmichael forsook the Anti-Burgher Seceders for the same fellowship in 1762. They remained with this group only a year, withdrawing because of dissatisfaction over the handling of certain disciplinary problems. The churches they established after their withdrawal followed the doctrinal pattern of the Glasites in most points. However, they did repudiate infant baptism and practiced immersion instead of sprinkling. From Scotland the Scotch Baptists spread into England and Wales. This body was later greatly disturbed and divided over the necessity for pastors in the constitution of a church and the right to celebrate the Lord's Supper when no elders were present.

The Haldane brothers, Robert and James, began a movement for reform in the Church of Scotland resembling that of John Wesley in the Church of England in its original purpose, but eventually paralleling the Glasites in doctrinal emphases. They were wealthy businessmen and used their money freely in attempts to revitalize the spiritual life and to promote evangelistic and missionary fervor in the established church. Efforts to promote missionary programs for India and Africa were unsuccessful. They organized the "Society for Propagating the Gospel at Home" and brought to Scotland Rowland Hill, the great English evangelist, to stir their countrymen with his earnest evangelism. Lay preaching was encouraged, and theological schools established for the training of these preachers. The Haldanes left the Church of Scotland in 1799 and organized an Independent Church in Edinburgh, James becoming the pastor. They made many converts, and churches multiplied rapidly. Ten years had not passed, however, before the Haldanean forces were split over baptism. Out of the controversy over baptism eventually came the Congregational Church and the Baptist Church Union. The Haldanes themselves were immersed.

AN UNUSED COMMUNION TOKEN

The study of the philosophical systems of John Locke and Thomas Reid, of the Scottish "Common Sense" school of philosophy, undoubtedly had its effect on Campbell. His concept of faith as the belief of testimony and the reasonable nature of the Christian system and the Bible, as opposed to, the irrational concept of faith he encountered in the Calvinistic system and the mystical and allegorical interpretations of the Word, were furthered by these eminent philosophers.

Alexander had opportunities to become acquainted with the teaching of the Independents through representatives who visited Rich Hill, including such men as Rowland Hill, James Haldane, Alexander Carson, and John Walker. He later indicated that his own doctrinal positions were much like those of John Walker.

While at Glasgow, Campbell was again exposed to Haldanean teaching through Greville Ewing, who was an associate of the Haldanes. While Ewing agreed with them in most doctrinal points, including their emphasis on restoring the church as it is set forth in the New Testament, he differed from their immersionist views, holding that sprinkling was equally acceptable as the fulfillment of this ordinance. Campbell often joined others in the Ewing home for informal discussions of various religious issues. He also attended Ewing's Sunday evening services quite frequently, listening to sermons which for clarity and warmth contrasted greatly with the cold and stilted messages he heard from the Seceder preacher on Sunday mornings

Campbell became more and more sympathetic with the independents' position and more and more dissatisfied with Seceder Presbyterianism. But it seemed that he could not bring himself to sever his connection with this body. How much the fact that his father was a sincere Seceder minister affected his thinking we do not know, but in all probability this was one of the factors which he gave consideration, since he respected and honored him so greatly.

Although he was greatly concerned over his changing religious concepts and though he disapproved of many doctrines and practices of the Seceders, he successfully passed the examination that preceded the semiannual Communion service and was given a metallic token that entitled him to commune.

The hour for Communion came. A perplexed and uncertain Alexander Campbell was present with his Communion token. Could he conscientiously commune with others in a religious system that he no longer accepted? He waited until the last table in order to postpone his decision as long as possible. When he could delay no longer, he cast his token into the plate and left without communing!

This act, which to the casual observer might have seemed trivial and unimportant, marked Alexander Campbell's break from Presbyterianism and his determination to follow a new course. Perhaps in the uncertain light of this early, dawn of the all-importance and all-sufficiency of Biblical truth Campbell could see only the dim outlines of the new road he had chosen to follow, but the light of God's Word was to grow brighter and brighter until it clearly illuminated even the far reaches of the highway of religious reformation, which he was to travel until death ended his journey.

REUNION OF THE CAMPBELL FAMILY IN AMERICA

Following the close of the session at the university, Campbell spent five weeks at Helensburgh tutoring children of some of his newfound friends in Glasgow. He returned to the city to complete arrangements for the trip to America. The family left Scotland aboard the Latonia on August 3, 1809. Although the ship sprang a leak and had to ride out several rather severe storms during the voyage, they arrived safely in New York on September 29, 1809.

The Campbells took the stage from New York to Philadelphia, arriving on October 7. After spending Sunday and a major portion of Monday in Philadelphia, they departed by wagon for Washington, some 350 miles away. Meanwhile, Thomas Campbell had set out to meet his loved ones. On October 19, 1809, somewhere on the road in western Pennsylvania, the family was reunited. Their journey ended at their new home some three days later.

At the time of the reunion neither father nor son knew that the other had renounced Presbyterianism. There may have been some reticence on the part of the son to make known his changed religious views. The father soon recounted his experiences in America, including his trials before presbytery and synod, his repudiation of both, and his continuing work as an independent minister. In turn, the son shared his religious experiences and his decision at Glasgow. They rejoiced greatly because of their unity of religious convictions. Alexander was delighted with the principles and program incorporated in the Declaration anti Address. While Thomas Campbell had outlined the principles of restoration, his son was to propagate and defend them.

INFANT BAPTISM—A PERPLEXING PROBLEM

When the principle, "Where the Scriptures speak, we speak; where the Scriptures are silent, we are silent," was first announced in the home of Abraham Altars, as already noted it was quickly pointed out that this would put an end to the practice of infant baptism. At that time, Thomas Campbell said, "Of course, if infant baptism be not found in the Scripture, we can have nothing to do with it." But apparently he made no attempt to justify infant baptism on Scriptural grounds, relegating it to the realm of the "non-essentials" as a matter of private opinion. He said that he saw no reason to baptize those again who had been sprinkled in infancy; this was to take them out of the church in order to bring them in again.

James Foster, a member of the Christian Association, had become convinced that infant baptism was without Scriptural warrant before leaving Ireland for America. He believed that Campbell's rule should be applied to infant baptism. Richardson records the following conclusion to a discussion of infant baptism between Foster and Campbell:

> "Father Campbell, how could you, in the absence of any authority in the Word of God, baptize a child in the name of the Father, and of the Son, and of the Holy Spirit?" ... [Campbell's] face colored, he became for a moment irritated, and said in reply, in an offended tone: "Sir, you are the most intractable person I ever met."[2]

Thomas Campbell strongly opposed divisions in the body of Christ. If at all possible, he wanted to avoid accusations of opposing divisions while fostering a new one through the Christian Association. Therefore, with the consent of the Association and a disregard for his son's pessimistic attitude concerning the venture, he presented the plan and program of the Christian Association to the Presbyterian Synod of Pittsburg and petitioned that body "to be taken into Christian and ministerial communion." The synod considered the petition, refusing admittance on the grounds that the course proposed by the Association would promote division instead of union, degrade the ministerial character, permit errors in doctrine, and corrupt discipline. "And further," they added, "for the above and many other important reasons, it was resolved, that Mr. Campbell's request to be received into ministerial and Christian communion cannot be granted."[3]

When Campbell asked for a clarification of the "important reasons" indicated in this statement, among other things the synod indicated his irregular position concerning infant baptism: "For declaring that the administration of baptism to infants is not authorized by scriptural precept or example, and is a matter of indifference, yet administering that ordinance while holding such an opinion."[4]

Alexander Campbell preached his first sermon July 15, 1810, and soon became a popular preacher. He preached strictly as an independent. Though nominally a Presbyterian, he had affiliated with no religious body after coming to America. He preached without ordination or license, dedicated to the propagation of "simple, evangelical Christianity."

This young preacher was to become the leader in the application of the rule announced by his father. He had expressed full agreement with the principles set forth in the *Declaration and Address*. Yet, at this time, he was not quite ready to have this rule strictly applied to infant baptism. In a sermon on November 1, 1810, he argued that infant baptism was nowhere expressly enjoined, and that it should be made a matter of forbearance, even as circumcision was in the apostolic church. Again in June of the following year he said: "As I am sure it is unscriptural to make this matter a term of communion, I let it *slip*. I wish to think and let think on these matters."[5]

Alexander Campbell discussed baptism with a Baptist preacher in the home of his future father-in-law, but was unsatisfied with his showing. He examined the case for infant baptism as presented in the published works of its advocates and then turned to the Greek New Testament. But, although convinced that infant baptism and sprinkling had no Scriptural foundation or support, he was unwilling to make a practical application of his conclusions.

IMMERSION OF THE CAMPBELLS

The baptismal issue was climaxed when Alexander Campbell's first child was born and the matter of her baptism was considered. Further study of the subject, action, and purpose of baptism led him to repudiate infant sprinkling and accept believer's baptism. He was *now* ready to act on his conviction.

Matthias Luce, a Baptist preacher, finally agreed to baptize Alexander Campbell and his wife upon the profession of their faith in Christ and without the relation of a "religious experience" according to Baptist custom. Thomas Campbell and his wife and their daughter, Dorothea, also decided to be immersed. Both father and son addressed the assembled crowd before the baptisms. Two others, Mr. and Mrs. James Hanen, requested baptism. These seven then were baptized by Mr. Luce in Buffalo Creek.

QUESTIONS

1. Describe the early life and education of Alexander Campbell.

2. When and how did he decide to become a minister?

3. What was the significance of the year he spent at Glasgow—educationally? religiously?

4. What significance may we attach to his refusal to use the Communion token just before coming to America?

5. Why were Thomas and Alexander Campbell so reluctant to give up the practice of infant baptism?

6. What event led Alexander Campbell to study infant baptism in the light of the New Testament?

7. Who baptized Alexander Campbell?

8. Name the others who were baptized at the same time. Describe the occasion and the baptisms.

---

[1] Richardson, *Memoirs of Alexander Campbell*, Vol. I, p. 49.

[2] *Ibid.*, p. 240.

[3] *Ibid.*, p. 327.

[4] *Ibid.*, p. 328.

[5] *Ibid.*, p. 392.

ASSOCIATION WITH THE BAPTISTS

Thomas Campbell found fellowship and opportunity for spiritual service in the Christian Association after his separation from the Seceder Presbyterians. Those of the Association who were church members continued to hold membership in different congregations, while joining together for the promotion of "simple evangelical Christianity." Rebuffed by the Presbyterian Synod of Pittsburgh, representing the main body of Presbyterians, and having little hope of finding acceptance elsewhere, Campbell and the Association were forced to consider their future course.

BRUSH RUN CHURCH

Brush Run Church Constituted

Alexander Campbell, in his reply to the statement of the Synod of Pittsburgh at the semiannual meeting of the Christian Association in November, following the rejection of the petition for admission into the synod, intimated that if all doors were closed the Association might be compelled to organize and function as a church. No other course seemed to be open to them, so on May 4, 1811, the Brush Run Church was constituted. At this meeting Thomas Campbell asked this question of those who desired to become members of the new congregation: "What is the meritorious cause of a sinner's acceptance with God?" Thirty of the prospective new members gave satisfactory answers to the question and were enrolled as members; two were rejected.

Thomas Campbell was chosen the first elder, four deacons were selected, and Alexander Campbell was licensed to preach at this organizational meeting. Eight months later, January 1812, Alexander Campbell was ordained to the gospel ministry. His ordination certificate was signed, "Thomas Campbell, Senior minister of the First Church of the Christian Association of Washington, meeting at Crossroads and Brush Run, Washington county, Pennsylvania."[1]

Brush Run Church and Immersion

The Brush Run Church began as an independent and autonomous church body. In their congregational capacity they selected their own leaders. The Lord's Supper was observed weekly. The Bible was designated their only guide in doctrine and life.

At the first service following the organization it was noted that some who had answered Thomas Campbell's question satisfactorily and were considered members of the Brush Run Church did not participate in the Communion. When questioned, they indicated an unwillingness to commune when they had not been baptized. Not one of the three— Joseph Bryant, Margaret Fullerton, and Abraham Altars—had been sprinkled when a child, or received baptism in any form later in life. They desired to be immersed.

While Thomas and Alexander Campbell were willing "to think and let think" on the validity of infant baptism, and had not been immersed themselves, the right of these to be immersed was recognized. At the appointed hour a large group gathered at a fairly deep pool in Buffalo Creek for the baptisms. In one respect at least these baptisms were rather unusual, as may be seen from the following account:

> The pool was narrow, and so deep that the water came up to the shoulders of the candidates when they entered. it. Thomas Campbell, then, without going into the water, stood on a root that projected over the edge of the pool, and bent down their heads until they were buried in the liquid grave, repeating at the same time, in each case, the baptismal formula.[2]

Alexander Campbell's decision to be immersed was significant for himself, his family, the Brush Run Church, and the Restoration Movement. His search for the truth in regard to infant baptism resulted in five conclusions: infant baptism is without Biblical command or example; a believer is the only proper subject for baptism; immersion is the only "mode" of baptism found in the Bible; Alexander Campbell had not been Scripturally baptized; and Alexander Campbell would be immersed.

The baptism of Alexander Campbell and his wife, his father and mother, his sister Dorothea, and Mr. and Mrs. James Hanen made seven more immersed believers in the Brush Run Church. The Sunday following their baptism thirteen more members of the church requested immersion. Within a short period of time still others expressed a desire to be immersed. No effort was made to force every member to be immersed, but those who did not want to do so withdrew.

The fact that the church at Brush Run became a congregation of immersed believers had two far-reaching results. First, it led to bitter antagonism on the part of pedobaptists in their area. The Presbyterians particularly took it almost as a personal affront and challenge. Mr. Richardson tells us that:

> Misrepresentations of all kinds were freely circulated amongst the people; friendships were broken off; the ties of family relationship were weakened; and the discord of religious controversy invaded the quietude of the most secluded habitations…. The opposition, however, by no means confined itself to private intercourse, or even to the pulpit, but manifested itself in business relations, in the withdrawal of custom from members whose callings were dependent upon public patronage, and in slights at public gatherings whenever it was supposed an indignity might be safely offered to any member present…. It happened, more than once, that while Thomas Campbell was baptizing individuals who came forward from time to time to unite with the church, sticks and stones were thrown into the water from amidst the crowd assembled; imprecations also would sometimes be heard, and even threats of personal violence.[3]

But if the repudiation of infant baptism and sprinkling, and the practice of immersion filled pedobaptists with hatred and animosity, it found for them some new friends among the Baptists. The Campbells had been baptized by Matthias Luce, a Baptist preacher; they were now "baptists" and protagonists for the Baptist position in relation to the form of this ordinance. Alexander Campbell was invited to preach in their churches. Members of the Redstone Baptist Association began to urge the Campbells to bring the Brush Run Church into their Association.

AFFILIATION WITH THE REDSTONE BAPTIST ASSOCIATION

The friendly overtures from members of the Redstone Association met with little interest or favor at first. While Alexander Campbell had been welcomed by the Baptist "laity," and was favorably impressed by their consecration and piety, he had little respect for most of the "clergy," whom he characterized as "narrow, contracted, illiberal and uneducated ... little men in a big office."[4] But he soon learned that the Baptists themselves were greatly dissatisfied with their leaders.

The question of affiliation with Redstone was finally laid before the Brush Run Church for their consideration and decision. The congregation applied for admission to the Redstone Association, providing they would be received on their own terms. A need was felt for fellowship and for avoiding, if at all possible, the accusation of creating another religious body while pleading for the union of Christians. Alexander Campbell later reported:

> Some eight or ten pages of large dimensions, exhibiting our remonstrance against all human creeds as bonds of union or communion among Christian churches, and expressing a willingness, on certain conditions, to co-operate or to unite with that Association; provided only, and always, that we should be allowed to preach and teach whatever we learned from the Holy Scriptures, regardless of any creed or formula in Christendom.[5]

While a few objected to receiving Brush Run on these conditions, an overwhelming majority favored their admission. So the Brush Run Church was welcomed into the Redstone Baptist Association in the fall of 1813.

"Likes" and "Unlikes"

There were a number of similarities in the faith and practice of the Brush Run Church and the Baptist churches composing the Redstone Association. Among these "likes" were the following: the Bible the final authority in religion; autonomy of the local congregation; observance of the Lord's Supper; repudiation of sprinkling; immersion of believers;

ordination of the ministry; divinity of Christ; the atonement; resurrection of the dead; the ultimate happiness of the righteous; and eternal punishment of the wicked.

There were also "unlikes" in relation to some of these points of agreement, as well as in other areas. They differed as to the utility and use of creeds, divisions of the Bible, the purpose of baptism, the administrator of baptism, frequency of the Lord's Supper, operation of the Holy Spirit in conversion, requirements for church membership. Many of these differences were made apparent through the preaching and writings of Alexander Campbell.

While professing allegiance to the Bible as final authority, the Baptists had adopted the *Philadelphia Confession of Faith*, a Calvinistic document, as the standard of Baptist orthodoxy and the basis for union and communion. Brush Run repudiated the authority and expediency of all such human documents, proclaiming the all-sufficiency of the Word of God.

The Baptists made little or no distinction between the Old and New Testaments, or between the Jewish and Christian dispensations. The *Declaration and Address* proclaimed the unique character of the New Testament for the Christian age. Alexander Campbell enraged his opponents and alienated others in the Baptist ranks with his clear distinction between the old and new covenants in his *Sermon on the Law* in 1816.

The Baptists immersed *because* the candidate's sins *were already forgiven*; Brush Run immersed *unto* or *in order to* the remission of sins. The Baptists held that only an ordained minister should baptize; Brush Run taught that any Christian might, in keeping with the commission of Christ, baptize a penitent believer.

According to the Baptists, the Holy Spirit operated *directly* upon the sinner in conversion, bestowing saving faith to those elected by God and predestined to eternal life. Brush Run taught that the Holy Spirit operated only through the Word in converting sinners, that faith came through believing the testimony found in the Bible.

The Baptists required the relation of a religious "experience," indicating the fact of their regeneration, before baptism and admission into the church by vote of the congregation. Brush Run simply called upon sinners to believe in Christ and, having confessed this faith, to be baptized. All those who believed and were baptized were extended "the right hand of fellowship."

Sermon on the Law (1816)

Alexander Campbell continued to preach among the Baptists. His reformatory doctrines were accepted by many but met with increased antagonism on the part of others.

A meeting of the Redstone Association was held at Cross Creek, Virginia, the last of August 1816. A petition was introduced for the admission into the Association of a small congregation of immersed believers gathered together by Thomas Campbell in Pittsburgh, where he was teaching. The petition was rejected because it was "not presented according to the constitution of this Association." However, Thomas Campbell was given a seat in the meeting, and an article on "The Trinity," which he had prepared by request of the Association, was accepted and ordered to be printed in the minutes.

Many of the people and some preachers, desiring to hear Alexander Campbell, nominated him as one of the speakers; but Elder John Pritchard, claiming the right as the host preacher to name the speakers, substituted the name of Elijah Stone of Ohio for that of Campbell. When Stone became ill Campbell was asked to preach, and delivered his now famous *Sermon on the Law*.

This sermon was based on Romans 8:3. In it he pointed out the meaning of "the law," limitations of "the law," reasons for these limitations, and how God remedied the defects of "the law" through Christ. He argued that the complete Law of Moses was nullified, superseded by the gospel of Christ. The old dispensation passed away, making room for a new dispensation having a new covenant, new sacrifices, new priests, and new forms of worship.

Campbell later told readers of the *Harbinger*, "This unfortunate sermon afterwards involved me in a seven years' war with some members of the said Association, and became a matter of much debate."[6]An immediate move to have the doctrine set forth in the sermon condemned by the Association failed. It was printed, however, and at the next meeting of the Redstone Association it was brought forth as sufficient cause to try its author on charges of heresy. While the charges were dropped at that time, they were repeated before the Association for several years.

Campbell considered his appearance before the Redstone Association in 1816 to deliver this sermon providential. He later wrote: "He [Stone, the speaker first selected] providentially was suddenly seized by sickness."[7]The sermon also had great importance for the future of the Restoration Movement according to Campbell: "It is, therefore, highly probable to my mind, that but for the persecution begun on the alleged heresy of this sermon, whether the present reformation had ever been advocated by me."[8]

ALEXANDER CAMPBELL'S DEBATES

Alexander Campbell engaged in five public debates on religious subjects. At first he was reluctant to enter into a public discussion of religion; he agreed with his father, who felt that Christianity required a demonstration rather than a debate. While limitations of space do not permit a discussion of the lines of argument in these debates, a list of opponents, their religious affiliations, places and dates of the debates, and subjects discussed is included here.

John Walker, Presbyterian. Mount Pleasant, Ohio; June 19, 20, 1820. Mode and subjects of baptism.

William L. MacCalla, Presbyterian. Washington, Kentucky; October 15-21, 1823. Mode and subjects of baptism.

Robert Owen, skeptic. Cincinnati, Ohio; April 13-21, 1829. Evidences of Christianity.

John B. Purcell, Roman Catholic. Cincinnati, Ohio; January 13-21, 1837. Roman Catholicism.

Nathan L. Rice, Presbyterian. Lexington, Kentucky; November 15—December 1, 1843. Mode, subjects, and purpose of baptism; operation of the Holy Spirit; creeds; Christian union.

In the first two debates, Campbell appeared as the champion of the Baptist cause, in the one with Owen, as the defender of Christianity, in his debate with Purcell, as the representative of Protestantism, and with Rice, as a leader of the Restoration Movement.

Most Significant Debate

All of these debates were important, but the first proved most significant for Campbell and the religious world for a number of reasons. It revealed his aptitude for and power in the public discussion of religious issues. It convinced Campbell that debating was a legitimate and excellent means for exposing error and disseminating truth. Doors were opened to him for preaching in Baptist churches. The challenge issued at the close of the debate led to the discussion with MacCalla, which served to enhance further the stature of Campbell among the Baptists and gave him entrance into many Baptist churches in Kentucky, where his reformatory views spread rapidly. Here, also, he first became acquainted with B. W. Stone. The publication of the debate spread Campbell's views on baptism much more widely than they otherwise might have been at this time.

Results

Some ten years later Campbell revealed two results of this debate, which were most significant for the Restoration Movement. In the concluding article of the *Christian Baptist* he wrote:

> An unsuccessful effort by my father to reform the presbytery and synod to which he belonged, made me despair of reformation. I gave it up as a hopeless effort; but did not give up speaking in public assemblies upon the great articles of Christian faith and practice. In the hope, the humble hope, of erecting a single congregation with which I could enjoy the social institutions, I labored. I had not the remotest idea of being able to do more than this.
>
> . . . .
>
> It was not until after I discovered the effects of that discussion that I began to hope that something might be done to rouse this generation from its supineness and spiritual lethargy. About two years afterwards I conceived the plan of this work, and thought I should make the experiment.[9]

WALTER SCOTT AND THE MAHONING ASSOCIATION

Walter Scott, successful teacher, evangelist, and editor, holds an important place in the early history of the Restoration Movement. He was born in Moffat, Scotland, in 1796. His parents were members of the Church of Scotland. He received his higher education in the University of Edinburgh. At the request of an uncle, George Innes, he came to New York in 1818, finding employment as a Latin tutor in an academy. He soon left this position to travel west, arriving in Pittsburgh in 1819, where he became assistant to George Forrester in the academy that he conducted.

Forrester, also a Scotsman, had received religious training under the Haldanes before coming to America. In addition to conducting the academy, he worked with a small congregation that he had established. Scott proved an apt pupil of Forrester in religious matters, soon forsook Presbyterianism, and was baptized by his teacher.

Scott devoted himself to his teaching and a study of the Bible. A tract issued by a Scottish Baptist Church in New York fell into his hands and he made a visit to this congregation. He was disappointed with their Calvinistic concepts. He was also disappointed with independent congregations that he visited in Baltimore and Washington. He returned to Pittsburgh and resumed teaching. The sudden death of Forrester by drowning gave Scott the oversight of the congregation in Pittsburgh. His study of the Bible led him to conclude that the messiahship of Jesus is the central fact of the Bible and the divine creed for Christians.

Scott and Alexander Campbell met in Pittsburgh in 1822; they became warm friends. It was at Scott's suggestion that Campbell named his paper *The Christian Baptist* instead of *The Christian*. His contributions to this paper appeared over the name "Philip." In 1826 he moved to Steubenville, Ohio, to open an academy. He attended the meeting of the Mahoning Baptist Association the same year.

Evangelism was almost dead among the churches of the Mahoning Association. In 1827 fourteen churches reported thirty-four baptisms. Two churches, Wellsburg and Hiram, were responsible for more than half of these. Alexander Campbell suggested that Scott be called to evangelize for the Association, and he accepted. At his best, the new evangelist was a superlative preacher, but on occasion he failed miserably.

Scott immediately began a careful and thorough study of the New Testament. He discovered the following "order" in conversion: faith, repentance, baptism, remission of sins, gift of the Holy Spirit (later to be known as Scott's "five-finger exercise"). He met with little success at first, but he persisted and was able to report some thousand additions at the annual meeting of the Association.

Under Scott's influence a great evangelistic movement based upon the messiahship of Christ and a clear presentation of the "plan" of salvation revealed in the New Testament swept the Western Reserve. There was no "mourner's bench," no call for a "religious experience." Individuals who confessed their faith that "Jesus is the Christ, the Son of God" were baptized "for the remission of sins." Baptist churches were being revitalized, and many Christian Churches (Newlight) were accepting Scott's program. Reports from the Western Reserve reached the Campbells, and Thomas went to see what was happening. He wrote his son:

We have long known the former (the theory), and have spoken and published many things correctly concerning the ancient gospel, its simplicity and perfect adaptation to the present state of mankind… but I must confess that, in respect to the direct exhibition and application of it for that blessed purpose, I am at present for the first time upon the ground where the thing has appeared to be practically exhibited to the proper purpose.[10].

At the meeting in Austintown in 1830, upon motion of John Henry, the Association voted itself out of existence and became merely an annual meeting.

SEPARATION FROM THE BAPTISTS

The union of the Brush Run Church with the Redstone Association was a shaky union at best. Refusal to abide by the *Philadelphia Confession* made permanent union doubtful. The *Sermon on the Law* alarmed many Baptists. Campbell's reform program, harsh criticisms of the clergy, and opposition to various practices of the Baptists were constant aggravations. His growing popularity and success angered many of the clergy. To many Baptists, Campbell was a dangerous man, guilty of heresy, and should be excluded from their fellowship. Special efforts were made to discredit him in the Redstone Association in 1823. He frustrated the attempt by obtaining letters for himself and about thirty members of the Brush Run Church and organizing a new congregation in Wellsburg. Since the new congregation did not belong to the Redstone Association, he was beyond its jurisdiction and power.

But the opposition would not be satisfied as long as Alexander Campbell and those tainted with "Campbellism" remained within the Baptist fold. In 1825 ten churches of the Redstone Association adhering to the *Philadelphia Confession* excluded thirteen churches, including Brush Run, from their fellowship. Baptist Associations in Kentucky, Pennsylvania, and Virginia soon purged their ranks of "Campbellites." By 1830, although the work of separation was not yet fully complete, the exclusion of the "Reforming Baptists" was rather well accomplished and the lines clearly drawn.

Alexander Campbell had said: "I do intend to continue my connection with this people so long as they will permit me to say what I believe; to teach what I am assured of, and to censure what is amiss in their views and practices." "This people" had determined that Alexander Campbell's program was intolerable.

QUESTIONS

1. Discuss the organization of the Brush Run Church. What question was asked each prospective member?

2. Describe Thomas Campbell's first immersions as minister of the Brush Run Church.

3. How did the Brush Run Church become a body of immersed believers? How did this affect the religious community?

4. On what basis did the Brush Run Church affiliate with the Redstone Baptist Association?

5. How were Brush Run Church and the Baptist churches alike? How did they differ?

6. What was the "Sermon on the Law?" What was its significance?

7. With whom did Alexander Campbell have public debates? What issues were discussed?

8. What contribution did Walter Scott make to the Restoration Movement?

1 Richardson, *Memoirs of Alexander Campbell*, Vol. I, p. 391.

2 *Ibid.*, pp. 372, 373.

3 *Ibid.*, p. 431.

4 *Millennial Harbinger*, 1848, p.-345.

5 *Ibid.*, p. 346.

6 *Ibid.*, 1846, p. 493.

7 *Ibid.*, 1846, p. 494.

8 *Ibid.*, 1846, p. 493.

9 *Christian Baptist*, Burnet edition., p. 664.

10 William Baxter, *Life of Eder Walter Scott*, pp. 158, 159

UNION OF THE REFORMERS AND THE CHRISTIANS

The Stone movement in Kentucky antedated that led by the Campbells. It had been under way for a number of years before Thomas Campbell arrived in America. *The Last Will and Testament of the Springfield Presbytery* preceded the *Declaration and Address* by five years. While there were some differences between the Reformers under the leadership of the Campbells and the Christians who were associated with Stone, there were enough similarities to give hopes for a successful union of the two groups.

Barton Stone was a determined foe of partyism and an ardent advocate of Christian union. In a letter to the *Christian Palladium* in 1840 he stated his great concern for union in these words: "Christian union is my polar star. Here I stand as unmoved as the Allegheny mountains, nor can any thing drive me hence."[1]

Stone found some of the Presbyterians in North Carolina crossing party lines to associate with those of other denominations. The Orange Presbytery, which licensed Stone to preach, was rather liberal in the interpretation of certain Presbyterian doctrines, being influenced by such men as David Caldwell, William Hodge, and Henry Pattillo. And while teaching in Succoth Academy, at Washington, Georgia, Stone was closely associated with Hope Hull, who had been a sympathizer with James O'Kelly but had remained with the Methodists when the break finally came. Undoubtedly, he heard from Hull much about O'Kelly's fight for religious freedom and his plea for a return to the Bible. It is not particularly strange, then, to find Stone co-operating with

Methodists and Baptists in the Kentucky revival, ignoring doctrinal issues and party lines in the evangelistic fervor of the hour.

Stone and others were unwilling to sacrifice their freedom in Christ and loyalty to His Word for Presbyterian exclusiveness and party standard. Withdrawal from the jurisdiction of the Synod of Kentucky and organization of the Springfield Presbytery were significant events. The new presbytery was much more liberal in its sentiments than those which had been forsaken. The growing conviction that division and partyism were destructive of vital Christianity soon led to the dissolution of the new presbytery. The will of this body, expressed through *the Last Will and Testament*, was "that this body die, be dissolved and sink into union with the body of Christ at large."

Alexander Campbell was also exposed to formative influences of Biblical emphasis and the unity of Christians. These were dominant notes in the preaching and work of his father, both in Ireland and America. The Haldanean concepts of Biblical Christianity, which he first heard at Rich Hill, were renewed through association with Greville Ewing and others while at Glasgow. In the *Declaration and Address*, with its Biblical and unitive emphases, Alexander Campbell found religious sentiments and aspirations that paralleled his own.

SIMILARITIES OF THE REFORMERS AND THE CHRISTIANS

Generally speaking, we find the views of Barton Stone reflected by the Christians and the views of Alexander Campbell representative of the Reformers.

All-sufficiency of the Scriptures and the Rejection of Creeds

Both Reformers and Christians insisted that the Bible must be the final authority, the deciding voice in all religious matters. Human creeds as tests of fellowship were vigorously opposed.

These positions are clearly stated in the *Last Will and Testament*: "We *will*, that the people henceforth take the Bible as the only sure guide to heaven; and as many as are offended with other books, which stand in competition with it, may cast them into the fire if they choose; for it is better to enter into life having one book, than having many to be cast into hell." Factions and party, spirit within the body of Christ were believed to be "principally owing to the adoption of human creeds and forms of government."[2]Stone suggested that all creeds should be given to the "moles and bats."

In the *Declaration and Address* we find these expressions: "The Divine word is our standard"; "Nothing ought to be inculcated upon Christians as articles of faith; nor required of them as terms of communion, but what is expressly taught and enjoined upon them in the word of God"; the New Testament is a perfect "constitution for the worship, discipline, and government of the New Testament Church."[3]

Emphasis on Unity

Thomas Campbell characterized divisions in the church as anti-Scriptural, anti-natural, and anti-Christian. Lest they be accused of starting a new party, he sought fellowship for himself and the Christian Association with the Synod of Pittsburgh. It was only after rejection of this petition, and there seemed no other alternative, that the Brush Run Church was organized. And when the opportunity came, the new congregation joined forces with the Baptists in the Redstone Association.

Nature of Faith

Stone and the Campbells had rejected the Calvinistic doctrine that faith is a miraculous gift of the Holy Spirit. Stone taught that. there can be no faith without testimony. The "word of God is the foundation of faith," offering "sufficient evidence in itself to produce faith," which is "*simply believing the testimony of God.*"[4] Alexander Campbell, whom many believe indebted to Locke for his concept of faith, defined faith as "the belief of testimony," or "the certainty of the experience of other persons.[5]

Baptism

Baptism was not an issue when Stone and others renounced the jurisdiction of the Synod of Kentucky. Before this break Robert Marshall became convinced that immersion of believers was Scriptural baptism. Attempting to correct his concept of baptism, Stone became convinced that Marshall was right. The excitement attending the Kentucky revival and the separation from the Presbyterians pushed consideration of baptism into the background for a time. Later, the matter came before the Kentucky Christians again. It was agreed that all who desired to do so should be immersed. Stone immersed David Purviance, Purviance baptized Reuben Dooley, and these baptized others. Stone was not immersed until later, although he and the other preachers continued to immerse their converts. While immersion was not made a test of fellowship among the Christians in Kentucky, it became the common practice.

Stone, through continued Biblical study, concluded that baptism was associated with the remission of sins and should be "administered in the name of Jesus to all believing penitents." While he preached this doctrine on occasion, he did not grasp its full significance. He later wrote: "Into the spirit of the doctrine I was never fully led, until it was revived by Brother Alexander Campbell, some years after.:[6]

Alexander Campbell struggled with the doctrine of baptism, but once fully convinced that infant baptism was unscriptural and that immersion was Scriptural baptism, he immediately sought out a Baptist preacher to immerse him. (Some point to the immersion of the Campbells as the time when the mantle of leadership in the Campbellian reformation passed from the father to the son.) The meaning and design of baptism in the Christian dispensation became increasingly clear to him, and through sermon, private discussion, public debate, and periodical contributions Campbell constantly challenged the religious world to give it the place and importance in the conversion of sinners that it was given in apostolic preaching and practice. The Reformers made immersion a requisite for church membership.

Autonomy of the Local Church

The Springfield Presbytery "willed" that the church resume her right of internal government, and the Christians continued to emphasize the freedom of the local congregations from all other sources of ecclesiastical authority. The Reformers were also jealous of the freedom of the local church. When Brush Run entered the Redstone Association, it was with the understanding that this Association had no authority to determine its doctrines and practices. The death of the Mahoning Association through the influence of

Walter Scott was due to the repudiation of all extra-congregational bodies.

DIFFERENCES OF THE REFORMERS AND CHRISTIANS

Trinity

While both Reformers and Christians pointed out that the word "trinity" does not appear in the Bible, the former group were predominantly Trinitarian in theology while some of the latter seemed to be Unitarian.

Alexander Campbell conceived of God as having one divine nature and three manifestations. He writes of God's "plurality, relation, and society in himself" and of the "holy and incomprehensible relations in the Divinity."[7] In a critique of the Unitarians' doctrine of God published in the *Millennial Harbinger* for 1846, he wrote:

> But who, of good sense, argues that these three persons are one person—one being! That God is one and plural, is just as evident as that he can be every where and no where ... But we have a manifestation of God out of humanity in the Father, of God in humanity in the Son, and of God with humanity in the Holy Spirit.[8]

Stone was greatly confused by the doctrine of the Trinity as outlined, in the *Westminster Confession*. He believed the orthodox Trinitarian theology to be unreasonable, without Scriptural revelation or support, and involving a divine relationship for which no suitable earthly analogy can be found. Yet he unhesitatingly affirmed his belief in the living God and in the pre-existence and divinity of Christ.

Because of his "unorthodox" view of the Trinity, which was shared by many of the Christians, Stone was opposed not only by Campbell and other Reformers, but also by many of the Protestant denominational leaders. Fundamental differences in this area of theology were to become a major factor in defeating overtures for unity between the Reformers and the New England Christians, as well as many congregations in other sections of the country.

Atonement

Stone's rejection of a vicarious or substitutionary atonement, a doctrine which he felt would justify either the Calvinistic concept of a limited atonement or the Universalists' teaching of salvation for all, led to extended oral and written discussions with Presbyterians and Reformers, including Alexander and Thomas Campbell. For Stone, the atonement was an "at-one-ment"; through the life and death of Jesus, God and men are reconciled.

According to Alexander Campbell, atonement is the cause and reconciliation the effect of the death of Christ. Concerning the sacrifice of Jesus, the Lamb of God, he wrote:

> Sacrifice, as respects God, is a propitiation; as respects sinners, it is a reconciliation; as respects sin, it is an expiation; as respects the saved it is a redemption…. As a propitiation or atonement it is offered to God: not, indeed, to move his benevolence or to excite his mercy, but to render him propitious according to law and justice.[9]

The Name

Rice Haggard was convinced that the name "Christian" given to the disciples at Antioch (Acts 11:26) was the "new name, which the mouth of the Lord shall name" (Isaiah 62:2). He influenced both the O'Kelly secessionists from the Methodist Church and those who renounced Presbyterianism with Stone in Kentucky to adopt and use this name to the exclusion of all others. Alexander Campbell denied that the word translated "called" in Acts 11:26 indicated "divine appointment." Any Scriptural name was acceptable to Campbell, but he preferred the name "Disciples" or "Disciples of Christ" as being more ancient, more descriptive, more Scriptural, and more unappropriated. In the amplification of the fourth point he wrote: "Unitarians, Arians, and sundry other newly risen sects abroad, are zealous for the name Christian; while we are the only people on earth fairly and indisputably in the use of the title *Disciples of Christ*."[10]

"Disciples," "Disciples of Christ," and "Christians" were used to designate the followers of the Lord, and to some extent these names were used in referring to the adherents of the Restoration Movement. "Christian Church" and "Church of Christ" have been almost exclusively used to designate local congregations.

Evangelism

The Christians were intensely evangelistic. The fervor of the Kentucky revival continued to characterize their work. On the other hand, the Campbells had done little to foster evangelism. Walter Scott, as the evangelist for the Mahoning Association, inaugurated an effective evangelistic program. His sane, logical, Scriptural approach to the conversion of sinners was radically different from the early emotional "mourner's bench" type of evangelism of the Christians.

UNION EFFORTS

The Christians, under the influence of Stone and others, antedated the Campbell movement among the Baptists in Kentucky by almost twenty years. The Campbellian influence, augmented by debate, personal tours, and the *Christian Baptist*, spread rapidly in Kentucky from about 1823, the time of the Campbell-MacCalla debate, and his reform doctrines became the cause of dissension among the Baptists. By 1830 the Campbells and all those suspected of "Campbellism" were being excluded from the Baptist fellowship.

Efforts Begin in Kentucky

Serious efforts to effect a union between the Reformers and the Christians began in Kentucky about 1831. Already there had been some e association and fellowship between certain preachers of the two groups in Ohio. Recognizing their similarities and willing to forbear in their differences, the two congregations representing the Reformers and the Christians in Millersburg, near Cane Ridge and Paris, Kentucky, began communing together and finally became a united body in April 1831.

John T. Johnson, who had been greatly influenced by Alexander Campbell, attempted reforms in the Baptist Church at Great Crossings, of which he was a member. Failing to accomplish his desires, he withdrew and established a church on reform principles. Barton Stone was the preacher of the Christian Church in nearby Georgetown. Personal contacts led to mutual esteem and love. Campbell wrote of the situation at Great Crossings: "We rejoice to hear that the utmost harmony and Christian love prevail, not only amongst the disciples composing this congregation, but between them and the disciples meeting under the Christian name in connexion with brother Stone in Georgetown, notwithstanding the sparrings between us editors."[11]

Union Discussed at Georgetown

In November 1831, Raccoon John Smith, who was waging a battle for reform among the Baptists in Kentucky, was called to hold a meeting at Great Crossings. Johnson, Smith, Stone, and John Rogers (Christian) began discussing a union of the Reformers and Christians, and determined to make an effort to effect it. They announced meetings for the discussion of union at Georgetown on December 23-26, 1831, and for Lexington, December 30, 1831, through January 2, 1832.

At the meeting in Georgetown, Smith was selected to speak for the Reformers and Stone for the Christians. Smith had been opposing sectarianism and urging union in his preaching throughout this region. He expressed a willingness to forego all opinions or speculations in order to promote union and made clear his determination to use only Biblical terms for Biblical doctrines. He said:

> While there is but one faith, there may be ten thousand opinions; and hence, if Christians are ever to be one, they must be one in faith, and not in opinion.
>
> ·   ·   ·   ·   ·   ·   ·
>
> While, for the sake of peace and Christian union, I have long since waived the public maintenance of any speculation I may hold, yet not one Gospel fact, commandment, or promise, will I surrender for the world!
>
> Let us, then, my brethren, be no longer Campbellites or Stoneites, New Lights or Old Lights, or any other kind of lights, but let us all come to the Bible alone, as the only book in the world that can give us all the Light we need.[12]

Stone was deeply moved by the words of Smith. He expressed regret for his own speculations in the past and for their harmful effect upon himself and the church. He concluded: "I have not one objection to the ground laid down by him as the true scriptural basis of union among the people of God; and I am willing to give him, now and here, my hand."[13]

Union Achieved

While a hymn was being sung hand met hand in a pledge of brotherhood and fellowship. All joined together about the table of memory as one body on the Lord's Day. Williams writes of this union:

> It was an equal and mutual pledge and resolution to meet on the Bible as on common ground, and to preach the Gospel rather than to propagate opinions. The brethren of Stone did not join Alexander Campbell as their leader, nor did the brethren of Campbell join Barton W. Stone as their leader; but each, having already taken Jesus the Christ as their only Leader, in love and liberty became one body; not Stoneites, or Campbellites; not Christians, or Disciples, distinctively as such; but Christians, Disciples, saints, brethren, and children of the same Father, who is God over all, and in all.[14]

In order to cement the union and to encourage it elsewhere, Stone took John T. Johnson (Reformer) as co-editor of the *Christian Messenger*. John Smith (Reformer) and John Rogers (Christian) were selected to ride together and visit the churches, in order to make them acquainted with what had happened and to persuade them to similar action.

Union in Indiana

About this time a union was being effected between the Christians and Reformers in eastern Indiana under the labors of John Longley (Christian) and John P. Thompson (Reformer). Longley wrote to Stone on December 24, 1831: "The Reforming Baptists and we are one here." An earlier movement for union had developed in southern Indiana under the leadership of John Wright, a Free-Will Baptist. Wright held that "all human creeds are heretical and schismatical," and that the Bible was a sufficient guide for all Christians. In 1819 he persuaded the Blue River Baptist Church to drop its creed and sustain itself on the Bible alone. Within two years the churches forming the Blue River Association had accepted Wright's position and disbanded as an association. The Dunkards and Newlights soon joined these reformers. By 1828 union was practically complete among these groups. Uniting with them later were the Regular Baptists forming the Silver Creek Association, influenced by Absalom and John T. Littell and Mordecai Cole.

Union in Tennessee and Illinois

The union movement reached into Tennessee. E. Sweat wrote from Lebanon: "On last Lord's day in July at a camp-meeting on Lock's Creek, Rutherford Co. Tenn. The Christian and reforming brethren united."[15]

In his report of a tour through the west in the fall of 1832, Stone indicated that union was under way also in Illinois:

> We had very interesting meetings in Lawrenceville, Jacksonville, Carrolton, Rushville, Springfield, &c. of Illinois. In Jacksonville we witnessed a happy union of the two societies, Christians and Reformers, in one body or church. This church consists of 80 members.—There are many more who were not present.—In Jersey prairie about 50 of these two societies would unite on the same foundation the next Lord's day following. In Carrolton the same union was to take place at the same time.[16]

SOME CHRISTIANS REFUSE UNION

But the union was not to be consummated in some areas. The leadership of the eastern Christians, especially in the New England States and in some areas of Ohio, were opposed to any union with the "Campbellites." They objected to union on the grounds of Campbell's legalism and, particularly, his doctrine of baptism, which they chose to call "baptismal regeneration." Alexander Campbell was equally opposed to union with them. He classed them with the Unitarians and accused them of failing to give Christ His rightful place, of not recognizing His full deity.

Stone was under fire from both sides, but particularly from some of his "Christian" brethren who did not like Campbell. To their accusations that he favored "the errors of the Reformers," Stone replied:

> I would prefer death to such a practice. The Reformers have, doubtless, errors, as fallible men—no doubt, we have also.... You may think I have seceded from the C. Church, because the Reformers and we, being on the same foundation, and agreeing to take the same name Christian, have united as one people. Is not this the very principle we have been pleading from the beginning? Is uniting with any people in this manner seceding from the church? In thus uniting do we agree to unite with all the opinions and errors of each other?

… Have we by such union agreed to receive all their errors? No. In the great leading principles, or facts of the New Testament we agree, and cheerfully let each other have his opinions, as private property.[17]

Some years later, looking back on these early efforts for union, Stone indicated one reason for the failure to bring about a union of all the Christians and the Reformers. "This union, I have no doubt, would have been as easily effected in other States as in Kentucky," he wrote, "had there not been a few ignorant, headstrong bigots on both sides, who were more influenced to retain and augment their party, than to save the world by uniting according to the prayer of Jesus."[18]

QUESTIONS

1. Who were the Reformers? Who were the Christians?

2. How were the Reformers and the Christians alike?

3. How did the Reformers and the Christians differ?

4. Describe the union meetings at Georgetown and Lexington, Kentucky. Who were the leaders?

5. In what two ways were these efforts at union promoted?

6. What difficulties would be encountered in a union of two such religious bodies as these?

7. Why did the union efforts succeed so well in Kentucky?

8. Why did the efforts at union not succeed with the Christians in the east?

---

[1] Christian Palladium, p. 286.

[2] Young, *Historical Documents Advocating Christian Union*, 21, 22, PP. 24

[3] *Ibid.*, pp. 117, 108, 109.

[4] Rogers, *Biography of Eld. Barton W. Stone*. pp. 205, 206.

[5] *Millennial Harbinger*, 1837.

[6] Rogers, Biography of Eld. Barton W. Stone, p. 61.

[7] The Christian System, pp. 8, 12.

[8] *Millennial Harbinger*, 1846, p. 394.

[9] *The Christian System*, p. 23.

[10] Millennial *Harbinger*, 1839, p. 403.

[11] *Ibid.*, 1832, p. 29.

[12] J. A. Williams, *Life of Elder John Smith*, pp. 453, 454.

[13] *Ibid.*, p. 455.

[14] *Ibid.*, p. 456.

[15] *Christian Messenger,* 1832, p. 345.

[16] *Ibid.*, p. 347.

[17] *Ibid.*, 1833, p. 6.

[18] Rogers, *Biography of Eld. Barton W. Stone*, p. 78.

ORGANIZATIONAL DEVELOPMENTS

EARLY ATTITUDES

In breaking away from the established ecclesiastical order of their day, the early leaders in the Restoration Movement renounced the jurisdiction and questioned the legitimacy of authoritative religious organizations outside the local congregation.

The eastern Christians, both those in Virginia and North Carolina under the leadership of James O'Kelly and William Guirey, and those in the New England States led by Abner Jones and Elias Smith, insisted upon the autonomy of the local congregation. Smith opposed associations of churches and missionary societies, believing that all such organizations were contrary to the New Testament.

The Springfield Presbytery, having determined that the New Testament was to be their only standard, "soon found that there was neither precept nor example in the New Testament for such confederacies as modern Church Sessions, Presbyteries, Synods, General Assemblies, etc." They were convinced that consistency of profession and practice necessitated the following item in their will: "We will, that our power of making laws for the government of the church, and executing them by delegated authority, forever cease."[1]

In 1813 the Brush Run Church, holding the New Testament as the perfect "constitution for the worship, discipline and government of the New Testament Church," and so stated in the *Declaration and Address*, was accepted into the Redstone Baptist Association as an independent congregation, over the protest of some of its members. The Mahoning

Baptist Association of Ohio, influenced by Walter Scott, disbanded in 1830, but continued its fellowship through an annual meeting of Christians having no status as "an advisory council" or "ecclesiastical tribunal."

Another restoration movement, independent of the Stone and Campbell movements in its origin, affected the Free-Will Baptists, Dunkards, Newlights, and Regular Baptists in southern Indiana.

John Wright was responsible for the Blue River Baptist Association disbanding about 1821. Joseph Hostetler contributed to the death of a Dunkard Association about 1828. The preaching of Absalom and John T. Littell, who had adopted reform principles, so upset the churches of the Silver Creek Baptist Association that in 1837 it ceased to meet as an association.

In Kentucky a similar religious revolution was taking place among the Baptists. One example of this religious upheaval may be found in the action of the North District Baptist Association. Greatly influenced by the eccentric and powerful preacher, Raccoon John Smith, the North District Association concluded that there was no authority in the Word of God for this Association to meet at all.[2]

Alexander Campbell began the publication of the *Christian Baptist* in 1823. The opening article of this new periodical was entitled "The Christian Religion." In discussing the life and organization of the early church Mr. Campbell states:

> The *order* of their assemblies was uniformly the same. It did not vary with moons and seasons.... Their churches were not fractured into missionary societies, Bible societies, Education societies; nor did they dream of organizing such in the world.... They knew nothing of the hobbies of modern times. In their church capacity alone they moved. They neither transformed themselves into any other kind of association, nor did they fracture and sever themselves into divers societies. They viewed the church of Jesus Christ as the scheme of Heaven to ameliorate the world; as members of it, they considered themselves bound to do all they could for the glory of God and the good of men. They dare not transfer to a missionary society, or bible society, or education society, a cent or a prayer, lest in so doing they should rob the church of its glory, and exalt the inventions of men above the wisdom of God. In their church capacity alone they moved.[3]

These words were to be urged against Campbell by many of his followers when he began his strong advocacy of co-operation.

CHANGING ATTITUDES

For a time the members of the new movement were too occupied with defending themselves against attacks by leaders of older religious bodies, with arriving at a correct understanding of their own position, and with the proclamation of "simple evangelical Christianity", to give much consideration to the broader aspects of their personal and congregational relationships as parts of the body of Christ.

The movement was composed of a group of self-conscious, autonomous churches, having similarities but also having differences. The dawning consciousness of a brotherhood with a common task and common responsibilities indicated the need for closer fellowship and co-operation. They were faced with the problem of coordinating their efforts for effective service without jeopardizing the freedom of the local congregations. Efforts for co-operation were soon made for purposes of consultation, fellowship, and spreading the gospel.

The eastern Christians began co-operative meetings quite early: Kentucky, 1804; Ohio, 1808; Virginia, 1814; Indiana, 1817; Illinois, New York, Vermont, and Maine, 1818. A United States Christian Conference was organized in 1820.[4]

Alexander Campbell contributed both voice and pen to the growing sentiment favoring responsible co-operation among the churches. He continued to advocate such united efforts despite charges of inconsistency, of reversing his attitude toward extra-congregational associations as set forth in the *Christian Baptist*. In replying to his critics, Campbell insisted that his earlier statements in the *Baptist* had been misunderstood, that they were aimed at the sectarian character of existing organizations; that it was the abuses of such organizations which he opposed; and that the corruption of legitimate means and agencies for the advancement of Christian work in the past history of the church was no valid argument against their rightful use.

In an article entitled "Five Arguments for Church Organization," which appeared in the *Millennial Harbinger* for 1842, Campbell called for "a more rational and scriptural organization."[5] He proposed that

91

organization is essential to Bible distribution, the carrying out of home and foreign missions, the improvement and elevation of the Christian ministry, the protection of the churches from irresponsible preachers, and the best use of the total resources of the church.

Campbell found Scriptural precedent for the co-operation which reason suggested and justified. A group of churches could, and must, do what the individual congregations found impossible. References in the New Testament to the "Churches in Galatia," the "Churches of Macedonia" and similar expressions, were taken as illustrative of his contention that "the churches were districted in the age of the Apostles." The churches of Galatia and Achaia co-operated in raising money for the poor in Judea; churches united in choosing and appointing persons for certain religious purposes (2 Corinthians 8:19). Those thus chosen, according to Campbell, were "the messengers of the churches" from the districts which chose them. As early as 1831 he proposed a widening circle of co-operation among the churches. Beginning with the county, co-operative organization would ascend through the districts and states to a national level."[6]

EXAMPLES OF EARLY CO-OPERATIVE EFFORTS

The co-operative idea spread rapidly, although not without considerable opposition. It found fertile soil and diligent cultivation in Kentucky, Ohio, Indiana, Illinois, Missouri, Tennessee, Alabama, Virginia, and other states.

As already noted, the Mahoning Baptist Association, infiltrated by restoration concepts, disbanded as an association in 1830, but was continued as an annual meeting. A group estimated at five or six hundred met for three days (Friday through Sunday) at New Lisbon, Ohio, in August 1831. The time was spent in worship and reports. Walter Scott and Alexander Campbell preached. Eight were immersed. Reports from the preachers present showed about five hundred baptisms during the past year. The matter of cooperation was discussed, resulting in a resolution to co-operate on a county basis. The recommendations were:

These county meetings shall have nothing to do with any church business, of any sort whatever; but shall spend the time in public worship and edification, in hearing reports from the churches and those who labor in the word, of the success attendant on their operations, and to devise ways and means for giving greater publicity to the word in such places as may require their particular attention.[7]

Christians from several counties in Kentucky gathered at Mays Lick in May 1830, for a general meeting to promote fellowship and co-operation.[8] Matthew Winans reported a co-operation meeting composed of "messengers" from the churches in Clinton and Green counties, Ohio, in the early part of 1835.[9]

The "Eastern District of Virginia and the neighboring counties of Ohio" held a co-operation meeting in Wheeling, March 19, 1836. After listening to reports from the churches, the expediency of co-operation was affirmed. The area was divided into five districts; each was to support an evangelist if possible. It was also recommended that "a general meeting of Messengers from all the churches in co-operation be held annually for mutual information and interchange of sentiments?"[10] The report of this meeting was made by Alexander Campbell.

A County Co-operation for Hancock County, Indiana, was held in April 1836. Peter Roberts and Gabriel M'Duffie were appointed to "ride as evangelists." There were three baptisms during the time of the meeting.[11]

Early co-operative efforts in Indiana led to a state meeting in Indianapolis in June 1839. Education, co-operation, and the sustaining of evangelists were discussed. Reports and statistics of the churches were presented by messengers and letters. The report of this meeting led Campbell to suggest "an annual meeting in some central point of each state in the union, conducted on similar principles, exhibiting the statistics of the churches united in the primitive faith and manners, would in many ways greatly promote the prosperity of the cause." He added, "Co-operation and combination of effort is the great secret of success."[12]

SOCIETIES

The continued emphasis on co-operation eventually led to the organization of societies as the best means or agencies for furthering the interests and work of Christ's kingdom.

American Christian Bible Society

The first society to appeal to the brotherhood for support was the American Christian Bible Society, which was organized in Cincinnati in 1845. The purpose of the society was to "distribute the Sacred Scriptures without notes, or comment." David S. Burnet was elected its first president. The board of managers was made up largely of men from Cincinnati. Alexander Campbell was not present, but was selected as one of nine vice-presidents. He remained somewhat cool toward the society, however, suggesting that it would be better to co-operate with the Baptist Society, the American and Foreign Bible Society, in the distribution of Bibles than to have another society for the same purpose.

A contribution of one dollar per year entitled the contributor to membership; payment of twenty-five dollars constituted a life membership; and one hundred dollars made the donor a life director. Conduct of society affairs was invested in a board of managers consisting of the executive officers and twenty-five members chosen by the society. Reports and an accounting of funds were to be made at the annual meeting of the society in Cincinnati. The constitution also provided for auxiliary societies, with "surplus funds" to be placed in the treasury of the parent society.

American Christian Publication Society

Shortly after the organization of the Bible Society, Christian leaders in Cincinnati launched the Cincinnati Tract Society. Later the name was changed to the Christian Tract and Sunday School Society. In 1851 it became the American Christian Publication Society, publishing the *Christian Age* as its official organ. Efforts to make it the "brotherhood" publishing house failed.

American Christian Missionary Society

Agitation for a more representative co-operative program led to the call for a meeting of messengers or delegates from the churches in Cincinnati (October 1849). In the August issue of the *Millennial Harbinger*, Campbell stated the importance of such a meeting and described what it should be.

> ... a Convention of messengers of churches, selected and constituted such by the churches—one from every church, if possible, or if impossible, one from a district, or some definite number of churches. It is not to be composed of a few self-appointed messengers, or of messengers from one, two, or three districts, or States, but a general Convention....
>
> The purposes ... a more efficient and Scriptural organization—for a more general and efficient co-operation in the Bible cause, in the Missionary cause, in the Education cause.[13]

Eleven states were represented at this meeting. One hundred and fifty-six delegates represented one hundred churches. The Indiana State Meeting sent delegates. Alexander Campbell was not present, but was elected president. Among the twenty-five vice-presidents, representing fifteen states, were D. S. Burnet, Walter Scott, W. K. Pendleton, John T. Johnson, and Tolbert Fanning.

The new society was to be composed of "annual delegates, Life Members, and Life Directors." An annual contribution of ten dollars entitled a church to one delegate. Life members were those who paid twenty dollars at one time; one hundred dollars made the giver a life director. Duties of an executive board, composed of the duly elected officers, life directors, and twenty-five others elected by the society annually, were:

> ... [to] establish such agencies as the interest of the Society may require, appoint agents and missionaries, fix their compensation, direct and instruct them concerning their particular fields of labors, make all appropriations to be paid out of the Treasury, and present to the Society at each annual meeting a full report of their proceedings during the past year.[14]

According to Article 10, "all the officers, managers, missionaries and agents of the Society, shall be members in good standing of the Churches of God."

The new society recommended the Bible Society to the brotherhood. An organizational pattern consisting of quarterly district meetings and annual state meetings was recommended; the churches were urged to use care in selecting those to be ordained to the ministry; the organization of Sunday schools was encouraged; and a committee of five was appointed to co-operate with the Tract Society in providing Sunday-school books. The first missionary sent out was Dr. James Barclay, who went to Jerusalem in 1851. His stay in this city showed little in the way of tangible results.

While objections continued to be raised about the Scriptural warrant for societies, and especially to the monetary basis of membership and direction, the American Society continued to function until its merger with others in the United Christian Missionary Society. The report of "the mother society" in 1916, shortly before the merger, showed 4,137 churches established; 225,133 baptisms; and $3,040,560.15 disbursed.[15]

Christian Missionary Society

Organization of the Christian Missionary Society was motivated by the abolitionist sentiments of many Disciples. Barclay, the first missionary of the American Society, was a slaveholder. Many felt that a more definite stand needed to be taken on the slavery issue. Unwilling to co-operate in a society where this was ignored, they called a meeting to consider the formation of another society. The name suggested was "Northwestern Christian Missionary Society," but when the meeting convened in Indianapolis in 1859, "Northwestern" was deleted. Pardee Butler was supported as a missionary in Kansas. This society never gained much popularity; the annual receipts seldom exceeded a thousand dollars. The Civil War turned the attention of its advocates to actual conflict, and after the war was over and slavery was abolished by governmental decree, those interested in missions co-operated in the American Society.

Foreign Christian Missionary Society

Dissatisfaction with some aspects of the American Christian Missionary Society, coupled with a desire for some more definite and concentrated efforts in foreign missions, resulted in the organization of the Foreign Christian Missionary Society in 1875, with Isaac Errett as president. Work was carried on in many foreign countries: England, Denmark, France, Turkey, India, Japan, China, Africa, the Philippines. Archibald McLean, as corresponding secretary, did much to "put missions on the map" and popularize the work of the Foreign Society.

Christian Women's Board of Missions

This phase of organized missionary activity began in Cincinnati in 1874. The first president was Mrs. Maria Jameson. Article II stated its object:

> ... to maintain preachers and teachers for religious instruction, to encourage and cultivate a missionary spirit and missionary effort in the Churches, to disseminate missionary intelligence and to secure systematic contributions for such purposes; also, to establish and maintain schools and institutions for the education of both males and females.

The organization of local and state societies was encouraged, each to be subject to the parent society. New life was infused into the missionary work of the churches. Missions were sustained both at home and abroad, and an educational program in mountain areas and among the Negroes was established.

United Christian Missionary Society

Each society and board directed appeals to the churches for the funds needed to carry on their work. The number of these appeals and the competitive struggle for support called for a coordination of efforts in the co-operative program, resulting in the creation of the United Christian Missionary Society in 1919. Headquarters, first located in St. Louis, were later moved to Indianapolis. Merging to form the new society were the American Christian Missionary Society, Foreign Christian Missionary Society, Christian Women's Board of Missions, National Benevolent Association, Board of Ministerial Relief, and Board of Church Extension. The official publications of these older organizations were combined in a new organ, *World Call*.

A leadership inclined—at least in many instances—toward liberalism and a changing attitude toward the validity of the plea to restore New Testament Christianity, has tended toward the development of a denominational organization. Criticisms and defences of the United Society have abounded almost from its beginning, primarily involving the development of an ecclesiastical body designed to control and speak for the churches, comity agreements, and the practice of open membership by some of its missionaries.

INTERNATIONAL CONVENTION OF THE CHRISTIAN CHURCHES

The annual meeting of the American Christian Missionary Society, which absorbed the Bible and Tract Societies in 1856, served as a general convention for the Christian brotherhood and became the sounding board for many controversial issues.

The organizational pattern was changed somewhat with the adoption of "The Louisville Plan," which was worked out by a committee of twenty and accepted at the meeting in Louisville in 1869. The changes were designed to facilitate action and to alleviate the criticism that the American Society was representative of individuals and not of the churches.

The "Louisville Plan" involved a delegate system of representation in district, state, and national conventions. The national convention was called the General Christian Missionary Convention. It was to be composed of two delegates from each state, plus one delegate for every five thousand members. Each church was to make its report and present its offering to the district convention, which retained half of the offerings and sent half to the state convention, which, in turn, sent half of the money received to the national organization. Diminished receipts led to appeals for individual gifts in 1873 and a return to a paid membership in 1881.

The national gathering was actually a group of consecutive meetings representing the various societies. The need for a more definitive coordinating agency for the work led to the setting up of a "General Convention of Churches of Christ" at Louisville in 1912. The constitution was revised and the name changed to "The International Convention of the Disciples of Christ" in 1917 at Kansas City. The name was again changed in 1956, becoming "The International Convention of the Christian Churches (Disciples of Christ)."

The International Convention was designed to serve both as a delegate convention and a mass meeting of Disciples. All legislation must pass through a Committee on Recommendations, composed of delegates elected by the state conventions, the number of delegates being based on the total membership in the state. This committee presents all matters to the convention, with recommendations for approval or rejection. According to the constitution (but not in actual practice), any missionary, educational, or benevolent agency which submits its annual report to the convention and keeps its books open for inspection may become "a co-operating organization" in the convention, and thus qualifies to make appeals to the brotherhood for continued support. The International Convention has a secretary, who heads up its work; publishes the *Year Book of the Christian Churches (Disciples of Christ);* and publishes the reports of those organizations which report to the convention.

QUESTIONS

1. What three basic attitudes have been taken toward extra-church organizations such as missionary societies?

2. What did Alexander Campbell have to say about such organizations in 1823? What five arguments did he use to promote organization in 1840?

3. How may free, independent, autonomous churches co-operate?

4. What were the primary purposes of the early "co-operation" meetings?

5. Describe the organization and show the significance of the American Christian Bible Society.

6. Discuss the organization of the American Christian Missionary Society. Name and show the particular purpose of later organizations.

7. What organizations came together to form the United Christian Missionary Society? When?

8. What purpose does the International Convention serve?

[1] Young, *Historical Documents Advocating Christian Union*, pp. 24, 20.

[2] Williams, *Life of Elder John Smith*, p. 416.

[3] *Christian Baptist*, p. 20; Burnet ed., pp. 6, 7.

[4] M. T. Morrill, *History of the Christian Denomination in America*, pp. 122, 477-479.

[5] *Millennial Harbinger*, 1842, p. 523.

[6] *Ibid.*, 1831, pp. 436-438. See also a series on "The Nature of the Christian Organization in the *Harbinger* for 1842.

[7] *Ibid.*, 1831, p. 446.

[8] *Ibid.*, 1830, p. 238.

[9] *Ibid.*, 1835, pp. 119, 120.

[10] *Ibid.*, 1836, p. 185.

[11] *Ibid.*, 1836, p. 287.

[12] *Ibid.*, 1839, p. 353.

[13] *Ibid.*, 1849, p. 691.

[14] *Ibid.*, 1849, p. 691.

[15] *Year Book,* 1917.

SOME EARLY EDUCATIONAL VENTURES

The "big four" of the Restoration Movement in America—Thomas Campbell, Alexander Campbell, Walter Scott, Barton W. Stone—were all well-educated men and teachers, knowing the value of education for themselves and seeking to share its benefits with others.

Thomas Campbell received his early education in a military academy near his home. He was privileged to study at Glasgow University for three years. He later attended the theological school of the Anti-Burgher Seceder Presbyterians for the equivalent of another academic year of study (forty weeks). He taught in southern Ireland for a brief period, then at Sheepbridge, near Newry. In addition to his preaching as a probationer among the Seceders, he taught school at Market Hill. While minister of the church at Ahorey, he established an academy in his home at Rich Hill. His career as preacher and teacher continued in America. After his unfortunate experiences with presbytery and synod, he taught near Cambridge, Ohio; at Pittsburgh, Pennsylvania; and Burlington, Kentucky. With his son he taught in Buffalo Seminary.

Alexander Campbell received his early education in an elementary school in Market Hill, in the academy at Newry, conducted by his uncles, Archibald and Enos, and under the personal supervision of his father. One year was spent in study at Glasgow just before coming to America. He was associated with his father in teaching in Ireland and assumed the responsibility for the school at Rich Hill when Thomas Campbell left for America. He was responsible for starting two

101

education institutions in which he taught, Buffalo Seminary and Bethany College.

Walter Scott received his education in Scotland. After preparatory training in an academy, he attended the University of Edinburgh. He came to New York in 1818 and almost immediately became a Latin tutor. He joined George Forrester in the school which he was conducting in Pittsburgh. When Forrester drowned, Scott took charge of this school. Later he taught in Mays Lick and Covington, Kentucky. He moved to Steubenville, Ohio, in 1826 to establish an academy. Scott was selected as a trustee of Miami University, Oxford, Ohio, in 1834. When Bacon College was founded in Georgetown, Kentucky, in 1836, Scott was selected as its first president and professor of Hebrew Literature. He was president less than a year, primarily in name only, contributing little to the actual conduct of the school.

Barton Stone received his higher academic training in the school of David Caldwell in North Carolina. He accepted a position at the age of twenty-two in Hope Hull's academy in Washington, Georgia. He later taught in Lexington, Kentucky, and served as principal of Rittenhouse Academy in Georgetown, Kentucky.

Leaders in the Restoration Movement have been greatly concerned about education. This concern is shown by the great number of educational institutions that they started. One research worker has compiled a list of more than 250 schools established by those associated with this movement.[1] Others have estimated the number at a much higher figure. These schools include institutes, academies, colleges, and seminaries. An emphasis on education for women led to the foundation of a number of academies for women.

BUFFALO SEMINARY

Motivated by the "importance of obtaining the assistance of instructed and cultivated minds in the work to which he was devoted," Alexander Campbell began Buffalo Seminary in his home in 1818. According to Robert Richardson, Campbell had two objectives in mind when he established this institution: "He hoped to be able thus not only to confer a benefit upon the neighborhood in giving to the youth a better education than they could otherwise obtain, but also to have the opportunity of preparing some young men for the ministry of the Word."[2]

A number of students came from Pittsburgh, and some from Ohio. Those students living in the immediate neighborhood attended the day classes. Both men and women were accepted. Board and room were provided for $1.50 per week, and tuition was $5.00 per quarter. The curriculum included French and Hebrew. Thomas Campbell assisted his son in the Seminary for some two years after he left Burlington, Kentucky.

Buffalo Seminary continued for four years, 1818-1822. At least three factors were involved in Campbell's decision to close the school: very few of the young men showed any interest in becoming preachers; the close confinement required by his teaching was proving detrimental to his health; and his popularity as a preacher was bringing so many calls for preaching appointments that he could not give the necessary time to the Seminary.

At least two young men from Ohio who studied in this school gave themselves to the ministry. Jacob Osborne, who already had begun preaching, attended the Seminary for two years. He returned to Ohio to preach, but died at Warren in 1839. Joseph Freeman also returned to Ohio to preach reform doctrines among the Baptists. Some of the students attained success in other fields, such as law and medicine.

BACON COLLEGE

Bacon College opened its doors to students in a dwelling house in Georgetown, Kentucky, largely through the efforts of Thornton Johnson, on November 14, 1836. Walter Scott became president, at least in name, for about a year. He was succeeded by David S. Burnet. Financial inducements resulted in the college being moved to Harrodsburg in 1839, where, under the direction of Samuel Hatch, sessions were held in a dwelling. James Shannon became president in 1840. He was a well-educated, talented, and conscientious educational leader. Shannon occupied a number of important positions in the educational world, including the presidency of the University of Missouri. Insufficient support led to the suspension of the school in 1850. It was revived in Kentucky University, and Robert Milligan began service as the president of the collegiate department in 1859. The buildings burned in 1864. In 1865 Transylvania University merged with Kentucky University and the school was relocated in Lexington. The Academy and the College of Liberal Arts were continued; a College of Law and a College of the Bible, to educate young men for the ministry, were added.

COLLEGE OF THE BIBLE

This constituent college of Kentucky University, the first Bible college in the Restoration Movement, was organized in 1865, with Robert Milligan as president. Milligan and J. W. McGarvey, a graduate of Bethany College, comprised the first faculty. I. B. Grubbs, another Bethany graduate, was added to the faculty later. Because of different concepts of the purpose of the school held by John Bowman, regent of the University, and the faculty of the College of the Bible, particularly J. W. McGarvey, conflicts arose. McGarvey was asked to resign. He refused and was discharged in 1873.

Robert Milligan died in 1875. Robert Graham succeeded to the presidency, and McGarvey was recalled to serve as Professor of Sacred History. When Graham resigned in 1895, McGarvey became president. Under the dynamic leadership of McGarvey and a faculty composed of such men as S. M. Jefferson, Charles Louis Loos, and I. B. Grubbs, the College of the Bible sent forth a stream of young men into the ministry who were faithful to the Word and the principles of the Restoration Movement.

With the death of McGarvey in 1911, plans to continue the school on a conservative basis ran into difficulties when R. H. Crossfield was made president of the College of the Bible as well as president of Transylvania. The "old faithful" on the faculty were replaced by such "liberals" as A. W. Fortune, W. C. Bower, G. W. Henry, and E. E. Snoddy. H. L. Calhoun, who had become dean of the College of the Bible, fought to hold the line, but finally surrendered to the inevitable and resigned. The "liberals" had won the battle and the school.

BETHANY COLLEGE

Nineteen years after the closing of Buffalo Seminary, Alexander Campbell launched a more ambitious educational program. The new institution was chartered as Bethany College in 1840; the first classes were held the following year. According to the charter, Bethany College was to be "a Seminary of learning for the instruction of youth in the various branches of science and literature, the useful arts, agriculture, and the learned and foreign languages."[3]

Campbell donated the land for the campus of Bethany College, gave generously to its establishment, and served as the first president. The areas of teaching assigned to the five men who composed the first faculty were Alexander Campbell, mental philosophy, evidences of Christianity, moral and political economy; A. F. Ross, ancient languages and ancient history; Charles Stewart, algebra and general mathematics; Robert Richardson, chemistry and geology; W. K. Pendleton, natural philosophy and natural sciences.

The student body during the first term numbered about a hundred and fifty. Classes began at 6:30 in the morning and continued until 4:30 in the afternoon. Campbell's morning lectures on the Bible were stimulating, provocative, and challenging. W. T. Moore speaks of the "easy manner, comprehensive sweep, and intense earnestness" which characterized these lectures.[4] The long list of graduates who have been influential in the Restoration Movement include Thomas Munnell, Robert Graham, Moses E. Lard, J. W. McGarvey, J. S. Lamar, and Charles Louis Loos. Graduates of Bethany have also attained prominence in politics, law, medicine, and education. Later presidents include W. K. Pendleton, W. H. Woolery, Archibald McLean, Hugh McDiarmid, and B. C. Hagerman.

At the time Bethany College was launched Alexander Campbell declared his purpose to give the remaining years of his life to the development of his particular theory and program of education. His "Plan of a Literary, Moral, and Religious School; or the Union of Four Institutions in one—the combination of the Family, the Primary School, the College, and the Church in one great system of Education" was published in the *Harbinger* for 1839 (pp. 446-451). A more extended discussion of his program is found in a series on "New Institution," which appeared in the *Harbinger* during 1840.

Campbell proposed a four-part program: a preparatory and elementary school for boys 7-14 years of age; an academy of arts and sciences for boys 14 years and older (designed to prepare young men as farmers, mechanics, manufacturers, merchants, etc.); a college, in which a literary and scientific education could be obtained; and a normal school for the preparation of teachers. He proposed a "liberal and comprehensive institution" and stated its purpose:

> ... to model families, schools, colleges, and churches according to the divine pattern shown to us in the oracles of reason, of sound philosophy, and of divine truth; and to raise up a host of accomplished fathers, teachers of schools, teachers of colleges, teachers of churches, preachers of the gospel, and good and useful citizens, or whatever the church or the state may afterwards choose to make of them.[5]

This educational program was designed to cultivate the physical, intellectual, moral, and social areas of life; but the particular emphasis was on moral education. "The formation of moral character, the culture of the heart, is the supreme end of education, or rather is education itself," according to Campbell.[6] All courses were to be developed and taught in the light of this purpose.

The Bible, as "the basis of all true science and true learning," was to be at the center of the educational system. Every mind was to be "enlightened with divine revelation." This applied to those who entered secular fields of service as well as those who desired to preach. Campbell's purpose was not to present a doctrinal system, but to acquaint the student with the Biblical records and spiritual truths. "Bethany College is the only College known to us in the civilized world, founded upon the Bible," Campbell wrote in 1850. "It is not a theological school, founded upon human theology, nor a school of divinity, founded upon the Bible; but a literary and scientific institution, founded upon the Bible as the basis of all true science and true learning."[7]

HIRAM COLLEGE

Hiram College had its beginning as Western Reserve Eclectic Institute at Hiram, Ohio, in 1849; instruction began in 1850. The name was changed to Hiram College in 1867.

The first president was A. S. Hayden. Among the later presidents were James A. Garfield, the only preacher-President of the United States; H. W. Everest; B. A. Hinsdale; and E. V. Zollars. Hinsdale later became the superintendent of schools in Cleveland and a professor of education in the University of Michigan. Zollars, who already had taught in Bethany College and two schools in Kentucky before going to Hiram, later became president of Texas Christian University and Oklahoma Christian University (Phillips University). Isaac Errett suggested the original name and was one of the incorporators. For a short period beginning in 1865, he was principal and teacher of evangelism, pastoral work, homiletics, and church polity.

Alexander Campbell gave the new school his blessings. Two aspects of the institution may point to the influence of Campbell: a philosophy of education that made the Bible central, and the morning Bible lectures. According to the charter, "the Holy Scriptures shall forever be taught in the institution as the foundation of all true liberty, and of all moral obligation."[8] During Garfield's presidency the morning lectures of the school were not confined to the Bible, but covered a wide range of subjects, including history, morals, education, books, geography, geology, current events.

The first year the school enrolled 313; attendance reached 529 in the 1852-53 academic year.[9] Hayden, in his farewell address, pointed to the fine record and the educational impact of the Institute, both of which he felt compared favorably with any similar institution in the nation. The collegiate division included offerings in the classics, Hebrew, French, and German. According to Hayden, the school "encourages no hothouse scholarship.[10]

Hiram has had a great number of graduates serving with honor and distinction to themselves and to their college in secular and in religious work. Among the latter we find E. B. Wakefield, F. M. Green, Jessie Brown, Pounds (the hymn writer), Charles Reign Scoville, W. R. Walker, and P. H. Welshimer.

BUTLER UNIVERSITY

A conviction "by the prominent men among the Christian brotherhood in Indiana, that the prosperity of the Christian cause, as entrusted to their hands, was very intimately blended with the cause of education" led to the discussion of and agitation for the establishment of an institution of higher learning in the Indiana state meetings.[11] The meeting for 1849 voted to establish "Northwestern Christian University" in Indianapolis. A charter was granted in 1850, and a program for selling seventy-five thousand dollars in stocks began immediately.

A preparatory school, under the direction of Allen R. Benton, formerly with Fairview Academy (established in 1843), was opened in the spring of 1855. Buildings were completed, and the university began classes in November of the same year. Like other educational institutions associated with the Restoration Movement, the Bible was made a part of the curriculum. The school was coeducational from the beginning. John Young, president, with A. R. Benton and James Challen composed the first faculty. S. K. Hoshour became the second president in 1858, and A. R. Benton the third in 1861.

The college was first located on a campus of twenty acres just beyond the city limits, north of Indianapolis. In 1875 a new campus was obtained, and the school moved to Irvington. The name was changed to Butler University in 1877, in honor of Ovid Butler, who had contributed heavily and was closely associated with the school. In 1928 the university moved to Fairview, in north Indianapolis. Originally an institution sponsored by and related to the Christian Churches in Indiana, in later years it has gradually assumed the status of a municipal university.

The School of Religion, a graduate school, was begun in 1925, with Frederick D. Kershner as dean. O. L. Shelton succeeded Kershner as dean. In 1958 the name was changed to Christian Theological Seminary, and it became a separate institution, with Shelton as the first president. A new campus adjacent to the university was purchased. B. A. Norris became president of the Seminary in 1959.

Northwest Christian University did not entirely escape the controversy that surrounded the slavery issue, nor did the school receive the unqualified blessings of Alexander Campbell. When the school was chartered in 1850, Ovid Butler sent a report of the project to Campbell, which was published in the *Millennial Harbinger*. In this communication Butler made the following statement concerning Campbell and Bethany College: "Influenced, it may be, by its local position, as well as by other controlling circumstances, you have apparently, and, we suppose wisely, relied upon the south for its principal support." He closed his letter with an invitation: 'We are anxious that you should visit the interior of this State, and especially Indianapolis, but we fear that further importunities would prove as unavailing as the past has been."[12]

Campbell's comments on the project were not particularly friendly. He accused the brethren in Indiana of manifesting a sectional spirit in establishing a "Northwestern" Christian University. As to visiting Indiana, he explained that he often had planned such a tour, but had encountered difficulties which made it impossible for him to visit the state. And by way of further explanation he added: "My tours have been, of necessity, almost universally either in autumn or winter. In autumn, Indiana has been celebrated for fevers, and in winter, for impassible roads."[13]

Campbell denied any sectionalism on his part in beginning Bethany College, in purpose, location, or name. He warmly defended the position of Bethany in the brotherhood, pointing to its beautiful and healthful location, its well-qualified and experienced faculty, and the splendid record of its graduates. He concluded his reply to Butler with these words:

> I hope most satisfactorily to show, what I believe to be capable of satisfactory demonstration, that one good institution, well-organized, well furnished with an able cohort of teachers, well-patronized by the brethren and the public, is better than ten such as we are likely to have got up and spirited into life by such arguments and efforts, that tend much more to schism, rivalry, and false ambition, than to union, harmony, and successful action. I hope the brethren will hasten leisurely, and hear all the premises and arguments before they act in such a way as to create half-a-dozen of ill-begotten, mis-happen, club-footed, imbecile schools, under the name and title of Colleges and Universities. They may strike, but hear me; and if they will only

concede a candid hearing, I will give them a candid homily or sermon, either on their own premises or on mine.[14]

OTHER EDUCATIONAL INSTITUTIONS

Limitations of space make it impossible to do more than mention some of the other educational institutions: Milligan College, Eureka College, Culver-Stockton College, Drake University, Chapman College, Texas Christian University, Lynchburg College. These, and many others, may well have received some attention.

The Churches of Christ (non-instrumental) have followed an educational philosophy and policy closely akin to that of Alexander Campbell, and have been responsible for a number of very fine schools and colleges. Among these are Abilene Christian College, Oklahoma Christian College, Florida Christian College, Harding College, Freed-Hardeman College, David Lipscomb College, and George Pepperdine.

Christian Churches and Churches of Christ have also established "Bible Chairs" in a number of universities, including the Universities of Michigan, Virginia, Pennsylvania, and Texas.

In total impact, through specific educational institutions which have been established, and through individual disciples teaching in secular institutions, the Restoration Movement has made and still continues to make most significant contributions in the field of education.

QUESTIONS

1. What was the educational background of Thomas Campbell, Alexander Campbell, Barton Stone, and Walter Scott?

2. What attitude have leaders in the Restoration Movement taken toward education?

3. What two schools did Alexander Campbell start? Why did he start these schools?

4. What particular place was given the Bible in the early schools, such as Bethany, Hiram, and Butler?

5. Name some of the other colleges founded by leaders in the Restoration Movement. Who were some of the prominent educators?

1 James DeForest Murch, *Christians Only*, p. 200.

2 Richardson, *Memoirs of Alexander Campbell*, Vol. I, p. 491.

3 *Millennial Harbinger*, 1840, p. 176.

4 *Comprehensive History of the Disciples of Christ*, p. 364.

5 *Millennial Harbinger*, 1839, p. 449.

6 *Ibid.*, 1840, p. 157.

7 *Ibid.*, 1850, p. 291.

8 A. S. Hayden, *Early History of the Disciples in the Western Reserve*, p. 264.

9 F. M. Green, *Hiram College and Western Reserve Eclectic Institute*, p. 51.

10 *Ibid.*, p. 92.

11 Madison Evans, *Biographical Sketches of the Pioneer Preachers of Indiana*, p. 414.

12 *Millennial Harbinger*, 1850, pp. 330, 331.

13 *Ibid.*, pp. 332, 333.

14 *Ibid.*, p. 335.

PERIODICALS IN THE RESTORATION MOVEMENT

"The tongue of the eloquent orator and the pen of the ready writer are the two most potent instrumentalities of moral good or moral evil in the world"—Alexander Campbell.[1]

EDITORS AND THE RESTORATION MOVEMENT

The place of the editor was, and is, very important in a reformatory movement such as the one under consideration. This was especially true in the earlier, formative years. Each editor determined the character of the periodical for which he sought the public favor and support. He established its purpose and policy. Through personal contributions and articles from the pens of others, he set the tone and fulfilled the destiny of his paper.

Each editor also created a constituency substantially in agreement with the particular emphases of his publication; and, in turn, this constituency supported °the paper. While it may be true that some subscribe to a periodical with which they are not in agreement simply because they "want to know what is going on," most people take a paper because it gives them what they want. Cancellations are the strongest protests against changes in editorial policies.

Most of the earlier editors were self-appointed. It must be remembered that in the Restoration Movement there has been no agency for controlling the periodical press, no individual or ecclesiastical body having authority to say to one man "You can edit" and to another "You cannot edit." So, while in a sense representing the movement, editors spoke only for themselves.

As early as 1839 Alexander Campbell expressed concern about the number of papers and the choice of editors. "How much the cause we have espoused has suffered by young and inexperienced men assuming the responsibilities of preachers and editors on their own motion, is not for me nor any one else to say," he wrote; "but that it has suffered much injury from such hands I am as fully persuaded as I am of the truth of the gospel."[2]

In 1852 he became more outspoken in his criticism of the "voluntary, and only partially educated scribes and irresponsible editors" in the Restoration Movement.[3]

> The unlicensed press of the present day, and especially in our department of reformation, is the most fearful omen in my horizon....
>
> As a community we have been the most reckless in choosing our editors, our scribes, our elders and our preachers....
>
> We have had a brood of periodicals the most voluntary and irresponsible that I have ever known.[4]

PERIODICALS AND THE RESTORATION MOVEMENT

Positive Contributions

General religious information was included in periodicals on a limited scale. The activities of the religious bodies of the day received some attention from editors, particularly where such events had significance for or bearing on the message of the Restoration Movement. *Devotional articles* were published as an aid in developing devotional life and stimulating spiritual growth. *Exposition of the Scriptures* was a major concern of editors, for a knowledge of the Word was vital to a program dedicated to the restoration of New Testament Christianity. *Dissemination of news*— such as the reports of evangelists, successes in local congregations, establishment of new churches, periodicals, educational and benevolent institutions, and announcements and minutes of co-operation meetings—was an important function of periodicals. *Propaganda for the Restoration Movement* was found in the periodicals. The principles of the movement were stated and explained, attacks were repelled, misrepresentations pointed out and the truth revealed, and misunderstandings clarified. *Errors in the interpretation of the Bible* were refuted and the "errorists" rebuked.

Negative Contributions

The *statement and propagation of speculations and opinions* were made possible by editorial freedom. *Partyism* developed and "camps" grew up within the movement, each having its own periodical standard and authority. *Intolerance and dogmatism* were fostered, in some cases at least, by self-appointed judges bent on exposing the errors of others. *Liberty of opinion was denied,* and every matter, however small or insignificant, became an issue fraught with vital and eternal significance. *Crystallization of thought and vocabulary* led to stagnation and enforced immobility. *Editorial jealousy and envy* minimized personal faults and magnified the faults of others. *Love and forbearance often died* in the heat of the various controversies.

HOW MANY PERIODICALS?

This is a question no one has been able to answer satisfactorily. Many have desired to occupy the editorial chair. Two motives have contributed to this desire: service for the Lord and the glory attached to the office and name of editor. There are three ways to limit the number of periodicals: voluntary restraint on the part of would-be editors, mergers of existing periodicals, and lack of support. Perhaps the last has been most significant. A great number of the early periodicals lasted only a short time, being eliminated by the economic sword, the subscribers failing to pay or discontinuing their subscriptions. Alexander Campbell described the editing of a periodical as "a benevolent enterprise."

In 1839 Campbell spoke out against the "periodical zeal" being manifested in the Restoration Movement. His arguments against the multiplicity of papers centered in the poor stewardship involved: poor stewardship of time—too much time being spent in editorial duties which could be used to greater advantage in evangelism; poor stewardship of money—a few periodicals well supported were better than many struggling for existence; poor stewardship of the truth—there was a tendency to confuse through many voices and through errors involved in the new idea which each editor felt impelled to give his readers.[5]

At this time (1839) Campbell advocated two papers: "a Monthly Quarterly Review, and a large Weekly News-Letter." When he again approached the problem in 1852 he suggested three papers, "one weekly, one monthly and one quarterly." The weekly would be a newssheet, the monthly devoted to fuller discussions of important issues, and the quarterly given over to scholarly matters. Such a program, he said, "would save the community many thousands of dollars per annum for better purposes than for the reading of diluted ideas in Homeopathic doses, as we now have them dispensed in invisible pills, in the ratio of one to a gallon of water."[6] But even Mr. Campbell had little success in persuading men to forego the editorial chair or forsake the editorial fraternity.

SOME RESTORATION PERIODICALS

The earlier publications of the Restoration Movement were monthlies. W. W. Eaton sent forth *The Sower* weekly from Pittsburgh in 1854; Benjamin Franklin began the weekly appearance of his *American Christian Review* in 1858; and Elijah Goodwin issued the *Weekly Christian Record* beginning in 1862; other weeklies soon followed. There have been few quarterlies in the Restoration Movement, and these few have had a comparatively short life span.

Christian Baptist (Monthly, 1823-1830)

This publication was said to be "the periodical which produced the greatest revolution in thought in this century."[7]

The *Christian Baptist* was a small monthly, the issues of one year making a bound volume of some three hundred pages and measuring about four and one-quarter by seven inches, begun by Alexander Campbell in 1823. During the years of its publication the editor was a Baptist, and the paper, at the suggestion of Walter Scott, went out under the Baptist banner. However, the work itself was an independent journal devoted to a search for Biblical truth. No one could say that the editor failed to fulfill the promise he made in the prospectus for the *Baptist*: "The 'CHRISTIAN BAPTIST' shall espouse no religious sect, except the Ancient Sect, called 'CHRISTIANS FIRST AT ANTIOCH.'

Its sole object shall be the eviction of truth, and the exposure of error in doctrine and practice."

The principles of the Campbellian reform movement, which had been incorporated in the *Declaration and Address*, were again given to the public in the *Christian Baptist*, amplified and ably defended. The significant series, "A Restoration of the Ancient Order of Things," which began in volume two and continued through the remaining volumes, included discussions of the Restoration principle, creeds, nomenclature, order of worship, Lord's Supper, fellowship, washing of feet, elders, deacons, singing, discipline. The series on the dispensations in volumes six and seven emphasized the dispensational divisions of the Bible, making distinctions which were so vital and necessary to "rightly divide" the Scriptures.

The *Christian Baptist* was the lash with which Campbell gave the clergy their "forty stripes save one"—most of the time they received their full forty stripes! His "Sermon on Goats," a satire on the clergy, appeared in the first issue. It was followed by a series on "The Clergy," and the ironical "Third Epistle of Peter." Creeds also received considerable editorial attention. Two articles in the series on "Restoration of the Ancient Order" deals with creeds. The "Parable of the Iron Bedstead" pointed to the inconsistency and tyranny of creeds with inescapable logic.

The vitriolic character of the *Baptist* is often referred to. The editor tells us that the tone of the *Baptist* was so by predetermined policy. Efforts of his father at reformation had met with little success. The irenic *Declaration and Address* had made little stir in the religious world. Convinced that "desperate diseases require desperate remedies," Campbell launched the *Christian Baptist*, the first volume of which he describes as "the 'most uncharitable,' the most severe, sarcastic, and ironical he ever wrote." According to the editor, "it was an experiment to ascertain whether society could be moved by fear or rage—whether it could be made to feel at all the decisive symptoms of the mortal malady which was consuming the last spark of moral life and motion."[8]

It would be difficult to overestimate the place of the *Christian Baptist* in the Restoration Movement. Through this paper such men as Joseph Hostetler in southern Indiana, John P. Thompson in eastern

Indiana, Chester Bullard in Virginia, and countless other men were led to a deeper understanding of and great efforts for restoring New Testament Christianity. Later, the words of this periodical were to become a wedge, separating brethren on the validity of co-operation in such projects as missionary societies and Christian colleges. When the *Christian Baptist* began, Alexander Campbell was a popular and influential young Baptist preacher, having just successfully defended the Baptist cause in a debate with John Walker and preparing for his encounter with another Presbyterian, W. L. MacCalla. When it closed, the Baptists had contributed hundreds of members, including entire congregations and associations, to the Restoration Movement, and all "Campbellites" were being expelled from the Baptist fellowship as rapidly as possible.

Christian Messenger (Monthly, 1826-1845)

The *Christian Messenger*, comparable with the *Christian Baptist* in size and make-up, was first published at Georgetown, Kentucky, and later at Jacksonville, Illinois, when Stone moved there in 1834. This periodical is irenic in tone, breathing some of the gentleness, tenderness, and warmth of the "apostle of unity." It contributed greatly to Stone's leadership among the western Christians.

Christian unity, which Stone says he took as his "polar star;" is a recurring topic in the Messenger. The editor began a series on union in the first issue. At the time of the union between the Reformers and Christians in 1832, Stone took John T. Johnson, Reformer, to labor with him in promoting union between the two bodies.

The *Messenger* was opposed to slavery. The anti-slavery sentiments of the editor revealed in the periodical, including some articles on this vexing problem copied from the *Harbinger*, caused many in the south to cancel their subscriptions.[9] Stone had owned some slaves at one time, but had given them their freedom.

Here, too, Stone discussed various theological concepts, including election and predestination, the Trinity, and the atonement. His unorthodox views of the Trinity and the atonement, particularly the latter, led to extended discussions with the Campbells, and made many of the Reformers somewhat reluctant to freely accord Stone and his followers full fellowship.

Millennial Harbinger (Monthly, 1830-1870)

The *Millennial Harbinger* was somewhat larger in size and expanded in number of pages, compared with the *Christian Baptist*. Under the militant editorial policy of Alexander Campbell, the *Harbinger* was the dominant voice in the Restoration Movement for many years. W. K. Pendleton was its editor from 1865-1870.

The change from the *Christian Baptist* to the *Millennial Harbinger* was due, in part at least, to the actions of the Baptists against Campbell and those associated with him. Campbell had determined to remain with the Baptists just as long as they would tolerate his independent New Testament position; the point of "no toleration" had been reached. By 1830 those opposed to him had succeeded in having "Campbellism" anathematized in many local congregations and Baptist associations, so that the editor of the *Christian Baptist* was not welcome in their churches or associational meetings. The paper had fulfilled its mission; there was no longer any need for maintaining the name "Baptist" in his editorial labors. A new era was beginning; a new paper with a new name was called for.

Essays, Biblical expositions, discussions, news—these formed the major portion of each issue. The exposition and defense of the basic principles of the Restoration Movement were continued in the *Harbinger*. During the first decade the editor published a number of "extras," which were essays on such matters as remission of sins, regeneration, kingdom of heaven, education, order, and the loaf. These were later put together in a volume having the binder's title *Christianity Restored*; still later they appeared as *The Christian System*.

In the *Harbinger* Campbell reveals a growing interest in bringing order to a group of independent churches having both likenesses and differences, which were jealous of their congregational liberty. When the editor campaigned in behalf of co-operation and united brotherhood action, and cast his vote for co-operative agencies as legitimate means through which the church could function, the course of the movement in such areas was practically decided.

Why did Campbell choose the name *Millennial Harbinger* for his new paper? He was convinced that a successful restoration of Biblical Christianity would usher in the millennium.[10] In 1840 he wrote, "When we put to sea under this banner we had the port of Primitive Christianity, in letter and in spirit, in profession and practice, in our eye; reasoning that all the Millennium we could scripturally expect was not merely the restoration of the Jerusalem church in all its moral and religious character, but the extension of it through all nations and languages for one thousand years."[11] In keeping with this view, Campbell worked for the annihilation of partyism, restoration of pure speech, preaching of the original gospel, restoration of the Christian ordinances, and the reception of larger measures of the Holy Spirit.

American Christian Review (Monthly and Weekly, 1856-)

Benjamin Franklin, who had published a monthly periodical for a number of years under the names *Reformer, Proclamation and Reformer*, and *Western Reformer*, began the *American Christian Review* in Cincinnati in 1856. For two years it was published as a monthly and then was changed to a weekly. Daniel Sommer became the editor when he bought the paper from Franklin. Sommer changed the name to *Octographic Review* and later to *Apostolic Review*. It is currently published in Indianapolis as the *American Christian Review*, the editors having returned to the original name.

Franklin and his periodicals lack the polish manifested in some of the other papers, yet they do not suffer greatly by comparison. He had little formal education. His writing was simple and clear; his readers certainly could understand his meaning. He was sincere, straightforward, and thoroughly committed to Restoration ideals. Franklin wielded great influence, both as a preacher and as an editor.

The editor of the *Review* vacillated for a time when the agitation for societies was strong: He was present in Cincinnati when the American Christian Missionary Society was formed, and he co-operated in the work. He served as corresponding secretary with C. L. Loos in 1857. He helped to establish the short-lived American Christian Publication Society in 1851. For a time he rejoiced over the adoption of "The Louisville Plan" and its provisions for church representation in the co-operative program. But he later became the foe of the organized pattern for church cooperation. He also threw the weight of the *Review*, often referred to as "The Old Reliable," against the use of instrumental music in worship and contributed to the division over this issue.

Christian Standard (Weekly, 1866-)

Dissatisfaction with the growing legalistic attitude in the Restoration Movement, especially as expressed by the *American Christian Review*, led to the formation of the Christian Publishing Association, a joint stock company chartered January 2, 1866, which immediately called Isaac Errett to become the editor of a new periodical, the *Christian Standard*. The office was first located in Cleveland, but was later moved to Cincinnati. The first issue, dated April 7, 1866, carried an obituary of Alexander Campbell. Purchase of the Weekly Christian Record, published in Indianapolis by Elijah Goodwin, provided a nucleus of some two thousand subscribers. Financial difficulties led the directors to turn the company and the Standard over to Errett within two years.

Errett committed the *Standard* to a policy that made it an outstanding religious journal: a bold and vigorous advocacy of New Testament Christianity; emphasis on the plea for union; challenge to practical piety; support of worthy missionary, educational, and benevolent institutions; review of Christian literature, education, moral and political science, and commerce; analysis of important religious movements in America and elsewhere, with particular emphasis upon their significance for the message and mission of the Restoration Movement.[12]

The new paper was to be "Scriptural in aim, catholic in spirit, bold and uncompromising, but courteous in tone." It would "seek to rally the hosts of spiritual Israel around the Bible for the defense of truly Christian interests against the assumption of popery, the mischiefs of sectarianism, the sophistries of infidelity, and the pride and corruption of the world."[13]

If the editor of the *Millennial Harbinger* had a successor, his mantle fell on Isaac Errett. He had served for two years on the staff of the *Harbinger*. His first series of articles on "A Plea for Reformation," which appeared in the *Harbinger* during 1861, revealed the same analytical ability, grasp of essentials, and breadth of treatment which marked the writing of Alexander Campbell. His later work continued to manifest the same spirit and ability.

While Errett joined those favoring missionary societies and instrumental music, he refused to make these tests of fellowship, pleading for understanding and forbearance where differences prevailed. Later the *Standard* opposed the rising tide of liberalism in education. J. W. McGarvey's ably conducted department of "Biblical Criticism" was both an answer to destructive criticism and an apologetic for Biblical trustworthiness. The *Standard* also has publicized and opposed the practical repudiation of the plea of the Restoration Movement manifested in the development of ecclesiastical concepts and practices in conventions and missionary societies, and the practice of open membership in local congregations and on the mission fields.

Gospel Advocate (Weekly, 1855-   )

The *Gospel Advocate* was begun by Tolbert Fanning and William Lipscomb in 1855. Except for a short period when it was suspended during the Civil War, it has continued to the present. David Lipscomb and E. G. Sewell are among its distinguished editors; B. C. Goodpasture is the present editor. From its beginning the Advocate has opposed "innovations" in the work of the church, including the use of instrumental music in worship. It has become more liberal in its attitudes toward missionary and benevolent enterprises, and has favored the fine educational system promoted by the Churches of Christ.

The Christian (Formerly, Christian-Evangelist; weekly, 1882)

Genealogy of the *Christian* is often traced through editorial succession to the *Christian Messenger* of Barton Stone. The *Christian*, edited by J. H. Garrison in St. Louis, and the *Evangelist*, edited by B. W. Johnson in Chicago, united in October 1882, to form the *Christian-Evangelist*.

During the lifetime of Garrison and Errett the *Christian-Evangelist* and the *Christian Standard* were somewhat similar in tone and emphases. Divergencies began following the death of Errett. The *Standard* has continued in a conservative direction, while the *Christian*, particularly in recent years, has been inclined toward a more liberal reinterpretation of the principles held by the early reformers. As "The Brotherhood Paper," it has been more and more closely identified with the agencies of the Disciples and with interdenominational organizations.

Quarterlies

Lard's Quarterly (1863-1868) is filled with the editor's vigorous, and often bitter, "anti" sentiments, especially in his opposition to instruments in worship. The *Christian Quarterly* (1869-1876) was marked by a broader and less strict interpretation of the principles of the Restoration Movement. It was a scholarly journal. Under the able editorship of W. T. Moore it was recognized as an outstanding religious periodical, both in America and Europe. The *New Christian Quarterly* (1892-1899) was edited by J. H. Garrison and W. T. Moore. In character and policy it resembles the older *Christian Quarterly*.

QUESTIONS

1. How have men been chosen to serve as editors in the Restoration Movement?

2. What factors were involved in a man continuing as an editor?

3. How have periodicals served to advance the principles and objectives of the Restoration Movement?

4. In what ways have periodicals hindered this movement?

5. Characterize and show the importance of the following periodicals: Christian Baptist, Millennial Harbinger, American Christian Review, Christian Standard, The Christian.

6. How may periodicals best serve the local congregation?.

---

[1] *Millennial Harbinger*, 1852, p. 390.

[2] *Ibid.*, 1839, p. 550.

[3] *Ibid.*, 1852, p. 494.

[4] *Ibid.*, 1852, pp. 390, 391.

[5] *Ibid.*, 1839, p. 550.

[6] *Ibid.*, 1852, p. 391.

[7] Baxter, *Life of Elder Walter Scott*, p. 73.

[8] *Millennial Harbinger,* 1831, pp. 419, 420.

[9] Cf.. *Christian Messenger*, 1832, p. 223.

[10] Cf. *Christian Baptist*, Burnet edition, p. 128.

[11] *Millennial Harbinger*, 1840, p. 561.

[12] J. S. Lamar, *Memoirs of Errett*, Vol. I, pp. 305, 306.

[13] *Ibid.*, p. 306

TWENTIETH CENTURY DEVELOPMENTS — PART I

A number of issues disturbed the peace and impeded the progress of the Restoration Movement. Three of the most significant of these have been instrumental music, liberalism, and open membership.

INSTRUMENTAL MUSIC

Cause for Division

Should instrumental music be permitted in the worship of Christians? This issue was brought into the Restoration Movement at a comparatively early period, but did not receive too much attention until the latter half of the nineteenth century. Although the controversy arose during the closing years of the nineteenth century, it bore its bitter fruit of division in the early dawn of the twentieth. The tragedy of division in a movement committed to unity was formally recognized in the United States Religious Census for 1906. In that year those churches using the instrument were listed as "Disciples of Christ," and those rejecting its use as "Churches of Christ."

The use of an instrument in worship was discussed widely and earnestly, quite often with unrestrained emotion and bitter feeling. In reading the literature produced by this controversy one finds it difficult to escape the conclusion that much of the discussion and debate has been concerned with maintaining a position rather than searching for the truth. Alexander Campbell wrote in 1851: "To all spiritually-minded Christians, such aids would be as a cow bell in a concert."[1] Moses E. Lard, one of the most determined opponents of instrumental music in worship, writes of those who "condemn the authority of Christ by resorting to will worship," suggesting that it would be better to "live out of a church than go into such a den" where there was an instrument.[2]

Beliefs of Opposing Sides

Those favoring the use of the instrument offered the following justification for this practice: it is expedient; there is no prohibition of its use in the New Testament; it has Scriptural sanction through its use in the worship of God by the Jews and in the worship of God in heaven (Revelation 5:8,9; 14:2,3); it violates no teaching or command of Christ or His apostles; it does not void the command to sing, but is merely an aid to singing.

Those who opposed the use of the instrument argued: it is an "innovation"; there is no evidence of its use in apostolic times; the Scriptures enjoin singing, but give no command to play and sing; without "express command" or "approved precedent" it can have no place in the worship of Christians.

Basically, these arguments involved two different attitudes toward the silences of the Scriptures. Is Scriptural silence equivalent to prohibition? The opponents of instrumental music said "yes." Moses Lard writes: "In all acts of worship we must do only what is prescribed in the New Testament, or was done with divine sanction by the primitive Christians."[3]

On the other hand, there were those who believed that Scriptural silence involved the "law" of freedom. "I must still contend, therefore," wrote J. S. Lamar, "that 'within the Word is authority—all beyond is liberty.' "[4]

Later, O. E. Payne, in a work entitled *Instrumental Music Is Scriptural* (*Standard Publishing Company*, 1920), approached the problem through an examination of the Greek word *psallo*. In his study of Greek lexicons Payne found that the root meaning of the word was "to pluck, as the strings of an instrument," and that it was the word used by a writer when he wished to indicate singing with an instrument.

In recent years the argument that every *element* of worship is prescribed in the New Testament, and to use an instrument is to introduce a *foreign element* into worship, has received some attention.

Those using the instrument have called for the Scripture which establishes *singing* as an *element of worship*. If the list given in Acts 2:42 is a list of such elements, then singing is not included. Furthermore, the two passages most often cited by opponents of instrumental music, Ephesians 5:19 and Colossians 3:16, have no reference to *public worship* and must be taken out of their context of *personal admonitions* to make them apply to such worship.

Hopes for Reconciliation

Through the years some continued to hope that a restoration of fellowship between these divergent groups was possible. In recent years some definite steps have been taken in an attempt to realize these hopes. Under the direction of James DeForest Murch (instrumental) and Claude Witty (non-instrumental) representatives of both groups came together in Cincinnati in 1937 to discuss the situation. Other meetings were held later in different parts of the nation.

These exploratory conferences were designed to get the leaders acquainted with each other; to establish some basis for fellowship, even on a limited scale; to find areas of agreement; to discuss areas of disagreement as Christians concerned about the division; and to pray for unity. A National Unity Meeting was held in Detroit in 1938 and another in Indianapolis the following year. Witty and Murch began publishing the *Christian Unity Quarterly* (later, *Unity Quarterly*) in April 1943, to further the efforts for unity. After about ten years a number of factors combined to discourage these particular efforts for unity.

However, efforts to do something about the situation did not cease entirely. In 1950 Ernest Beam, a minister of the Church of Christ, but who refused to limit fellowship by the use of an instrument, began the Christian Forum, a periodical designed to destroy partyism and promote fellowship with the instrumental brethren. Carl Ketcherside, editor of the *Mission Messenger*, has led in a significant movement, promoting "brotherhood" meetings in an attempt to emphasize the basic areas in which fellowship lies and to approach the problem with sympathetic understanding.

LIBERALISM

Development

Liberalism is a rationalistic, humanistic philosophy that attained prominence during the latter half of the nineteenth century, becoming particularly prevalent in America during the first half of the twentieth century (1900-1935). Its rise and development was influenced by the modern scientific method, the evolutionary theory of Charles Darwin, the philosophies of Kant and Hegel, and the historical-critical approach to the study of the Bible. Liberalism vitally affected every area of Christian emphasis. Liberals challenged the traditional faith of evangelical Christians, including their concepts of the Bible, God, Christ, man, sin, the church, salvation, immortality, heaven, and hell.

Christianity was assigned a place as one of many religions, similar to and comparable with the other religions in many respects, having no particularly unique or revelatory character.

Biblical inspiration, in any real meaning of inspiration, was denied. The Bible had validity for the people of its day only; its primary value for the modern day is historical rather than normative, a document showing one phase of man's religious development and illustrative of the evolutionary process, by which man is inclined ever upward in the scale of life. Miracles mentioned in the Bible were attributed to natural causes or otherwise explained away.

God was considered an immanent force in the world, a view of God which, in some instances at least, was difficult to distinguish from pantheism. The Jehovah of the Hebrews was merely a tribal deity.

Christ was not the divine Son of God. There was a Jesus of history, but no supernatural Christ. This Jesus was the natural development of the ages; a good man, a prophet, the exponent of splendid ethical concepts, but not divine.

The church is an evolutionary development, having no fixed doctrine or laws. It must be changed and adapted to meet the needs of every age. There can be no "going back"; it must be ever "onward, forward."

Man was exalted in proportion as God was minimized. The rejection of Biblical authority was followed by the establishment of human experience as the authoritative standard for life. The development of the "social gospel" followed.

The Christ of the cross has no redemptive significance for the world, only ethical significance. Salvation is reformation. Man needs no "sacrifice" for his sins, he merely needs to be challenged to bring out the good inherent in everyone. All men are potentially divine, not because of something God does for them, but because of what they can do for themselves.

Since nothing concerning the hereafter can be verified through experience or scientific investigation, then nothing positive can be said concerning heaven, hell, or the ultimate destiny of man.

Introduction to Colleges and Universities

Liberalism was introduced into the colleges and universities of America, heralded as the new approach to the understanding of man and his religion. Of particular significance for the Restoration Movement was the capture of Yale University by the liberals and the commitment of the University of Chicago (organized in 1892) to the "new learning." Many of the ministers and other leaders of the Christian churches were educated in these two institutions and were thoroughly indoctrinated in the tenets of liberalism.

A number of related factors—in time, emphasis, and purpose—contributed to the spread of liberalism in the Restoration Movement. The Disciples Divinity House was established at the University of Chicago, with Herbert L. Willett as dean, in 1894. The Campbell Institute was organized in 1896. Herbert L. Willett, Burris Jenkins, and E. S. Ames were among the incorporators. *The Christian Oracle* was purchased in 1901 and later became the *Christian Century*. A series of Congresses (1899-1926) were set up to discuss problems pertinent to the brotherhood.

The leaders of these various enterprises were college men committed to keeping the "scholarly spirit" alive, to being "sympathetically" aware of developments in the new approach to man and Christianity. The *Bulletin* of the Campbell Institute became the Scroll. The *Scroll* and the *Christian Century*, which was purchased by C. C. Morrison in 1908, became propaganda sheets for liberalism and open membership. The Congresses of the Disciples publicized the new doctrines and brought them into wider acceptance. They were so completely dominated by members of the Campbell Institute that the conservatives soon ceased to participate in them.

The schools of the Disciples were soon infiltrated by men holding the new theology. One by one, with hardly an exception, the old order was superseded by the new. For example, the College of the Bible, long a bulwark of faith under the direction of men thoroughly committed to New Testament Christianity, fell to the liberals. Ministers and leaders trained in the new atmosphere carried its conclusions and emphases into the churches and the missionary societies.

Effect of Liberalism Upon Restoration Movement

The controversy caused by a leadership committed to liberalism has been a major factor in at least two developments in the Restoration Movement: a division into two "camps," liberals and conservatives, having little love and little or no fellowship, and the creation of a new educational institution designed to provide a Biblically sound leadership for the churches, the Bible college.

OPEN MEMBERSHIP

"Open membership" is the reception of the "pious unimmersed" who transfer membership into a local congregation without being required to be immersed. Immersion may still be, and usually is, required of all "non-Christians" for church membership.

Immersion the Common Practice

The Brush Run Church gave no consideration to baptismal requirements for membership at the time of its organization. Within a few months, however, the practice of immersion was adopted and required for membership. It was on this basis—they were "baptists"— that the congregation and its ministers were welcomed into the Redstone Baptist Association.

Under the influence of Alexander Campbell, Walter Scott, and, to some extent at least, Barton Stone, immersion "for the remission of sins" (Acts 2:38; 22:16) was the practice of the preachers and churches associated in the Restoration Movement. Immersion, preceded by faith, repentance, and confession, was required for church membership; even the "pious unimmersed" transferring membership from other religious groups were immersed. Those of the Kentucky Christians who united with the Reformers beginning in 1832 followed the same practice.

The Lunenburg Letter

This letter, written by a "conscientious sister" from Lunenburg, Virginia, was published in the *Millennial Harbinger* for 1837, accompanied by the editor's discussion of the issue it raised. The concluding question of this brief letter was: "Does the name of Christ or Christian belong to any but those who believe the *gospel,* repent, and are buried by baptism into the death of Christ?"[5]

Campbell's reply involved him in considerable controversy with many of his brethren. It is frequently quoted by advocates of open membership in support of this practice. It seems difficult to reconcile some statements in his discussion at the time and in later articles. For example, note these two statements:

> Who is a Christian? I answer, Every one that believes in his heart that Jesus of Nazareth is the Messiah, the Son of God; repents of his sins, and obeys him in all things according to his measure of knowledge of his will.
>
> · · · · · · · ·
>
> He only has praise of God and man, and of himself as a Christian, who believes, repents, is baptized, and keeps all the ordinances, positive and moral, as delivered to us by the holy Apostles.[6]

According to Mr. Campbell, there are "Christians" who have not been immersed—imperfect Christians. Some have an imperfect knowledge of God's plan; imperfect knowledge leads to imperfect obedience; and imperfect obedience makes an imperfect Christian. He makes a distinction between the Christian *state* and *character*; one may have the latter without the former; he may be an *inward* Christian without having become an *outward* Christian (through baptism).

Campbell's ultimate answer to his critics was that he had expressed an opinion, adding, "My *opinion* is no rule of action to my brethren."[7] The editor of the *Harbinger* might readily express his *opinion* that there are "Christians among the sects," but he did not advocate admitting the unimmersed into the church. In 1831 he criticized Stone and the Christians for making "immersion of non-effect by receiving persons into the kingdom of Jesus, so called, irrespective of their being legitimately born."[8] And in *The Christian System* he asserts that "all that is required of Heaven for admission into the church"[9] is belief of one fact—Jesus is the Christ— and submission to one institution—baptism.

The Practice of Open Membership

For many years those associated in the Restoration Movement practiced immersion and admitted to church membership only those who were immersed. Contemporary with the rise of liberalism, however, was a growing sentiment in favor of open membership.

As early as 1869 L. L. Pinkerton advocated receiving the unimmersed into full fellowship. In 1889 R. L. Cave proposed the abolition of all restrictions on baptism. About five years later Thomas Munnell, a former secretary of the American Christian Missionary Society, suggested open membership as an aid in the promotion of Christian union. Samuel H. Church, grandson of Walter Scott, caused quite an uproar when he advocated open membership in the Centennial Convention at Pittsburgh in 1909.

W. T. Moore, in the *Christian Quarterly* for 1897 and again when speaking before the Congress of the Disciples in 1901, proposed a plan for promoting union. According to this plan, all Christians would come together, forming a united church, disregarding the baptismal issues, but afterward only immersion would be practiced. C. C. Morrison promoted open membership in a series of articles in the *Christian Century* in 1911. Some attempted to meet the problem by receiving the unimmersed into an associate membership.

A. T. DeGroot found nineteen churches *openly* committed to the practice of open membership in 1929.[10] Carl Ledbetter reported 120 churches practicing open membership in 1940.[11] DeGroot, as the result of a second study in 1948, reported about the same number as were found eight years earlier, but estimated the number committed to the practice either openly or "quietly" at about 500.[12]

Despite denials, there was little question that open membership had been instituted by missionaries with the Foreign Christian Missionary Society and later with the United Christian Missionary Society. Controversy centered first on practices in the China and the

Philippine missions. A long and often "bitter" struggle by "conservatives" to bring the practice on the foreign fields into harmony with the practice of the main body of Christians in America through the societies and through the International Convention proved unsuccessful. The result was withdrawal from these cooperative agencies and the inauguration of an "independent" or "direct-support" missionary program.

QUESTIONS

1. What was meant by the slogan, "Where the Scriptures speak, we speak; where the Scriptures are silent, we are silent"?

2. How has this slogan been used in the instrumental music controversy?

3. What efforts are being, or have been, made to heal the division over the use of an instrument in worship?

4. What is liberalism?

5. What basic principle of the Restoration Movement does liberalism affect?

6. Through what particular medium has liberalism gone into the churches?

7. What is open membership?

    How prevalent is the practice of open membership in churches which have been associated in the Restoration Movement?

---

[1] *Millennial Harbinger*, 1851, p. 582.

[2] *Lard's Quarterly*, 1864, p. 332.

[3] *Ibid.*, 1867, p. 395. Italics are the writer's.

[4] *Millennial Harbinger*, 1868, p. 666.

[5] *Ibid.*, 1837, p. 411.

[6] *Ibid.*, 1837, pp. 411, 508.

[7] *Ibid.*, 1837, p. 508.

[8] *Ibid.*, 1831, p. 392.

[9] *The Christian System*, p. 101.

[10] B. D. Thesis, Butler University.

[11] B. D. Thesis, Butler University, published, in the *Christian Standard* during 1940, 1941

[12] Garrison and De Groot, *The Disciples of Christ*, p. 440.

TWENTIETH CENTURY DEVELOPMENTS — PART II

The developments discussed in the preceding chapter—instrumental music, liberalism, and open membership—are primarily doctrinal. Two of them, instrumental music and open membership, are involved in congregational practices; but even these are rooted in specific doctrines, worship and baptism. All three reflect significant attitudes toward the Scriptures. Instrumental music is significant of the silences of the Bible; liberalism, the character and authenticity of the Bible as the divinely inspired Word of God; open membership—the purpose and authority of the Bible in governing the practices of the church.

The developments to be considered in this chapter—direct-support missions, North American Christian Convention, Bible colleges, and Christian service camps—are reactions to liberalism and its translation into the faith and practice of the church. At the same time they are objective expressions of deep convictions concerning the necessity for implementing the commission of Jesus to evangelize the world and bring Christians to maturity in Him; and to do everything in keeping with the spirit and teaching of the New Testament.

DIRECT-SUPPORT MISSIONS

Three attitudes toward missionary societies have had adherents in the Restoration Movement. The first is that societies are Scriptural, not necessarily as "societies," but as co-operative efforts to advance the Master's kingdom. They have precedent in the association of churches in New Testament times for benevolent and missionary purposes. The second attitude is that societies are anti-Scriptural, being contrary to the program of Christ. He established the church and the church alone. It is the missionary society; every Christian is a member and functions through *this* society.[1] The third is that societies are non-Scriptural, falling into the category of "expedients," to be established and perpetuated as occasion demands and as they prove useful and effective. They may be supported or not supported at the discretion of every Christian. The establishment of missionary societies as an expression of the co-operative life and missionary endeavor in the Restoration Movement has been based on the conviction that such organizations have New Testament precedent, or that they are expedient.

Societies Infiltrated by Liberals

These societies were later infiltrated by liberals, those liberal in their attitudes toward the Scriptures and in the interpretation of the principles of the Restoration Movement. The organizational life of the Disciples more and more assumed a denominational character. The status and operation of a denomination were accepted.

Comity agreements were entered into with other denominations. A comity agreement is an arrangement whereby two or more denominations accept boundaries for the area in which they work. Evangelistic, educational, and benevolent efforts are confined within these areas. Weak churches may be closed in communities where another has greater strength. Interdenominational projects, such as educational institutions, may be maintained on a co-operative basis.

While controversy engendered by liberalism and open membership had begun much earlier in the twentieth century, proposals for the union of the China Mission with the liberal "Church of Christ in China" (not the non-instrumental body) in 1920 brought to light the practice of open membership in the China Mission. A battle was waged through the International Convention to force the United Society to recall all missionaries committed to or practicing open membership, but the personnel of the society were able to circumvent every action of the convention.

John T. Brown, a conservative on the board of the newly-organized (1919) United Christian Missionary Society, made a trip to the various missions in an attempt to get the facts concerning the work of foreign missions. His report, indicating the practice of open membership in China and the Philippines, was published in the *Christian Standard* and in a pamphlet entitled The *U.C.M.S. Self-Impeached*.

Society Ignores Resolution

In 1925, at the meeting of the International Convention in Oklahoma City, Z. T. Sweeney introduced a "peace resolution": no individual out of harmony with the historic positions of the Restoration Movement, or committed to the practice of open membership, was to be employed by the United Christian Missionary Society, and all such then employed by the society were to be released. Although the resolution was passed by the convention with a strong majority, leaders of the society, particularly F. W. Burnham, so interpreted the resolution as to ignore and nullify any vital significance or application that it might have. Liberals and advocates of open membership, many of whom had prepared or were ready to prepare their resignations, were retained by the society. Another effort was made at the convention in Memphis in 1926 to induce the society to restore their policies to a sound Biblical basis; it also proved unsuccessful.

Individuals and churches began withdrawing support from the United Society in increasing numbers. These had completely lost confidence in the integrity of leaders who seemed determined to carry out their own policies—policies repudiated by the Disciples as expressed through the International Convention, the only agency through which an "official" expression of their disapproval could be voiced. Some still hoped, and worked from within the society in an attempt to salvage the investment which had been made through the earlier missionary societies.

Periodicals Begin

Three periodicals began in 1925 as a direct result of this controversy. The *Christian Standard*, which had been the principal medium for publicizing the policies of the United Society, began *The Touchstone* (first issued as *The Spotlight*). R. E. Elmore was chosen editor of this publication, which was dedicated to exposing errors in doctrine and practice in the Restoration Movement. The United Society's answer and antidote to this periodical was the United Society News, edited by W. M. Williams. The Christian Restoration Association was organized in September 1925. *The Restoration Herald*, with James DeForest Murch as editor, was launched as the organ of this Association and a medium for promoting home and foreign missions, education, and the work of the "associated free agencies" desiring to take advantage of its services.

Direct-support Missions

As early as 1891 Miss Loduska Winch was operating as an "independent" missionary in Japan. W. K. Azbill began working in Japan about the same time. W. D. Cunningham (Yotsuya Christian Mission), who for physical reasons was rejected for service with the Foreign Christian Missionary Society, began missionary work "on his own" in Japan in 1901. A great number of "independent" missions were organized in the twenties: Mexican Christian Missionary Society (E. T. Westrup), Philippine Mission Church of Christ (Leslie Wolfe), Osaka Christian Mission (M. B. Madden), Christian Mission to India (Dr. S. G. Rothermel), Central Provinces India Mission (Harry Schaeffer), Tibetan Christian Mission (J. Russell Morse).

The number of direct-support missionaries multiplied exceedingly following the twenties. New missions were opened, and the list of missionary recruits continued to grow. In spite of disruptions and setbacks occasioned by war, by 1963 the number of foreign missionaries in Africa, Asia, Europe, various islands, Mexico, and South America had grown to 329. Add to this number 170 working in missionary projects in the United States and nine in Canada and we have a total of 508 engaged in missionary activities at home and abroad.[2]

A missionary society, the Christian Missionary Fellowship—proposing "to evangelize the non-Christian people of the world in the order, manner, and fashion of a missionary society"—was incorporated in 1949. In 1957 William L. Thompson was called to serve as the General Administrator, with headquarters in Aurora, Illinois. Mission work has been carried on in Brazil, Japan, and India.

The expanding program in the United States includes missions among the Indians and Negroes, children's homes and homes for the aged, and ten Christian day schools. In addition to local use of radio and television, on a broader scope the Christian's Hour, the Gospel Broadcasting Mission, and Christian Television Mission, which produces "Homestead U.S.A.," are maintained. New church evangelism in metropolitan areas in various sections of the nation is a part of the growing evangelistic emphasis. In the years 1960-1963 approximately two hundred new congregations were established.

NORTH AMERICAN CHRISTIAN CONVENTION

The conduct of the International Convention during its sessions in Memphis in 1926 left many thoroughly disgusted with the deportment of this body. Those who felt that the leaders of the convention and the United Christian Missionary Society were acting in bad faith and out of harmony with the expressed wishes of the great body of the Christian brotherhood, came together to discuss the situation. A Committee on Future Action was selected, consisting of P. H. Welshim.er, W. R. Walker, Mark Collis, W. E. Sweeney, O. A. Trinkle, Robert S. Tuck, and F. S. Dowdy. This committee issued a call for a national gathering of Christians in a "North American Christian Convention."

The North American Christian Convention was to do more than create an occasion and provide the platform for critical analyses of or bitter tirades against the International Convention and the United Society. It was to be marked by a positive rather than a negative emphasis; the wranglings associated with recent national gatherings had left a deep sense of dissatisfaction and a longing for something more edifying. There was a feeling of need on the part of those thoroughly committed to "the old paths" to walk in them again, to hold up the Scriptures as the divine and all-sufficient revelation of God and to emphasize the great doctrines of the Christian faith.

Convention Begins in 1927

About 3,500 gathered for the first "North American," which was held in Cadle Tabernacle, Indianapolis, October 12-16, 1927. Those who gathered for this convention were made more effective servants of Christ through the sharing of ideas relative to Christian service, were warmed by great fellowship, and were inspired by great preaching.

Enthusiasm ran high. A continuation committee was selected to plan for another meeting the following year. With few exceptions, the North American Christian Convention has continued to meet each year. On occasion, registrations have been more than double the number at the first gathering. The North American has continued to be marked by selection of great themes, well-conceived and well-delivered messages showing depth of conviction and breadth of vision, and the same warm fellowship so in evidence at the first gathering, a fellowship in faith and in service.

BIBLE COLLEGES

The capture of American religious educational institutions by the liberal and critical school, including those founded by Disciples, could not fail to affect the Restoration Movement, for the preachers were being educated in these institutions. The humanistic and rationalistic teaching, which made Christianity and its message of Christ primarily an ethical pattern rather than the redemptive program of God, was translated in varying degrees into the congregations in which these men served.

There was need for a rebirth of Biblical preaching, a re-emphasis upon the inspiration of the Bible, the deity of Jesus, and the necessity and program for salvation from sin. This called for a new leadership having faith in and committed to these basic Christian doctrines. And the preparation of this new leadership called for new educational institutions. The answer to this need was the Bible college.

Colleges Established

Johnson Bible College, Kimberlin Heights, Tennessee, first known as "School of the Evangelists," was established by Ashley S. Johnson in 1893, and was an expression of the deep and abiding faith of its founder. Three more schools were organized during the first twenty years of the twentieth century: Minnesota Bible College, Kentucky Christian College, and Phillips Bible Institute (Canton, Ohio). (The latter school, although short-lived, contributed much to the movement.) The twenties saw three new schools: Cincinnati Bible Institute and McGarvey Bible College, merging after one year to form The Cincinnati Bible Seminary; Manhattan Bible College; and Pacific

Bible Seminary, now Pacific Christian College. During the thirties Atlanta Christian College and San Jose Bible College came into existence.

The years 1940-1950 were fruitful Bible college years, producing Boise Bible College, Central Washington School of the Bible, Colegio Biblico, Dakota Bible College, Great Lakes Bible College, Intermountain Bible College, Lincoln Bible Institute (now Lincoln Christian College), Louisville Bible College, Midwest Christian College, Midwestern School of Evangelism, Nebraska Christian College, Ozark Bible College, Roanoke Bible College, Southern Christian College, Southwest Christian Seminary, Dallas Christian College, Puget Sound College of the Bible, and Mexican Bible Seminary.

The number of schools continued to grow during the next decade: Central Christian College of the Bible, Church of Christ School of Evangelism, Eastern Christian College, Grundy Bible Institute, Memphis Christian College, Platte Valley Bible College, St. Louis Christian College. In 1962 Paducah Christian College was begun.

Alberta Bible College is the oldest of the Canadian schools. Canada also has Toronto Christian Seminary and Maritime Christian College.

Two schools for training Negro workers have been established: College of the Scriptures and Winston-Salem Bible College.

Two graduate schools, the Graduate School of The Cincinnati Bible Seminary, granting the B.D. degree; and Lincoln Christian Seminary of Lincoln Christian College, granting the M.A. and B.D. degrees, are maintained.

Curriculum and Growth

Bible colleges, designed to prepare workers for Christian service, have formed a curriculum of basic liberal arts, including courses in English, literature, science, logic, philosophy, world history, psychology, foreign language (Greek and Hebrew). In addition to these are the introductory, expository, and exegetical courses on the Bible, speech, homiletics, apologetics, hermeneutics, Christian doctrine, church history, Christian education, and music.

A liberal amount of criticism, some justified but much of it unjustified, has been leveled against the Bible college and its educational program. The name "glorified Sunday school" has been used in an attempt to ridicule the teaching program. Many schools have struggled for support, and some have died.

A number of the Bible colleges have taken on an educational stature comparable with that of other educational institutions in America in facilities, library, quality of teaching, and preparation of faculty. Several Bible colleges have been accredited by the Association of Bible Colleges, recognized agency for accrediting such institutions, and others are seeking accreditation. Academic hours earned in some of the Bible colleges have been accepted for transfer by schools accredited by other agencies, including state colleges and universities.

The Bible colleges have assets of more than thirteen and a half million dollars. The annual enrollment exceeds four thousand. A full-time faculty of over three hundred is maintained, supplemented by a part-time faculty of more than 150.

The contribution of the Bible colleges and justification for their teaching program, may be seen in the souls won to Christ, the closed churches opened, the weak churches strengthened, the new churches established, and the preachers, teachers, and missionaries now serving at home and abroad.

CHRISTIAN SERVICE CAMPS

Coming out of the same general background and conditions in the Restoration Movement as direct-support missions and Bible colleges, and closely paralleling their rise and development, are the Christian service camps. Among the earliest developments were at Erieside (Ohio) and Lake James (Indiana). (A list of camps and the weeks scheduled appears in The Lookout sometime in May or early June, and reports of the camps in a later issue.)

Christian service camps have had an almost unbelievable growth. In 1939 the number of students attending camps was about five thousand; in 1962 the number exceeded thirty-six thousand. The fifty weeks of camp provided in 1939 had grown to 458 weeks in the same period. A faculty of five thousand provides instruction and leadership.[3]

These camps provide instruction, inspiration, and recreation for Juniors, Junior High, and Senior High young people; some offer one or more weeks for adults. While primarily designed for Christian young people, a large number who are not Christians attend. Confessions and baptisms have averaged fifteen hundred or more in recent years.

The emphasis in these camps is upon Christian service in the local congregation or in wider areas. The challenge to commitment of life in specialized Christian service as preacher, teacher, missionary, director of music or Christian education, and church secretary has had over a thousand responses in some years and approximately this number in other years. At least ten camps have set up Life Recruit weeks in their camp schedules. From these life recruits have come many of the Bible college students.

QUESTIONS

1. What is meant by "direct-support" missions? How do such missions differ from other missionary programs?

2. What has led to the development and growth of direct-support missions?

3. What factors contributed to beginning the North American Christian Convention?

4. What gave rise to the Bible college movement? What is the basic purpose of the Bible college?

5. Name some of the Bible colleges.

6. What is a Christian service camp? What contribution do these camps make to the Restoration Movement?

---

[1] Cf. *Millennial Harbinger*, 1850, pp. 282-287.

[2] 1963 *Directory of the Ministry.* In 1962 Mr. Murch, *Christians Only*, p. 305, reports six hundred missionaries in eighteen lands.

[3] Cf. 1963 *Directory of the Ministry.*

RETROSPECT AND PROSPECT

The Restoration Movement is a Biblically-based and Christ-centered religious movement It proposes that all Christians, and all who desire to become Christians, submit themselves completely to the Lord Jesus Christ, individually and collectively taking the New Testament as the standard for doctrine and conduct.

REFORMATION AND RESTORATION

The two words, "reformation" and "restoration," have been used indiscriminately in referring to this religious movement. Alexander Campbell, although continuing to use both words in referring to the movement, was careful to indicate its essential restorative character. In the first article of a series in the *Christian Baptist* entitled "A Restoration of the Ancient Order of Things," he wrote:

> Since the New Testament was finished, it is fairly to be presumed that there cannot be any reformation of religion, properly so called....
> Human creeds may be reformed and re-reformed, and be erroneous still, like their authors; but the inspired creed needs no reformation, being, like its author, infallible.... Human systems, whether of philosophy or of religion, are proper subjects of reformation; but Christianity cannot be reformed....
> A restoration of the ancient order of things is all that is necessary to the happiness and usefulness of Christians.[1]

The writer is certain that the following distinction has not been adhered to when using "reformation" and "restoration," but it is suggested as legitimate and proper when speaking about this movement. It is a "reformation" or "reformatory" movement when referring to the religious bodies, their creedal standards and ecclesiastical systems, to be affected; it is a "restoration" movement when referring to the divine standard by which changes are to be effected, the extent of the changes to be made, or the ultimate goals to be kept in sight. The "Restoration Movement," then, is a movement designed to bring about a *complete* "reformation" or renovation of religion according to *the divine standard, the New Testament.*

RETROSPECT

When the Christian Association, and later the Brush Run Church, adopted the principle, "Where the Bible speaks, we speak; where the Bible is silent, we are silent," they committed themselves to a course which would lead to conflict with their religious neighbors. Obviously, the adoption of this slogan as the principle for reformatory action was indicative of a conviction that, in a large measure at least, the religious world was not speaking where the Bible speaks and was not silent where the Bible is silent.

Controversy Inevitable

Controversy was inevitable; for people, especially religious people, do not abandon practices or move out of well-established patterns of thought or action without great difficulty. Both offensive and defensive battles were fought. Occasions for condemning anti Biblical practices and defenses against critical accusations brought by the established religious groups were frequent. Presbyterians, Baptists, Methodists, Universalists, Mormons, even a Roman Catholic, were met in public debate. A well-defined and extensive body of apologetic and polemic literature exists today as the fruit of these controversies.

Human Creeds Condemned

Human creeds were condemned as standards of faith and fellowship. They were opposed as being un-Scriptural, unnecessary, presumptuous, and factional. The "horrid evil" of a divided church, with its warring parties, was decried. Thomas Campbell, in the *Declaration and Address*, wrote of the "awful and distressing effects" of division: aversions, reproaches, backbitings, evil surmisings, angry contentions, enmities, excommunications, persecutions. A divided church did not rightly honor the Christ who was its head, ignoring His prayer for the unity of His followers as recorded in John 17; nor could it be an effective witness for Him in the world. Ecclesiastical systems, such as presbyteries, synods, general assemblies, and associations, holding disciplinary authority over the faith and conduct of individuals and churches, were considered anti-Scriptural and detrimental to the cause of Christ. But the movement was more than "anti-creed, anti-council, or anti-sectarian," as Alexander Campbell points out.[2] It is not just "anti," it is "pro"—pro-Bible, pro-Christ, pro-gospel, pro-union.

Much confusion and many errors had resulted from the failure to "rightly divide the word of truth," to differentiate between the dispensations covered in the Biblical record. Alexander Campbell's Sermon on the Law, which was an attempt to point out differences between the law and the gospel and to show the superiority of the latter, resulted in a "seven years' war" with the Baptists.

Doctrines of Calvinism Rejected

The basic doctrines of Calvinism—human inability, election, limited atonement, irresistibility of grace, and perseverance of the saints—were repudiated and rejected as unscriptural. Men were not to be considered puppets manipulated by God, or "totally depraved" creatures incapable of any good, but those whom God "so loved" and for whom Christ went to Calvary. The Calvinistic theology was charged with responsibility for the loss of countless numbers of souls who might have been saved by preaching the simple plan of salvation found in Acts. A sane evangelism, conforming to the pattern and examples found in the New Testament, was opposed to the emotional "mourner's bench" type of conversion.

Movement Criticized

Much criticism was leveled against the message and the messengers of the movement. They were accused of bigotry, of claiming to be the only Christians; to which they replied, "We are not the only Christians, but we are Christians only." The practice of immersion "for the remission of sins" was proposed as evidence that these Christians believed in "baptismal regeneration" or "water salvation." The preaching of a plan of salvation—faith, repentance, confession, baptism, forgiveness of sin, gift of the Holy Spirit—which did not involve a period of anxiety and agonizing prayer, brought cries of "a heartless religion." The emphasis on man's ability to co-operate with God in his redemption was considered salvation by works and opposed to salvation by grace. And because they taught that the Holy Spirit operates through the Word in conversion rather than directly upon the sinner, they were accused of denying the Holy Spirit.

Name Discussed

The matter of the name to be worn was widely discussed in the formative period. Alexander Campbell urged the use of "Disciples" or "Disciples of Christ"; others—including Thomas Campbell, Walter Scott, and B. W. Stone—were convinced that "Christian Church" or "Church of Christ" was to be preferred as giving more honor to the Christ. While the latter names have been used to designate local congregations, those suggested by Alexander Campbell have been widely used to refer to the body of people.

Communion

Participation in the Communion was also discussed. Should Communion be open or closed? In particular, controversy centered in whether or not the unimmersed should be admitted. In their final decision most of the churches chose to make a different emphasis: Communion was neither open nor closed; no invitations were extended, and no prohibitions announced. The individual rather than the corporate character of the Lord's Supper was stressed. No pre-Communion examinations were held to determine the fitness of communicants; there was no "policing" of those present at the hour of Communion. The Lord's table was prepared in the Lord's house each Lord's Day, and each individual present was called upon to consider' the admonition of Paul: "Let a man examine himself, and so let him eat of that bread, and drink of that cup" (1 Corinthians 11:28).

Biblical Terminology Emphasized

An emphasis on using Biblical terminology led to the rejection of "Sabbath" when referring to the Lord's Day. "Trinity" was rejected because it was not found in the Bible. "Reverend" was not considered a proper tide for preachers, since it is used only once in the Bible and then with reference to God (Psalm 111:9). Furthermore, since *all* believers are priests, there should be no division into "clergy" and "laity," no ministerial class to be set apart and designated as "reverends."

Slavery Issue

The controversy over slavery raged in a number of the prominent religious bodies, resulting in divisions into northern and southern bodies, each having its own standard and medium for co-operation. But while there was a strong anti-slavery sentiment, a sentiment sufficiently strong to lead to the organization of the Christian Missionary Society in which those opposed to slavery could conscientiously co-operate, no permanent division was created in Restoration forces. The position taken by Alexander Campbell played a prominent part in preventing division.

Legalism

Legalism marked the movement in some areas of thought and practice. The silences of the Scriptures were given a prohibitory character. Thomas Campbell's principle, designed to make a place for faith and opinion, in essence was rephrased to read: "Where the Bible speaks, we speak; where the Bible is silent, it speaks in prohibition." No room was left for opinion. The impact of this concept was manifested in the reaction to missionary societies and instrumental music in worship, which resulted in division among the churches.

Legalistic views further divided the Restoration Movement, particularly the non-instrumental fellowship. The listing in Acts 2:42—apostles' teaching, fellowship, breaking of bread, prayers—was taken by some to be the divine *order* in worship, an order which would not be varied without violating New Testament teaching and incurring the wrath of God. Divergent views of the "lawfulness" of church buildings, orphan's homes, colleges for training preachers, divided classes for Bible study, use of lesson helps (such as quarterlies) brought divisions. Different concepts of the millennium were responsible for further severing fellowship.

An example of the extremes to which legalism has been pushed is found in two camps rising out of interpretations of the words of Jesus when He instituted the Memorial Supper, "He took the cup." Some hold that since Jesus took a *cup*; only a container having *handles* (which distinguishes a cup from a glass) may be used in the Communion. Others contend that Jesus took the cup, indicating that only *one* cup was used; therefore, more than one cup cannot be used.

Liberalism

Liberalism also has left its marks on the movement. Those adopting modern critical attitudes and methods of interpreting the Bible and its message gained sufficient influence to dominate the co-operative life of the movement, resulting in division into "liberals" and "conservatives" or "Co-operatives and Independents." The acceptance of the tenets of liberalism, although often covered over with other issues, has been the basic factor affecting the movement in the twentieth century. The influx of liberalism resulted in the development of the direct-support missionary program, Bible colleges, Christian service camps, the North American Christian Convention, and other conventions. These programs now display a remarkable vitality.

Movement Biblically-based

The Restoration Movement was begun by men thoroughly convinced that the Bible was the Word of God, a unique book, divinely inspired and given to make known God's will to men. They were committed to understanding and preaching its message of redemption and oneness in Christ to an unsaved world and a divided church. Their plea was a Biblical plea, and it was, and is, valid only if the Scriptures are valid.

Modem critics may approach God's Word with a skeptical attitude, but these men approached it in reverent faith. Alexander Campbell dedicated the *Christian Baptist* "to all those, without distinction, who acknowledge the Scriptures of the Old and New Testaments to be a revelation from God; and the New Testament as containing the Religion of Jesus Christ: —who [are] willing to have all religious tenets and practices tried by the Divine Word."[3]

The normative character that Thomas Campbell conceived the Bible to have is seen throughout the *Declaration and Address*. In this historic document we have such expressions as: "conform to the model and accept the practice of the primitive church"; "the original pattern laid down in the New Testament"; "the divine Word is our standard"; "making a rule of it and *it alone*"; "what is expressly revealed and enjoined in the holy Scriptures." He characterized the Bible as "divinely revealed truths" and "legible and authentic records." Here was not just a rediscovery of the Bible; it was a re-emphasis upon its centrality and all-sufficiency in the Christian system.

The Bible, by charter, was included in the educational program at Bethany College. Alexander Campbell considered the place that he had assigned the Bible in the curriculum and teaching program made Bethany College unique among educational institutions of his day. Later schools made the same provision in their charters. A. S. Hayden, speaking of Western Reserve Eclectic Institute, indicated the high value placed upon the Bible by the founders of this institution:

> The Bible is the foundation of all morality in the world. It contains all moral power for the improvement and refinement of the human race. Its counsels are eternal wisdom. Its morality is perfect. It cannot, therefore, be hazardous to lay the Bible as the moral basis of the Eclectic Institute.[4]

Movement Christ-centered

Christ is central in the Scriptures. He moves through the Word from the first promise of His coming in Genesis 3:15 to the close of Revelation. He is associated with the events of the first chapter of Genesis in the prologue of John's Gospel and the opening verses of Hebrews. Following the example of the apostolic messengers found in the Book of Acts, the preachers of the Restoration Movement put Christ at the center of their preaching and activity.

According to Alexander Campbell, "the very soul, body, and spirit of the gospel—the marrow and fatness of Christianity—is in the proper answer to the question,. *What think you of Christ? Who is He! What is He!*" And concerning the broader implications of the right concept of Christ he wrote, "Is not an agreement in the doctrine concerning Christ, or a declaration of our faith in the person, mission, and character of Jesus Christ, essential to Christian union—indeed, to an admission into any Christian community!"[5] Campbell refused union with Unitarians, who denied the deity of Jesus.

Walter Scott made the messiahship of Jesus the focal point of the entire Christian system. He wrote, "The proposition of the Mesiahship [sic] forms the basis or foundation of our religion." And again, "This is the master revelation, the primum mobile of the Christian Religion, the power that gives life and motion to all the other parts of the evangelical machinery.... Jesus is the Messiah the Son of God."[6]

PROSPECT

It has been said that the Restoration Movement was born to die. And this is true ... when its work is finished. Any movement that has lost its purpose or fulfilled its mission no longer has any reason for existence. But has the Restoration Movement lost its purpose or fulfilled its mission? Do those factors which called it into being no longer exist?

Are there standards other than the Bible in Christianity today? In the early days human creeds were challenged as rightful standards for Christian conduct. While these historic symbols do not figure so prominently in the thinking of the "laity," they still continue to exist and to regulate religious bodies. Today, too, liberalism and humanism continue to challenge the Bible as a legitimate guide, suggesting that men follow the individual conscience or human experience. There is a trend, however, even among Biblical scholars, toward recognition of the validity of the Biblical record.

Is the church still divided? And is a divided church today any less a "horrid evil" than it was in 1809? A divided church fails to honor the Christ and fulfill His will as much today as it failed in these respects yesterday. Today we hear much about unity: the ecumenical movement, the National Council of Churches, the World Council of Churches. The unity proposed, however, is not unity of Christians, it is the federation of denominations, the peaceful co-existence and collaboration in practical expression of Christianity. But, as Alexander Campbell observed in 1839, "The union of sects, and the union of Christians, are not identical propositions."[7]

Are there still unsaved men and women? Has the babel of voices directing sinners given place to the language of God? There are religious programs today as far from Biblical Christianity as those in the earliest days of the Restoration Movement. Every sincere seeker after God has the right to and should be given, a clear, Biblical answer to the question, "What must I do to be saved?"

CONCLUSION

As a fitting conclusion to this study of the Restoration Movement we propose the following evaluation by Alexander Campbell:

> The ground assumed in the proposed reformation is the highest ground which can be assumed at any time or under any circumstances, and it is the only rational and lawful ground which human ingenuity and Christian integrity can propose.... If we fail it cannot be in the object proposed: for in this no people can excel us— none can claim higher, more rational, or more scriptural ground.... If, too, Christianity is ever to be restored ... if the disciples of Jesus Christ are ever to be united, if sectarianism is ever to be put down, if the world is to be regenerated and its kingdoms to bow to the sceptre of Jesus... it must be by placing the Apostles upon the thrones which Jesus promised them, by making them the infallible arbiters of every question of faith and morals... If there be a rock, if there be a sure and well-tried foundation on which to build in the moral and religious desolations of Christendom, this is the foundation.[8]

QUESTIONS

1. What is the difference between the concepts of "reformation" and "restoration" in religious matters?

2. What issues have been the cause of controversy between leaders of the Restoration Movement and other religious groups?

3. What issues have been the cause of controversy within the Restoration Movement?

4. Show how the Restoration Movement is Biblically based.

5. Show how the movement is Christ-centered.

6. Is there still need for the Restoration Movement? Why?

---

[1] *Christian Baptist*, Burnet edition, pp. 127, 128.

[2] *Millennial Harbinger*, 1831, pp. 390, 391.

[3] *Christian Baptist*, Burnet edition, dedication page.

[4] Green, *Hiram College and Western Reserve Eclectic Institute*, p. 52.

[5] *Millennial Harbinger*, 1846, p. 222.

[6] *Gospel Restored*, pp. 131, 187.

[7] *Millennial Harbinger*, 1839, p. 344.

[8] *Ibid.*, 1831, pp. 417, 418.

SUGGESTED PROJECTS

1. Promote a church library or some other means whereby biographical, historical, and doctrinal books relating to the Restoration Movement are made available for reading to the congregation.

2. Gather, or help in collecting, materials for a history of your congregation.

3. Promote the writing of this history in conjunction with the minister and others in the congregation who are interested.

4. If possible, make available interesting historical and doctrinal information for the church bulletin or paper.

5. Have a church historian appointed or elected who will be responsible for direction in the collecting and preservation of historical materials such as the following:

    a. Pictures—preachers, missionaries, church groups, classes, buildings, etc.

    b. Local church papers, weekly bulletins, etc.

    c. A scrapbook from local newspapers and religious journals concerning the church, its organizations, its ministry, activities, members. Be sure to indicate date, title of article, and name of paper in each instance.

6. Perhaps the congregation would be interested in a campaign to obtain subscribers for a religious periodical related to the Restoration Movement, such as the *Christian Standard.*

7. Plan some special services relating to the movement, such as a hymn service in which the writers and hymns of those associated with the Restoration Movement might be featured.

8. Keep a missionary file or scrapbook.

9. Keep a Bible college file of a number of Bible colleges.

10. At some suitable time, have a report on some interesting volume of Restoration Movement literature, such as *The Fool of God* (Cochran), Raccoon John Smith (Cochran), or *"P.H." the Welshimer Story* (Arant).

11. Have someone review one of the early documents.

BIBLIOGRAPHY

· BOOKS ·

BAXTER, WILLIAM. *Life of Elder Walter Scott.* Cincinnati: Bosworth, Chase and Hall, 1874.

CAMPBELL, ALEXANDER. *The Christian System.* Cincinnati: Standard Publishing Company, 1835.

CAMPBELL, ALEXANDER. *Memoirs of Elder Thomas Campbell.* Cincinnati: H. S. Bosworth, 1861.

COCHRAN, LOUIS. *Raccoon John Smith.* New York: Due11, Sloan, and Pearce, 1963.

COCHRAN, LOUIS. *The Fool of God.* New York: Duell, Sloan, and Pearce, 1958.

COREY, S. J. *Fifty Years of Attack and Controversy.* Des Moines: Committee on Publication of the Corey Manuscript, 1953.

Directory of the Ministry. Springfield, Illinois: Directory of the Ministry, 1963.

EVANS, MADISON. *Biographical Sketches of the Pioneer Preachers of Indiana.* Philadelphia: J. Challen & Sons, 1862.

GARRISON, W. E., and DEGROOT, A. T. *The Disciples of Christ: A History.* St. Louis: Christian Board of Publication, 1948.

GATES, ERRETT. *Early Relation and Separation of Baptists and Disciples.* Chicago: Christian Century Company, 1904.

GREEN, F. M. *Hiram College and Western Reserve Eclectic Institute.* Cleveland: O. S. Hubbell Printing Company, 1901.

HALEY, J. J. *Debates That Made History.* St. Louis: Christian Board of Publication, 1920.

HANNA, W. H. *Thomas Campbell, Seceder and Christian Union Advocate.* Cincinnati: Standard Publishing Company, 1935.

HAYDEN, A. S. *Early History of the Disciples in the Western Reserve.* Cincinnati: Chase & Hall, 1875.

HAYDEN, EDWIN V. *Fifty Years of Digression and Disturbance.* Joplin, Missouri: Hunter Printing Co., n. d.

JENNINGS, W. W. *Origin and Early History of the Disciples of Christ.* Cincinnati: Standard Publishing Company, 1919.

KERSHNER, F. D., and PHILLIPS, WOODROW. *The Restoration Handbook.* Five series. San Antonio: Southern Christian Press, 1960.

LAMAR, J. S. *Memoirs of Isaac Errett. Vol. I.* Cincinnati: Standard Publishing Company, 1893. 127

LEWIS, GRANT K. *The American Christian Missionary Society.* St. Louis: Christian Board of Publication, 1937.

MACCLENNY, W. E. *The Life of Rev. James O'Kelly.* Indianapolis: Religious Book Service, 1950 (reprint).

MOORE, W. T. *A Comprehensive History of the Disciples of Christ.* New York: Fleming H. Revell, 1909.

MORRILL, M. T. *A History of the Christian Denomination in America.* Dayton, Ohio: Christian Publishing Association, 1912.

MURCH, JAMES DE FOREST. *Christians Only.* Cincinnati: Standard Publishing Company, 1962.

RICHARDSON, R. *Memoirs of Alexander Campbell.* 2 vol. in one. Cincinnati: Standard Publishing Company, r.d.

ROGERS, JOHN. *The Biography of Elder Barton Warren Stone.* Cincinnati: J. A. & U. P. James, 1847.

SCOTT, WALTER. *The Gospel Restored.* Cincinnati, Ohio: Donogh, 1836.

WARE, C. C. *Barton Warren Stone.* St. Louis: Bethany Press, 1932.

WELSHIMER, P. H. *Concerning the Disciples.* Cincinnati: Standard Publishing Company, 1935.

WILLIAMS, J. A. *Life of Elder John Smith.* Cincinnati: R. W. Carroll & Company, 1870.

WITMER, S. A. *The Bible College: Education With Dimension.* Manhasset, New York: Channel Press, 1962.

YOUNG, C. A. *Historical Documents Advocating Christian Union.* Chicago: Christian Century Company, 1904.

· PERIODICALS ·

Christian Baptist, 1823-1830. Alexander Campbell, ed.

Christian Messenger, 1826-1845. Barton W. Stone, ed.

Millennial Harbinger, 1830-1870. Alexander Campbell, ed.

APPENDIX

A BRIEF HISTORY OF THE CHRISTIAN RESTORATION ASSOCIATION

BY LEE MASON

To understand fully the Christian churches/churches of Christ in the twentieth century, one needs to know about the Christian Restoration Association. Although the CRA is mentioned in book three of this trilogy, more information is needed and hereby given.

To begin the story of the CRA we begin with the estate of one Sidney S. Clarke. Sidney S. Clarke was a Christian gentleman who left part of his estate to the keeping of the Richmond Street Christian Church, Cincinnati, Ohio, for the purpose of helping to establish new churches in "destitute places," meaning "communities where there is no church of Christ." The elders of the Richmond Street church immediately put the money to good use and within a two-year period the estate helped establish thirty congregations in Ohio, Oklahoma, Illinois, Arkansas, Virginia, Michigan, and Iowa. Two hundred weak congregations in seven states received assistance, with over six thousand people baptized into Christ.

News of this plan spread through the brotherhood and people thought that more work could be done if the estate had more money. Money began to flow to the Richmond Street church to add to the estate, only to find that the court would not allow money to be added

i

to the estate. The problem was not insurmountable as the elders of the church simply started the Clarke Fund to act independently of the Clarke Estate. The Clarke Fund came into existence officially on November 1, 1922, with the following men serving as a Board of Trustees: James DeForest Murch, C.D. Saunders, Horace W. Vaile, John 0. Chappell and Edwin R. Errett. These men then chose an Advisory Board to help them administrate the Fund; P.H. Welshimer, Mark Collis, C.J. Sharp, Byron Cassell, and J.E. Davis. At this point the trustees decided that a publication was needed to tell of the on-going work of the fund. Volume I, Number 1, of The Facts was published in December 1922. Later this publication changed its name to *The Restoration Herald.*

The work grew until it became obvious that it was too large for a local congregation to administer. It was proposed and accepted that the Clarke Fund become a separate institution from the local congregation with a self-perpetuating board of trustees, support of which would be dependent upon the contributions of Christian people. Such support would depend upon the merit of the program, fidelity to the purpose that brought it into existence, and steadfastness in the faith. This also brought a change in name from the Clarke Fund to the Christian Restoration Association and from The Facts to *The Restoration Herald.* This separation was effected in October 1925. James DeForest Murch was named president, and continued as editor of *The Restoration Herald.*

The Clarke Fund was established with its objective carefully written in its constitution: "To receive and distribute monies for the preaching of the gospel of Jesus Christ and the organization of Churches of Christ according to the New Testament pattern, and other church, educational, missionary and benevolent enterprises." This was continued by the CRA.

NEW CHURCHES

The original intent of both the Clarke Estate and the Clarke Fund was to help establish congregations set after the New Testament pattern. The Christian Restoration Association sent evangelists out from coast to coast. Some of the first CRA evangelists were C.C. Root, who went to California and helped establish over thirty-five congregations and the Southern California Evangelistic Association; Thomas Adams to Arizona; Edward Clutter to Colorado; J.S. Raum who seemed to work all over the country including Georgia, Illinois, Missouri, Michigan, North Carolina, and Pennsylvania; J.B. Pickel who went to Iowa; and L.G. Tomlinson who went to Ohio. Often the plan used was to enter a community and have a protracted meeting (what we often call revival). Before the evangelist would leave, he would have started a new church.

For the next decade, literally scores of churches were established and reopened in one-half to two-thirds of the United States of America.

THE CINCINNATI BIBLE SEMINARY

Because of the infidelity being spewed out in the preacher training schools, the trustees of the CRA realized that a school was needed which would produce Bible-believing preachers who would stand for the faith once delivered to the saints. In 1923, two schools had begun, one in Cincinnati and one in Louisville. It was felt that better stewardship would be shown if these two schools could merge. In 1924, the schools merged and formed The Cincinnati Bible Seminary. The trustees of the Clarke Fund were the trustees of the new school. H.F. Lutz was considered the first president of the new school, although on an interim basis. He died that first year and James DeForest Murch became interim president because of his position as President of the Clarke Fund. In 1928, the CRA trustees helped set up another board of trustees for the Bible college and helped established it as a separate institution from the CRA. The first official president was Ralph Records.

DIRECT SUPPORT MISSIONS

The time in which all of this was taking place was a time of great change among the Christian churches/churches of Christ. Liberals and infidels had taken over some of the great institutions. Colleges no longer taught the inerrant Word of God. The United Christian Missionary Society of the Disciples of Christ had embraced open-membership and comity agreements as acceptable practices.

People loyal to Christ no longer trusted the UCMS and sent money to the CRA. At this same time, missionaries working under the banner of the UCMS found that they could no longer work with those who nullified the Great Commission. Many missionaries worked without support when cut off from the UCMS. In 1926, Leslie Wolfe wrote the CRA stating his dilemma and need. The CRA immediately underwrote his salary. Then petitions came from C.B. Titus in the Union of South Africa; the Cunninghams from Tokyo, Japan; Russell Morse from Western China; and others. These were aided, but it did not take long to realize what a great financial task this was.

The trustees of the CRA wrote to nine of our larger congregations in America with the idea that they would assume the living-link support for these missionaries. The Indianola Church of Christ, Columbus, Ohio responded, as did the First Christian Church of Canton, Ohio; the West Side Christian Church, Springfield, Illinois; and the Dodge City, Kansas congregation. This began the "direct support" way of financing missions. From now on each individual congregation was able to take charge of the stewardship entrusted them and wholesome relationships developed between missionary and congregation.

CHRISTIAN SERVICE CAMPS

In 1926, it was decided that there needed to be some way to influence more young men into the full-time vocational Christian ministry. At that time we had just a few Christian services camps and some of them were run by single congregations. The trustees began an effort to have a series of Christian Youth Conferences around the country. That first year there were twelve camps in twelve states, and the next year fourteen camps in fourteen states. These were not the first camps, but by this means a nation-wide impetus was given to the Christian camping movement of today. It is unfortunate that many of those leading camps today have gotten far afield from the original intent. To compare the curriculum of those early camps with the curriculum of today is to compare a steak dinner to a glass of dirty water. There is no comparison and the latter is void of nourishment.

LENDING MONEY

The CRA continues to be a "Helping Hand to the Churches." Today it has money that has been left in its keeping to administer in agreement with the terms of those who have left the funds. Some money is available for small loans to help young and struggling congregations get established and perhaps enter a building program. The Recycled Riches program is another lending fund that uses missions money to help congregations. A cotton baron in Texas named A.D. Milroy left funds to be used for evangelism. This fund is used to help support preachers in newer congregations.

TRAINING LEADERSHIP

In the 1960's, Pearl Willis covered the country training elders and deacons with his Elders and Deacons Clinic, and helping preachers through the Advanced Ministers Seminars. Complete figures were not kept, but over 6,000 men were trained the first year of these clinics.

Leadership training has continued through the terms of all of the directors of the CRA and is still a part of the present program.

CHRISTIAN BIBLE INSTITUTE

Another part of leadership training has been carried out through the Christian Bible Institute of the CRA. In 1966, the CRA assumed the oversight of the CBI, which was a correspondence school for men and women desiring to further their training in Christian work, but unable to attend a Bible college full-time. Trustee Milton Dills directed the program until 1978. Norval Campbell was in charge of the CBI from 1979 to 1996. Paul Pratt began his ministry with CBI in 1996.

DEFENDING THE FAITH

In the 1940's, director Robert E. Elmore was sued for libel by Disciples of Christ leadership. When Elmore won his case, it brought a virtual end to a rash of lawsuits being instituted by various Disciples groups in several states in an effort to control congregations by controlling their properties.

In the 1960's, under the capable leadership of director Harvey C. Bream, Jr., the CRA provided expert counsel to scores of congregations who sought to disassociate themselves from the Disciples denomination because of the infamous "Restructure" action taken by that body.

For two decades, through the legal expertise of attorney Luther D. Burrus, of Louisville, Kentucky, who was a CRA trustee; the expert testimony of the scholarly Dr. Lewis A. Foster of the Cincinnati Bible Seminary, also a CRA trustee; and Harvey C. Bream Jr., trustee and Director of the CRA, and editor of the *Restoration Herald,* independent congregations won a rash of legal battles in which these congregations were the defendants.

PUBLISHING

The CRA has published the *Restoration Herald* for over seventy-five years. This monthly periodical has proven to be a valuable asset to the people of the Restoration Movement congregations. It has chosen by design to publish the whole counsel of God without compromise. Over the years it has taken stands that have not always been popular but have been true to the Word. It has often spoken where no other publication would speak. This publication reaches around the world and is currently being sent to forty-four foreign countries.

Eight men have served as editor of the *Restoration Herald* and director of the CRA: James DeForest Murch, Leon Myers, Robert E. Elmore, Harvey C. Bream Jr., James Greenwood, H. Sherwood Evans, Thomas Thurman, and H. Lee Mason.

The CRA has also published soul-winning tracts, doctrinal booklets, and a variety of educational books and other materials, including books such as the one you are currently reading.

A HELPING HAND TO THE CHURCHES

The history of the CRA is one of helping the churches. When there was a need, the CRA tried to meet that need. It has never sought to be a controlling body, but a serving body. The only authority it has is speaking where the Bible speaks. The CRA depends upon the faithful support of the brethren in the churches. It realizes that its support is contingent upon its faithfulness to the purpose of its organization, the merit of the program, and its steadfastness in the faith.

Today the CRA still follows the original purpose of those who brought her into existence. That purpose is expressed in the pages of *The Restoration Herald* each month on its masthead where the words of Nehemiah 2:18 are printed: *"**Let us rise up and build**."*

May that continue to be our motto until Jesus returns. "Amen. Come, Lord Jesus."

Made in the USA
Columbia, SC
06 January 2023

74237566R00251